MW00723500

The North American
HIGH TORY
TRADITION

———

The North American
HIGH TORY
TRADITION

RON DART

AMERICAN ANGLICAN PRESS
New York

Copyright © 2016 by Ronald Samuel Dart

All rights reserved. No part of this publication may be reproduced, stored in a retrieval system, or transmitted in any form or by any means—electronic, mechanical, photocopy, recording, or any other—except for brief quotations used for purposes of review or scholarly citation, without permission in writing from the publisher.

Published by American Anglican Press, Empire Building, 71 Broadway, Level 2B – No. 149, New York, New York 10006

ISBN 978-0-9963248-4-7

Publisher's Cataloging-in-Publication Data

Dart, Ron (Ronald Samuel), 1950-
  The North American high Tory tradition / Ron Dart.
    pages cm.
  Includes bibliographical references and index.
  ISBN 978-0-9963248-3-0 (hardback)
  ISBN 978-0-9963248-4-7 (paperback)
  1. Canada—Politics and government—1980- 2. Canada—Politics and government. 3. Conservatism—Canada—History. 4. Nationalism—Canada—History. 5. Canada—Relations—United States. 6. United States—Relations—Canada. I. Title.
  F1034.2.D369 2016
  320.520971

Cover design by Peacock & Pen Graphic Design
Front cover illustration: *Forest Scene* by Barend Cornelis Koekkoek, 1848, courtesy of Rijksmuseum, Amsterdam

If Lockian liberalism is the conservatism of the English-speaking peoples, what was there in British conservatism that was not present in the bourgeois thought of Hamilton and Madison? If there was nothing, then the acts of the Loyalists are deprived of all moral significance. Many of the American Tories were Anglicans and knew well that in opposing the revolution they were opposing Locke. They appealed to the older political philosophy of Richard Hooker. They were not, as liberal Canadian historians have often described them, a mixture of selfish and unfortunate men who chose the wrong side. If there was nothing valuable in the founders of English-speaking Canada, what makes it valuable for Canadians to continue as a nation today? — GEORGE GRANT

Posterity may know we have not loosely through silence permitted things to pass away as in a dream ... — RICHARD HOOKER

TABLE OF CONTENTS

PREFACE

No public intellectual today gives more breadth and life to the older way of being 'North American' than does Ronald Samuel Dart (b. 1950), yet, his is not a name known outside of Canada. There is no reason to wonder at this, because in the authorized narrative promulgated by the American Republic, there are no real Ron Darts, nor, for that matter, is there even a real Canada. The exceptionalist mind which dominates the popular culture of North American society knows only the classical liberalism, universalism, and absolutism of its own Manifest Destiny, a dream of progress in which the invasion of 1812 did not need to end in success, because that which Canada–British North America stood for, and in fact is, can only be understood as something of the past to be forgotten. The popular American mind operates in a state of advanced amnesia—it is now not even sure that there ever was a 'Canada', and so the Canadian Tory-Nationalist tradition moves forward as a thing invisible to the majority to its south. The reverse is not, however, the case, and the High Tory tradition in Canada has grown up knowing how and why it is not the American republican way, and why a people would want to live in North America outside of the United States. In 1999 Ron Dart published his *The Red Tory Tradition: Ancient Roots, New Routes*, providing an entry into the fundamentals that have come to define the North American High Tory tradition as preserved and matured in Canada. This was followed by two other important works on the subject, *The Canadian High Tory Tradition: Raids on the Unspeakable* in 2004, and the more concise *Keepers of the Flame: Canadian Red Toryism* in 2012. This present additional collection is an effort to draw out the work of Ron Dart, and the tradition it represents, from the confines of Canada and present it in a broader North American context and in doing so to make it more accessible to a non-Canadian audience. To the south of Canada there are fewer and fewer, day by day, who are willing to march along to the war-drums beat by the American Republic without pausing to question whether there is a different, and perhaps even better, way somewhere out there to be found. Many are those who look to the east, across the Atlantic, or to the west across the Pacific, in search of finding a way to again become something altogether new. Very few, however, have looked carefully to the north, but if they do they will find in the High Tory way that remains there, a way which was once their own, but which they have forgotten. In its content, *Keepers of the Flame* represents the best-made Canadian map which will bring the reader to the finest of the older High Tory way—*The North American High Tory Tradition* is intended to broaden the scope of that map, that it might serve also to lead those who would begin their journey on the High Tory trail from locations well below the 49th parallel. The prophetic voice of the other 'North America' is speaking clearly to the whole of the world, if they would only but listen for it.

FOREWORD

With the publication of *The North American High Tory Tradition*, Professor Ron Dart has offered a remarkable narrative of English Canadian political thought. Canadian national identity consists of assertions that the nation's culture comprises both British and French heritages in complex contradistinction to American republicanism. From Samuel de Champlain's explorations to the Nova Scotia landing of the ship *Hector*, Canadian settlement became marked by these two legacies. With the 1763 defeat of Montcalm and Quebec's resultant incorporation into a British Canada, both Upper and Lower Canada's governments owed their loyalty to the British Monarch. In this allegiance, they were joined by the Eastern Seaboard's Thirteen Colonies. However, the 1763 Stamp Act Crisis began a series of events that resulted in Boston's Battle of Bunker Hill and the 1776 American Declaration of Independence. At this point, the developing political thought of the Canadian provinces and the American rebelling colonies began to widely separate. Always sparsely populated, the British Crown proved able to defend their Northern holdings and repel Benedict Arnold's attack on Montreal. With the 1781 defeat of Lord Cornwallis at Yorktown and the subsequent 1783 Treaty of Paris, the American–Canadian border solidified along with distinct political dichotomies separating the two nations. Professor Dart's historical study begins not with Confederation in 1867 and John Macdonald's prime ministership but rather in the political rupture that the American Revolution created within North America. The War for American Independence produced thousands of exiles loyal to the British Crown who fled the emergent American republic for the West Indies and Canada. Within Upper Canada and Nova Scotia, these exiles became known as the United Empire Loyalists and brought with them both political monarchism and a defensive Anglicanism. Thus the intellectual and cultural origins of Canadian nationalism engendered continued loyalty to the British Empire partly due to inherent opposition to the United States. Professor Dart's detailed monograph delineates this Anglocentric Canadian nationalism throughout Confederation and into the early twenty-first century. His work illustrates numerous aspects of

Canadian identity ignored by American historians and frequently neglected even by contemporary historians of Canada.

Professor Dart rightly acknowledges that the collective experience of the United Empire Loyalists as exiles in shock and outrage at the American War for Independence shaped Canadian political institutions. Canadian elites became stridently pro-British and this sentiment only further increased with the War of 1812—if the Canadian provinces were to survive and not be menaced by the United States, then a continued alliance with the United Kingdom would prove vital. Along with such allegiance, Canadian culture must become uniformly Anglophile in tone and content.

Such sentiment led to the 1839 *Report on the Affairs of British North America*. Presented to the British government by Governor General John George Lambton, First Earl of Durham, it warned of separatist elements within French Quebec and recommended forced assimilation of the French population. Lord Lambton intended to remove surviving seigneurial influence within Quebec and curb Jesuitical influence within educational and intellectual circles. His report resulted in the 1840 Canadian Act of Union passed by Parliament, which coalesced Upper and Lower Canada into a single province with a unitary government. This governmental system continued until the 1867 Constitution Act, which reversed unification and established both Ontario and Quebec as provinces within a united dominion state. Professor Dart correctly notes that Confederation created the instrumental political structures for a British Canada. Along with a bicameral parliament composed of a House of Commons and Senate, the Constitution established the regnant British monarch as Head of State and provided for representation with an appointed Governor General. Serving in the monarch's absence, this official opened and closed Parliament with throne speeches from an *in absentia* Queen Victoria.

The North American High Tory Tradition perceptively discusses the importance of Prime Minister John A. Macdonald in creating the new nation and shaping its early statecraft. Macdonald served as a foundational *pater auctoritas* for the new nation and articulated a political philosophy grounded in loyalty to Crown and Parliament as opposed to American republicanism beyond the nation's southern border. Such Toryism became expressed with the newly founded Conservative Party. Professor Dart's narrative expertly discusses fundamental philosophical differences between Canadian and

American conservatism. He rightly notes that Canadian conservatism draws from a far older wellspring of Anglican political thought predating Burkean political analyses. Unlike the Protestant Episcopal Church in the United States, the Anglican Church in Canada enjoyed greater social prominence and continued stronger linkages to the Church of England. This led to the perpetuation of Anglican political theory through such Tory bishops as the Right Reverend Charles Inglis (1734–1816). Consecrated as the first Anglican bishop of Nova Scotia, he previously served as rector of Trinity Church in Manhattan before the Loyalist retreat from New York in 1783. As very much a Loyalist, King George III selected Inglis precisely because of his Crown allegiances. Inglis worked tirelessly to develop Canadian Anglicanism and founded King's Collegiate School, which later became King's College in Halifax. The College originated with a strong Anglican identity and served to educate and cultivate young men from Canada's prominent Eastern families. Inglis's legacy continues within the College's continued existence and within the Conservative Party in Nova Scotia and New Brunswick. Professor Dart's historical study thus rightly examines Canadian Anglican ecclesiology in addition to political history when discussing the nation's Tory traditions.

By extending discussion of Canadian Toryism into the twentieth century, it proves only right that Professor Dart concludes that Liberal William Lyon Mackenzie King's (1874–1950) long premiership resulted in the diminution of Tory sentiments within Canadian culture. King believed that Canada's future lay in greater alliance with the United States as the dominant Western power. Noting the decline of the British Empire and the United Kingdom's waning influence, he believed that closer American ties would solidify Canada's position within North America and thus lessen its colonial and subsidiary allegiance to the Crown. Mackenzie King and his Liberal successor Louis St. Laurent (1882–1973) progressively articulated an increasingly independent Canadian public culture as distinct from the British experience. This eighteen-year period of Liberal governance witnessed the collapse of the Raj, the formation of the North Atlantic Treaty Organization and the embarrassment of the Suez Crisis. The United Kingdom's advancing debilitation appeared evident to the international community and Canadian Liberalism wished the country to emerge from colonial status into a fully mature nation. However, conservatives such as

George Grant argued that by accepting American dominance, the nation risked abandoning its political and cultural patrimony in favour of United States suzerainty. When elected in 1957, Conservative prime minister John Diefenbaker (1895–1979) attempted to articulate a renewed Canadian Toryism; one respectful of the United States but fully consonant with the nation's British origins and continued heritage. However, Diefenbaker's popular Tory nationalism conflicted with exigent Cold War realities and Canada's junior military partnership with the United States. Diefenbaker's initial support for Canada's involvement in the North American Aerospace Defense Command's intercontinental ballistic missile tracking system later changed into opposition towards American nuclear missiles on Canadian soil. He correctly perceived that this would lead to further declines of Canadian national sovereignty. This controversy offended the American Kennedy administration and proved instrumental in Diefenbaker's 1963 electoral defeat against the pro-American Liberal Party leader Lester Pearson. This defeat marked a key event in the decline of Canadian Toryism as loyalty to the Crown within a British-oriented Canada lost to a Liberal, American-allied vision of the nation's future.

Almost immediately after the fall of Diefenbaker's Conservative government, the nation faced a tempestuous national debate over its own identity. In 1964, the Great Canadian Flag Debate erupted over proposed changes to the national flag. Lester Pearson's Liberal government favoured replacing the Red Ensign flag with a new design that did not incorporate the Union Jack. The Red Ensign had symbolized Canadian nationhood since Confederation and its possible retirement incensed many Canadian veterans of the First and Second World Wars. As leader of the opposition, Diefenbaker led the Tory resistance and fiercely argued against the proposed flag alterations while contending that the Union Jack's removal constituted a betrayal of Canada's founding culture. Despite intense opposition, the bill passed through the House of Commons and mandated the Maple Leaf Flag's adoption. As a show of final resistance to the Liberal Pearson government's retirement of the Red Ensign, Diefenbaker dictated that his coffin be draped with it during his state funeral. For many Canadians, this echoed a continued leitmotif of Canada's dominion status within the once extant British Empire.

Such resistance to Americanization along with the decline of British cultural identity also became expressed through the writings of historian Donald Creighton (1902–1979). Born into a Toronto family, his intense academic studies resulted in his academic appointment to the University of Toronto's history department. Remaining there for the rest of his professional career, Professor Creighton produced numerous historical works studying English Canada's history. His greatest work consisted of the two-volume biography of Prime Minister John A. Macdonald. Creighton lionized Macdonald as the founder of Confederation and an ardent British imperial patriot. Subsequent works included *The Story of Canada* and *The Road to Confederation: The Emergence of Canada 1862–1867*, published in 1959 and 1964. These contained narratives supporting allegiance to Church and King along with hagiographic descriptions of the United Empire Loyalists' settlement of Canada. Towards the end of his career, Creighton served as a political speechwriter for Diefenbaker and helped articulate Canadian Toryism in opposition to the Liberal Party. He energetically opposed both bilingualism and the Maple Leaf Flag because of their effects on the reconstitution of Canadian national identity. Creighton's influence on Diefenbaker is apparent in the Prime Minister's collection of speeches *Those Things We Treasure: A Selection of Speeches on Freedom and in Defence of Our Parliamentary Heritage*, published in 1972. Diefenbaker defended Canada's British legacy and wrote of the need to preserve and protect it against Liberal-supported continentalist thought.

Creighton latterly published his *The Forked Road: Canada, 1939–1957* in 1976 and his only novel *The Take-Over* in 1978, with his essay collection *The Passionate Observer: Selected Writings* appearing in 1980 shortly after his death. In all of these publications, Creighton argued against the Liberal Party's continentalist foreign policy and increasing coordination with the United States of America. He wrote passionately about Canada's parliamentary government and the role of the Governor General as the Queen's representative. What most incensed Creighton about Canadian subordination to American prerogatives proved to be the increasing strain of liberal politics and *laissez-faire* economic thought within both the Liberal Party and increasingly the Progressive Conservative Party. Creighton identified strongly with the 'Red Tory' element of Conservative politics rather than the business-oriented and American-supporting 'Blue Tory' faction. In this, he was joined by the eminent political philosopher George Grant (1918–1988). From the perspective of Western philosophical inquiry, Grant defended a traditionalist vision of Canada indebted to the Tory and Anglican traditions.

Grant descended from a prominent Toronto Conservative family and excelled in his academic career with the reward of a position at Dalhousie University. He attracted mass public attention with the 1965 publication of his political tract, *Lament for a Nation: The Defeat of Canadian Nationalism*. In this work, Grant defended a Tory tradition of social organicism, cultural traditionalism and respect for Canada as a sovereign nation partly formed in contradistinction to the United States of America. He regretted the fall of Diefenbaker's government and the installation of American nuclear missiles on Canadian soil. Grant combined political analysis with his own philosophical reflections and famously compared liberalism to cobwebs and cultural perennialism to honey. Grant metaphorically posited that liberals draw out webs of rationalist argumentation from their own selves whereas traditionalists draw from the Western 'Great Tradition' in order to make honey. Therefore, Grant was appalled to witness the rise of liberalism within the Progressive Conservative Party during Brian Mulroney's premiership. He believed this constituted an abandonment of Canada's intellectual and cultural patrimony. During the final decade of Grant's lifetime, a gulf opened between cultural traditionalists and Anglophile nostalgics, and the business-oriented Blue Tories whom they increasingly opposed. Grant wrote from a Red Tory perspective and criticized the Mulroney government for its closeness to the Reagan administration. His 1988 death deprived Canadian conservatism of an important Tory voice during a period of discontent from Western Canada which took the form of Preston Manning's Reform Party.

Professor Dart appropriately concludes his narrative with a discussion of Preston Manning's influence within Canadian conservatism and the role of his protege Stephen Harper as prime minister. The Reform Party's rise and the rapid decline of the Progressive Conservative Party resulted in a transformation of Canadian politics. The Reform Party and subsequently the Canadian Alliance party favoured *laissez-faire* economic policies combined with devoted support for American foreign policy. These policies combined with Stockwell Day's evangelical fundamentalism alienated older Red Tories who feared the influence of this new electoral force. The 2003 merger of the Progressive Conservative Party and Canadian Alliance into the current Conservative Party of Canada resulted in a Blue Tory victory and the long Harper government of 2006 to 2015. Whether it appears doubtful in the contemporary political culture that an older Tory vision of Canada can be revived, nevertheless it exists as a complex genealogy of political thought that needs only to be renewed. *The North American High Tory Tradition* serves as a passkey to this patrimony through its expert exegesis of essential texts and figures from Canada's history. Professor Dart's work therefore has earned a rightful place on university syllabi and among curious readers eager to know more of Canada's proud history. In future years, it will become a vital text for students of Canadian political traditions.

JONATHAN M. PAQUETTE

St. Andrews, 2016

INTRODUCTION

2017 signals, formally, the 150th anniversary of the birth of Canada. There has been a tendency to falsely assume that Canada, like the United States, is a liberal fragment from Europe: Locke, Paine, Hobbes and Burke (a Rockingham Whig) being the intellectual English liberal visionaries that brought into being the political vision of North America. The Tory historian, Donald Creighton, has called this the authorized version of Canadian history. This liberal read of the origins, development and contemporary forms of Canadian intellectual and political life can be found in William Lyon Mackenzie, Goldwin Smith, Kenneth D. McRae, John Ralston Saul and, from a more telling and sophisticated perspective, Janet Ajzenstat and Peter J. Smith in their edited 1995 classic, *Canada's Origins: Liberal, Tory or Republican?* The burden of *Canada's Origins* was to debunk the notion that Canada had a Tory touch in a way the United States did not, but methinks Ajzenstat and Smith protested too loud.

There can be no doubt that in pre-Confederation Canada there was certainly a Tory touch. The Family Compact has often been roundly criticized by the liberal establishment as being too Tory, and such an ideological class tend to flatter themselves as the bearers of what it means to be Canadian (while denigrating the Toryism of the Family Compact). But, such a simplistic read of Canadian history is much too dualistic. Yes, there can be no doubt that there is a distinct liberal tradition and ethos in Canada, but there is also the Tory touch. Bishop John Strachan, Stephen Leacock and George Grant, to name but three different types of Tories, do reflect a way of being Canadian that cannot be ignored or dismissed in the telling of the Canadian drama. If it had not been for the United Empire Loyalist Tories who fled to Canada after 1776, and the Tories who opposed the invasion of Canada by the Americans in 1812, Canada would be, today, a star on the flag of the United States. The Tory tradition in Canada is certainly not a monolithic one. There are distinct differences between Bishop Strachan, Stephen Leacock and George Grant, but there is also a family resemblance that differentiates them from the liberal tribe. There are, also, essential points of concord between First Nations leaders such as Tecumseh, Joseph Brant and the French political thinker and commentator, Henri Bourassa, and Strachan, Leacock and Grant. Those who have eyes to see can see the connections and their ongoing relevance. The tale of such early Canadian thinkers was also carried forward, in different Tory ways, by Mazo de la Roche, Hilda Neatby and Robertson Davies. Many are the names on the family tree that will be pondered in this book.

It would, of course, be patently silly to equate the High Toryism of classical Canadian thought with the Blue Toryism that has dominated much of Canadian political thought and life over the last twenty years. The right-of-centre Blue Toryism of Preston Manning and Stephen Harper is, in many ways, at the opposite end of the spectrum from the High Toryism of Stephen Leacock and George Grant. Ernest Manning's *Political Realignment: A Challenge to Thoughtful Canadians* (for which Preston Manning did much of the research) embodies a different understanding of conservatism than George Grant's *Lament for a Nation: The Defeat of Canadian Nationalism.* Manning stands very much within the right-of-centre liberal tradition whereas Grant holds high a much older understanding of what is meant to be conserved (and what has been lost with the coming to be of liberalism).

There has been a tendency within the United States since World War II to equate conservatism with the life and writings of William F. Buckley, Jr. and Russell Kirk. Those who have pondered political philosophy at a deeper and more demanding level (and who see themselves as having decided conservative leanings) often turn to Leo Strauss, Allan Bloom or Eric Voegelin as their guides and mentors. But, Buckley, Kirk, Strauss, Bloom and Voegelin did not have any serious understanding of the distinct synthesis in Canada of English, French and First Nations origins—the form of Toryism that emerged north of the 49th of North America cannot be equated with the versions of Anglo-European conservatism that did much to inform the thinking of Buckley, Kirk, Strauss, Bloom, Voegelin and clan.

Anglicans have been called 'Tories at prayer' and when Toryism is properly understood as a concern for the common good (commonweal) and the role of both state and society in bringing into being such a commonwealth, the religious-political vision of Toryism is being approached in a more meaningful manner. There is much more to Toryism than this, though. The purpose of this book is to introduce the reader to the deeper philosophical prejudices and principles of Toryism (liberalism has its own principles and prejudices) and the consequences of banishing such a way of thinking and being from the public square. Liberalism has a way of being imperialistic and colonizing other worldviews while trotting out the slogans of diversity, pluralism and tolerance. It is not very liberal of a liberal not to critique liberalism but many liberals (being enfolded within their ideological perspective) do not do so. Why is this? This book will attempt to answer such a question. May the 150th birthday of Canada awaken those interested in the depth, breadth and perennial significance of the unique Canadian High Tory way and, thereby, see through the ideology and dominance of liberalism in all its crude and subtle shapes, sizes and chameleon-like guises and colours.

RON DART

Abbotsford
Trinity Season 2016

A TORY MANIFESTO

What are the principles and content of historic Anglo-Canadian Toryism and how can such a vision take us beyond the malaise of modernity? The philosophical and political roots of historic Toryism go deep and thick into the well-watered soil of Western culture, and space prevents a thorough discussion of these principles, but in brief, let us look at ten points:

First, Tories are concerned about the wisdom of tradition, the insights of the past and the truths learned about the human condition by those who have gone before us. Bernard of Chartres summed up this Tory way of seeing quite nicely when he said: 'If we see further than those who have gone before us, it is because we are children on the shoulders of giants'. The eagerness of Tories, indeed generous openness of Tories, to hear and heed the past stands in startling contrast to so many in the modern world who have clear-cut the past and lack any sense of direction in the present and for the future.

Second, Tories have a passion for both the commonweal and the commons. The good of the people, of the nation, of each and all is the foundation of Tory thought. The individual truly becomes a person as they find their place in the whole. Tories often compare the nation to a body, and it is as each and all (gifts and nature discovered and lived forth) find their place within the organic life of the whole that life bears much fruit. John Donne, in 'Meditation 17', summed up the integrative and holistic vision that Tories are committed to: 'No man is an island, entire of itself: every man is a piece of the continent, a part of the main … Any man's death diminishes me, because I am involved in mankind'. Thus, the Tory notion of our being connected with one another comes as a challenge and affront to the liberal notion of the primacy of the individual and their freedom to shape their future as they choose. The concern for the commonweal is why Tories within Canada have created a strong federal government; it is the role of the state to think about and protect the well-being of each and all from coast to coast.

Third, Tories do not separate ethics from economics. When the ledger of profit and loss becomes the dominant criterion we use for evaluating the wealth, health, prosperity and development of a people, we become moral cripples. The tendency to divorce ethics and economics runs contrary to the best of historic Toryism that grounds political life in the classical virtues of courage, wisdom, justice and moderation. The cleavage between the rich and poor is a natural product of elevating trade and commerce and ignoring or subordinating an ethical plumb-line by which wealth is earned and distributed. Dante, for example, placed the greedy in the lowest level of hell. It is rather ironic that many neo-conservatives make trade, commerce and economics a virtue; the classical tradition would resist such a move with a passion.

Fourth, the English High Romantics (Coleridge, Wordsworth, Southey) were deeply conservative, and their High Tory conservatism led them to not only oppose the way economics was dominating the political scene, but equally, the way the captains of industry were destroying the environment for a crude and short-sighted notion of profit. In short, much of the Tory tradition has a deep and abiding respect for the land and recognizes, only too keenly, that the environment is the branch we sit on—if we cut the branch off, we will fall and experience great hurt and harm. Therefore, Tories are most ecologically minded.

Fifth, Tories do not separate and artificially oppose state and society. The state has a vital and vibrant role to play in creating the common good as does society. Tories hold together, in a most judicious manner, the role and importance of the state and the essential role of society. The notions of mediating structures, sphere sovereignty, voluntary organizations and subsidiarity highlight the role of society, but such notions must also walk hand in hand with the national role of the state. The excessive badmouthing of the state and the consequent turn to a lighter state (with all the deregulation) is more of a liberal move that serves the interests of a market economy—it is only a strong state that can oppose and stare down the dominance of multinational and transnational corporations. Tories always find a middle ground between capitalism and communism. High Toryism, at its best, has much affinity with aspects of socialism.

Sixth, if a Tory is concerned with the commonweal, such a concern leads to a concern for the commons. There is, obviously, a place for private property and possessions, but there must also be much public space and place that we share in common. C. B. Macpherson, in his classic work, *The Political Theory of Possessive*

Individualism, highlighted so clearly how liberalism is very much about the rights of the individual to compete in the marketplace and possess and keep what was caught in the hunt. The building of ever-greater private barns and dwellings has done much to erode and undermine the commons, the public virtues—such is the liberal inheritance. It is the role of the state to ensure and protect the commons for the good of the people, those living and those yet to live. The modern liberal addiction to possessions–property and protection of such does much to fragment and isolate people from one another into affluent and indulgent bourgeois ghettoes. These notions of commonweal and commons run against the streams of both classical liberalism and neo-conservatism with their singular interest on the marketplace as the venue from which property and possessions can be accumulated.

Seventh, education is about being grounded in the best that has been thought, said and done in the past. The classics and epics are read, digested and internalized as a means of alerting and attuning students to that which is worth living for and that which is to be avoided. Education is not, in its deepest and most significant sense, about teaching some skill or techne so that the naive and gullible will uncritically fit into a dehumanizing and, in many ways, dehumanized culture. The task of education is to awaken the conscience to the important things, to stir the will into action and to point to the wisdom that calls forth to be heard. Just as ethics should guide and be the north star for economics, so wisdom and insight guide and lead knowledge and technical skills for a Tory.

Eighth, according to the Tory's view of human nature we are imperfect, finite and fallible beings. This means, then, that we need to hear from those who differ with us, respect and honour their insights, but be firm with what we stand for. There is always the danger, in life as in politics, of ideology rather than dialogue dominating the day. When this occurs politics become reduced to tribalism and those who don't salute at the flagpole of a certain clan are viewed as heretics and excommunicated. Tories recognize that human nature can go bad, we live east of Eden and even the best of intentions can be fraught with complex motives and riddled with the quest for inordinate power. This is why Tories have a certain wariness of the concentration of too much power in any one place.

Ninth, Tories are convinced that the foundation stones of a good state are built with bricks of ethical firmness and religious depth. The religious institutions that bear the ancient myths, memories and symbols of the community past and present are imperfect, but to negate, ignore or destroy such institutions is to cut ourselves off from the deeper wisdom of the past. Anglicans have often been called Tories at prayer, and there is still much to probe in such an alluring statement—just as the spirit of historic religion needs the ship of the institution to carry it through time, so the Tory vision of politics needs the ship of political party to bring the political vision into being. In short, Tories do not spurn the old institutions that carry their ideas into material form. Those who separate ideals and ideas from the institutions that embody such ideas are most short-sighted and doomed to unfulfilled longings.

Tenth, Tories are committed to the notions that there is a good, better and best, and, equally so, there are such things as bad, worse and worst. Reality cannot be dumbed down to the lowest common denominator. There are ideals worth knowing and aspiring to; there is an order worth knowing and attuning oneself to, and a vision worth remembering and living. This means, therefore, that the ongoing liberal debate about liberty, equality, individuality, choice, communitarianism and other liberal dogmas and creeds at the level of principle can often become a diversion and distraction. If there is no higher good or reality beyond such principles that shapes and guides such principles, liberals become enclosed in their own cage with no way out. A Tory calls out in the streets to one and all to lift their eyes, hearts and heads to the heavens and truly see what needs to be seen and lived for.

SECTION I

THE TALE OF TWO NORTH AMERICAS

CHAPTER ONE

ANGLO-CANADIAN TORYISM AND ANGLO-AMERICAN CONSERVATISM: WE CHOSE A DIFFERENT PATH AND THAT HAS MADE ALL THE DIFFERENCE

A man that should call every thing by its right name, would hardly pass the streets without being knocked down as a common enemy. — George Savile, First Marquess of Halifax[1]

The American republic was founded, consciously and deliberately, on a graphic and clear break from historic English Toryism. The United States was carefully built, brick by brick, by the close alliance of Puritans and Liberals. Both had much in common and were convinced of five essential virtues: 1) the primacy of the individual (and conscience) to choose, in good faith, the right, 2) the importance of enterprise and the Protestant work ethic, 3) the sacredness of property rights and possessions, 4) a suspicion of the state, hence the contract relationship between the citizen and the state, and 5) a commitment to build a new world (manifest destiny) on middle class values. The founding of both the American Revolution and the republic was grounded in liberalism, and this is a basic notion we must be clear about as we compare Canada and the United States.

The Glorious Revolution in 1688 was applauded by Puritans and Liberals alike. The arrival of William and Mary consolidated the Protestant vision in England and set the stage for the founding of a liberal ethos in the fledgling republic across the ocean. The Calvinist work ethic of Holland combined with the protesting spirit of the Puritans worked their wonders. Men like Locke, Hume, Smith, Burke and Paine (in their different ways) voiced the vision of this liberal revolution both in ideas and actions. The American Revolution of 1776 was to echo and further advance the Glorious Revolution of 1688; both revolutions were fully liberal, and they sought to challenge and end the dominance of Toryism. Life, liberty and estates (property–possessions) and life, liberty and the pursuit of happiness were decided by the autonomous and free individual. Many Tory loyalists fled to Canada to find refuge from such liberalism, and, in the process, build and create a more conservative society, a culture much more founded in an older Tory vision of the common good.

Canada, therefore, unlike the United States, did not make a conscious break from English Toryism and the deeper principles that define and shape the Tory vision of the commonwealth. In fact we clearly and deliberately committed ourselves to an older, more time-tried conservative vision that dared to differ with the emerging liberalism that was in vogue at the time. The intellectual–political DNA, then, of the Canadian identity is more complex than that of the United States. Such a reality has been succinctly traced in *Canadian Identity* and *The Canadian Intellectual Tradition* by Robin Mathews. Mathews, in his more recent book, *Treason of the Intellectuals: English Canada in the Post-Modern Period*, continues to track and trace how our intellectuals have betrayed our unique tradition. Our Tory tradition in Canada has been quite willing to both (in the past and present) interrogate and deconstruct the liberal myth.

The much older Tory tradition from which Canada has, historically, dipped its bucket deep is centred in an organic vision of the good society in which a partnership exists between each and all. The founding of our original vision viewed the state, religion, and the people as one, as dependent on one another, reliant on one another for spiritual, emotional, economic, social and political good. We do not need to read too far into Jewel's *Apology of the Church of England*, the Thirty-nine Articles of the Book of Common Prayer or Hooker's *Of the Laws of Ecclesiastical Polity* to get a keen sense that the state has an essential role in building and creating a good and just society. The Conservative tradition, then of Jewel and Hooker (and earlier, More, Colet, Ridley, Cranmer, Latimer) and those who followed Jewel and Hooker from within such a Magisterial tradition (Andrewes, Taylor, Laud, Walton) had a high view of the state. This much older conservative tradition played an essential role in the founding of Canada. If and when the state ceases to rightly fulfil its duty, historic Toryism does not become reactionary and insist that we need a lighter state; this is more of a liberal move and manoeuvre. A classical Conservative will, consistently, call the state to live up to its high calling, insisting that abuse does not prohibit use.

The initial clash between two different visions of what a good and just civilization might be can be found in two of the earliest confrontations between the United States and Canada. It is important to note at this point, though, that Burke (much a dutiful child of

Locke and Smith) strongly supported the American Revolution; he, in short, would not have been one of the loyalists that came to Canada after 1776. The drama, in short and capsule form, finds its fittest and most poignant expression in 1776 and 1812. Thomas Paine published one of his first books in 1776; more than 120,000 copies of *Common Sense* were published in the first three months of 1776. Paine, as most know, trashed the English state (and there were legitimate criticisms to be had), then he argued that government was a necessary evil that did more to fill the coffers of the rich and wealthy than produce real justice. Society, on the other hand, is a legitimate product of our human needs. When Paine's argument is fully decoded, society is seen as a good and the state as evil. This means, then, for Paine (and those who followed him) that the newly emerging republic must break away from England, and it must be forever suspicious of the state. The reply to Paine came from the eminent Tory Anglican Charles Inglis (1734–1816).[2] Inglis became the first bishop in Canada. Inglis argued against Paine, insisting that state, tradition and commonwealth must play a central role; this does not mean that 'society' is not important. The conservative tradition holds together, in a sort of triangle, the individual, society and the state. Inglis, and those like him, were forced to flee the United States; they came to Canada in search of a better way than that offered by the 'Sons of Freedom'. Inglis, of course, was grounded in the world of Jewel and Hooker. This was summed up quite nicely by Nelson in *The American Tory* when he said, 'In the shelter of the Church it was possible to escape the shadow of Locke, even possible to catch occasionally a glimpse of the lost Catholic world of Hooker.'[3] The invasion of Canada in 1812, by the United States, signalled the true intent and nature of the liberal spirit. The republic was convinced it was the way, truth and life and those who differed with it would suffer. Canada, to its credit, stood up against the United States, and to its credit won the day. The War of 1812 signalled that Canada would not be taken or held captive by the manifest destiny to the south. Bishop John Strachan (1778–1867) stood on the front lines, opposing the invasion and, in doing so, linking an older Toryism and nationalism—the blending of a passion for the commonwealth versus the individual, balancing of the state, society (with such notions as sphere sovereignty, mediating structures, subsidiarity, voluntary organizations) and the individual are a vital part of the Canadian Tory heritage. But, deeper than the forms by which the good country can be built, Toryism takes us to a moral and religious grounding. Political theory, at the present time, is often stuck in either recycling class analysis or balancing the rights–responsibilities tension. But, deeper than those two approaches, is the time-tried turn to the virtues as an undergirding of everything. If we have no notion of who we are or what human nature is, then, it is impossible to think the common good in any minimal manner much less to act or live it in the public place. The Tory tradition dares to raise the notions of natural law, the virtues toward whose ends we might move if we ever hope to live an authentic existence.

When we hear American republicans (whether of a sophisticated, popular or crude variety) such as Kirk, Buckley, Nisbet, Kristol, Himmelfarb, Bennett, Novak, Neuhaus, Friedman, Reed, Dobson, or Rush Limbaugh (the crude variety), we need to realize that they are not conservatives in any deep, significant or substantive sense; they are merely trying to conserve the first generation of liberalism that we find in the Puritans, Locke, Hume, Smith, Burke, and Paine. Those who stand within such a tradition of first generation liberalism target the second generation liberalism of Keynes and the welfare state as the problem. A Classical conservative, though, sees this as merely an in-house squabble between two different types of liberalism. But, more on this in the in the following chapters.

CHAPTER TWO

JANUS, TERRORISM AND PEACEMAKING

For it was a witty and a truthful rejoinder which was given by
a pirate to Alexander the Great. The king asked the fellow,
'What is your idea, in infesting the sea?' And the pirate
answered with uninhibited insolence, 'The same as yours, as
in infesting the earth! But because I do it with a tiny craft, I'm
called a pirate: because you have a mighty navy, you're called
an emperor'.[1] — Saint Augustine of Hippo

Emperors and Pirates

Janus was, in Roman myth, the god who had two faces, one at the
front and the other at the back of his head. Janus looked in both
directions, and, being able to do so, could not be taken in by a single
perspective. The language of terrorism is very much with us these
days, and the political use of the term has certainly intensified since
9-11. Janus can very much be a guide for us in this chapter, as we
ponder how the language of terrorism is employed, who uses it and
to what end. In short, it is essential to gaze in all directions as we
dissect the functional use of the language of terrorism.

The apt and insightful passage from St. Augustine in *City of God*
mentioned above can, if heeded, clarify some often ignored realities.
Terrorists are usually defined as those who threaten and disrupt the
national security of the state. This does beg an important and
significant question, though. What have been the decisions made by
a state, at domestic and foreign policy levels, that threaten national
security? The terrorists, like the pirates, are usually seen as the
problem, but the state, like Alexander, is exempt from such
questioning and scrutiny. And yet, it is often the state, like Alexander,
that has much greater capacity to silence opposition and use greater
violence against the pirates–terrorists. Many states often, in domestic
and foreign policy, oppress and terrorize others through the use of
death squads and the military, but when those who have been
terrorized dare to fight back (with fewer arms and less sophisticated
technology), they are branded with the terrorist term. Alexander can

inflict massive hardships and brutality on people, but because he is emperor, he cannot be defined as a terrorist. The small-scale pirates that oppose the emperor are called the terrorists. This simple yet often ignored point must be held front and centre in our understanding of how 'terrorism' is used. The large and vicious sharks are not seen as such, but the smaller fish, when they, in their limited sort of way, attack the sharks, are seen as the enemies of state security. Let me offer a few illustrations of this point.

I was on a sabbatical when 9-11 occurred. Our university hosted an event to discuss the terrorist threat. I was invited to be on a panel to ponder how 9-11 should be interpreted. Most on the panel deplored the terrorist event, and suggested more security was needed. My question was rather simple yet direct: why did such an event take place? What was the nature of historic United States foreign policy in the Middle East that created such a response? I listed the many post-World War II Central Intelligence Agency (CIA) covert (and not so covert) operations in the Middle East that destabilized states. I suggested one and all read William Blum's *Killing Hope: U. S. Military and C. I. A. Interventions since World War II.* I then asked how those of us in North America might respond if we had had all sorts of Middle Eastern states attempting to threaten and destabilize our regime order and drain our natural resources. I'm sure those in North America would fight back if a foreign invasion and occupation occurred. But, we are often blind to the fact that what we do to others we would never allow to be done to ourselves. If the Middle East had become home to the dominant empire after World War II, and Middle Eastern states needed our resources (and we refused to offer them up), Americans would be called the terrorists for seeking to protect their own. There is no doubt that the United States after World War II had become the dominant empire on the stage of world politics. The United States was the Alexander the Great, and those who dared to oppose it (with lesser might and power) were defined as the pirates and terrorists.

It was virtually impossible after 9-11 to raise questions about historic American complicity in that tragic day. I am Canadian, and in Canada, the major media were all pro-American after 9-11. There was rarely a serious question asked about the deeper reasons for 9-11. Sunera Thobani (a significant west coast academic and activist) had the public courage to say that American foreign policy was 'soaked in blood', and the United States was 'the most dangerous and powerful global force unleashing horrific levels of violence'.[2]

The national media in Canada turned on Thobani as public enemy number one. Surely, such comments were not true, and even if true, should not be publically spoken. Was this not a case, though, of a friend of the pirates–terrorists blowing the whistle on Alexander the Great?

Terrorism: Retail, Nefarious, Benign, Constructive

Edward Herman has made a valuable distinction in *The Real Terror Network: Terrorism in Fact and Propaganda* between three ways of understanding how the language of terrorism is employed: constructive terror, benign terror and nefarious terror. Constructive terror is that which fulfils the aims and ambitions of the United States. The actions of the United States in Indonesia in bringing Suharto to power and overthrowing Sukarno in 1965-1966 (and the countless lives lost), the political murders in Chile in 1973-1974 when Pinochet was in power, the carnage of Vietnam, the support of the Shah of Iran from 1953 to 1979, the American support of the State of Israel (and the impact on the Palestinians), and the invasions of Afghanistan and Iraq are just a few instances of terror unleashed by the United States for national security reasons. But, because the use of violence was done for the United States, it is not deemed a terrorist activity. It is seen as a constructive activity because done by Alexander. Benign terror is something not directly done by an imperial power, but by a client state of the United States to consolidate power in an area. The Indonesian invasion of East Timor in 1975 is a case in point. The United States supported Indonesia, hence little was said when Suharto invaded the island. American support of Israel means that the terror unleashed by political Zionism on the Palestinians (although not explicitly sanctioned by the United States) is rather benign in terms of direct American involvement. Nefarious terror is what enemies of the First World do to other states that play into the larger propaganda system. The Pol Pot regime in Cambodia proved how vile communism could be and why vigilance must ever be attentive. The same notion of nefarious terror could be applied to the Soviet Union and its client states in the Cold War. We could also argue in the post-Cold War and 'clash of civilizations'–9-11 era we are in,

Islamism has become the new focus of nefarious terror. Nefarious terror is, in fact, what the enemies of the West do to the West or others. The fact that constructive terror has killed millions of people since World War II is often ignored. Alexander does it, he is emperor, so the actions taken cannot be deemed terrorist. But, when enemies of the West (pirates) threaten the West, they are nefarious and called terrorists. The fact that the United States has far greater power and can either directly or indirectly prop up, or destabilize states that do not please it, and does so in a violent way, does not justify the use of the term terrorist being applied to it. Only opposition states or small activist cells that use violence are terrorists.

We need, perhaps, to further unpack how and why the language of terrorism is used the way it is. Hannah Arendt was one of the finest political philosophers of the twentieth century. Arendt's *The Origins of Totalitarianism*, published in 1951, became a sort of Cold War text book on what the United States and the First World opposed. The First World had fought totalitarian states in World War II (Japan, Germany, Italy) under the banner of liberty and democracy, and post-World War II totalitarian states such as the Soviet Union and China were questionable political regimes. *The Origins of Totalitarianism* is a complex and dense tome, and needs many a reread, but the language of totalitarianism was often linked to the terror done by those 'nefarious' states that threatened the First World. Many horror stories could be drawn forth to amply illustrate how these totalitarian states in foreign or domestic policy terrorized their people. The merging of totalitarian states and nefarious terror was a hand-in-glove fit for planners in the First World. The fact that the world is not neatly divided (and never has been) into free and democratic states and totalitarian regimes meant that the United States after World War II had to make some hard decisions. There is no doubt totalitarian states were the enemy and problem, but choices had to be made. A distinction was made between those states which were totalitarian and those which were authoritarian. Authoritarian states could be worked with even though such states were quite willing to terrorize opposition groups and deem such opposition terrorists. But, this was constructive terror, that is terror done in the name of Alexander. So, just as totalitarian states were viewed as agents of nefarious terror (real terrorists), authoritarian states were agents of constructive terror (that is, violence done that serves the aims and ambitions of the First World). The litany of authoritarian states supported by the United States in the twentieth century is a long list: Guatemala (Montt), Indonesia (Suharto), Chile (Pinochet), Nicaragua (Somoza), Philippines (Marcos), Iran (Shah), Saudi Arabia (Saud family), Iraq (Hussein in the 1980s), Greece (Tsaldaris), South Korea (Rhee), Haiti (Duvalier), Cuba (Batista), Portugal (Salazar), Spain (Franco), Thailand (Phibun), Pakistan (Zia) and many other authoritarian states. The amount of terror unleashed in these states is not seen as such for the simple reason it is constructive. The American state has subverted other states such as Guatemala (Arbenz), British Guyana (Jagan), Iran (Mossadegh), Dominican Republic (Bosch), Indonesia (Sukarno), Brazil (Goulart) and Chile (Allende). The level of terror and violence perpetrated by the authoritarian regimes backed by the United States when such regimes were aligned with Alexander's own ambitions cannot be denied or ignored. The shortest reading of Amnesty International annual reports or special publications brings the ominous facts to gruesome and graphic light.

The language and use of terrorism has often been reduced to the actions of violent opposition groups such as the Irish Republican Army, Shining Path, and Palestine Liberation Organization—this can be called retail terrorism. When this approach to terrorism is used, state terrorism tends to be left out of the discussion. But, it is states that have the greatest power to inflict the greatest amount of damage on citizens. The fact of small-scale retail terrorism cannot be denied, but there is much more to the terrorist story than this. The way large scale terrorism works is through a more subtle form of propaganda. States that are totalitarian (communist in the Cold War world, Muslim in the 9-11 world) are viewed as nefarious terrorists for the simple reason their agenda and use of violence (which cannot be denied) threatens the Alexander of the West. The use of equally brutal violence by authoritarian states is accepted and approved by the West for the simple reason it aids in the constructive vision and agenda of Western leaders.

An examination of the history of the United States' use of violence both at home and around the globe over the past three centuries reveals a painful tale. Those who have taken the time to read through the annals that recount these deeds cannot help but get the overwhelming feeling that Alexander, indeed, has terrorized many, but most are either unaware of the facts or simply ignore them because of who Alexander is in the global village. *Captain America and the Crusade against Evil: The Dilemma of Zealous Nationalism*, by Robert Jewett and John Shelton Lawrence, amply illustrates in a philosophical manner the underpinnings in American religious and political thought that have created the 'Captain America' syndrome. Alexander and 'Captain America' are now one and the same. A read of Ziauddin Sardar and Merryl Wyn Davies's two books, *Why Do People Hate America?* and *American Dream, Global Nightmare* clarifies much for the curious and confirms why many faced with Alexander's deeds see through the language surrounding constructive terror, particularly those that are the victims and recipients of them.

The Clash of Civilizations and Orientalism

Samuel Huntington published a controversial article in *Foreign Affairs* in 1993 called 'The Clash of Civilizations?'.[3] The article was developed into a book that was published in 1996 with the title *The Clash of Civilizations and the Remaking of World Order*. The burden of the article–book was rather simple, and the implications of the article–book ominous. Huntington argued that the 'clash of ideologies' that dominated the post-World War II era had come to an end in 1989. Capitalism had defeated communism, and those in the West had much to be grateful for. But, a new war was in the making. Huntington argued that world politics was about to enter a new phase, and the West had better be prepared for this tougher challenge. The West was about to face the incoming fact that civilizations were arising again to challenge the dominance of the West, and of the many civilizations Huntington mentioned that will threaten the Alexander of the West, Islam is the dominant one.

The rise of Islamism and the violence and terrorism that could and would emerge from such a civilization must be noted and guarded against. Huntington had dipped his bucket in the well of a better known Western Islamic scholar, Bernard Lewis, for his Western read of Islam. Lewis had published many books on Islam, and central to many of his arguments is the notion of 'Muslim rage'. Islam was on the march again, and the West had best prepare for a new war. This time the enemy was not communism but Islam. This negative view of Islam by Lewis and Huntington certainly played into the

Alexander–pirate, authoritarian–totalitarian model and dualism that so shaped much of American thought. The 'clash of civilizations' argument also reinforced, from another perspective, Edward Said's 'Orientalism' thesis.

Said had argued, in his classic tome, *Orientalism*, that the West had a historic habit of depicting the Orient in a way that was thick with cliches, caricatures and, for the most part, negative. The many images the West constructed about the Orient served, in an imperialist manner, to see them as a lesser people that needed to be civilized by the more advanced West. The Orient was a threat to the West, and the way the West fabricated images of the Orient further reinforced this cultural read of the Orient. The thinking of Lewis and Huntington merely perpetuated Said's main thesis. The West and Islam could not be reconciled, and the clash between these civilizations was inevitable. The clash model of Lewis and Huntington and the co-existence and humanistic model of Said do have serious implications when fleshed out in the real world of activism and politics.

Is Islam, by its very nature, aggressive and violent, and must the Christian West be vigilant and on guard against Islam? It does not take a great deal of thought to realize that Islam is a complex religious tradition, and the form Islam takes in Turkey and Indonesia is quite different than the form Islam has taken in Southern Russia and the Balkans. Islam in Iran and Sudan is quite different than Islam in Egypt and Saudi Arabia. Islam in Pakistan and India takes on different forms than Islam in the United States and Europe. In short, as Judaism and Christianity, Hinduism and Buddhism, Confucianism and Sikhism are not homogenous groupings, Islam does not stand apart as an exception. There is no doubt that there are tendencies towards violence within each of these traditions, but these religions also have strong and committed peacemaking heritages that are more committed to co-existence than a perpetual clash with one another. It is simply false and wrong to merely see Islam and Islamism in a negative and violent way. The Christian West, as I have mentioned above, has certainly exerted a great deal of constructive terror on those that have dared to oppose 'Captain America'. Those whose minds are locked within a Christian West–Islamic Orient dualism (the former often idealized, the latter demonized) rarely use their critical thinking on their own tradition in the way they use it ruthlessly on the tradition of 'the Other'. There can be no doubt that the Christian West in the twentieth century has used a great deal of violence on the Orient. Why is it, then, that the Islamic Orient is seen as the terrorists? Is this not a classic case of the mote–beam syndrome?

Constructive terror wielded against those that oppose American interests is rarely viewed as terrorism.

Modern Islamism is now targeted and defined as an agent of nefarious terror: the Taliban, Hamas, Al-Qaeda, the Muslim Brotherhood, and Hezbollah are all seen as terrorist groups and their various sleeper cells are seen as spreading far and wide.

The West has often caricatured and demonized the Orient and idealized and romanticised its own heritage. But, just as in the souls of one and all, the good, mediocre and evil wage warfare, the same is the case in civilizations. The British Broadcasting Corporation production, *The Power of Nightmares: The Rise of the Politics of Fear*,[4] makes this fact poignantly clear and obvious. *The Power of Nightmares* demonstrates how a form of Islamism is violent, and how an ideal can lead to the worst form of ideology. The same is true, though, for the United States and Britain. The line and lineage of Reagan–Bush–Blair was as ideological in its views of communism and Islamism as were the Islamists towards the West. Both groups viewed political reality through a simplistic black–white lens, both thought the other was dark and menacing, both groups thought their own vision the truest and best, and both groups were prepared to use violence on the other. The point to be noted here is this, though: the West, like Alexander, had the overwhelming power. Muslims, like the pirates, had minimal ability to seriously match or oppose the West. But, when the Muslim pirates dared to use violence against Alexander, terrorism was the charge levelled against them. *The Power of Nightmares* makes it more than obvious that variations of the Muslim Brotherhood (and their line and lineage) and the political philosophy of Leo Strauss (and his academic and activist children) are merely mirror images of one another.[5] The film does not press the point, though, that in this clash of civilizations, one tribe has much more power than the other, and this is an important point to realize. Alexander has the political will and power to define the terms in a way the pirates do not—Sardar and Davies's *American Dream, Global Nightmare* takes the argument beyond *The Power of Nightmares* and illustrates my point quite well.

Augustine, Just War and Peacemaking

There is a predictable habit by many in the West to see Augustine as the Christian Father of the 'Just War Tradition', hence the merging of faith and war under certain conditions. Thomas Merton had this to say about Augustine in *Peace in the Post-Christian Era*: 'St. Augustine is, for better or for worse, the Father of all modern Christian thought on war', or, again, 'Thus Augustine becomes also the remote forefather of the Crusades and the Inquisition'.[6] The 'Just War Tradition' can be interpreted in a variety of ways when principles are applied to a particular historical context, and this is where the nub of the issue remains a perennial problem. Jean Bethke Elshtain, for example, in *Augustine and the Limits of Politics*, and of much more importance *Just War against Terror*, has been more than willing and eager to use Augustine's notion of 'Just War' to legitimate American invasion and occupation of independent and sovereign states. Elshtain and many other American political theorists on the soft republican right in the United States use Augustine in a way that can be seriously questioned. *Just War against Terror* remains the landmark book of the last decade on the use of the 'Just War Tradition' for American imperial purposes in their constructive use of violence against the neo-pirates and nefarious terrorists that threaten America in the clash of civilizations.

There is an argument that the Christian tradition was a peacemaking and pacifist tradition until the coming of Augustine. This argument is problematic, but it tends to hold the attention and commitment of some in the Christian peace tradition. Is this argument true and faithful to the more complex Christian peacemaking heritage? And, can peacemaking be equated with pacifism? This is what Augustine was trying to make sense of at a time when Roman civilization was under siege and wanton violence was spreading. How should communities respond to those that are committed to the burning of villages, towns and cities and, worse yet, the rape, pillage and slaughter of men, women and children? Can, under certain conditions, defensive violence be used? This is what Augustine was pondering in his Christianized version of the Roman 'Just War Tradition'. Augustine did not idealize the Roman Empire. He knew in his bones the aggressive violence that Rome perpetuated on others that were not Roman. He, like Janus, knew how to look both ways. Augustine was also keenly aware that the various tribes and clans that were in the process of destroying the Roman Empire in the fifth century could be just as vindictive and violent as Rome. Rome was the Alexander that defined the terms. The pirates that assaulted Rome in this classical clash of civilizations were the terrorists. Augustine held high the 'City of God', but he was also aware that humanity lives in the 'City of Man', and the difficult task was to know how, in trying times, to live in both. The issue of war and peace was one of the issues that had to be thought through and lived forth in this fragile dilemma. The issue of war and peace was more poignant in Augustine's era for the simple reason that the 'Pax Romana' was deteriorating and many were vulnerable to the warlike tendencies of the barbarians (pirates).

There is no doubt that Augustine's attempt to articulate a theory of 'Just War' must be set within the context of the rapacious nature of his time. Augustine was no supporter of a holy war ideology or the imperial nature of 'Pax Romana'. He would, if living, be opposed to 'Pax Americana'. The passage from Augustine that I began this chapter with makes it clear that Augustine saw quite clearly how terms could be used by the powerful to define who the terrorist–pirate was and why. Alexander–Rome–United States of America could not be the terrorist because it is they who have the power to define the terms. Yet, ironically, it is they who have the power and use it to commit more violence than those they accuse of being the pirates, terrorists or barbarians. Augustine had this to say about kingdoms and empires that are not grounded and rooted in justice. 'Remove justice, and what are kingdoms but gangs of criminals on a large scale?'[7] Such a statement and incisive comment very much reinforces the kingdom–pirate motif that St. Augustine was only too well aware of in his time. But, there still remains the legitimate discussion of peacemaking, pacifism and just war.

There have been, as I mentioned above, those that, rightly so, see Augustine as the father of the Christian 'Just War' tradition. The next step tends to be more worrisome, though, and Augustine is often seen as a key component of this secondary step. The 'Just War Tradition' often gets equated with the ambitions of nationalist or imperial politics when states or empires are threatened by pirates–terrorists. Constructive terror and 'Just War' are often linked within such a scenario, and Augustine is seen as the father of such a questionable approach to peacemaking. I'm not sure Augustine can be used to service such a position, but he often is, sadly so.

It is significant to note that the English Humanists of the sixteenth century (John Colet, Thomas More, Erasmus, Juan Vives) were at the forefront of peacemaking at the time, and most of the English Humanist peacemakers were quite fond of Augustine's *City of God*. More gave lectures on the massive tome as a young man, and Ronald Musto has this to say about Vives:

> Vives's edition and commentary on Augustine's *City of God*, commissioned by Erasmus for Froben's Basel press in 1520, is one of the great Humanist texts. Vives saw Augustine's work as a basic commentary on Christian peacemaking amid the fall of empires and warring kingdoms.[8]

The fact that Augustine could be and was used by the English Humanists in the sixteenth century in their peacemaking quest speaks much about an alternate read of the *City of God*. Musto's *The Catholic Peace Tradition* is, of course, a must read for those interested in the long and complex nature of peacemaking (past and present) within the Roman Catholic tradition. I think it can be legitimately argued that the 'Just War Tradition' cannot be equated, obviously, with various types of pacifism, but there are various ways to interpret the principles of 'Just War' in particular historical contexts. The English Humanists were certainly not absolute pacifists, but their stringent and dovish read of the 'Just War Tradition' made it virtually impossible for many of the wars of their time to be called just. The same read of the 'Just War Tradition' can be applied in our time. The 'Just War Tradition' need not be taken captive by right-of-centre politics to justify the going to war in Iraq, Afghanistan and beyond.

Counter-Terrorism

There are, as I have mentioned above, various ways of understanding and defining terrorism and peacemaking. The dominant imperial strategy tends to be 'peace through strength', and the state that has the largest and most imposing military can make peace through the strength, might and power of the military. Those that threaten the peace of an empire or large state through violent actions are targeted as the terrorists. When 'Pax Romana' was threatened, the Roman military and centurion guards were quick to counter the terrorist threat. When 'Pax Americana' is threatened, counter-terrorist threats are monitored by the Central Intelligence Agency–Federal Bureau of Investigation (CIA–FBI), then acted upon to preserve the peace. Such an approach, of course, elevates the peace of one people, state, or regional alliance over and against another rogue state or terrorist cell–terrorist movement. It is often non-state terrorist movements that are defined as terrorists. Walter Laqueur's *A History of Terrorism* did much to create this establishment position in the peace–terrorism tradition. Once Laqueur's approach to terrorism is accepted, states can, will and do define those who oppose them in violent ways as the terrorists. The state which opposes such terrorists in a counter-terrorist way is a maker and broker of peace for innocent citizens and civilians. The language of counter-terrorism, therefore, feeds nicely into the constructive approach to the terrorist problem. This model is, obviously, played out in the Russian state peacemaker–Chechen Muslim terrorist or Post 9-11 American peacemaker–Al-Qaeda Muslim terrorist motifs. The language of peace, like terrorism, is malleable and often defined by the user to serve larger political and propaganda ends and purposes. There is no doubt that terrorist movements use violence to achieve their ends, but terrorist movements tend to be quite limited in their capacity to inflict violence in comparison to militaristic states (whether of a totalitarian, authoritarian or democratic nature). It is essential, therefore, when we hear the language of counter-terrorism that we ponder who is using the language and whose political ends it is serving.

Conclusion

Augustine's distinction between Alexander and pirates must be kept in mind. The powerful kingdoms and emperors often see those that challenge them as the terrorists. There is no doubt that the clash of civilizations plays nicely into this view of the world. Constructive terror by the powerful is often seen as a categorical imperative against those pirates who use nefarious terror against the powerful. It is often needful for Alexander to align himself with authoritarian states to oppose terrorist and totalitarian states. The fact that Alexander has committed many crimes against humanity need not be noted by the followers of Alexander. The task is to locate the pirate–terrorist and use all manner of military might against the pirates to preserve order in the world. Constructive terror is not seen to be terror, and if it is, it must be used to protect the world against nefarious terrorists like Islamists. Sadly so, the 'Just War Tradition' is often used to legitimate the actions of Alexander and his military deeds of constructive terror. Augustine has been frequently used by the mild and sophisticated hawks like Jean Bethke Elshtain to justify the aggressive actions of the empire they inhabit and feed well off of. But, can Augustine be used in this way? Is there a dovish read of the 'Just War Tradition' that cannot be co-opted for hawkish purposes? In sum, the English Humanists can be seen as guides, mentors and models in a way that blends and synthesizes the 'Just War Tradition' with a firm and solid commitment to peacemaking. Books such as Ronald Musto's *The Catholic Peace Tradition* and Hildo Bos and Jim Forest's *For the Peace from Above: An Orthodox Resource Book on War, Peace and Nationalism* illustrate and illuminate how peacemaking in the Roman Catholic and Eastern Orthodox traditions has taken place, at the level of theory and praxis, in the past and present. Such books highlight, in the clearest possible manner, how peacemakers have confronted the duplicity of terrorism by being Janus-like (having the wisdom and discernment to look both ways), hence refusing to be taken in by the ideological narrowness of any tribe, clan, state or empire.

CHAPTER THREE

NOAM CHOMSKY AND THE CANADIAN WAY: ANARCHISM OR NATIONALISM?

Even the dissident ones speak as members of an Empire
— John Newlove[1]

We have seen, in the last fifty years, the waxing of Noam Chomsky as a darling and superstar of sorts of the dissident and anarchist left both in the United States and Canada. There have been lean and barren years for Chomsky, but in these times he gathers many to his lectures and presentations. The hive does buzz and bees do gather whenever and wherever Chomsky turns up to expose the folly and bully-like nature of the American empire. The truth is told in a clear and distinct manner, and the chasm between the kindness of American rhetoric and brutality of American reality is graphically articulated and demonstrated.

Chomsky has published more than a mountain of books and articles in the areas of linguistics and American foreign policy. There is probably no American of his stature today that has, since the 1960s, clearly illustrated in both a popular and scholarly manner, the carnage the United States has wrecked in the global village we live in. Chomsky has walked the extra mile to reveal, in the most painstaking detail, the intimate connections between the major media, government and political parties, the military and corporations. It is this power elite, Brahman, Mandarin and Family Compact class that have done much to create much sadness and tragedy for many in the world. Chomsky claims to stand and speak for the oppressed people against such a sophisticated *mafia*, and he should be heard and heeded for doing so. There is no doubt that Chomsky deserves his rightful and honoured due as a leading critic of dishonesty and injustice amongst all the high mucky-mucks.

It is interesting to note that many is the thoughtful and critical thinker that goes mute and silent when they sit at Chomsky's feet. Many is the fan and acolyte that genuflects at his every word, sigh and sound. This should raise some questions for those who, at least in principle, hold high the value and place of critical thinking. Many are those who would and do gag when the Pope speaks in an *ex cathedra* fashion, but when Chomsky speaks, most on the dissident and anarchist left treat his comments the same as the Roman Catholics treat those of the Pope.

There are many Canadians who see into and through the pretensions of the American empire, yet many fail to see how dissidents from within the empire can and do perpetuate its ideological underpinnings. Chomsky was asked to give the Canadian Broadcasting Corporation's (CBC) Massey Lectures in 1988 on the media. 'Necessary Illusions: Thought Control in Democratic Societies'[2] told the tale, in five compact lectures and many a detailed appendix, on how and why the media works the way it does in our democratic societies. Many was the Canadian who bowed and tipped the hat at each and every word from the master. It was Canadians, yet again, who put together the first full length video on the varied life and activism of Chomsky. *Manufacturing Consent*[3] was an instant hit and bumper-crop seller to many who were, rightly so, longing to hear another voice other than that from those of power, perks and privilege. There is no doubt that Chomsky has become the political guru and pope to many, and when he speaks (as he does often) his fans are silent and a hearty amen ends the sessions and seminars.

There is also no doubt that Chomsky gathers his followers from those who have a high sense of moral outrage about the way American foreign and domestic policy plays itself out. It is from such a clan that protest and advocacy politics is held high as a way of opposing and resisting a dishonest and oppressive state. Such a tribe tends to see the world of formal politics and party politics as beholden to corporate power, hence an ethos to be ever cynical and sceptical about—such an ethos can do little or no good, and truth and justice can be best seen by the people who do the peace walks, do protest, write many an article on such power politics and work in advocacy and a variety of network groups. In short, so this fable goes, the world of high politics is riddled with the abuse and misuse of power, but the world of grass-roots and people's politics is the world of justice, equality, freedom and all that is good, true and beautiful.

Needless to say, this way of understanding how to both think and act politically tends to idealize and elevate the people and demonize and denigrate the state. Such a tradition tends to be both cynical and sceptical of formal party politics (Democrats and Republicans both eat at the pig's trough of corporations) while pointing the way to a more decentralized and local way of bringing about the just, collegial and cooperative community. This either–or way of thinking and doing politics does need to be questioned, though. We might want to begin by asking, as Canadians, this rather simple question: what are the weaknesses and limitations of the anarchist way and what are the positive things the state offers and does? Needless to say, the misuse and abuse of power can appear in both the state and in anarchist cells and communities. Resistance and peace groups have a thick history of splitting, splintering and fragmenting in a variety of sad and sorry directions. It is this anarchist tradition of the left that sees itself as the pure St. George fighting the oppressive dragon of the state that does need to be questioned. Is some form of utopian anarchism, in short, the best way to oppose globalization and corporate power? What role does the state have to play in resisting such a reality?

I mentioned above that there are many Canadians who see into and through the pretensions of the American empire yet fail to see how dissidents from within the empire can and do perpetuate its ideological underpinnings. There is little or no doubt that the United States was formed and forged on the anvil of liberty, individualism, conscience and equality. Happiness, within such a perspective, was meant to follow and flow from such a creed and dogma. It is from within such a tradition and heritage that the state is seen as a problem and should be seriously limited. Both the anarchist left and the libertarian right tend to share these perspectives at the level of principle. The intellectual foundation stones of the United States, the radical democratic tradition and anarchism are liberty, individualism, conscience and critical thinking. The building blocks of the Canadian way tend to be the common good, order and good government. When Canadians buy into and bow to the anarchist way (and those who embody and are disciples of it), they, interestingly enough, slip into a more subtle form of colonialism.

It is one thing to use moral outrage and protest politics as a means of exposing hypocrisy in high places. It is essential and important to state in the firmest, cleanest and clearest manner what a people do not want. It is quite another thing to organize and deliver, at a political level, what a people do want. It is much easier to deconstruct and expose than it is to create and bring into being the good society. We do need to question whether the anarchist approach can actually deliver the goods given the fragmented history of anarchism.

There are many ways Canadians can be colonized and taken captive by an imperial power. Some of these ways are crude and obvious. It takes not a great deal of thought and minimal observation to see the gap between rhetoric and reality in American thought and action. But, there are many other more subtle and nuanced ways colonialism can and does work. It is some of these more subtle ways we do need to ponder and not flinch from. When Canadians doff the cap and bow the head to individualism and liberty rather than the common good and order, are we not genuflecting to more subtle forms of American thought which this nation was founded on resisting and opposing? When we see the state as the source, centre and bastion of abusive power are we not buying into an American view of things?

The fact that many Canadians turn to Chomsky as their north star should raise some eyebrows. The fact that Chomsky tends towards anarchist politics as the way to bring the good society into being should raise some questions for Canadians. The history of Canadian nationalism in Canada (whether in the Tory, Liberal, New Democratic Party or Maoist versions) tends to have a high regard for the state as a means to create the commonwealth from ocean to ocean.

Is the best way to resist, oppose and question the concentration of wealth in the media, military, party politics and corporations the anarchist way? Or, as Canadians, is not a strong and firm state the best way to oppose and stare down such obvious Goliaths? If, as Canadians, we hope to create and build a strong, just and affordable health care, educational, cultural, economic and political system to act as a counter to the United States, do we not need the counterweight of Ottawa to do so? The fact that anarchists are so cynical of the state (and the power embodied in it) means that the very vehicle and ship that could take us to the other shore is dismissed and not boarded.

When Canadians, therefore, turn to American anarchists (and there are many—Chomsky is just one of the better known), are they not being colonized in a more subtle and insidious way and manner? Dare we say that there just might be a Canadian colonial and comprador class that under the guise of opposing power reinforces the very power they oppose by refusing to become involved in the formal political means that could oppose it?

Thomas More wrote a fine missive in the sixteenth century. The tract for the times was called *Utopia*. *Utopia* probes and questions the nature of utopian idealism—the dialogue between More and the fictional Raphael is most instructive in this regards. Raphael had been to the new world and had come back with glowing reports. It was a paradise, so he reported, in which each and all shared the goods of the land. All were justly tended and cared for in a compassionate political system. Raphael returned from such an inspiring place to tell More of his find. More was most impressed. More was, like Raphael, irritated and vexed by all the injustices in England's fair and pleasant land. More was also the foreign minister and minister of finance, so he was in a position to bring some changes. More was also a lawyer of some note and significance. More asked Raphael if he would join him in reforming England and making her as she should be. It is at this point in the discussion that Raphael begins to trot out all sorts of reasons and excuses for not getting involved in the formal political process. Raphael was, in short, so cynical of the state and its ability to deliver that he turned his back on it. More realized, probably much more than Raphael, the imperfections of the state, and yet he worked within it to bring about the common good, and there was much good he brought about before his execution. More was a tamed cynic who believed the state could deliver justice, and he worked within it. Raphael was cynical of the state and turned his back on it. Both men had a vision, and shared such a utopian and idealistic vision. More thought that the state could deliver imperfect justice, whereas Raphael thought the state could never do such a thing. Anglo-Canadian nationalism tends to be grounded in the tradition of More. Anglo-American anarchism tends to have much affinity with Raphael.

We do need to ponder and answer, as Canadians, this rather simple and elementary question. Who are the Canadians that have thought through the nature of American imperialism in the same way Chomsky has and does? And, more importantly, who are the Canadians who have offered and do offer a more creative and political answer to injustice and globalization than moral outrage, protest, anarchism and advocacy and network politics? There is a steady and solid nationalist tradition within Canada that we do need to turn our ear to if we ever hope to step out of going round and round with the same simple and reductionistic formulas and answers. Is not this turning to someone who knows little about Canada just another way of turning to the imperial centre for our great and good place under the sun?

The stark contrast between the state and society (the former often denigrated and demonized, the latter elevated and idealized) was highlighted, in a visual form, in the recent *festschrift* for the beloved west coast anarchist, Jerry Zaslove. *Anarcho-Modernism: Toward a New Critical Theory* has on its cover pictures of both Stalin and an American stealth bomber. If, of course, the state is viewed simply and only this way, anarchism has a point to make. But, there is much more to the state (in a positive way) and society (it does have its dark and negative side) than this. It is significant to note that Chomsky has published most of his books in Canada through one of the leading anarchist presses in Canada (Black Rose Press). We need also ponder why Naomi Klein's *No Logo* was so popular when it appeared not that long ago. The book, rightly so, asked some good and hard questions about the negative nature of globalization, but when serious questions are asked about how such a process can be challenged, Klein tends to have little to say about the role of the state and formal party politics. In short, Raphael tends, amongst such people, to trump More.

George Woodcock was, for many Canadians, a hero of sorts. Woodcock waved high the banner of anarchism, yet, like most establishment anarchists, he was quite willing to take money from the federal government for his many writing projects. Anarchists tend to question the role of the state, yet it is often the very largesse and generosity of the state that underwrites and pays for all their educational and publishing ventures. Such inconsistencies do need to be faced in all honesty.

Is the state, *de facto*, unable to be just and bring about the common good? Is the state so riddled through with negative power it can never be trusted? This tends to be the position of the anarchist left and the libertarian right. It also tends, in some important ways, to be the position of our new republican party in Canada (the Conservative Party). Is society the best means to bring about the common good? What are the limitations of society and small decentralized groups in bringing about such a good? Power (its use and abuse) can be found at all levels of human and political life, and it does little good to project the misuse of power onto the state and locate the proper use of power to society. If only life was so simple? Those who have taken the smallest and shortest steps in life know only too well how power can be both abused and used well in both the state and society.

In conclusion, Canadians must be wary and aware about the more subtle ways we can be, and are often, colonized. There is a thoughtful anarchist comprador class in Canada that, rightly so, warns us about the dangers of American imperialism at one level, but, at another level, walks us into the very centre of the American web. It is our historical Canadian nationalist tradition that can keep the True North on guard both against the American military-industrial complex and, equally important, an American ideology that priorizes liberty and individualism against the Canadian heritage of the commonweal and good government. More or Raphael, Raphael or More? Nationalism or anarchism, anarchism or nationalism? Which shall we choose and why? The road taken will take us, when day is done, to very different places.

But we must remember that even the dissidents can speak as members of the empire.

CHAPTER FOUR

NOAM CHOMSKY MEETS ROBIN MATHEWS: AMERICAN ANARCHISM AND CANADIAN NATIONALISM

Judged in terms of the power, range, novelty, and influence of his thought, Noam Chomsky is arguably the most important intellectual alive. — *The New York Times*[1]

Mathews sees himself—accurately I think—as helping us gain an independent sense of ourselves. — *Books in Canada*[2]

Both Noam Chomsky and Robin Mathews emerged, in a public and published way, in the late 1960s as political writers. Both men had been active in the 1960s, but their activism began to take wings and leave the presses and publishing houses and homes in 1968 and 1969. When Chomsky's *American Power and the New Mandarins* and *At War with Asia* were published in 1968 and 1969, Chomsky emerged as a dominant critic of American foreign policy. When Mathews and Steele's *The Struggle for Canadian Universities* and Mathews's *This Cold Fist* were published in 1969, Mathews became a significant actor on the stage of Canadian political, educational and literary life. Chomsky and Mathews have, since the 1960s, continued to play a substantive and prophetic-like role in both the United States and Canada. And yet, if many Canadians were asked if they had heard of Chomsky, the answer would be a resounding 'yes'. If many Canadians were asked if they had heard of Mathews, a rather quizzical look would appear. Why is this the case?

Many bookstores in Canada carry many of Chomsky's books, and Chomsky is taught in many Canadian university classes. It is a rare bookstore in Canada that carries any of Mathews's books, and few students at Canadian universities have heard of Mathews. Why is this so? Why is it that Canadians know more about American political activists and writers than they do about some of the more important Canadian activists and writers? What is it about the Canadian publishing ethos that bows deep and low to American anarchists yet keeps Canadian nationalists far from the public attention and limelight?

Both Noam Chomsky and Robin Mathews have spent much of their academic and public lives exposing the questionable rhetoric of the American empire. Both have seen Leviathan for what it is, and told all who would hear that the emperor and the empire have no clothes on. Chomsky has used the political principles of the empire to point out the chasm between rhetoric and reality. Chomsky has defended liberty, individualism, conscience and equality to one and all. He, in many ways, sees himself as the true patriot and defender of the American founding principles. Mathews has, like Chomsky, walked the extra mile to clarify and point out that the American empire has a predictable tendency to act like a predator and bird of prey. Mathews, unlike Chomsky, has pointed out how many Canadians have been taken in by both American principles and American imperial ambitions, and, as such, have acted as dutiful colonials and compradors.

Chomsky has been a consistent critic of the state, and as an anarchist, has, much of his life, argued that society rather than the state is the best and finest way to bring in the good community. Chomsky has been most suspicious of the power that is invested in the state, and he has spent most of his days pointing out how such power is abused and misused.

Chomsky has become a guru and mentor of sorts to the anarchist and protest left in both the United States and Canada. Many Canadians, who see themselves as radical, readily genuflect to Chomsky, and, in doing so, fail to see how they are welcoming a more subtle form of the empire into their midst. Mathews started a nationalist party in Canada (before Mel Hurtig), and he is a firm believer in the role of the state as a means of bringing into being the just society. Why do so many Canadians follow the cynical path of Chomsky and his view of the state, and fail to heed and hear the insights of Mathews when he urges Canadians to engage the state at the level of political parties? The liberty-loving individualism of Chomsky and clan has, buried at its centre, a worrisome cynicism and scepticism. It is this cynicism that creates political paralysis at the level of formal party politics. Do Canadians truly want to hike down this dubious path? Is indifference and apathy in regard to formal party politics the wisest and sanest way to go? What are the limitations of anarchist and advocacy politics and what are some of the positives of the state? Until these sorts of probes are sent out, we will be in danger of slipping into a comic book way of seeing and doing politics. Who, as Canadians, should we heed and hear? Chomsky or Mathews? Mathews or Chomsky? And, what does it say about us as Canadians when we turn to Chomsky to teach us how to be political?

There is no doubt that moral outrage, protest and advocacy politics have their place, but when formal political parties (and their role in guiding the ship of state) are seen only in a negative way, the very goals the idealists so long to attain are undercut and undermined.

Mathews has never pitted society against the state in quite the same way Chomsky and many anarchists have. In fact, Mathews has argued, quite convincingly, in both *Canadian Identity: Major Forces Shaping the Life of a People* and *The Canadian Intellectual Tradition* that the delicate Canadian dialectic holds together both the role of the individual and community, and the society and the state. The individual and society can go astray and slip into individualism and splinter groups just as the state and community can slip into collectivism and the abuse of power. But, both society and the state, the individual and community can also do much good. Those who only concentrate on the negative role and function of the state distort social reality. Much good is brought about by the state, and, in Canada, as privatization and globalization continue to make insidious inroads, the only way to restore a shared and national sense of the common good is through a strong state. Those who perpetually badmouth and take shots at the state might just sink or cripple the very ship that can take them from one shore to another.

Mathews would agree with Chomsky that the American empire is an empire, and, as such, does need to be exposed for all its brutal deeds in various parts of the world. Mathews would, though, question some of the American principles that Chomsky holds so near and dear. Mathews would ask Canadians why they are so keen and eager to embrace such principles when, in Canada, we hold high such notions as the common good and the positive role of the state in bringing about such a good.

The Canadian tradition has often held order in tension with liberty, the commonweal in tension with individualism, the organic nature of society with equality, tradition with conscience and the role of the state and society in bringing into being the True North. When we, as Canadians, snap the tension and turn to the reactive and reactionary

American way as our north star, we become obedient colonials of the empire. Mathews has made this process quite clear in his challenging and razor sharp missives, *Treason of the Intellectuals: English Canada in the Post-Modern Period* and *Being Canadian in Dirty Imperialist Times*.

Treason of the Intellectuals is divided into five compact and challenging sections. The 'Introduction' lays bare the problem many Canadians face in an all too frequent way. Most of our intellectual class has betrayed the Canadian way again and again. This comprador class, with its commitments to the United States, anarchism, or its firstborn child, postmodernism, has no sense of any common heritage, identity or nationhood. The underlying principles that shape and guide these prejudices are extreme notions of individualism, liberty and equality (all part of the American genetic code). What seems to be a form of dissidence and radicalism is, in fact, a deeper and more worrisome attitude of Canadian capitulation to American founding principles and priorities. Chapter I, 'Political Lies, Canadian Cultural History and the Post-Modern' takes a surgical knife to the deceptions of much of cultural history and the postmodern way that can only fragment, divide and separate. Mathews has little interest in such an intellectual way of seeing things, and he blows the ram's horn on the failures and futility of the postmodern project and ideology. Chapter II, 'Regionalism: Imperialism in a Small Pond' continues the assault on the shaky and dubious foundations of the postmodern way. The turn, in Canada, to regionalism, Mathews argues, is a turn away from the larger vision of what Canada might and could be. Mathews is very much a poet and thinker of the large picture, of the epic vision, of the Canadian meta-narrative. He has little patience for those who hide away in ever smaller and smaller views of what the common good might and could be if we had but the fullness of mind to see what we share in common. Chapter III, 'Iago in the Colony: Resentment as a Reactionary Force in Canada' turns to many Canadians who, like Iago, are driven by resentment and have no sense of Canada as being more than a colony to serve imperial interests and ambitions. Chapter IV, 'The New Treason of the Intellectuals in English Canada' pulls no punches and refuses to capitulate. Our intellectual class has, again and again, betrayed us, and Mathews walks the extra mile to identify who such intellectuals are and how this betrayal process works (in crude, subtle and sophisticated ways). *Treason of the Intellectuals* is a must read for any Canadian who has lost their national way and realizes the implications of such a lostness. There is, in short, a way out of the dark, deep forest where light is thin and shadows many. It is to such clearings that Mathews points.

Being Canadian in Dirty Imperialist Times is a poetic manifesto that just will not quit. Mathews probes, in poem after poem, how Canadians are colonized, how Americans mesmerize and take captive the Canadian mind and imagination and what Canadians can do to resist the empire in its multifaceted ways of taking captive the Canadian ethos. *Being Canadian in Dirty Imperialist Times* draws together many of Mathews's earlier poems and adds a few new ones. The tract for the times is both a poetic *magna carta* and a historical overview of the Canadian journey. The initial poem, 'Pre-History Lesson' sets the stage for the drama that is about to unfold, and the final poem, 'Marina: Saturna Island' brings the book to a fitting conclusion. Many is the poem between these two bookend poems that explores and unpacks the way Americans just assume they have a right to shape and assimilate the Canadian way. The language Mathews uses is accessible, for and to the people, and spoken in such a way that Canadians can see themselves caught in the dilemma they are in. The missive is thick with struggle and hope, critical of the empire (like Chomsky), yet capable of speaking with a Canadian voice (unlike Chomsky).

Hegemony or Survival: America's Quest for Global Dominance, published in 2003, tells much the same sort of tale that Chomsky has been telling for the last five decades. The United States is an empire, and, as an empire, it seeks to dominate the globe. Chomsky's approach tends to be straightforward and stays on the same goat trail again and again. It is one thing, though, to expose the pretensions and violence of the United States. It is quite another thing to sort and sift through how Canadians are to respond to such a quest for global dominance. Chomsky does not know the Canadian tradition (most Americans suffer from the same problem), he has no real solutions for Canadians (most Americans don't), and he has no real solution to the American empire (beyond a sort of thoughtful and probing anarchist solution). Why then do Canadians turn so dutifully to an American who knows little about the Canadian way? Why, in short, do so many turn to Chomsky and so few turn to Mathews?

Mathews has, in a variety of ways, been faithful and true to the Canadian nationalist tradition, but many is the Canadian dissident or self-perceived radical that knows little about Mathews's yeoman's service in and for Canadians since the 1950s. It seems to me that if Canadians are ever going to get a serious and substantive sense of their own unique and vivid tradition, they do need to hear and heed Mathews as a primer and starter, at least. Those who think that protest and advocacy politics can bring down the American empire or resist and oppose the forward march and juggernaut of globalization are short-sighted and naive. Canadians who bow and genuflect to Chomsky and the American anarchist way might just be paving the way for the weakening of the state and the undermining of such Canadian institutions as health care, education, the CBC, employment insurance and pensions. Those who turn to Mathews (and his more nationalist vision) might be the true radicals who are at the forefront of offering a serious and substantive challenge to the United States and globalization in a way that can, through national and institutional means, oppose such Goliaths in our time.

Should we, as Canadians, turn more to the American liberal and anarchist way of Chomsky (and his followers, kith and kin) as our north star? If so, are we just not perpetuating and deepening our colonial way of being? Or, should we, as Canadians, gaze deeper into our communal and collective tradition and see, in such a way of being, that we need not follow the American lead into the future? The choice, as ever, is ours.

Anarchism (and its underlying principles of liberty, individuality, equality, anti-statism, conscience and a suspicion of the past) or Nationalism (and its underlying principles of order, the common good, justice and a respect for tradition and the state). Canadians have, in their history, lived with the dialectic and tensions of liberty and order, individuality and commonweal, equality and justice, and society and state, and with a respect for the accumulated wisdom of tradition and history. There are many ways Canadians have been and continue to be colonized. Those who uncritically bow to Chomsky perpetuate this worrisome process. Those who have taken the time to heed and hear Mathews might just see an old way, a way that is much older and nuanced than the American way, a way that is truly Canadian, a way that upholds and seeks to defend the best of the True North strong and free. It is by turning our ears to such a way that we truly might be able both to expose the follies and pretensions, in thought, of the United States and globalization, and, in deed, support the Canadian institutions that can fight the good fight and stay the course of opposition to such large and imposing forces. Canadians have done such things in the past. There is no reason we cannot do such things in the present and future.

CHAPTER FIVE

ALLEN GINSBERG AND GEORGE GRANT: HOWL AND LAMENT FOR A NATION

It is sixty years now this last autumn since the Beat movement was launched at Six Gallery in San Francisco on 13 October 1955. Some of the American Beats from the East Coast (Jack Kerouac and Allen Ginsberg) and the West Coast (Kenneth Rexroth, Gary Snyder, Philip Whalen, Lawrence Ferlinghetti) met and read together at this gathering. John Suiter rightly says, 'The Six Gallery reading has sometimes been called the first synthesis of the East and West Coast factions of the Beat Generation'.[1]

Kenneth Rexroth had hiked to many of the peaks in the North Cascades in the 1920s. His rambling and tramping tales are well told in *An Autobiographical Novel*.[2] Gary Snyder worked on lookout peaks (Crater and Sourdough Mountains) in 1952-1953, but he could not get work in the North Cascades in 1954 because of his affiliations with unions and anarchist left groups. These were the McCarthy years, and Snyder was a victim of such a red scare. Philip Whalen worked on lookout peaks (Sauk and Sourdough Mountains) between 1953 and 1955. Jack Kerouac, a year after the Six Gallery reading, in 1956, spent a summer on Desolation Peak in the North Cascades. *The Dharma Bums, Lonesome Traveler* and *Desolation Angels* all reflect much of what he saw and experienced on Desolation Peak.

The Six Gallery reading of 1955 was, therefore, a pivotal event in bringing together the ecological Beats of the West Coast and the Bop and Beat tradition of the East Coast. Allen Ginsberg attended and participated in the Six Gallery reading, and a year later, *Howl and Other Poems* was published. The back cover of *Howl*, from City Lights Books, says:

> Allen Ginsberg's *Howl and Other Poems* was originally published by City Lights Books in the Fall of 1956. Subsequently seized by the U. S. Customs and the San Francisco police, it was the subject of a long court trial at which a series of poets and professors persuaded the courts that the book was not obscene. Over 150,000 copies have since been sold ...[3]

There is no doubt *Howl* created a commotion and stir in the San Francisco area at the time.

Fifty years have passed since George Grant's (1918–1988) *Lament for a Nation* was published in 1965. *Lament for a Nation*, like *Howl*, created strong reactions. Many in the New Left and Counter-culture in Canada were drawn to *Lament for a Nation*. Many on the political centre and political right in Canada were offended by what Grant was saying in *Lament*. Grant was fully aware of what he was saying and doing at the time, and he knew that his criticisms of the American empire (and the Canadian colonial and comprador class) would not be taken well by the ruling establishment and high mucky-mucks at the time.

Lament has been called 'a masterpiece of political meditation',[4] and Darrol Bryant sees it as a tract for the times that stands within the Old Testament prophetic tradition of Lamentations.[5] Kenneth Rexroth has argued, in defending Ginsberg, that his poetry stands within the Jewish Old Testament tradition of testimonial poetry.[6] It is significant to note that Grant in his 1970 'Introduction' to *Lament for a Nation* refers twice to the image and metaphor of Moloch. Moloch was seen by the Jewish people as a devouring god that consumed and destroyed the life of one and all. Moloch is a central metaphor in Part II of 'Howl'. Grant also refers to the Beats and the Counter-culture in *Lament for a Nation*. Ginsberg and Grant seem, at first glance, to be lamenting and howling against the same Moloch. The American empire seemed to consume one and all. The best and the brightest did their best to oppose and resist such a monster and leviathan, but souls and bodies were required to feed the ravenous appetite of such a beast. Was it possible to live a meaningful life without bowing and genuflecting to Moloch?

Howl and *Lament for a Nation* seem to be on the same page and fighting the same enemy and opponent. But are they? Ginsberg and Grant do agree on what they want to be free from. Do they agree on what they want to be free for? It is by understanding this difference that we will understand the different paths taken between American anarchism (and Canadian devotees of such a tradition) and Canadian High Tory nationalism. The different paths hiked do lead to quite distinctly different places on the political spectrum. Let us, all too briefly, light and linger at *Howl* and *Lament for a Nation* to see how and why American anarchism and Canadian nationalism, although seeming to have much in common at one level, have less and less in common at more substantive levels.

It is significant to note, by way of beginning, who *Howl* and *Lament for a Nation* are dedicated to. Ginsberg offers up *Howl* to Jack Kerouac, William Burroughs and Neal Cassady; all three were East Coast Bop and Beat poets and activists. *Howl* was written for Carl Solomon, and William Carlos Williams wrote the introduction. Kerouac is very much in the lead in the dedication, and Ginsberg says, 'Several phrases and the title of *Howl* are taken from him'.[7] We need to ask ourselves this simple question if we ever hope to get a fix and feel for Ginsberg's drift and direction: what is the essence and core of the East Coast Bop and Beat ethos, and how did Ginsberg, Kerouac, Burroughs, Cassady, Williams and Solomon embody such an ideology? There tends to be six distinct points to be noted here: 1) individual feelings and emotions are paramount—reason and one-dimensional science are the problem, 2) protest and rebellion against the American empire and Puritanism are dominant, 3) uprootedness and unrootedness are welcomed—being on the road becomes a new creed and dogma, 4) eclectic spirituality becomes the new sacrament—a rather raw sexuality and spirituality are fused, 5) institutions—whether they are religious, political, cultural or economic—are seen as the problem, and 6) anarchism is seen as the liberating way in opposition to the authoritarian and repressive nature of all ideologies and institutions.

Liberty tends to trump order, individuality repels the common good, equality of desires is held high, raw experience banishes the wisdom of tradition, and spirituality is freed from the bondage of shackles of religious dogmas and institutions. Needless to say, such a position becomes its own ideology, creed and institution that cannot be doubted and must be defended at all costs by its guardians and gatekeepers.

There is no doubt that Kerouac, Burroughs and Cassady embodied such a vision. Carolyn Cassady dared to expose and question such an ideology in *Off the Road: My Years with Cassady, Kerouac and Ginsberg*. Even Kerouac was beginning to ask substantive questions about the Beats and distance himself from them in the early 1960s. He makes this quite clear in *Lonesome Traveler* when he said, 'I am actually not "beat" but a strange solitary crazy Catholic mystic',[8] and with the publication of *Vanity of Duluoz* in 1968, Kerouac made it clear that much of the Bop and Beat tradition was much more about a rather inflated vanity and egoistic and indulgent individualism than anything else. But Kerouac still remained the liberty-loving and solitary Catholic mystic. The American DNA and genetic code of individualism was still his master and guru.

Grant dedicated *Lament for a Nation* 'To Derek Bedson and Judith Robinson: Two Lovers of Their Country: One Living and One Dead'.[9] Who were Derek Bedson (1920–1989) and Judith Robinson (1897–1961), and how, as Canadian lovers of their country, were they different from Kerouac, Burroughs and Cassady? Derek Bedson, unlike many of the Beats, had a strong commitment to the Anglican High Tory tradition both in politics and religion. He was active in the Anglican Church of Canada (ever the gadfly to its emerging liberalism) and he worked in the areas of both federal and provincial politics. Bedson, unlike the Beats, realized that both political and religious institutions (although always imperfect), were important means to work within for the common good of the nation and the people. Society and the state (both have their distortions and demons) when understood aright should and can work together, in an organic, just, and ordered way, for the commonweal.

The philosophic tradition of liberalism, in either its American imperial form or its Beat reactionary form, was about individuals using their liberty in a unilateral way to undermine and deconstruct those things that, as people, we share in common. Grant turned to Bedson as a true teacher and mentor who loved his country. Judith Robinson was a feisty and fiery Red Tory who, as an animated journalist, challenged both liberalism and the Liberal Party in Canada. In fact, her relentless assaults on the Liberal Party led to the Royal Canadian Mounted Police (RCMP) bloodhounds being turned on her in the 1940s. Robinson thought the liberals were selling out Canada to the United States, and she would have none of it. The Liberal Party of St. Laurent and King was an anathema to her. The American way (both in principle and fact) was something she had little or no patience for. George Grant, therefore, when he dedicated *Lament for a Nation* to Derek Bedson and Judith Robinson knew what he was doing and saying.

Many Canadians have, I suspect, heard of Ginsberg, Kerouac, Cassady, Williams and Burroughs. I question whether many have heard of Judith Robinson or Derek Bedson. What does this tell us about our Canadian soul and how it has been colonized by the American matrix?

There is little doubt that Bedson, Robinson and Grant stood in a very different place on the political and personal spectrum than

Kerouac, Burroughs, Cassady and Ginsberg. Both clans could agree that American imperialism, corporate capitalism, consumerism, liberal bourgeois thought and Puritanism needed to be exposed and undressed. There was no depth to them. They embodied Nietzsche's 'last man' or Miller's 'wrong dream'. Surely there was more to the good life than defining and defending personal peace and happiness. In short, Canadian High Tories and American Anarchist Beats do agree on the fact the patient is ill and ailing. They have much in common in their diagnosis. But they have quite a different way of healing the failing and faltering patient. The prognosis takes Grant and Ginsberg down different paths and to different places. What then is this different prognosis? Let us turn to *Howl* and *Lament for a Nation* to see what is seen. It is in this different seeing we will come to understand some important differences at a root, core and genetic, philosophic and practical level between Americans and Canadians.

It is just now sixty years since *Howl* was published and fifty years since *Lament for a Nation* was published. It is at such remembering points we are offered the opportunity to see again what animates and tends to define the True North from the empire to the south.

'Howl' (the poem from which the book is named) is divided into three sections and a 'Footnote to Howl'. Section I opens with the memorable lines that none forget once heard and read: 'I saw the best minds of my generation destroyed by madness'.[10] The rest of the section is a prose poem that describes how these best minds were destroyed, and equally so, how the artistic and visionary nature of such minds were bent and broken on the anvil of the modern world. Section I is both tragic and sad, and the ruined and wrecked lives are amply laid out for all to see in the most graphic and poignant of ways. We might ask, as we read Section I, whether these are the best minds (given their end points), but Ginsberg has told us these are the best and the brightest, so we heed and hear.

Section II turns, in a penetrating manner, to the place that has savaged such minds, and the potent image that speaks of such an alluring and tempting place: Moloch, Moloch and Moloch becomes the destructive and dominant metaphor. The metaphor of Moloch is unpacked and unravelled in a variety of ways, but there is no doubt that the best minds are defeated victims of Moloch, and Moloch will devour one and all. Who is Moloch? Ginsberg makes this most clear. It is all forms of tyranny and authority that brutalize and are callous to the best minds. The United States is very much in the foreground, though.

Section III presses home the point in a more urgent and not-to-be-forgotten manner. Section III is directed to Carl Solomon in Rockland. The political left is held high and idealized, and the United States is seen as the place of repression and destruction. The language is raw and graphic in 'Howl', and social reality is neatly and crisply divided into a rather simplistic either–or way of looking at things. 'Footnote to Howl' walks the extra mile to shout from the rooftops the Holy, Holy, Holy theme: all is holy and needs to be seen as such. Ginsberg in this section is doing his best to fuse spirituality and sexuality, street life with city life. Nothing should be seen as unholy. All has goodness in and to it, and when this is seen, eternity is in our midst.

There are other poems in the *Howl* collection, also. 'A Supermarket in California' doffs the cap to Walt Whitman, and 'Transcription of Organ Music' takes the reader through and beyond the purpose of organ music. The transcription and the organ are meant to walk the attentive and alert to higher and deeper spiritual states. This poem points the way to what such a fusion of spirituality and sensuality might look like. 'Sunflower Sutra' tells the tale of Ginsberg and Kerouac as they see, through Blake's sunflower, a *sutra* of insight in hard places. 'America' is a longer poem, and true to form, turns on the United States. 'In the Baggage Room at Greyhound', like other poems in the collection, takes the reader into the underground and underbelly of America. 'An Asphodel', 'Song', 'Wild Orphan' and 'In Back of the Real' close off this final section in *Howl and Other Poems*.

It must be remembered that these poems were published in 1956. The United States was in the thick of the Cold War, and anyone with the mildest sympathies with the left was seen as communist. The raw sexual and sensual language that permeates and pervades most of *Howl and Other Poems* is a frontal assault and attack on both middle class bourgeois America and the Puritan ethos that shaped such an ideology. Ginsberg, in short, was pulling no punches. He thought the best minds in America had been driven mad by the combination of the military-industrial complex, anti-communist thinking and Puritan and bourgeois ethics. He howled against such a repressive way of being, and the state and police turned on him for doing so. *Howl* and *On the Road* became sacred texts and bibles for the Beat generation, and Ginsberg became a high priest to such a generation with his fusion of sensuality–spirituality, anarchist–protest politics and a raw and in-your-face assault on middle class values. *Howl* became a lightning rod missive for those who felt ill at ease with expectations laid on them they had no interest in. Ginsberg's *Howl* spoke what many felt but had not yet put to words.

What are the points of concord and convergence between Grant's *Lament for a Nation* and Ginsberg's *Howl*, and equally important, what are the points of discord and divergence?

The 1965 edition of *Lament for a Nation* is divided into seven chapters. In some ways it is a prose poem that deals with major political themes in Canada, and between Canada and the United States. George Grant added an 'Introduction' in 1970, and Sheila Grant (George's wife) added an 'Afterword' in 1997. I will stick with the 1965 edition of *Lament for a Nation*. I mentioned above that the very language of lament conjures up for the reader the tradition of Jewish political thought. The Jewish prophet Jeremiah wrote *Lamentations*. The fact that *Lament for a Nation* is divided into seven chapters reminds the reader of the seven days of creation in the Jewish tradition. The fact the seventh chapter is theological means that the political reflections have a deeper source than merely politics.

Chapter I in *Lament* deals with John Diefenbaker's (1895–1979) defeat by Pearson in the 1963 election. Grant saw this as a source of much concern, since Pearson was pro-American and Diefenbaker was a thorn in Kennedy's side. And, more worrisome for Grant, most Canadians were overjoyed to have Pearson as the new Prime Minister of Canada. What did this say about Canadian nationalism?

Chapter II and III ponder both the follies and foolishness of Diefenbaker and his nobility and heroism. Grant was no uncritical fan of Diefenbaker, but he did think that Diefenbaker stood on principles, and his nationalist political principles brought about his demise. Chapter IV touches on both liberalism and the Liberal Party in Canada, and why such a party has tended to dominate much of Canadian political life (and the consequences for Canadian nationalism).

Chapters V and VI, consciously so, walk the reader into the realms of political theory and political philosophy, and why at root and ground level, Canadian conservatism (in its English and French forms) is almost the opposite of American republican conservatism.

The fact that American liberalism (in its Democratic and Republican forms) seeks to dominate the world raises for Grant a worrisome question. Is there any way to oppose or resist this Moloch? Is this, as Canadians, our fate and necessity? What can we do given this stubborn fact? Chapter VII opens up a dialogue about the difference between fate–necessity and the good. How, as Canadians, can we live from something higher than what seems to be our dominant fate? Is it possible to get out of the matrix of American liberalism?

Lament for a Nation has been called a masterpiece, and it is for a variety of reasons. The tract for the times moves from the facts of Canadian and American political history, to Canadian and American political philosophy to theology. It is poignant and pungent prose writing in the best tradition of political pamphlets.

How, though, is *Lament for a Nation* similar and different from *Howl*, and what can these points of concord and discord tell us about the differences between Canadian and American thought and culture? There are five points of convergence, and five of divergence.

First, both *Lament* and *Howl* raise serious and substantive objections about the American military-industrial complex, the power elite in the United States and the damage done by such an elite in various parts of the world.

Second, both write in an intense, committed and accessible manner. Ginsberg can be raw, crude and excessively graphic. Grant was much more polished, incisive and delicately evocative. Grant and Ginsberg do communicate through plain and direct speech, though, as participants in the tough issues of the time rather than as detached and cool-headed observers. Both are on the ice. Neither is in the balcony or bleachers.

Third, both men were critical of the liberal bourgeois tradition and a form of American puritanism that justified such a smug view. Ginsberg rebelled against this by indulging all sorts of desires and interests, whereas Grant rebelled against the liberal bourgeois tradition by deepening and ordering his interests and desires towards the highest and noblest things. Both could agree that Locke's 'life, liberty and estates' and Nietzsche's 'last man' were something they did not want to be. They disagreed on the best path to hike when the Puritan–bourgeois–last man was left behind. Plato is quite different from Whitman, Coleridge from Blake. Grant was for the former,

Ginsberg the latter. Allen Ginsberg sent me a couple of letters in the late 1980s (1 January 1989 and 6 February 1989). The first discussed the Beats, his involvement with Naropa Institute, Buddhism, and Chogyam Trungpa Rinpoche and his rather negative and reactionary view of the Jewish God. The second letter was a copy of his small book on Blake (*Your Reason & Blake's System*). Both the long letter and the missive speak much about Ginsberg's commitments, and some of the distortions and caricatures he had of other traditions because of such commitments. Both Grant and Ginsberg rebelled against the American empire, Puritanism and the bourgeois tradition, but they turned to different wells to slake the thirst of their deeper longings and questions.

Fourth, both men are distinctively and consciously thinking from a religious and theological vision in more than merely a moral sense. Ginsberg begins *Howl* by saying 'All these books are published in Heaven',[11] and Grant begins *Lament* by reference to Anglican parish life and ends with a sustained theological reflection on the difference between necessity–fate and the good.

Fifth, neither Grant nor Ginsberg offer much of a way out of the problem. Ginsberg can howl and Grant can lament. This might be a good place to start, but it is hardly a positive, creative and constructive way to end. What lies on the far end and other side of howling and lamenting? There are, sadly so, many who begin and end in such a place.

If Grant and Ginsberg can meet and greet at this intersection place, where do they part paths and why? It is one thing to agree on what we oppose and desire to say a firm 'no' to. It is quite another thing to state what we wish to affirm and say 'yes' to. There are many who often agree on what is not wanted, but such people often part paths when a serious discussion (at both a philosophical and practical level) begins on what is desired and wanted. This is where Ginsberg and Grant go in different directions. What are their points of discord and divergence, then?

First, Grant was Canadian, and he had a commitment to Canadians and a concern for the way Canada is being colonized by the United States. Ginsberg was American, and he had little or no interest in the Canadian political tradition. *Lament for a Nation* deals with Canadian–American relations in a way *Howl* does not. When, as Canadians, we know more about Ginsberg than Grant, it speaks much about a way of being colonized.

Second, there is no doubt that both Grant and Ginsberg had deep commitments to a moral and mystical religious vision, but Grant, unlike Ginsberg, would have argued that it is important to hold together spirituality and religion rather than fragmenting them. There is a tendency in Ginsberg to fly off into the mystical, visionary and contemplative ether, and, in the process, such things as dogma and institutions are seen as the problem. Needless to say, such a position becomes its own dogma and institution. Ginsberg's models and teachers were those like Whitman and Blake, whereas for Grant thinkers such as Plato, Augustine, Hooker, Swift, Johnson and Coleridge were his teachers and guides. We can see, therefore, the anti-institutional mindset in Ginsberg, whereas, for Grant, institutions are important even though a critical attitude must always be held towards them. The ideas that underwrite this difference are important to note. Ginsberg's sense of liberty and individualism dominates the day (all so American) whereas for Grant order and institutions are equally important.

Third, although both Ginsberg and Grant howled and lamented the state of things in the 1950s and 1960s, Grant attempted through the Progressive Conservative Party, to challenge the American empire. Ginsberg never rose much beyond anarchism, protest politics and moral outrage. Grant pointed out, in *Lament*, how such an approach is both allowed and easily co-opted by the power elites. Those who step out of the formal political process merely facilitate, by their absence, the very thing they protest against. What might seem the moral high ground can be, in fact, a form of grave digging.

Fourth, Grant argued that, with the coming to be of liberalism, we faced an ominous challenge. Those like Daniel Bell had argued (and Grant noticed this) that we had come to the end of ideology with liberalism. Francis Fukuyama argued, in the 1990s, updating Bell's argument, that we had come to the end of history with the end of the Cold War and the victory of liberalism. There is no doubt that both Ginsberg and Grant opposed the unilateralism of American military and corporate power. The aggressive notion of liberty and rugged individualism that underwrote and justified such a stance was abhorrent to both Grant and Ginsberg. But—and this is the catch—Ginsberg used the same American notions of liberty and individualism in his anarchist and protest approach as did the power elites. He applied such principles in more of an anti-establishment and, of course, anti-authoritarian way, but the notions of liberty, choice, individualism, protest, dissent were all there.

Grant saw through this charade. Ginsberg was just the other side of the corporate elite. They just used their liberty and freedom in different ways, but neither disagreed about the priority of the American vision and dream: life, liberty, choice and individualism. Grant dared to question the very philosophic principles of American liberalism, and as such, hiked a different path than Ginsberg and the Beats. Canadian notions such as law, order and good government take the curious and thoughtful to different places than life, liberty and the pursuit of happiness. Grant realized that when Canadians uncritically genuflected to the American Beats, they were welcoming the American Trojan horse into Canada in a more subtle way. There are more ways to be colonized than mere military and economic pressures. The literary and cultural traditions of the United States (the Beats) have done much to colonize many Canadians, and there have been many Canadian cultural and literary compradors that have facilitated such a process. Grant would have said 'no' to Ginsberg for the simple reason that Ginsberg was as much a devout and committed American, like a Noam Chomsky, as the very Americans he howled against and opposed.

Fifth, Grant was a much more sophisticated thinker than Ginsberg, and there is no doubt that *Lament for a Nation* is a more substantive work than *Howl*. The level of political and philosophical depth in *Lament* opens up vistas of thought that are just not there in Ginsberg and *Howl*. *Howl* never rises much beyond rant and reaction, and sadly so, Ginsberg's intellectual world tends to polarize between the evil and nasty power elite and the good, pure and lovable anarchist, Beat and protest types. It is a simplistic interpretation of reality that Grant was much too wise to bow an uncritical head to. He saw too much, and saw too far to worship at such a shrine and with such reactionary priests, and he urged Canadians not to turn to such a comic book view of the world.

In sum, Ginsberg and Grant, at first glance, seem to have much in common, but on deeper and further inspection, have little in common. Both protest against many of the same things. Both agree on many of the things that must be opposed. But by day's end, the American Beat anarchism of Ginsberg is quite different from the Canadian High Tory vision of George Grant. It is by understanding such differences that we can see why and how the American and

Canadian traditions create and make for different national outlooks. It is somewhat sad and tragic when Canadians know more about American models and take their leads from such fashions than they do from their own kith and kind.

SECTION II

THE FLAME STILL BURNS IN THE TRUE NORTH

CHAPTER SIX

WHAT IS CANADIAN CONSERVATISM?

Nor does our future lie in Union with those that dwell to the Southward. — Stephen Leacock[1]

We were grounded in the wisdom of Sir John A. Macdonald, who saw plainly more than a hundred years ago that the only real threat to nationalism was from the South, not from across the sea. To be a Canadian was to build, along with the French, a more ordered and stable society than the liberal experiment in the United States. — George Grant[2]

We have, as Canadians, in the last few decades, come more and more within the gravitational pull of the United States. Our culture, economy, military and linguistic frame of reference have, increasingly so, been drawn into such an orbit. Since the late 1970s-early 1980s, when Thatcher and Reagan ascended the thrones across the ocean and to the south of us, the language of conservatism has been defined by their frame of reference. This Anglo-American understanding of conservatism is really a form of first generation liberalism that seeks to return to a lighter state, less taxes, more power to the individual (and the business sector) over and against the growing power of the state to protect its own sovereignty (in an age of globalization), and the role of the state in ensuring basic services such as health care, education, culture and employment.

There are important points of convergence between Canadian conservatism (with its concern for the common good) and second generation liberalism with its concern for the welfare of each and all (and the role of the state in ensuring such a good). It is this notion of the commonweal or the welfare state that has come under increasing attack in the last two decades. Those who have been the most vocal and persistent in their assault have called themselves conservative, and it is their use of conservative that has confused many who have little or no understanding of Canadian history or intellectual thought.

If we are ever going to seriously understand historic Canadian conservatism (rather than its present mutation and distortion), we need to go to the beginning of the Canadian drama to get a fix and feel for such a tradition. Anglo-Canadian High Toryism (from which conservatism was birthed and is a legitimate child) can be found within the Anglican heritage. Anglicans have often been called Tories at prayer, and the two most prominent Anglican bishops in Canada, Bishops Inglis and Strachan, were both deeply suspicious of American republican ideas and American expansionistic and imperial tendencies. Inglis was a United Empire Loyalist who fled the American Revolution of 1776, and Strachan was at the forefront of defending the fledgling Canadian way against the invasion by the Americans (of Canada) in 1812. So, we can see, the very birth of Canada was founded on a resistance to the American way of life.

It is this form of Canadian Toryism that gave us Sir John A. Macdonald (1815–1891), whose 'National Policy' was meant to build a true north strong and free. It was Macdonald who fought, again and again, against the liberals that sought to integrate and annex Canada with and to the United States. Most of the Conservative Canadian Prime Ministers (such as John A. Macdonald, Robert Borden, Arthur Meighen, R. B. Bennett and John Diefenbaker) exerted much effort and gave the best of their energies to defend Canada and define it in such a way that it could not be confused with or assimilated into the United States. It is this form of Toryism–Conservatism that has always contested the drift and direction of Republicanism–Liberalism.

We do not need to read too far or too deep into the writings of such Canadian literary worthies as Thomas Haliburton (1796–1865), Susanna Moodie (1803–1885), Catherine Parr Traill (1802–1899), William Kirby (1817–1906), Charles Mair (1838–1927), G. T. Denison (1839–1925), Mazo de la Roche (1879–1961) or Stephen Leacock (1869–1944) to get a feel for the texture of Canadian conservatives as they touch on culture and the larger questions of nationhood and sovereignty. The nineteenth century saw the emergence of the Imperial Federation League (IFL) and the Canada First movement. It is this type of conservatism that cannot be equated with either the so-called conservatism of Thatcher and Reagan or the way conservatism is used by Blue Tories in the Conservative Party; needless to say, such positions and ideologies are republican and liberal.

If we ever hope, as Canadians, to reclaim what it means to be a Canadian conservative, we, initially, need to expose and call into question how the word is being used today. Until this is done, there will be much confusion, and we will, increasingly so, march to the beat of the American way and tune. If we ever hope to free ourselves from the power of the American gravitational pull, much work is needed. The New Romans to the south will, understandably so, fight back (as will the comprador class in Canada that serves the empire's interests).

The first task, it seems to me, is to be grounded and rooted in Canadian history and the struggles we have fought not to be Americans. If we have no sense of history, if we have no memory, if Orwellian-like, all that is important is thrown away, we have no way to defend ourselves at a basic level of thought and language. It is by knowing our intellectual and political history that we can defend ourselves against its distortions. There is, of course, more to the struggle than this, but at a basic level if Canadians do not even know the difference between a conservative and a liberal, it is most difficult to get the thoughtful (with a concern for the commonweal and Canadian sovereignty) to join the Conservative Party.

There is no doubt that the major media do much to baffle the average reader, and it is equally true that much contemporary education does little to teach, in a serious way, a serious and substantive understanding of Canadian history. The conservative Canadian historian, Donald Creighton, often spoke about how the liberal authorized reading of Canadian history caricatured the authentic conservative way. Such an insight finds a true echo in John Ralston Saul's *Reflections of a Siamese Twin: Canada at the End of the Twentieth Century*, in which the liberal view of Canada is idealized and the classic conservative way is demeaned and distorted. Saul's authorized reading of Canadian history may serve and suit his interests well, but, as serious intellectual history it is weak and wanting.

Those who are interested in a further look at a more genuine Canadian conservatism beyond what is found in these pages might want to read Charles Taylor's *Radical Tories*, David Orchard's *The Fight for Canada*, Dalton Camp's *Whose Country Is This Anyway?*, George Grant's *Lament for a Nation*, Stephen Leacock's *The Unsolved Riddle of Social Justice* or any of my earlier books, *The Red Tory Tradition, The Canadian High Tory Tradition: Raids on the Unspeakable* and *Keepers of the Flame: Canadian Red Toryism*.

CHAPTER SEVEN

STEPHEN LEACOCK:
PIONEER OF THE CANADIAN TORY TRADITION

Stephen Leacock was part of that curious and perhaps indigenously Canadian species which has been given the name of 'Red Tory'. — Alan Bowker[1]

Many writers have asserted that there is a common ground between conservatism and socialism; perhaps the most frequently cited similarities are an organic view of society, distrust of pure individualism, and a willingness to use the state to assert the rights of society, as distinct from the interests of powerful individuals. When both ideologies have legitimacy within a political culture, a hybrid known as the 'red tory' may emerge. — Ian Robertson[2]

Introduction

When most of us hear the word conservative, we think immediately of Brian Mulroney, Stephen Harper, Ronald Reagan, George Bush and, of course, Margaret Thatcher. When we hear the word conservative, most of us think of Premiers Klein, Harris and Wall or Preston Manning's party, the Canadian Alliance. But, we need to pause for a second and ask whether such people and parties faithfully reflect the historic Canadian conservative way or whether the ideologies of those mentioned above are not more an embodiment of classical and republican liberalism.

What, in fact, were Mulroney, Reagan and Thatcher trying to conserve? What, in fact, were Harris, Klein, Manning and Stockwell Day trying to conserve? Is it not some variation of classical or republican liberalism? The language of a lighter state, less taxes, a market economy, more power to the individual, greater emphasis on law and order, the elevation of society and the demeaning of the state, ever-greater ties with the American empire and an uncritical cheerleading for globalization are all hallmarks of historic liberalism. But, are such ideas the centre and core of historic Canadian conservatism?

If we ever hope to understand the classical meaning of historic Canadian conservatism, we, of course, need a thorough feel for the English, French, and First Nations traditions from which Canada was formed and has been nurtured. Such a task is well beyond the scope of this chapter, but, for the rest of it, I will linger and hover about the life and writings of a well-known and much-loved Canadian, Stephen Leacock. We will need to ask, by chapter's end, whether Leacock's understanding of conservatism is even faintly similar to the conservatism of Harris, Klein and, of course, Manning and Stockwell Day. If Leacock's view of Canadian conservatism runs down a different track than Harris, Klein and Day, we then need to ask the deeper question of how this has happened? How and why has the American definition of conservatism come to define and shape the Canadian understanding of conservatism? Is this not just one more example of us, as Canadians, being colonized by the United States of America?

A Fuller Read of Leacock

We still need the 'holistic interpretation' [of Leacock] Ian Robertson called for in 1986. — Alan Bowker[3]

Those of us who grew up in Ontario were nurtured, breastfed and tutored on the humour of Stephen Leacock. The publication of *Literary Lapses* in 1910 initiated a series of short books that culminated thirty-four books later, in 1945, with *Last Leaves*. When Stephen Leacock died in 1944, Canada lost a gentle satirist that had, in an exquisite way, combined the best of Swift, Dickens and Twain. Laughter did, indeed, hold both its sides when Leacock was read and heard, but the laughter was laced with much social commentary and political bite at its centre and source. Most Canadians, when they think of Leacock, think of a thoughtful humourist and a sort of national court jester. Many of us remember, with much fondness, as a regular part of our childhood memories, either Leacock's many and varied short stories being read to us, or the actor, John Drainie, reading Leacock, on CBC.

The Stephen Leacock Medal for Humour has been presented annually since 1947, and, gratefully so, Leacock's home in Orillia (at the Old Brewery Bay) was restored and opened again in 1958; since then the property and site have become an important tourist attraction. Today, many stream to Leacock's famed Mariposa, just as many others visit Lucy Maud Montgomery's (a contemporary of Leacock) Green Gables in Cavendish, to get a feel for the texture of Canadian culture and a much older form of conservatism. It was an American though, Ralph Curry, that wrote the first Leacock biography, *Stephen Leacock: Humorist and Humanist* in 1959, and it was Curry that played a substantive role in restoring both Leacock and the Leacock home in Orillia to their rightful place in Canadian history. Curry was the curator of the Leacock museum until 1977. Leacock, good Anglican and Tory that he was (for the two cannot be easily separated) lies buried in St. George's churchyard in Sutton, Ontario, just a short distance, as the bird flies, from Orillia. What has this preamble to do with Leacock as a pivotal conservative theorist and pioneer of the Canadian Tory tradition, though?

I have mentioned the above for the simple reason that the real Stephen Leacock has been trimmed, domesticated, sanitized and reduced to a shell and shadow of who he really was in his long and active life. If most Canadians were told that Leacock spent his life teaching political economy at McGill University, and that he was, in his prime, a political activist of the highest order, they would be most surprised. Why has this thinned out portrayal of Leacock become the accepted one, and what can a revisionist reading of the real Leacock tell us about the nature of historic Canadian conservatism? The image of Leacock as a rather charming and quaint teller of amusing tales and anecdotes does much injustice to the real man. Leacock published, in his life, forty books that dealt with such seemingly diverse subjects as economics, education, history, literary criticism and political science. But, it must be remembered that Leacock, as a classical Tory and Anglican, was grounded in the best of an interdisciplinary, humanist and classical education, a tradition I might add, that has been, for the most part, lost and forgotten in an age of specialization, technical training and the dominance of the market and corporations in setting the agenda for public education. Leacock, for most of his busy life, as I mentioned above, taught in the political economy department at McGill University (from 1901 to 1936). It was from this creative department (which Leacock was the head of most of his academic life) that such well-known Canadians as David Lewis (former head of the New Democratic Party), and Eugene Forsey, who was 'a conscious ideological socialist with some "odd" Tory notions',[4] emerged. Alvin Hamilton (a conservative

Saskatchewan MP in the Diefenbaker government) who was a 'conscious ideological Tory with some "odd" socialist notions'[5] was responsible for bringing into being, in 1958, the restoration of Leacock's Old Brewery Bay home in Orillia.[6] Hamilton, like Diefenbaker, and Leacock before him, understood the meaning of conservatism in a way that would firmly oppose and contradict some of the more populist notions of conservatism that are in our midst these days. What did Leacock think when he thought 'conservative', and how is our contemporary understanding of this time-honoured term the direct opposite of what it meant within the historic Canadian context? The remainder of this chapter will track and trace the life of Leacock, and by doing so, unpack and unravel the original meaning of both historic Canadian conservatism and nationalism.

Early Years: 1869–1906

In Canada, I belong to the Conservative party
— Stephen Leacock[7]

Stephen Leacock was born in England in 1869 and died in 1944. Leacock's family moved to Canada in 1876 when the young and inquisitive Leacock was seven years of age. Leacock's father, like some Rip Van Winkle, had fared poorly as a farmer in South Africa, England and Canada, and he was rarely at home when kith and kin were in need of him. Leacock took both fate and history into his own hands in 1887, at the age of eighteen, when he took his truant father to the train station in Sutton, with a buggy whip in hand, and told him never to return home. Agnes, Stephen's mother, seemed somewhat grateful for her son's firmness, but such a difficult decision meant that Stephen, as the eldest son now at home, was forced to balance his studies with a keen sense of responsibility for the well-being of his family. Leacock had finished his high school studies at Upper Canada College (UCC) in 1887, and he enrolled at the University of Toronto for the autumn semester of 1887. Leacock had graduated from Upper Canada College with top honours, and he worked so hard and did so well at the University of Toronto that he was granted third year status after a full year of courses. The dire financial situation at home, though, took its toll on the young Leacock; he cut short his studies in classical and modern languages, did teacher training, and because of his high marks at Upper Canada

College and the University of Toronto, was offered a teaching position back at Upper Canada College in 1889. Leacock, never one to be deterred for long, taught during the day, took classes at the University of Toronto in the evening and completed his BA in classical and modern languages in 1891 at the age of twenty-two.

Leacock's years as a student and finally housemaster at Upper Canada College were crucial for his future. As a student and lecturer at Upper Canada College, he studied and taught with such Canadians as Pelham Edgar (who became a noted professor of English at the University of Toronto), W. Allan Neilson (who became a well-known Renaissance scholar) and Edward Peacock (the first non-British born director of the Bank of England and financial advisor to the Royal Family). One of Leacock's teachers at Upper Canada College was Major Charles Gordon who became the important Canadian novelist, Ralph Connor, author of the Glengarry novels. It is essential to note that Upper Canada College (and King's College in Nova Scotia) were formed and established to educate a leadership elite in Canada that would hold high a classical and Anglo-Canadian Tory nationalism against the intrusion and invasion of American cultural and political republicanism. Leacock grew up in an environment in which he was clearly aware that Canada was founded on a different foundation than the republic and empire to the south, and he knew it was the role and responsibility of the leaders in the True North to protect the Canadian way against the rampant and entrepreneurial individualism to the south.

Leacock came to see, though, that his future did not lie with Upper Canada College; he was restless at the place, and his interests (and he heeded them well) were becoming, increasingly so, political and economic. The fact that Sir George Robert Parkin (1846–1922), the grandfather of George Grant, became principal of Upper Canada College in 1895 must have worked its wonders in the ever-expanding, curious and growing mind of Leacock. Parkin, at the time, was a key figure in the Imperial Federation League, and he had spent many a demanding year, before coming to Upper Canada College, arguing Canada must no more be seen as a docile colony of the British Empire. Canada must, increasingly so, take its equal role with England round the Imperial table. Such a position and move was opposed and controversial, but the seeds of decolonization and nationalism had been sown and were growing in the soil. The Canada First movement and the Imperial Federation League were all part and parcel of a growing and indigenous Canadian nationalism that sought to, on the one hand, move beyond the colonial mindset and seek equality with England and, on the other hand, resist American annexation and imperialism. Leacock, in his final years of teaching modern language at Upper Canada College, would have absorbed much from Principal Parkin, but Parkin knew that Leacock's future had more to it than Upper Canada College could offer, and he told him so.

Leacock's growing interest in politics, economics and Canadian nationalism, his many meetings and conversations with Parkin and his weariness with being teacher of modern languages and housemaster at Upper Canada College, nudged him to hike down a new vocational route. The year was 1899, Leacock was almost thirty, he had taught for ten years at Upper Canada College and he knew it was time to move on to new challenges. Leacock applied to do PhD studies at the University of Chicago and he was accepted into the program; hence he began to hike, in a more serious way, down the path he would take for many more years. The University of Chicago had, at that time, over a thousand graduate students (the largest number in the United States), and it was well financed by John D. Rockefeller. There was, also, a dark side to Chicago life so well depicted by the slogans of white city and grey city.

Leacock saw most clearly what happened when Eugene Debs (a labour organizer) tried to form workers into unions, and fresh in the minds of most at the University of Chicago was the firing of Edward Bemis (a professor) who had argued for an interventionist state. In fact, the poverty within the grey city part of Chicago was so great that the underemployed and unemployed were often arrested and sent to prison for daring to protest the inhumane living conditions. Leacock saw this Dickensian world, and he would have no part of it; the tale of two cities was too much for him to bear.

The reality of the two cities in late nineteenth century Chicago, as in England, and the deeper economic and structural reasons for it, troubled Leacock. The conventional liberal economic wisdom of the time was that the marketplace, *laissez-faire* and the unseen hand would bring about the good and just society. The hard and obstinate facts, though, argued firmly against such a simplistic idea and conclusion. The Conservative Prime Minister of England, Benjamin Disraeli, like Dickens, poignantly pointed out the evils and horrors of free trade, physiocracy and industrialism; both argued, in different ways, for a more interventionist state. In Canada, the well-known liberal, Goldwin Smith, had published his manifesto, *Canada and the Canadian Question*, in 1891—Smith, like most liberals at the time, argued for a strong free trade position and annexation to or union with the United States. It is as we understand the English, American and Canadian context of late nineteenth century liberalism (and the consequences of it) that we can make sense of why Leacock chose the PhD thesis topic he did on 'The Doctrine of Laissez Faire'; the thesis was completed in 1903 when Leacock was, almost, thirty-four.[8]

Leacock finished his thesis, as I mentioned above, in 1903, and upon completing it he was offered a permanent position at McGill University. Leacock had hoped to teach at the University of Toronto, but earlier horn-butting incidences with a prominent faculty member meant that Leacock had to turn elsewhere for more permanent employment. Leacock had been teaching as a sessional at McGill since 1901, but now, thesis behind him, he was ready to yet further and more deeply argue and articulate the conservative and Tory way to the Canadian public. Leacock, then, thirty-four, was about to lift anchor, leave the cove and set out into the open waters of public, educational and political life. Much, indeed, had happened since Leacock had left Upper Canada College in 1899, and much more was about to unfold and occur in his life as a result of such a decision.

The Middle Years: 1906–1920

Leacock's mature view of *laissez faire* is contained in *The Unsolved Riddle of Social Justice* (1920), which he wrote as a social reformer following the tribulations and sacrifices of the First World War. — Carl Spadoni[9]

[I]n *The Unsolved Riddle of Social Justice* (1920) Leacock made a serious contribution to two significant categories of thought in Canada: 'red toryism' and, for want of a better term, social philosophy. — Ian Robertson[10]

The publication, in 1906, of Leacock's *Elements of Political Science* catapulted Leacock onto front and centre stage of Canadian political life. *Elements of Political Science* expands and develops ideas that were, in seed form, in his thesis. This timely text went into many printings, it was a standard class textbook in many political science classes in the United States and Canada and it went into many translations; in fact, it was Leacock's bestseller and a bumper crop for publishers. *Elements of Political Science* is neatly divided into three distinct yet overlapping sections: 'The Nature of the State', 'The Structure of the Government' and 'The Province of Government'. Leacock is quick to argue and insist that the state needs to play a more active and responsible role in the life of the nation. We can certainly hear the echoes of Disraeli and, more to the point, Macdonald, in all this. This did not mean that Leacock bowed to the shrine of Marxism, but he did reserve much of his ire and fire for the consequences of capitalism. Leacock was quite aware of the inner core of liberalism, and he, as a conservative, fought against it. Laurier was in power at the time, Smith's ideas were spreading far and wide across the Dominion and Leacock knew that liberalism had to be challenged and stopped. The success of *Elements of Political Science* worked its wonders on the elite of the time. Governor General Lord Grey contacted Principal Peterson at McGill, and both met with Leacock to offer him a broader forum for his nationalist and protectionist ideas. It is essential to remember at this time that the Liberal Party was in power, free trade was very much the talk of the town, and most conservatives could see the annexationist writing on the wall. Leacock seemed to be the best person to represent and argue the conservative position over against the growing dominance of liberalism in the Dominion of Canada.

Leacock was a committed conservative, an excellent scholar and writer, but true to the mark, he was a superb lecturer and had the ability to present difficult ideas in a digestible manner and hold audience attention. In fact, from 1905 to 1906, Leacock packed Massey Hall with his spellbinding lectures on the need for a nationalist conservatism. The enthusiasm that greeted Leacock wherever he went did not go unnoticed. Leacock was on his way to becoming the lightning rod for a growing Canadian nationalism. The crowds turned out in the thousands, the ideas spread like wildfire on dry tinder, and Leacock was much in demand. Leacock saw himself, as a faithful conservative, filling and fleshing out the time-tried ideas of such Loyalists and conservatives as Thomas Haliburton, William Kirby, Charles G. D. Roberts (1860–1943) and, of course, Sir John A. Macdonald. Leacock, quick of wit, keen of mind and grounded in the finest and fittest of the older conservative way was, without much doubt, replacing his first teacher George Parkin on the nationalist trail. In fact, Leacock went much further in his thinking (yet ever true to Tory principles) than either the Canada First movement or the important work of the Imperial Federation League.

Leacock, as the flagship of a fuller nationalism, did a tour of England, Australia, New Zealand, South Africa and Canada from April 1907 to March 1908, arguing and articulating the Tory and nationalist position. The tour was a success, but the success was costly. It became clear to the old guard Canada First–Imperial Federation League types that Leacock was not content to merely parrot the safe and cautious sentiments of the first generation Canadian nationalists. Leacock was as quick to critique the faltering British empire as he was the emerging American empire. Canada, and Canadians, were not going to be dutiful and compliant colonials of either the British or American empires; the taking of such a position did not bode well for Leacock, and yet he was convinced such a path was a valid form of conservatism. Leacock merely saw himself furthering Macdonald and Cartier's idea of the National Policy that had worked so well for the Conservative Party. It is important, as I mentioned above, to remember that Laurier's Liberal Party was in power at the time and had been for a few years (since 1896), but the liberal sheen was beginning to lose its lustre and glow. Leacock saw the drift and direction of the Liberal Party and he would have none of it, but he was, also, calling into question some of the tame and timid imperialist nationalism of the Canada First–Imperial Federation League clan, also.

Leacock's 1907-1908 trip caused quite a stir both at home and abroad. Leacock's emerging indigenous Canadian conservative nationalism refused and rejected colonial status whether it came from England or the United States. Lord Grey, true to form, found Leacock too strident, but Leacock would not be muzzled or intimidated. Leacock, while on tour in England, compared the country to an ailing farmer that refuses to let the young sons run the farm in his 'John Bull'—the parable goes like this:

> The old man's [England] got old and he don't know it; can't kick him off the place: but I reckon that the next time we come together to talk things over the boys have got to step right in and manage the whole farm.[11]

It was political parables like this, laced with a nationalist perspective, that disturbed those in power in London and their dutiful comprador class in the colony. Leacock reasoned that if the English and Americans can, rightly so, be patriotic and open to a nationalist vision, why can't Canadians? Why must Canadians bow before the nationalist ideals of another and remain as childlike colonials? Principal Peterson told Leacock that 'your friends here feel that you have gone far enough on that tack ... much of your offense consisted in rushing in where, by tacit compact, the genuine Canadian is afraid to tread.'[12] Peterson's comments, like many academics', were true to either the liberal annexationist position or that of the English comprador class. The young Winston Churchill called Leacock's position 'offensive twaddle', and the reaction to Leacock's nationalism could be filled out with many more tributes of obvious praise.[13]

The publication in 1907 of Leacock's *Greater Canada: An Appeal* clearly articulated Leacock's nationalism; he made it most clear that England must cease to see Canada as a colony. Canada is an equal to England and, in time, she might just exceed the mother land. Leacock also made it clear in this popular tract for the times that Canada must not follow the liberal lead of Smith and Laurier in the area of free trade and economic integration with the United States. In fact, a greater Canada should be able to forge its own unique and indigenous way. Macdonald and Cartier had set the standard at Confederation; it was the role and task of a new generation of conservatives to deepen the vision and carry the nationalist idea forward a step further. The work of the Canada First movement, the Imperial Federation League, the Conservative Party and the bolder form of nationalism formed a solid and time-tried phalanx against the ever-growing Canadian liberal ethos. Leacock finished *Greater Canada* with a firm and resounding 'no' to the United States and, in doing so, made it quite clear that the liberals were taking Canada down the wrong path. Leacock stated, in a most unequivocal way, 'Nor does our future lie in Union with those that dwell to the Southward. The day of annexation to the United States is passed.'[14] I wonder what Leacock would think of our modern conservatives who fawn before the notion of free trade and eagerly support the Free Trade Agreement (FTA), the North American Free Trade Agreement (NAFTA) and the Bretton Woods organization that bears such ideas, the World Trade Organization (WTO). The fact that so many who see themselves as conservative are keeners for all this would have Leacock, I am sure, writing many a tale with a humorous bent to it.

Leacock, from 1909 to 1911, continued to play a prominent role as an educator at McGill University and a popular speaker and writer on the theme of Canadian nationalism and a more robust conservatism. The election in 1911 focused on the question of free trade. The Liberal Party, true to form, held high the notion of free trade, and Laurier crossed the country doing his best to persuade as many Canadians as possible that this was the next step and take-off point for the growing and ever-maturing Dominion. G. T. Denison's *The Struggle for Imperial Unity*, published in 1909, was a vigorous apologia for the nationalist vision and the struggle for such a vision within Canada from 1867 to 1907. Denison had been in the thick of the struggle for many a decade, and *The Struggle for Imperial Unity* reflected such a struggle in a compelling and most challenging manner. Leacock was only too well aware of the fine work of Denison, and *The Struggle for Imperial Unity* yet further articulated the conservative reasons for opposing Laurier–Goldwin Smith and the liberal vision and Liberal Party in the 1911 election. Leacock, true to the conservative way of Sirs John A. Macdonald and Robert Borden (1854–1937), argued firmly and strongly against Laurier and the Liberals. Leacock, in 1911, at the age of forty-two, poured much time and attention into the election, travelling to varied and various places in the Dominion, arguing for a nationalist–protectionist position. Leacock was supported in his efforts by the Canadian Home Market Association which was a front for the Canadian Manufacturers Association. Canadian companies, Leacock was convinced, had to be protected, supported and subsidized rather than tossed out into a Darwinian survival-of-the-fittest world to fend for themselves. Borden defeated Laurier in the 1911 election, and the Conservative Party ruled Canada for the remainder of the decade (from 1911 to 1920). Leacock played a crucial role in his Orillia riding and on the national scene in the defeat of Laurier, and he was most delighted by the victory. Needless to say, the conservative stance that Leacock took in the 1911 election is the opposite of what most modern conservatives take. This is why it is much truer to Canadian political history to see the conservatism of those like Mulroney, Klein, Harris, Manning, Day and Harper as a variant of Anglo-American liberalism or, worse yet, republicanism.

The victory of the Conservative Party in 1911 is the historical context within which Leacock's two finest novels must be seen and are situated. Most Canadians have been warmed, charmed, delighted and entertained by *Sunshine Sketches of a Little Town* which was published in 1912. In fact, not to have read *Sunshine Sketches of a Little Town* or *Anne of Green Gables* is to have missed some vital aspects of the conservative and Canadian ethos. Leacock was not one to unduly romanticize or idealize the rural or Acadian way of life as did Antoine Gerin-Lajoie in *Jean Rivard* or, to an equally great extent, Longfellow, in *Evangeline*, but neither did Leacock see it as a bastion of oppression and backwardness as some modern social realists are wont to do. Leacock saw the foibles and follies of the small town, and he did, rightly so, see such a way of life disappearing into an urban, competitive, impersonal and inhumane existence that would wreak havoc on the human soul and human sanity. The deeper philosophical idea that supported such a destructive way, a way that would in time obliterate Leacock's little town of Mariposa, was the liberal notion of the independent and autonomous individual that was connected, rooted and grounded in nothing other than the whims and impulses of a totally disconnected existence. The battle against Laurier and the liberal ideology in 1911 was a much deeper battle than one about which political party would rule in Canada; it was about what view and vision was best for the human soul, community and nation.

Leacock's *Arcadian Adventures with the Idle Rich*, published in 1914, is a companion piece to *Sunshine Sketches*—the beauty, charm, elegance and humour of *Sunshine Sketches* is, consciously so, contrasted with the wealth, opulence, brutality (in subtle and crude ways), petty distractions, diversions and hard-hearted indulgences of the idle rich. *Arcadian Adventures* is such a strong indictment of capitalism and the lives of the idle rich that the Soviet Union translated and published the book as a classic example of the failings of bourgeois capitalism.[15] Leacock often felt he should have received a few roubles for the use of his book, but he was, true to form, amused by how it was used and who used it. *Sunshine Sketches* and *Arcadian Adventures* take the reader, consciously and deliberately so, down a trail that contrasts the differences between Canada and the United States. Mariposa and Plutoria are seen as two different types and interpretations of the good, meaningful and authentic life, and there is little doubt where Leacock tips his hat. The final chapter of

Arcadian Adventures tells its own tale, though.[16] Will Canadians go the way of all flesh, will they turn to the Carnegies and Rockefellers as their guides, will Chicago and New York become the new shining stars, will Plutoria and the Mausoleum win the day? Or will an older Canadian and conservative way dare to oppose, contest and interrogate the emerging empire to the south, an empire that was built on a liberal ideology, an ideology, Leacock feared, that was spreading like a cancer into the marrow of the Canadian bones? Leacock, true conservative that he was, saw the ominous writing on the wall, and the final chapter in *Sunshine Sketches* sums up in a most human and humane way the dilemmas and conflicts of both the individual soul and the soul of a civilization.[17] Both books are a must read for anyone who would like to get a sense and feel for the best of Canadian conservatism from a literary perspective. In many ways, Leacock combined the best of Thomas Haliburton's humour in *The Clockmaker* series, affirmed the limitations of the romantic hero in John Richardson's *Wacousta*, was true to William Kirby's *The Golden Dog* and his epic poem *The U. E.: A Tale of Upper Canada*, and carried forward the naturalism of Confederation poets such as Charles G. D. Roberts, Archibald Lampman and Duncan Campbell Scott.

The war from 1914 to 1919 took up a great deal of Leacock's time and attention, but a most important lesson was etched on Leacock's mind and imagination as a result of the war. Leacock, of course, anticipated Keynes in all this. The conventional liberal wisdom before the war was that a lighter state and the market economy was the yellow brick road to the new world. Leacock, as a true and classical conservative doubted the reigning creed and doctrine of such a liberal position. The war, though, made it abundantly clear that when the state interfered with the invisible hand of the marketplace, business could and did prosper. The old Tory notion of mercantilism was merely being revived to serve the interest of the active and interventionist state. The millions pumped into the economy by the state in World War I nudged Leacock to ask, why, after the war, the state could not continue to do this for all sorts of other economic and social concerns? William Lyon Mackenzie King had published *Industry and Humanity* in 1918, as the war raged thick and fierce. This timely tract urged and argued that the state had to be more active and interventionist. King, as a second generation liberal, keenly aware of the blind side of the first generation credo of the unseen hand, saw that the hand that would even things out only created an immense and growing chasm between the rich and poor. Leacock, like King, saw many coming home from the war, the dire impact of unrestrained capitalism (everything he saw so clearly in Chicago and depicted so well in *Arcadian Adventures*), the rise of the labour movement and the Winnipeg Strike of 1919, and he was moved to respond. Canadians returning from the war were in a trying time. Many who had fought for king and country came home to their country to find little support or solace. Leacock would not and could not be silent. The publication, in 1920, of Leacock's *The Unsolved Riddle of Social Justice* drew together, in a finely textured argument, the dilemmas of turning either too far to the Right or too far to the Left. *The Unsolved Riddle of Social Justice* is a classical tract of Canadian Red Tory thought, and it is an essential read for anyone interested in understanding both Leacock and the emergence of historic Canadian conservatism. The fact that Leacock goes much further than King in his argument that the state must intervene and be more active speaks much about a deeper and older conservatism that Leacock was tapping into and drawing from. *The Unsolved Riddle of Social Justice*, in many ways, continues the argument of Denison's *The Struggle for Imperial Unity* and in doing so, both texts offer the reader a feel for the fabric of Canadian conservatism.

Leacock attempted, in *The Unsolved Riddle of Social Justice*, to plot and chart a middle path between capitalism and communism; he was quick to probe and examine the underbelly of both ideologies. There is little doubt that the publication of *The Unsolved Riddle of Social Justice* highlighted the fact that such a popular pamphlet was a vital part of Leacock's reflection of economic issues that began with his PhD thesis in 1903, continued with *Elements of Political Science*, and was fleshed out in *Arcadian Adventures with the Idle Rich*. Leacock, though, was also going after King and the liberals. King turned to the emerging American empire as the fount and source of his hope and inspiration; he had little patience or interest in fading Britannia. King's gods and heroes were Rockefeller and Roosevelt. Leacock refused to take the typical liberal turn in the southward direction; he had fought Laurier in the 1911 election; now the battle would begin with a new generation of liberals led by William Lyon Mackenzie King. It was most unfortunate for the Conservative Party at the time that Arthur 'the Ready' Meighen was guiding the ship. The Winnipeg Strike of 1919 drew together the

Wobblies (Industrial Workers of the World, or the One Big Union), in a show of more than 35,000, to stand in solidarity with the workers. Many at this time saw communism and the reds spreading everywhere. Those like Meighen saw a Bolshevik conspiracy afoot. Meighen, following the lead of Mitchell Palmer in the United States, brought in the police (in this case the Royal Canadian Mounted Police), to quash the riots and end the threat of the red scare in the Dominion. The many failures of Meighen in 1920-1921 set the stage for King to become the new Prime Minister of Canada at the close of 1921.

The publication of *The Unsolved Riddle of Social Justice* must be seen and is situated within the context of the post-World War I tensions in Winnipeg and elsewhere, the red scare and Meighen's reactionary response. Leacock walked a delicate and middle path through this minefield, and in doing so, he continued the work of other more thoughtful Tories that had gone before him. Leacock had much sympathy for the strikers, and he did not walk side by side with Meighen's response. Leacock, as I mentioned above, did not follow King's lead either. The turn to the United States as the fount of support and all wisdom was not a turn Leacock was willing to make. *The Unsolved Riddle of Social Justice* argued, in seven closely reasoned chapters, the path a Red Tory should take. The language of Red Toryism was not used (this was to come much later in the Grant–Horowitz debate of the 1960s), but the ideas threaded through *The Unsolved Riddle* are unmistakably part and parcel of the Red Tory lineage. Those who take the time to walk through *The Unsolved Riddle of Social Justice* will see that Leacock's understanding of conservatism is the direct opposite, in many ways, of the modern varieties of conservatism that are, when decoded, variations of American liberalism or republicanism.

Leacock was fifty-one when *The Unsolved Riddle of Social Justice* was published in 1920. The Liberal Party was about to come to power and reign for the next decade and Leacock's brand of indigenous Canadian nationalism found little favour with the liberalism of King and tribe. Leacock turned more and more to his life at McGill and his many teaching and writing responsibilities. The new decade opened with Leacock very much in demand as a writer of humorous tales and anecdotes; he had become the Mark Twain of Canada, and Canadians were proud to have one of their own take a prominent place on the stage of the international literary scene. Leacock's literary output in the 1920s, for many, eclipsed his more serious and substantive publications in the areas of Canadian history, politics and economics. Leacock's turn to education and the important role of awakening Canadians to their rich natural tradition was central to his thinking and activism in the 1920s. Leacock contributed various and varied books to the nationalist series, *The Makers of Canada* and *Chronicles of Canada*. Leacock's tour of England in 1921 consolidated his position in Canada and abroad as a leading literary figure.

The Final Years: 1920–1944

After 1920 Leacock gave his attention increasingly to his career as a humorist. — Alan Bowker[18]

Leacock the man cannot be brushed aside in favour of Leacock the humorist. Leacock the man was concerned with social and political problems, deeply involved in the affairs of his age. He used all his many and varied talents to define these problems to himself and his contemporaries, and to advocate solutions to them as persuasively as he knew how. Only after 1922 did he see himself primarily as a humorist; before this time, in large measure, his humour was but one of the weapons he brought to bear on social problems. — Alan Bowker[19]

The comments mentioned above by Bowker, unfortunately, feed into the image of Leacock the humourist. Bowker has, at least, argued that we need to see Leacock the man, in his early years, as a person deeply concerned with the national, political and economic life of Canada, but Bowker then moves on to suggest that in the 1920s Leacock left behind such concerns and turned to literature and education; nothing could be further from the truth.

Leacock taught at McGill University in the busy 1920s when Montreal was very much the cultural and cosmopolitan centre in Canada. Toronto was still, in many ways, the Belfast of the North and a solid and firm bailiwick of the WASP way. Vancouver, at the time, seemed to be on the very edge of civilization, although the University of British Columbia (UBC) was finding its footings, in spite of having just emerged from under the watchful eye of McGill. World War I was now over, the quest and hope for a more prosperous, peaceful economy was in the air, and McGill was front and centre of the hot-button issues of the time. Leacock was in the midst of all this ferment as head of the political economy department at McGill and as a well-known Canadian literary figure.

It is important to note and remember that Leacock, along with Andrew Macphail, edited and contributed many an article to the much subscribed to *The University Magazine*; this was one of the most influential magazines in its time, and it reflected a Tory view. The 1920s brought to McGill a mix and blend of insights that must have delighted and challenged the ever-aging Leacock. The rise of the McGill Movement, led by such worthies as F. R. Scott, and A. J. M. Smith, was a force to be reckoned with. The initial publication of *The McGill Fortnightly Review* in 1925 ushered the modernist movement into Canada. How did Leacock–Macphail respond to those like Scott, Smith and the McGill Movement? The modernist movement sought to move beyond both the Romantic and Victorian ethos and create a new poetry in which the artist spoke to the people in their own language. This was a turn from nature poetry and rural romanticism to social realism. There were issues that had to be faced and it was not the role of the artist either to retreat, in solitude, into the life of the soul or turn to nature as the answer to the question of post-World War I Canadian life. It was men like Scott and Smith who founded the League for Social Reconstruction (LSR) and the Co-operative Commonwealth Federation (CCF), both forerunners of the New Democratic Party (NDP).

How did Leacock react and respond to the hopes and dreams, the visions and longings of Scott, Smith and the McGill Movement? How were *The University Magazine* and *The McGill Fortnightly Review* similar and different? These sorts of questions could take us into the core and centre of the debate between what it means to be a Red Tory and what it means to be a leftist Liberal. There is a large paper waiting to be written on the Leacock–Macphail and Scott–Smith approaches to social issues as such ideas were worked out in the two magazines named above. It is important to realize that many of the issues raised by the McGill Movement had been anticipated by Leacock, but there comes a place when there is a juncture in the road and such a cleavage takes the thinker and activist down a different trail. George Grant faced the same issues with the New Left in the 1960s. There is, obviously, much affinity between the Red Tory conservatism of Leacock and Grant and the leftist liberalism of Scott and the New Left. The more this question is probed, the more we find some telling areas of convergence between Red Tory conservatism and leftist liberalism, and equally so, points of substantive divergence.

Did Leacock, as Bowker suggests, turn more and more to humour and the delights of literature as the 1920s and 1930s moved ever on? I don't think so. In fact, Leacock wrote more books on Canadian history, politics and economics in the 1920s-1930s than he did in previous years. Leacock, although much older at the time, played his role in bringing Bennett to power in 1930, and Leacock wrote a foreword to Bennett's *The Premier Speaks to the People*.[20] Bennett's work is very much an updated version of Leacock's *The Unsolved Riddle of Social Justice*. The depression in the 1930s was demanding its dire due and Bennett, much to Leacock's chagrin, had been insensitive to some of the deeper problems of the era. With Bennett's turn of heart in *The Premier Speaks to the People*, Leacock was ready to support his chief and leader yet once again. Bennett lost the election of 1935, and King was returned to power again (where he would remain until 1948). Leacock saw only too clearly the direction King was taking the country. The liberal tradition was all about integration with and annexation to the empire to the south; whether it was Goldwin Smith, Laurier or King the liberal message and credo remained ever the same. This was not the Tory or conservative idea, though, and Leacock would have none of the liberal way.

Leacock was almost at retirement age when the 1935 election was won by the Liberals. McGill, much to Leacock's hurt and annoyance, insisted he take retirement. Leacock returned in his last and final years to his much-loved Mariposa in Orillia and his Old Brewery Bay home. Leacock turned more and more to his fishing and writing, and his fishing, in many ways, became the symbol of his life, a life of contemplation, a life of casting into the river of time and history from the contemplative place, a life of reeling in the big fish, the big issues of his time. Leacock's essay on Izaak Walton's *The Compleat Angler*,[21] a classical text of seventeenth century Anglican thought and life, threaded together many of his ideas; Leacock stood very much within such a large and organic view of life, a view and vision in which the life of religion, education–culture and politics were all organically connected and integrated. It is in this sense that Leacock is very much a Tory of the older way, a Tory who only too keenly realized that his Anglican faith was about being engaged in a nationalist way on political issues, but also being deeply concerned about persevering and protecting the classical way of humanist education.

Leacock has been called a 'Red Tory', 'a traditional Tory' and 'a Tory humanist'. Robertson Davis (another Anglican) once said of Leacock, 'A great countryman of ours: a man to thank God for'.[22] I might add, by way of conclusion, a man to remind us of what historic Canadian toryism and conservatism is and how such a tradition needs to talk back to those who would use such time-honoured language to distort most things that historic Tories have held near and dear.

In conclusion, Leacock has often been called the Canadian Mark Twain; nothing could be further from the truth. Twain's heroes are the epitome of American anarchist individualism. Leacock's aim is the very opposite of Twain's. Leacock, as a Canadian Tory, seeks to call a people and nation to the commonweal, the common good, and, as such, he opposed both corporate capitalism and American individualism. This did not mean Leacock idealized small rural Ontario life; in his earliest articles he poked fun at the silly romanticism of Wordsworth, Tennyson and Longfellow. Leacock saw, though, that without a strong state and nation to protect the good of the people and without the ever-fallible Mariposa to hold people together in community, liberal corporate capitalism and anarchism would win and rule the day. It is in this blend of community life and the organic connection between community life and national unity that the Red Tory stands; in standing in such a place, the classical High Tory resists two evils: corporate and competitive capitalism as embodied in multinational corporations that undermine the ability of the state to provide for its citizens and anarchist individualism that so deconstructs both the self and community that nothing but fragmentation dominates the day. Needless to say, the individualism of personalist anarchism feeds straight and centre into corporate planning. The more citizens are fragmented, disconnected, uprooted and depoliticized, the more easily the power of the corporation can take over. Leacock, as a classical Tory, resisted such a move in his day. Tories, true to the lineage of Leacock, cannot help but do the same thing in our day.

Leacock is buried at St. George's Anglican parish (with the rest of his family) on a hill overlooking Lake Simcoe by Sibbald Point. Many well-known Anglican Tories are buried in the same graveyard.

The battle for a sovereign Canada can be tracked and traced in a walk through the graveyard at St. George's. The Simcoe family donated the stained glass windows to St. George's, Maza de la Roche is buried at St. George's, Bishop Strachan (who fought for Canadian independence in 1812 against the Americans) consecrated St. George's and Susanna Moodie (our leading pink tory novelist of the nineteenth century) spent much time in the area. Peter Gzowski has suggested, in the St. George's parish pamphlet, that the birth of Canadian culture can be rightly understood by those who lived in the St. George's vicinity and area. Stephen Leacock, therefore, is buried in a place with an old lineage that very much reflects the older Tory way; to the degree we understand such a tale, drama and lineage, we can challenge the liberal–republican mindset that so often is equated with conservatism. An honest walk through St. George's will reveal what real Canadian conservatism is and how it is the direct opposite of much that passes for conservatism at this moment of Canadian history.

CHAPTER EIGHT

DONALD CREIGHTON AND EUGENE FORSEY: TORY HISTORIAN MEETS RADICAL TRADITIONALIST

I'm an unrevised, unrepented Sir John A. Macdonald conservative ... There aren't many of us left ... Just Creighton and me ... That is ... if Donald will admit me to the sacred precincts ... I'm sick of listening to pygmies trying to destroy what giants created! — Eugene Forsey[1]

When Brian Mulroney became Prime Minister of Canada in the early 1980s, most assumed Canada might return to a traditional form of Tory government. When Brian Mulroney went to Washington after his electoral victory, and assured President Ronald Reagan that Canada was open for business once again, a clear signal was sent across the land. The Progressive Conservative government of Mulroney was going to take Canada much closer to the United States than that of any other leader of the Conservative Party in Canada had ever done. Mulroney was, most came to see, cut from the same republican cloth as Margaret Thatcher and Ronald Reagan, and this type of republican conservatism had little in common with Canadian High Tory conservatism. Since Mulroney, the language of Canadian conservatism has come to ape, echo and reflect the American version of conservatism. Stephen Harper walks, for the most part, in the same footsteps as Mulroney, Reagan and Thatcher. This is why he was so supportive of the American invasion of Iraq, and most of the policies of the United States. He is a colonial of the most worrisome and activist type. He serves the interests of the American empire, and he has walked the extra mile to make sure Canadians do the same thing. All must bow and genuflect to Caesar to the south of us.

It was this disturbing shift in the meaning and understanding of Canadian conservatism in the early 1980s that created many a concern and worry amongst Canadian High Tory conservatives. It would just be a matter of time before some sort of response emerged. The first book that attempted, in a more popular way, to correct the image of conservatism that Mulroney was parading about was journalist Charles Taylor's *Radical Tories: The Conservative*

Tradition in Canada published in 1982. Taylor, in *Radical Tories*, pointed out in a clear-headed and historical manner, that there was a Tory tradition in Canada that could not be equated with Mulroney's brand of blue tory conservatism. Taylor listed the family tree and lineage in his missive and tract for the times in a series of short essays on important Canadian Tories that could not be squared with the Mulroney clan. The book came as a solid rebuke and firm-footed turning of the back on the blue tory way. Taylor, in his short profiles, showcased such worthies as Leacock, Sandwell, Deacon, Morton, Purdy, Grant, Stanfield, Crombie, Donald Creighton and Eugene Forsey. Taylor's chapter on Creighton was called 'The Northern Empire',[2] and his chapter on Forsey was called 'Red Tories and Social Justice'.[3] What did Creighton, the finest and noblest Canadian High Tory historian, have in common with Eugene Forsey, a noble and fine leftist intellectual and activist?

Donald Creighton (1902–1979), was, without much doubt, an eloquent and controversial Canadian historian. He argued, in book after book, that Canada was created and built, consciously so, in an East–West manner, and the most visionary of political leaders of Canada (which were Tories) waged many a battle to keep Canada from becoming a satellite and colony of the United States. Creighton's biography of Sir John A. Macdonald is a spirited and animated defence of Macdonald, and the way he gave his life to preserve and keep Canada firm and intact. Creighton wrote many other books on Canadian history, and in each of these books, he probes and examines the struggles within the Canadian soul to preserve its own way or integrate with and be annexed to the United States.

Creighton's book on Innis, *Harold Adam Innis: Portrait of a Scholar*, highlighted and reinforced Creighton's deeper passion. Innis had argued that societies shape and form themselves around two important ideas and concepts (space or time). Much hinges on whether the spatial or chronological idea dominates. A spatial society tends to be concerned and preoccupied with movement, mobility, change, a lack of history and tradition and a weak notion of boundaries. The sky above is a fit symbol for the metaphor of space. A time-bound and chronological society is more concerned about the past, the relationship between generations, the connections across time and what binds things together in and through time. A spatial culture tends to be more liberal, a time conscious society tends to be more conservative. Innis argued that, in an age of rapid change (as we are in now), we need to be more rooted and grounded in a more time-bound and chronological way.

Creighton drew together many of the insights of Innis and gave them a solid historical and political grounding. It was Innis's argument that Canadians, to be Canadians, need to think more in an East–West manner rather than a North–South way. The more Canadians think North–South, the more they will become Americans. Innis also argued Canadians need to think more in a time-bound and chronological way—when we think, mostly, in a spatial manner, we think more like the liberal Americans to the south of us.

Creighton had a great deal of fondness for the arguments of Innis, but he extolled the fine work of Eugene Forsey. Forsey was highlighted in Creighton's final book, *The Passionate Observer: Selected Writings*. 'Eugene Forsey: Political Traditionalist, Social Radical' holds high and offers many a kudo to the life and meticulous writings of Forsey. Forsey had been a student of Leacock at McGill University in the 1920s, and he taught in the political economy department at McGill in the 1930s. Forsey was a founding member of the League for Social Reconstruction and the Co-operative Commonwealth Federation. But, and this was a vital point for Creighton, Forsey, unlike many in the New Left, was grounded in the best of the English conservative way, and it was by mining the depths of this older conservatism that the gold of Forsey's social radicalism emerged. Creighton concluded his introduction to Forsey by saying, 'The truth is that he is indecipherable by Canadian criticism. If only there were many Canadians like him'.[4] Even though Creighton had his questions about Forsey, he saw in Forsey that unique Canadian ability to blend both conservatism and radicalism. It was in the living of this tension that the best of the Canadian vision is expressed and embodied.

When Charles Taylor was doing his interviews for *Radical Tories*, he asked Forsey if he would be interested in being interviewed with other Tories of an older tradition. Forsey's reply letter says much about the man:

I need hardly say I should be highly honoured to figure in such a distinguished company in your new book, though I fear George Grant looks upon me with a very jaundiced eye, and might jib at finding himself in such *bad* company. I am, however, very doubtful about whether you ought to bother with me, at any rate in anything more than perhaps a few footnotes. Leacock, Creighton and Grant are towering figures; I am simply not in the same class.[5]

Eugene Forsey (1904–1991), had his autobiography, *A Life on the Fringe: The Memoirs of Eugene Forsey*, published in 1990. His days were near an end, but he still had much to say. The tale told in *A Life on the Fringe* highlights just how Forsey managed to combine and integrate the deeper and fuller aspects of the Anglo-Canadian way with a searching and probing passion for justice and peace at a legal, economic and political level. The drama that Forsey recounts takes the curious Canadian into an intellectual world in which distinctions such as left, right and sensible centre make little or no sense. Forsey was too big a man to be captured by such a small ideological net. It is most interesting to note that in the last few years of his life Forsey gave a talk to the Anglican Prayer Book Society. The Prayer Book Society (PBS) tends to be seen by many as the last bastion of a reactionary and out-of-touch English traditionalism. What was Forsey, the social radical, doing giving a presentation to the Prayer Book Society? For Forsey, grounded as he was in the best of the Anglo-Canadian religious and political tradition, such simple and brittle distinctions lacked depth and substance. Forsey saw in the Prayer Book the very religious and political resources for building a just society and the True North. The Prayer Book Society magazine, *The Machray Review*, published Forsey's lecture. It was called, 'What Have These Reformers Wrought?'—the article is vintage Forsey.[6] Traditionalism and Radicalism are like the left and right hand. When either is lopped off, much hurt and harm comes to the body politic.

Donald Creighton was the finest High Tory historian Canada has produced. He often lamented the way liberals distorted and misinterpreted Canadian history to serve their agenda. He called the liberal read of Canadian history, playing on the old and new translations of the Bible, the authorized reading of Canadian history. Liberal Canadian historians tended to idealize the liberal interpretation of Canadian history and thereby offer gullible and naive Canadians a distorted view of both Toryism and the Canadian intellectual and political journey. Creighton realized that genuine

Canadian Toryism was not averse or opposed to a concern for the common good and the protection of the Canadian way over and against the American. Creighton knew his Tory tradition well enough to turn to Forsey as an ally and friend on the journey. Forsey, on the other hand, was so well rooted in the High Tory way that he knew that such rooting could hold up the trunk and branches of a radical social agenda. In short, for Forsey, the fruit of political radicalism could only be sustained and nourished by being rooted in the soil of the ancient conservative way. Sadly so, conservatism and radicalism have diverged and both have suffered for it.

We are in a desperate need for historians and intellectuals like Creighton and Forsey to rebuild and rebind what has been broken and injured. Until this is done, we will never recover the genius and visionary quality of what it means to be a Canadian. We will, sadly so, if such giants are ignored, either genuflect before the American empire, or, in reaction to such a position, reduce politics to soft liberal left protest or advocacy politics. The former tends to see little unique or good in the Canadian way, whereas the latter is so cynical of formal party politics that it elevates the role of civil society and denigrates the important role of party politics. Interestingly enough, the liberal protest and advocacy left shares some worrisome leanings with the libertarian right. Both the anarchist left and the libertarian right are suspicious of formal party politics and the state, and both clans elevate society as the antidote and answer to the ills of the state.

Donald Creighton and Eugene Forsey would never have thought in such a reactionary and short-sighted manner. Both men held high the role of both society and the state, formal party politics and the civic sphere. Both men realized that both society and the state are at their healthiest when they dwell together in an organic way. Needless to say, there will be tensions in the state–society relationship, but better to live with the tensions than to idealize society while denigrating the state, or romanticizing the state while demeaning society. It is in the living of this tension that the High Toryism of Creighton and Forsey can still teach and tell us much.

CHAPTER NINE

THE TROJAN HORSE OF LIBERALISM IN THE TORY CAMP

When we hear the language of 'conservatism', most of us immediately think of Mulroney, Harper, Thatcher, Reagan, Harris, Klein and Wall. Then, of course, there was the more extreme form of self-styled conservatism of Manning, the Reform Party and the United Alternative. We need, however, to ask ourselves this rather simple question: are such people and parties in any significant, consistent or substantive sense historic Canadian conservatives? My answer to this pressing question within the Canadian political tradition is a firm and obstinate 'no'.

Many of those who use the time-tried language of conservatism today are fiscal liberals, cheerleaders for free trade and, more to the worrisome point, fans for ever-greater annexation to the United States and the global market. Is this, then, the conservatism of Macdonald, Leacock and Grant? Hardly!

Such men would be appalled by the way the language of conservatism has been betrayed and taken captive by entrepreneurial liberals and American-style republicanism.

It is this liberal redefinition of conservatism that has led Robin Mathews, in *The Canadian Intellectual Tradition*, to state, in the most poignant way that:

At the end of the 20th century, the Progressive Conservatives are more like the U. S. Republican Party than perhaps ever before in their history. The Reform Party—which swept up a large number of previously Progressive Conservative votes in the 1993 federal election—described a conservative philosophy increasingly similar to the U. S. Republican Party ... we now live with a 'new conservatism,' which is, in fact, a distinctly different political philosophy that rushed in to fill the vacuum left by a retreating and untenable set of beliefs. Sir John A. Macdonald's conservatism—the conservatism of the last decades of the 19th century—is more interesting for its differences from contemporary conservatism than for its continuity with the kind announced with the prime ministership of Brian Mulroney and continued since then.[1]

It must be admitted at the outset, then, that historic Canadian conservatism has been hijacked by an American form of reactionary liberalism. It is the American republican way that places high value on a lighter state, less taxes, regionalism and an emphasis on a larger military and police to deal with crime and punishment in a swift and lethal manner.

Jack Granatstein, in his national bestseller, *Who Killed Canadian History?* highlighted in a graphic, convincing and telling manner how and why most Canadians know little about their rich and robust history and the reasons for such tragic amnesia. We might take Granatstein's concerns a step further, however. How many Canadians know what historic conservatism has been, how its heart and mind have been plucked out in the last few decades and how an insidious form of American philosophical and political liberalism dominates the stage of Canadian culture, economics, education and legal and political life these days? Needless to say, we will not learn much of historic conservatism from Granatstein. The authorized version of Canadian history forbids such a telling. But Granatstein is spot on when he laments, protests and calls for a renewal and resurrection of Canadian history and tradition. Whose interpretation of Canadian history–tradition will we heed and why, and, more to the point of this chapter, what bard will sing forth to us the conservative and High–Red Tory tale and drama once again?

It is essential, at this juncture in our history, that we remember and revive the perennial significance of the conservative and Red Tory vision as an antidote to the toxins of liberalism in our body politic. The future of Canada hinges on such a reflective retrieval of a wise and prudent Tory way. In short, the time has come for conservatives and Red Tories in Canada not to be silent about the Trojan horse of liberalism in the camp.

Liberalism, within Canada, has been about free trade, annexation to the United States and a turning against a free, independent and true north. Liberalism has also been about elevating the whims, impulses and rights of the individual against community and the nation, competition against cooperation, society against the state, secularism against religion and the notion of progress and technology against the wisdom and insights of the elders and tradition. We need not read too far or deep into the writings and lives of George Brown, Richard Cartwright, Goldwin Smith, Sandy Mackenzie, Wilfred Laurier, W. L. M. King, Louis St. Laurent and Jean Chretien to get a firm and solid feel for historic liberalism. The ghosts of Adam Smith, John Locke, Herbert Spencer and Cobden–Bright still brood over their children by day and by night. The fact that some liberals in the mid-1960s and early 1970s (such as Walter Gordon and Eric Kierans) and in the 1980s and 1990s (such as Mel Hurtig and Maude Barlow) became more nationalistic speaks more about adopting a conservative perspective than any sort of consistent or historic liberalism.

The Canadian Tory tradition has, from the beginning, been wary and suspicious of both American republican principles and American imperialistic ambitions. Canadian High Tories, unlike the Liberals, have never been as keen to bow the knee to Uncle Sam to the south of us—this High Tory tradition has had an abiding passion for the common good of Canadians and the role of the federal government in protecting such a good. How, then, did conservatism come to be identified with the historic content and position of liberalism? How, in short, did the Trojan horse of liberalism get such a firm footing in the Tory camp? There are those like Donald Creighton who see the forked road opening up in 1939, and others like George Grant who see the Port Hope conference of 1942 as a significant turning point in redefining conservatism to serve the interests of the business elite. The emergence of the Blue Tory tradition and the receding of the Red Tory tradition found much support in the Bracken–Drew era of the 1940s-1950s. But, the election of Diefenbaker as party leader in 1956, then his leadership role as prime minister from 1958 to 1963, restored an older Tory vision. There was, obviously, much folly, inconsistency and foolishness in the old chief, but, as George Grant rightly noted in *Lament for a Nation*, Diefenbaker did stand for a noble Tory ideal that was being eroded by Yankee individualism and imperialism.

The fact that Diefenbaker appointed a Blue Tory (Donald Fleming) as Minister of Finance and a Red Tory (Howard Green) as Secretary of State for External Affairs highlighted his dilemma and the tightrope he walked. The balancing act, for Diefenbaker, became impossible. Pearson beat Diefenbaker in 1963 on an annexation–nationalist issue and Pearson, true to liberal form, genuflected to President Kennedy and the American empire.

Stanfield did his best to hold high a sort of 'pink toryism', but Trudeau's blend of charisma and soft social-nationalist liberalism won the day for most Canadians. The fumblings of Trudeau, the distorted interpretation of the debt–deficit crisis and the attack on our social programs by the right led the Progressive Conservative Party to alter its historic perspective to get and stay in power—*voila* Brian Mulroney and clan.

But need we lament, wring our hands and claim that nothing can be done? Such a way of thinking leads to political paralysis and furthers the very thing we are concerned about.

Have we not been here before? History can teach us much if we care to listen. The 1940s-1950s saw both the Progressive Conservative Party dominated by Blue Tories and Canada led by the Liberal leadership of King and St. Laurent. And true to historic liberal form, our leaders graciously allowed the American to woo, wed and bed us. Yet, in 1956, Diefenbaker took the Progressive Conservative Party back to its deeper Tory roots and, from 1958 to 1963, led the country, against much opposition, down a different path. The 1950s were a time of intense and rigorous debate within the Progressive Conservative Party. The Red, 'Pink' and Blue Tories each sought to define what it means to be a conservative. John Farthing, Judith Robinson, Davie Fulton, Donald Fleming and many others were in the thick of the fray. The point to note, though, is that it was as voices were raised, as the fight for Canada took front stage, as apathy, indifference and defeatism gave way to courage, struggle and hope that the Progressive Conservative Party found itself again and went on to rule the country, challenge American imperialism and articulate what it means to be the True North. David Orchard's *The Fight for Canada*, revised and republished in 1998, makes it quite clear, by numerous examples, that Tories have played a key role in protecting the True North, and, the fate of this country hinges on those who are willing, in each generation, to fight for it against much opposition. In short, mere lamenting is an indulgent pose engaged in by sentimentalists and bruised idealists. It takes courage to carry on with the vision when self-pity, despair, cynicism and bitterness tempt the soul.

The question before us is, then, what is the Tory vision and how can it take us out of the maze of our postmodern malaise?

CHAPTER TEN

GEORGE GRANT:
LAMENT FOR A NATION AND RED TORYISM

Introduction

Lament for a Nation is a classic missive within the genre of Canadian political philosophy—when the book was published in 1965, Grant ignited the nationalist New Left in Canada, challenged and questioned the notion that conservatism is necessarily right-of-centre and exposed the vulnerable core of liberalism. *Lament for a Nation* emerged from the 1963 federal election in which Tommy Douglas (New Democratic Party) supported Lester Pearson (Liberal Party) to bring down the minority Conservative government of Prime Minister John Diefenbaker. President J. F. Kennedy backed Pearson's bid for power contra Diefenbaker in 1963 and Grant saw in this liberal alliance of Kennedy–Pearson the death knell of a deeper and older conservatism that had played a significant role in the shaping of the Canadian ethos. It was the passing away of such a 'Tory touch' that Grant lamented, jeremiad-like, that is at the core of *Lament for a Nation*. Grant moves in a deft and firm-footed way, chapter by chapter, in *Lament* from the actual historic election, to an analysis of Diefenbaker (the good and bad) to the history of and differences between liberalism and classical conservatism to political philosophy, philosophy and theology. The book embodies a distinctive and unique way of doing political philosophy and the conclusions Grant reached earned him the honorific title (given by Gad Horowitz but never fully embraced by Grant) of 'Red Tory'.

This chapter will discuss the historical background to *Lament for a Nation*, the way Grant does political philosophy in *Lament*, the content of *Lament* and Grant's ambiguous attitude towards the language of Red Toryism.

Historical Context

I remember quite distinctly (as if it were yesterday) the animated conversations around our dinner table in the late 1950s when Claude Bissell (1916–2000) had been appointed president of the University of Toronto. Bissell was president of the University of Toronto from 1958 to 1971, and he embodied a way of being (as did many others in the post-World War II era) in the next phase of the Canadian nationalist tradition. Bissell had been involved, when president of Carleton University from 1956 to 1958, in coordinating a series of lectures that was published as *Our Living Tradition: Seven Canadians*. Bissell stood, in many ways, on the solid and firm shoulders of the first Canadian-born governor general in Canada, Vincent Massey, who held the office from 1952 to 1959. Vincent Massey was George Grant's uncle, and the Massey Commission[1] was central in shaping and defining the way forward for Canada after World War II. George Grant was asked to contribute the paper on 'Philosophy' for the Massey Commission, and in the essay he challenged the drift and direction of most forms of modern philosophy and called, prophet-like, philosophers to return to a more ancient and contemplative approach to doing philosophy.[2] Grant's paper in the Massey Commission deeply offended the leading philosopher in Canada at the time (Fulton Anderson—the chair of philosophy at the University of Toronto), and Anderson (and other Canadian philosophers) organized their 1952 annual conference to debunk Grant (and those of his ilk). There can be no doubt, though, that with the Massey Commission a new form of mature Canadian nationalism was emerging in the post-World War II era in which Vincent Massey, Claude Bissell and George Grant were to take serious leadership in forging and making—this form of Canadian nationalism had a lingering attachment to the older tradition of England and was profoundly suspicious of the United States as an emerging empire. This way of thinking was, obviously, to play a significant role in *Lament for a Nation: The Defeat of Canadian Nationalism*.

The Liberal Party of Canada had dominated Canadian politics after World War II, and William Lyon Mackenzie King (the longest serving Canadian prime minister) and Louis St. Laurent guided the Liberal ship throughout most of the 1940s-1950s. King had a pronounced distaste for the English tradition and heritage (it had much to do with the way his prominent yet distant relative, William Lyon Mackenzie, was opposed by the more British oriented Family Compact in the 1837 Rebellion). King tended to turn to the United States as his north star, and Rockefeller and Roosevelt were his decided mentors. The fact that King was pro-United States and

Massey doubted such an imperial turn meant that there were heated clashes between King and Massey. King, St. Laurent and C. D. Howe also played a significant role in hitching Canada's economic and military future to the United States. It was this typical annexationist or integrationist perspective of the historic liberal tradition in Canada that collided with those like Massey, Bissell and Grant.

Canada, in the 1940s-1950s, had been drawn into the gravitational field of the United States. Foreign investment amounted to 65 percent, manufacturing was 56 percent foreign owned, mining 60 percent, pulp and paper 80 percent and petroleum 90 percent foreign owned. It was this excessive dependence by Canada on, mostly, American ownership, that brought down, temporarily, the Liberal annexationist position (which Grant would eventually call—drawing from Alexandre Kojeve—the universal and homogenous state[3]). John Diefenbaker came to power in 1957 committed to retrieving a Canadian nationalist political position that was not beholden to the Americans. Prime Minister John Diefenbaker did not have the philosophic depth of Grant, but he dared to challenge, and for a few years, from 1957 to 1963, redirect Canadian domestic and foreign policy. Diefenbaker has been called a 'rogue tory'[4] and there can be no doubt that Diefenbaker, in his imperfect and often erratic way, attempted to reclaim a form of conservatism in Canada that challenged the powerful influence of liberalism in Canada and its various forms and guises in the United States. Diefenbaker's brand of conservatism was, in many ways, at the opposite end from the American republican tradition and had affinities with the National Policy of J. A. Macdonald and Disraeli. Diefenbaker, again and again, stood up to Kennedy, and Kennedy had no patience for Diefenbaker. The clashes and animosity between Kennedy and Diefenbaker are amply illustrated in Knowlton Nash's *Kennedy and Diefenbaker: Fear and Loathing across the Undefended Border*.

The federal election of 1963 in Canada was, largely, fought over whether Canada would take warheads for Bomarc missiles or whether Canada would refuse the American demands. Pearson bowed the knee to Kennedy and the Kennedy administration backed Pearson in the election. Diefenbaker refused to take warheads for the Bomarc missiles, he had opposed Kennedy on a variety of contentious issues before the election and his nationalist vision was held high in opposition to Pearsonian integrationism. Pearson won the 1963 election and with the defeat of Diefenbaker, Grant was convinced that a way of being Canadian was passing away. It was this death of an older notion of conservatism (of which the actual election was but a portal and metaphor) that Grant lamented in *Lament for a Nation: The Defeat of Canadian Nationalism.* When *Lament* was published in 1965 it became an immediate bestseller. The compact missive sold 7,000 copies in the first six months and more than 50,000 copies in the next twenty-five years.[5] The language of Red Toryism emerged in Canada with the publication of *Lament,* and to the structure and content of *Lament* I now turn.

Lament for a Nation

Lament for a Nation was, originally, written in seven chapters (seven being a sacred number), and in later editions George Grant added an 'Introduction' in 1970 and Sheila Grant added an 'Afterword' in 1997.

Chapter I in *Lament for a Nation* is a frontal assault on all those who turned on Diefenbaker. The opening lines sum up Grant's passion well:

Never has such a torrent of abuse been poured on any Canadian figure as that during the years from 1960 to 1965. Never have the wealthy and the clever been so united as they were in their joint attack on Mr. John Diefenbaker.[6]

Grant turned on the liberal corporate and media power elite for maligning and defeating Diefenbaker. Grant uses two graphic illustrations to illuminate his poignant point. The life of a child is a good, and when a child dies, a legitimate lament is needful. Diefenbaker stood for something that was good in the Canadian historic way, his defeat and passing was like a death, hence a lament was in order. The second metaphor complements the tragic image of the death of a child. A fish survives within the reality of water— when the water is removed, the fish will die. The water that supported the fish (the ethos that supported the older Tory vision) has now been drained and many are like 'gasping political fish'.

Grant links the older conservative vision of Sir John A. Macdonald to Diefenbaker's last stand contra Pearson in the 1963 election:

We were grounded in the wisdom of Sir John A. Macdonald, who saw plainly more than a hundred years ago that the only threat to nationalism was from the South, not from across the sea.[7]

There can be no doubt that Grant is holding high an Anglo-Canadian political vision in the above statement in contrast to an Anglo-American political perspective. The deeper meaning and significance of this will be unfolded, at the level of political philosophy, as Grant develops his argument in *Lament for a Nation*.

Grant brings to a brief conclusion a couple of main points in Chapter I. There were few in the early 1960s that dared to compare the United States to an empire—many do this today. Grant makes it quite explicit that the United States is an empire that is enfolded in certain principles and, equally so, Canadians are being drawn uncritically into the fold of such liberal principles and practices. The final lines of the chapter turn to Richard Hooker (Anglican divine of the sixteenth century). Hooker's grounding in an older history in the midst of theological and political chaos had some affinities with the position of Grant in the 1960s. The unpacking of the sentence from Hooker will, in many ways, be the core of *Lament*—'Posterity may know we have not loosely through silence permitted things to pass away as in a dream'.[8] Grant feared, with the coming to be of the American imperial way (and Canadian colonials and compradors serving such an agenda) that things that were once goods and held dear could 'pass away as in a dream'. Grant refused, in the passing, to be silent.

Chapter II in *Lament*, once again, turns to the liberal power elite and establishment in Canada and clarifies, in poignant and not-to-be-forgotten detail, how and why such a ruling class became committed to a continentalist perspective. There are 'conflicts over principles' in the defeat of Diefenbaker, and the Canadian liberal classes were pro-American, whereas Diefenbaker was torn between an Anglo-Canadian-American form of liberalism and a unique Anglo-Canadian Toryism (or, as Horowitz would call it, the 'Tory touch'). The initial part of Chapter II describes, in a historical way, how Canadian liberals after World War II turned from England as their north star and turned to the United States as their master and mentor. This turn was philosophic, economic, military and political and the implications were obvious. The commitment by the liberal power elite hastened and further immersed Canadians into the ideology of American liberalism. Those with no memory merely assumed that American liberalism was the alpha and omega of political thought and action—Grant dared to question such an unthinking and uncritical position.

Grant was not an uncritical fan of Diefenbaker. Most of Chapter II makes it abundantly clear that Diefenbaker was pulled in inconsistent directions and this was his fault and failing. There was, in Diefenbaker, the older nationalist Tory vision that was suspicious of Anglo-American liberalism, but there was also the Anglo-Canadian-American liberalism that dwelt in Diefenbaker. It was this inner struggle as it worked itself out in Diefenbaker's life that led to his defeat. When push came to shove in the 1963 election, Diefenbaker held high the older Tory tradition contra Kennedy–Pearson against both those in his party and in the Liberal Party. Pearson was much more the predictable Canadian liberal who fawned at the feet of the ideology of liberalism and the embodiment of such a position in Kennedy. Grant dissected, in the bulk of Chapter II, how Diefenbaker's inconsistencies and glaring mistakes led to his defeat. Grant did, therefore, like many, challenge and criticize Diefenbaker, but he thought that Diefenbaker was pointer and cairn to an older way of being Canadian.

If Chapter II in *Lament for a Nation* probes the way Diefenbaker was torn between liberalism and a more classic form of nationalist conservatism, Chapter III is a spirited and animated defence of Diefenbaker and Howard Green's (Secretary of State for External Affairs) nationalism. Canada had a history of being rooted in the English way, and as Canada became more independent, the task was to find a middle way between the waning of the British empire and the waxing of the American empire. The Cuban Missile Crisis of 1962 and the federal election of 1963 (which was about warheads for Bomarc missiles being placed on Canadian soil) raised the question of Canadian identity. The problem, as Grant rightly noted, was this: the English had, since World War I (and more since World War II) turned to the United States as their north star. The power centre was, increasingly so, the United States, and American military organizations—the North Atlantic Treaty Organization (NATO) and the North American Aerospace Defense Command (NORAD). The less important and more conciliar idea of the British Commonwealth had become secondary to British foreign policy. Diefenbaker and

Green were still committed to an older notion of the commonwealth rather than American unilateralism.

Grant saw in the post-World War II emergence of the American empire the continuation of Jeffersonian liberalism: will (power), liberty and reason were at the core of such a creed and the American empire of Kennedy embodied such a reality. The fact that C. D. Howe and William Lyon Mackenzie King had prepared Canadians well to accept such a vision and Pearson merely oiled the wheels of such a continentalist approach was at the core of Grant's concerns. Were there options to this worrisome integration of willing, liberty and reason? The fact that Green and Diefenbaker (Green more than Diefenbaker) dared to oppose the liberal alliance of Kennedy–Pearson raised the question about the grounds for doing so. Did Green and Diefenbaker think from a counter tradition that saw through the pretences and rhetoric of liberalism? What did they see that most did not see? Was the Jeffersonian liberalism that Kennedy and Pearson espoused more about liberty for the powerful than about a form of liberty that was an extension of the good? Certainly, the liberal tradition of Locke and Jefferson (of which Kennedy and Pearson imbibed) had turned its back on an older form of conservatism. The 1962 Cuban Missile Crisis and the 1963 federal election were, for Grant, about more than merely a military and economic clash of interests—they reflected and embodied two different ways of understanding what it meant to be human, political and Canadian— there was, in fact, a parting of ideological paths. Grant was convinced that in the 1963 election more than Diefenbaker was defeated—in fact, an older notion of the political good had been defeated and died.

Chapters I–III in *Lament for a Nation* dealt, mostly, with the political events of post-World War II Canada and the Canadian turn to the liberal United States and away from an older English conservatism. It is important to note, of course, as I mentioned above, that English liberalism was the founding political philosophy of the United States and played a significant role in the origins of Canada, also. So, when Grant turned to an alternate political vision, he was calling forth a counter tradition that had almost been forgotten and vanished as the hegemony of liberalism came to dominate English-speaking Canada. Chapter IV begins, in a more focussed and definite manner, to clarify the nature of liberalism as a form of political theory and how such an imperial ideology has muted an older Anglo-Canadian Toryism.

Chapters IV–VI in *Lament* walk the reader into the centre and core of Grant doing political philosophy at a high level. The Anglo-American-Canadian liberal tradition is unpacked and unfurled both in underlying principles and content. Most of the mainstream liberal theorists and activists are brought on historical front stage for one and all to see as they act out their parts in England and North America. Grant's clear and poignant probes of both the appeal and imperial nature of liberalism are clearly articulated and enucleated. The crude and subtler forms of liberalism that, like roots on a tree, hold the trunk and tree up yet often remain invisible, are unfolded in thought and deed. Grant also makes it clear what a historic Toryism is when compared with various forms of Canadian and American conservatism. The High Tory line and lineage of Coleridge, Johnson, Swift and Hooker are held high, and Grant does not flinch from placing Burke in the Whig camp (most American conservatives turn to Burke as their mascot and bearer of the conservative way). Grant was much too grounded in history and in an older understanding of Toryism to doff the cap to Burke and tribe. The fact that Grant, rightly so, placed Edmund Burke in the liberal clan meant he had many an affinity with the much-respected leftist political philosopher, C. B. Macpherson, who also argued that Burke was a Rockingham Whig.

Chapter IV pondered and dissected the Canadian Liberal Party and liberal establishment, insisting that liberalism had become the dominant political philosophy in Canada. The option to such a political Sanhedrin was Leftist Castroism or French nationalist Gaullism—both forms of political thought were willing to use the state for the common good of citizens—both forms, in short, of leftist statism had much in common with High Toryism. The American conservative and republican idea that a lighter and minimal state is best ran contrary to the Anglo-Canadian High Tory notion that a strong state, at its best, exists to ensure, in an organic manner, that all citizens within the state are guaranteed basic goods necessary for a civilized existence. Chapter V further unpacked the complex nature of social and entrepreneurial liberalism. The level of philosophic depth and detail that Grant goes into in his various and varied probes of liberalism in Chapters IV–V prepare the reader well for his investigation of the history of French and English High Toryism in Chapter VI. Chapter VI is truly the must-read chapter in *Lament* both for an understanding of historic Toryism and why Grant thought such a way of being, in an age of progress, was an impossibility. The dynamo of liberal principles had won the day, and Hegel sat on the victor's throne. This did not mean, though, Grant took a defeatist view—like a prophet of old, he both lamented yet pointed, in a creative and constructive way to other, older possibilities. Chapter VI points the way to Grant's more complex argument in Chapter VII about 'necessity' and the 'good' which many readers simply ignore in their appropriation of *Lament for a Nation.*

Grant and Red Toryism

When *Lament for a Nation* left the publishing tarmac in 1965 many was the conservative that was startled by Grant's position. The Blue Tories in Canada (classical economic liberals) insisted Grant was not one of them. The New Left thought Grant's form of nationalist Toryism had many an affinity with their agenda. Gad Horowitz coined the term 'Red Tory', and he applied it to Grant after reading *Lament.* Horowitz and Grant engaged in many a public dialogue about the use of 'Red Tory', and Grant was always suspicious about the term being applied to him. The New Left in the 1960s (of which Horowitz was a comrade) was both nationalist and socialist—Grant had nationalist leanings, but he was not a socialist—he was committed to the lived tension of state and society working together for the common good—the New Left socialists leaned more in a strong statist direction. Red was the colour, of course, of the socialist left and Grant had his doubts about the secular socialist left. The historic High Tory tradition is certainly not secular nor is it socialist—there seemed to be affinities between the New Left and High Tories, but Grant made it clear, again and again, he was not a Red Tory in the sense in which Horowitz and the New Left understood Red Tory. Grant was, in most ways, a High Tory which most in the New Left lacked the historical depth to comprehend. The 'Tory touch' that, Horowitz suggested, made Canada different from the United States, was not, as Horowitz thought and argued, a red tory touch—it was more High Toryism—much more nuanced than the ideology of Red Toryism.

The ongoing debate and dialogue about Canadian Red Toryism, Horowitz and Grant, misreads of both of them and the ongoing interest in Red Toryism have certainly not ended. *Lament for a*

Nation brought to the fore a unique and distinctive Canadian way of understanding the political good that did not rest easily with either the right or left, conservative or liberal political ideologies. It was Grant who unearthed this older Anglo-Canadian Tory tradition in the 1960s, but Grant realized, only so well, that he stood on the shoulders of many who had gone before him.

SECTION III

GEORGE GRANT: A RADICAL ORTHODOXY

CHAPTER ELEVEN

GEORGE GRANT AND RADICAL ORTHODOXY

I teach him [Grant] now—but oddly only started to read him around 2010. So only since then any direct influence—but no doubt indirectly much before then. — John Milbank[1]

Conrad Noel continued the Headlam–Hancock sense that the church was the true society and extended earlier intuitions about the links between liturgy and social order. He surely realized the powerful links between beauty and justice, social and natural harmony. — John Milbank[2]

The Dethronement of Secular Reason: Grant and Milbank

I remember, with much fondness, a lunch spent with John Milbank at Peterhouse (founded in AD 1284) in Cambridge in May 1995. I was doing, at the time, research on the Anglican High Romanticism of S. T. Coleridge and the Anglican High Toryism of T. S. Eliot. I was on my way to Little Gidding for a few days to ponder Eliot's *Four Quartets*. John Milbank had published, in 1990, his innovative and plough-to-soil tome, *Theology and Social Theory: Beyond Secular Reason*. Radical Orthodoxy did not exist at the time, but the seeds of the movement had definitely been sown with *Theology and Social Theory*. Needless to say, we chatted much at Peterhouse (the definitive High Church college at Cambridge—Milbank made sure I realized this was Laud's college) about Milbank's demanding read of a book and how his challenge to secular reason opened up new yet much older terrain in which to do theology, philosophy, social theory and, in time, political philosophy. I did, a few days later, when at St. John's College, Oxford, attend a lecture by Professor Patrick Collinson, who spent most of the time bashing Archbishop William Laud (but such were his puritan and protestant prejudices). I was fortunate at the time also to be spending time with David Nicholls (rector of St. Mary and St. Nicholas Church, Littlemore—the church Cardinal Newman built and where he crossed the Rubicon to Rome)—quite a different read on Laud and politics than that offered by Collinson.

It should be noted that Milbank was not particularly new on the stage in his creative dethronement of secular reason—most postmodernists had challenged the hegemony of 'logo-centrism', the romantic and humanist wings of the Enlightenment had also questioned how secular reason was reductionistic and narrowed the range of thought—cutting edge scientists also doubted the ability of secular reason to deliver the goods as did those grounded and rooted in the contemplative theological and philosophical tradition of Plato–Aristotle and the Patristic Fathers of the Church (West and East). The turn, therefore, by Milbank to an older and deeper understanding of thinking was but part of a larger movement in the West to doubt the pretensions of a narrow definition of reason—needless to say, Coleridge's turn to a form of High Romantic Platonic Anglicanism meant he was engaged in the same process in the nineteenth century as was Eliot in his read of the wasteland of the twentieth century—Milbank was, in short, standing on the wise shoulders of those Anglicans who had gone before him, although Coleridge and Eliot were not front and centre in his thinking at the time.

George Grant is considered to be one of the most important public intellectuals in the latter half of the twentieth century in Canada. Grant died in 1988, but most of his thinking and prolific published writings dealt with the way secular reason revealed but concealed much. The task of good philosophy and theology (as Grant saw it) was twofold: to free reason from its secular bondage to a narrow notion of empirical thinking and release the mind (*nous*) to be open yet again to the contemplative wisdom offered by the sacred. Grant, like Coleridge, Eliot and Milbank was immersed in a much older and more comprehensive understanding of the mind as a contemplative faculty and organ of meditative insight. All of these men were acutely aware that when the secular dims and silences the sacred, the secular, in time, leads to disenchantment of nature, soul and society. The bully-like tendencies of secular reason had to be opposed by a more nuanced and refined understanding of reason which was not irrational but the very waiting and attentive nature of contemplative reason. Most of Grant's vocation was given to challenging secular reason by a turn to contemplative philosophy as a constructive antidote and healing balm to the soul injuries caused by a brittle understanding of reason, intellect and thinking. I don't remember John Milbank and I talking much about Grant at our lunch at Peterhouse, but my ongoing research on Grant at the time made me think of their multiple affinities—Grant was, in many ways, the departed elder in the ancient tribe—Milbank was waxing in his recall of the old ways. Both men, in their different ways, saw in the writings of Francis Bacon the theoretical magus for both empirical rationalism and a naive scientific utopianism—*Novum Organum* (*Instauratio magna*) and *New Atlantis* were deeply troubling for the simple reason that reason and science were set on the throne as the new guardians of intellectual and public reality—Grant exposed this hegemony and imperial way of knowing in the 1950s—Milbank, of course, much later.

Athens and Jerusalem

There has been, unfortunately, a tendency amongst some Christian thinkers to argue that Hebrew thought is integrated and holistic and Greek thinking is dualistic (spirit–mind is held high and body–matter denigrated). Needless to say, such ways of reading the Hebraic and Hellenistic mindsets and worldviews are both excessively simplistic and decidedly dishonest. Both the Jewish and Greek traditions are sophisticated and complex. The fact that the early Christian tradition (West and East) was quick to heed and internalize the Greek contemplative and philosophical way meant that post-apostolic and patristic Christianity saw much in the best and noblest of Greek thought that had a revelatory nature in a way the Jewish tradition did not. Again, the simplistic distinctions of Jewish-revelatory and Greek-rationalist approaches to reality distort both cultural heritages. The fact that George Grant and John Milbank hold high the Greek contemplative way contra secular reason speaks much about their radical (cutting to the roots) turn to the source and fount (*ad fontes*) of the historic Christian way of knowing and being. We live in a period of time in which the *vita activa* has become an opiate of sorts that drugs most against a slowing down and a seeing from another more listening and attentive stance. If secular reason has had a tendency to banish contemplative reason, then the *vita activa* has played a substantive role in marginalizing the *vita contemplativa*. The fact that both Grant and Milbank turned their gaze to the Platonic contemplative way in opposition to secular reason and the *vita activa* does, as I mentioned above, take them to a radical critique of the modern mood and ethos. There is, in fact, a sort of prophetic *metanoia* at work in Grant and Milbank's call to a change of heart and mind.

It is one thing to urge those of faith and a deeper vision of the soul and society to question the dominant paradigm of the West that tends to define what is worth living for, where citizens should turn for meaning, what education, church and public life should look like in a more healthy sense—the digging to the roots is but part of the prophetic task and calling. It is quite another thing to articulate the content and lived social context of an authentic and genuine faith journey.

Grant, Radical Orthodoxy and the Church

I have, up to this point, mentioned, mostly, the role and significance of two Anglicans worth the heeding: George Grant and John Milbank. The 1990s was the decade in which both the thinking of Grant and Milbank continued to ripple forth. The turn and deeper meaning of the 'radical' and 'orthodox' became part of the constructive recovery role of 'the Great Tradition', and the church (many have faulted the Radical Orthodox for not seriously grappling with the role of the church in their theology) does come to the fore. The publication of Catherine Pickstock's *After Writing: On the Liturgical Consummation of Philosophy* in 1997 was a fit and fine answer to such a questioning and queries. Grant, like Milbank, points to a way of doing philosophy and theology that is participatory and existential—Pickstock, in her evocative tome, clarifies the unique relationship between philosophy and liturgy. Philosophy and theology are not merely about the moving around of ideas and images of God in a sort of intellectual chess game. The heart, centre and core of contemplative thought is immersion and participation in the very being of God, and such a process is best shaped and formed by dwelling within the time-tried and historic liturgy of the life of the church—Plato, for Pickstock, is a fine and wise guide in articulating the role of liturgy in educating desires and reforming the soul and body towards the good, true and beautiful. When Pickstock is rightly read, the liturgical and ecclesial aspect of Radical Orthodoxy takes on a significant communal dimension.

Grant lived, often in an anguished way, within the life of the Anglican Church of Canada as the liberal drift ever hastened and demanded its ideological due. There could be no doubt that the broad church was winning the ecclesial and intellectual battle. The catholic party in the Anglican Church was becoming more liberal at the core and centre, and classical catholic Anglicans were being marginalized. The low church was battling a rearguard fight and most within the reformed–evangelical–charismatic party were either turning on one another or lacked the substantive intellectual resources to expose the weak underbelly of liberalism. Grant saw more clearly than most what the heart of the issue was, and he named it well and wisely: a form of ideological liberalism in the church and society, culture and politics that priorized, back of the rhetoric of tolerance and openness, a commitment to the rights of the individual to use their agency (power–will), all being free and equal, to define reality as they saw fit. Grant drew from Swift's analogy in 'Battle of the Books' between bees and spiders—bees took the pollen from that which is and created honey—spiders spun webs of reality out of their womb—the ancients were the bees, moderns the spiders.[3] Grant enucleated, ever so clearly, how the spiders were crawling to and from in the church and society. There can be no doubt, though, from Grant's joining the Anglican Church of Canada in 1956 until his death in 1988, he unconcealed and revealed, in a succinct and compact manner, a subtle seduction in the making—in this sense, Grant read and deciphered the writing on the wall decades before many—few heard, heeded or listened to him, though.

The theological, philosophical and liturgical roots of Radical Orthodoxy do work themselves out in the praxis of the life of the church. I quoted, to begin this chapter, Milbank's notion of the church as the catalyst and motivator of the new and true society. Milbank does draw, mostly, from the parochial role of the radical catholic Anglicans in his thinking such as Conrad Noel of Thaxted (where the Chesterton brothers attended when young), Headlam, Hancock, Dearmer and many others—it is this communal and social faith vision embodied and incarnated in the life of the church and community that Milbank and many from the Radical Orthodox tradition draw from—such a way of being church 'links liturgy and social order ... beauty and justice, social and natural harmony'. There are Anglicans who know not this more radical socialist position, but it has a long line and lineage. I was fortunate for a time to live with Kenneth Leech in East London—Leech, in his life and writings, threads together a high and catholic view of the church, a sacramental socialism and a radical commitment to parish life as the vehicle of justice, peace and environmental transformation. Needless to say, such a radical vision was not new to catholic Anglicanism—

Essays Catholic and Radical: A Jubilee Group Symposium for the 150th Anniversary of the Beginning of the Oxford Movement 1833– 1983, edited by Kenneth Leech and Rowan Williams, brings together some of the main thinkers of a tradition that Milbank and the Radical Orthodox turn to for insight and inspiration. It is, therefore, quite unfair and inappropriate to accuse the Radical Orthodox of sidelining or marginalizing the role of the church in their understanding of catholic orthodoxy—it is more apropos to argue that parish and church life are front and centre in their integrated notion of reform and renewal. Grant, Pickstock and Milbank are all one on this pertinent point—the anarchist contra church position will not be found in such a classical mother church position.

There can be no doubt that by the late 1990s Radical Orthodoxy had become, for many, the *cause du jour* way to do theology. Radical Orthodoxy challenged both the reformed–evangelical and liberal ethos within the Anglican Communion. The rather thin, insipid and trendy form of liberal Anglicanism embodied by Bishops John Spong in the United States and Richard Holloway in Scotland simply lacked depth—Grant had faced, in his time, the same dilemma of a form of ideological liberalism that simply and uncritically capitulated to modern liberalism—thinking and the church became a plaything of the newest trends and tendencies. If the broad church seemed to lack any substantive resistance to modern liberalism, then the low church form of Anglicanism (reformed and evangelical) tended to be too Biblicist and lacked a deeper classical grounding. Grant, Milbank and Pickstock were pointing the way to a classical participatory way of knowing and living from the centre of the Christian faith that was absent in the broad and low church forms of Anglicanism—in this sense, there were some affinities with the Tractarians of the nineteenth century, but the Radical Orthodox should not be equated with the Anglo-Catholics—there is something more radical about them (and even more orthodox).

The publication in 1999 of *Radical Orthodoxy: A New Theology* summarized, in a series of compact and succinct essays, the direction John Milbank, Catherine Pickstock and Graham Ward were going and why. It should be noted at this point that much of the thinking of the Radical Orthodox in the latter years of the last decade of the twentieth century and in the first decade of the twenty-first century tended to be in the disciplines of philosophy and theology—clearings had to be made, overgrown ways of doing theology had to be pruned, a recovery and rethinking was afoot—arts, culture, parish life, theology and philosophy were offered an alternate way of being. The mining of the ancient way was being recovered in a way that had not been done in quite the same way. Kant and Hegel were to go. The mystery of the sacred path was opened again for spiritual pilgrims— for those thirsty, the divine wells were refound. Many were the conferences, books, dialogues and debates, pro–contra, from 2000 to 2010 that focussed on the innovative approach of the growing adherents of Radical Orthodoxy.

Red–High Toryism

Radical Orthodoxy: A New Theology launched, in some ways, the Radical Orthodox movement, and in 2009, *The Radical Orthodoxy Reader*, edited by John Milbank and Simon Oliver, summarized in a congealed and succinct manner, the ongoing relevance of the Radical Orthodox position. Many of the essays in the two books are compact arguments, from a variety of angles, for the notion of being radical and being orthodox. The Twenty-four Theses of the Radical Orthodox brought the core ideas together in a compressed manner. We can see the important role of the church (Nos. 15 and 17), concerns about the low church tradition (No. 14) and approaches to politics (Nos. 15 and 20). There have been, as expected, many criticisms of Radical Orthodoxy—some of these critiques tend to begin with a caricature of a more complicated position, then dismiss the caricature—other criticisms have more weight and validity. The typical postmodern dismissal of Radical Orthodoxy can be found, for example, in *The Poverty of Radical Orthodoxy* edited by Lisa Isherwood and Marko Zlomislic and published in 2012. Sadly so, most postmoderns only have the thinnest understanding of the Classical heritage (which they often caricature, then curtly dismiss). *The Poverty of Radical Orthodoxy* tends to reflect more the impoverished perspective of the writers than a more rigorous read of Radical Orthodoxy. There have also been many critiques of the Radical Orthodox from within the Modern paradigm and some from within the emerging Patristic 'ressourcement' movement. There has been a generous reception by some within the Roman Catholic and Orthodox forms of Christianity, but others have their hesitant doubts. Even the reformed and evangelical clan has entered the evaluative fray, as in James Smith's *Introducing Radical Orthodoxy: Mapping a Post-Secular Theology*, published in 2004. There can be no doubt, though, that Radical Orthodoxy has had an impact on both the living Anglican tradition and ways of doing theology that extend far beyond the Anglican fold.

There had been hints within the Radical Orthodox tribe that there is a larger economic, social and political vision that bears fruit from their theological, philosophical, liturgical and ecclesial position, but it was not until Phillip Blond's *Red Tory: How the Left and Right Have Broken Britain and How We Can Fix It* was published in 2010 that what was implicit became more explicit. It is significant to note that the political language of 'Red Toryism' emerged within the Canadian context in 1965 following the publication of George Grant's controversial *Lament for a Nation: The Defeat of Canadian Nationalism*. Grant lamented, in this modern jeremiad of sorts, not only the defeat of the Conservative Prime Minister John Diefenbaker in the 1963 election by the combined alliance of Lester Pearson (who became the Liberal Prime Minister) and President John F. Kennedy, he also argued that in the defeat of Diefenbaker more than a political vision had been eclipsed (indeed died). In fact, Grant suggested that an older way of knowing and being had disappeared in the 1963 election—Canadian High Toryism had been replaced by the incoming tidal wave of liberalism at both the level of theory and political praxis—Grant lamented in this historical, political, philosophical and theological tract for the times the reality of such a transition and the implications of it. The fact that Grant lamented the passing away (a death of sorts of High Toryism) meant that, for many, at the political level, he must be a Goldwater republican of the sort that Russell Kirk might have applauded and approved—this was not the case, though. Grant made it abundantly clear that his understanding of the Anglo-Canadian way (of which he had significant roots) did not disparage the role of the state in bringing into being a variety of social goods such as health care, public education, social services and many other civic structures. This did not mean that Grant demeaned the role of society and the Burkean small platoon—he merely, as a High Tory, thought state and society, in a civilized country, should work together for the good of one and all (common good, commonwealth or commonweal). It was this notion that society and the state are in a living partnership to bring into being the needful goods of citizens within a country that distinguishes classical Toryism from its deviation and distortion within the republican way. After the publication of Grant's *Lament for a Nation*, the well-known Canadian political theorist, Gad Horowitz, called Grant a 'Red Tory'. The language of Red Toryism, therefore, emerged within the Canadian context in the mid-1960s.

The publication of Blond's *Red Tory* does raise some interesting questions about the relationship between Grant, Blond and the public expression of Radical Orthodox thought and practice. Is Blond's (and for that matter the Radical Orthodox) understanding of Red Tory on the same page as Grant's? It should be noted that Grant would agree with the Radical Orthodox in their critique of capitalism and the rise of multinational corporations (and the role they have played in undermining historic communities). Grant was as stringent a critic of Thatcher as are the Radical Orthodox. But, when Blond juxtaposes the state to society, with the former being a problem and the latter the answer, Grant would part paths with such a move. Grant, as I mentioned above, saw society and the state working together, in principle and imperfectly in fact, in a harmonic and symphonic way. Both society and the state were imperfect means of bringing into reality goods for one and all, and each needed one another to do so. It was simply naive to bash the large state (as another mega institution like a corporation) and idealize society. The realm of the political at the local and municipal level was as important as the higher levels—each sphere had tendencies towards imperfection, hence the need of all spheres to check and correct those inherent limitations of community, social life and the state. This means that the High–Red Toryism of Grant would have some affinities with Blond and the Radical Orthodox, but he (and other Canadian High Tories) would definitely differ with the too simplistic contrast of state and society that tends to dominate the Radical Orthodox political, civic and public vision. I should note, though, that in a variety of correspondences with John Milbank, he is much more nuanced in his read of parish, community, society and the state than is Phillip Blond in *Red Tory*—there are certainly decided affinities between Grant and Blond in the way they see the role of the church interacting at various levels of society and the state—certainly no 'state is evil', 'society is good' dualism—such is the Laudian magisterial Anglican way: radical and orthodox, catholic and publically engaged (at both the civil and political levels).

George Grant and Radical Orthodoxy

Many are the affinities (implicit and explicit) between the classical Platonic Anglicanism of George Grant, John Milbank and the Radical Orthodox: 1) secular reason is dethroned and contemplative theology–philosophy rethroned, 2) the classical thinking of Plato is held high as a way of knowing and being as a corrective to either caricatures of Athens or an either–or attitude to Athens–Jerusalem in which Athens is demeaned and Jerusalem idealized, 3) the church, in her prophetic essence, is honoured as the bearer of the new society— this means, of course, renewal is an ongoing process in which an older classical way reverses the dominance of liberalism in society and the church, 4) the church should not be beholden, under the guise of conservatism, to serving a right-of-centre political, economic or social ideological construct and fiction. In fact, if the church is true to her high calling, she will transcend the tribalism of the right, left and sensible centre with a more consistent vision, in principle and practice, of the higher good of the church and society, community and the state—such are the contributions of George Grant, John Milbank and Radical Orthodoxy. Needless to say, a much longer chapter (indeed a whole book) could be written on Grant, his affinities as well as differences with the Radical Orthodox, differences among the Radical Orthodox and critiques of the Radical Orthodox from a variety of directions and angles. In many ways the thinking of George Grant anticipated the Radical Orthodoxy movement and there is much to be gained by a turning to Grant as an elder voice within the greater tradition to which they both belong.

CHAPTER TWELVE

C. S. LEWIS AND GEORGE GRANT: A TALE OF TWO ANGLICAN TORIES

What sense! What clarity! What importance! It was just what I had come to Oxford to hear. My breath was taken away with gladness. From then on the Socratic Club was a centre for me. — George Grant.[1]

Grant wanted to learn how to argue the case for Christianity in the context of contemporary ethical, political, and economic struggles. How could modern human beings come to know God's love in their actions and their contemplation, even though they operated within a way of thinking and acting which excluded God? He attended C. S. Lewis's Socratic Club at Oxford. There he heard arguments for and against Christianity advanced and debated 'directly, clearly and lucidly.' Lewis, himself a convert, as has been said, first from secular thought to religion, and then to Christianity, was for Grant an example of a religious thinker who took the experience and language of modern people seriously. — Arthur Davis.[2]

Introduction

There is no doubt that C. S. Lewis has had a significant influence on many in the twentieth century, and his insights continue to ripple forth in many directions and reach diverse shores. George and Sheila Grant were quite active from 1945 to 1946 in the Socratic Club at Oxford that was run by Lewis, and George Grant has become one of the most important Canadian thinkers of the twentieth century, and his ideas continue to bear much fruit. The fact that the University of Toronto Press has published the *Collected Works of George Grant* in four volumes is yet further proof that Grant has played a most important role on the stage of Canadian thought and public life. David Cayley, in *George Grant in Conversation*, summed up Grant's public contribution in

Canadian life when he said, 'Altogether, his contributions to the CBC probably exceeded those of any other Canadian thinker of his generation, except perhaps Northrop Frye'.[3]

There are few, though, who realize that George Grant (and his wife Sheila) were most active in the Socratic Club at Oxford between 1945 and 1946, and many of Grant's more mature ideas were very much a reflection and echo of Lewis's older Tory perspective. Lewis was in his mid-forties when he met Grant, and Grant was in his mid-twenties. Lewis and Grant were, in many ways, on the same intellectual trail; Lewis was just twenty years further down the same path. Lewis had not, by 1945-1946, attained the fame he now has (he did not appear on the front cover of *Time* until 1949), and Grant was very much feeling and groping his way towards a vision of life worth living for. Grant, to the end of his days, looked back to his time at the Socratic Club with much fondness, and the ideas of Lewis did much to point Grant to cairns and a trail worthy of the trek.

There are many who claim Lewis as one of their own (particularly those from the American Evangelical and Roman Catholic republican traditions), but few see Lewis as a Classical Anglican Tory, deeply grounded and rooted in the ancient Anglican humanist and catholic way. Those who uproot Lewis from such a context and soil, predictably so, wither the plant of his worldview. George and Sheila Grant, after leaving Oxford (where Sheila was studying English literature), moved to Halifax, and throughout the 1950s, George taught philosophy at Dalhousie University. George and Sheila were confirmed as Anglicans in 1956, and George, in much of his thinking, teaching and writing, for the rest of his life, grappled with and clearly articulated many of the Tory ideas that were so much a part of the fabric of Lewis's mind and imagination.

If, as I am suggesting, Lewis and Grant are very much traditional Anglican Tories, what does this mean? Is there an obvious affinity between their ideas? Do they come to many of the same conclusions about the clash between the ancients and the moderns, conservatism and liberalism? And what can such men still teach and tell us about what we have lost by discarding the true and tried paths of those who have gone before us? Where, in short, is the Classical Tory Anglican well in which Lewis and Grant dipped their buckets so deeply, and dare we drink from the water they offer us?

Tory Tendencies: The Turn to Tradition

First, Tories are very committed to the accumulated wisdom of the past. Our elders who have gone before us still have much insight to impart to us if we have but the ears to hear, eyes to see, hearts to receive and minds to mull over. In short, the mother lode and deposit left to us, by those who have gone before us, is ignored to our personal and cultural peril. It tends to be the modern and liberal notion of history as progress, of the past as a dark and unenlightened era, that has done so much to shape and mould the modern mind. Lewis and Grant, like modern sages and prophets, call us to remember and retrieve that which can still nurture and nourish us.

This turn to the ancient sources (*ad fontes*) for wisdom and insight is the first and essential fact that distinguishes a Tory from a Liberal. But, the curious might rightly ask Lewis and Grant, what source or sources should we turn to and why? Lewis and Grant were both clear about one thing—the Reformation of the sixteenth century wreaked much havoc in the West, and there was much in the Protestant Reformation that set the stage for the modern liberal world. This turn to the pre-Reformation world (and its notions of natural law, the virtues–vices, the good, true and beautiful, ideas such as good, better, best, bad, worse, worst, and a thorough discussion of human longings, hungers and desires, their orientation, end, purpose and direction) and the historic Anglican Church were very close to the thinking of Lewis and Grant.

C. S. Lewis has been summarized aptly as proposing in his *English Literature in the Sixteenth Century, Excluding Drama* that 'it was the rise of Puritanism in late Elizabethan England, the advancing tide of Calvinist theology and ethics in the last two decades of the sixteenth century, not the Renaissance literary movement of the early and middle decades of the century, that marked the real rupture with medieval culture.'[4] In short, Lewis argued that it was the Reformation not the Renaissance that shifted the seismic plates of the West. The fact that Lewis would smile and doff his cap to the Renaissance (which he neither read nor interpreted in a Promethean manner, as man being the measure of all things) and frown and turn his back on much of the Reformation places him in a very different place than most Evangelicals (who call Lewis one of their own) call home. The Renaissance was merely a continuation of the best of the Classical and Medieval

Christian tradition for Lewis; it is in this sense that Lewis was most catholic and humanist in his thinking.

When I was at Regent College from 1979 to 1981, I was a teaching assistant for Jim Houston and I did my MA thesis with him. Jim Houston studied with C. S. Lewis, and he was only too well aware of the well from which Lewis dipped his bucket. Houston made this quite clear in his lecture 'Reminiscences of the Oxford Lewis', when he said, 'His [Lewis's] friends were all Anglo-Catholic or Catholic'.[5] Houston, in the same article, mentioned that most English Evangelicals from the 1930s until the late 1950s had little or nothing to do with C. S. Lewis. It was only with Clyde Kilby's interest in the late 1950s-early 1960s, and the fact Wheaton College created a special collection of Lewis's writings in 1965, that he became so popular with the American Evangelicals in the late 1960s-early 1970s. The fact that Lewis was deeply catholic in his thinking and imagination means that the Evangelical appropriation of him has often distorted some of the deeper insights of Lewis. The catholicity of Lewis and his grounding in the classical tradition come out quite clear in one of his final books. *The Discarded Image: An Introduction to Medieval and Renaissance Literature* argues that it was the Medieval–Renaissance Christian tradition that synthesized the wisest and best of the Classical heritage, and, it is as we have discarded this image, we have lost much.

There is much more that could be said about the way Lewis turned back of the Reformation for insight and wisdom about faith and culture, but did Grant do much of the same thing? There is no doubt he did.

Grant's first book, *Philosophy in the Mass Age*, is very much a missive that compares and contrasts the past and the present, and there is no doubt where Grant tips his hat. Grant is aware of the appeal of the modern liberal idea of liberty and individualism, and some of the good it has done, but he is only too aware of its dark and foreboding side. Does Grant, though, see the Enlightenment of the eighteenth century as the source and fount of such notions as liberty and individualism? No, not for a moment! Grant argues quite clearly, like Lewis before him, that it was the Reformation that let the cat out of the bag. The Enlightenment, therefore, for Lewis and Grant, was merely an extension and fleshing out of Reformation principles. The liberalism we live with today is merely the mature and fully grown child that was born with the Reformation. Protestant Christians who tend to toss stones at our modern and postmodern liberal ethos are often blind to the fact such a tradition gave birth to such principles as liberty, individualism, equality and conscience while turning against such classical notions as order, the commonweal, the organic nature of society and the wisdom of tradition (not to be confused with traditionalism). Grant was convinced, as Cayley suggests, that notions such as history as progress, freedom and individualism 'had begun in the Reformation with the overthrow of the church's power to interpose its dogmas, rituals, and hierarchies between the believer and God; but by the Enlightenment, European thinkers had already begun to chafe at the bonds imposed on thought by the very existence of God'.[6] Grant further argued 'the great central thought that I have tried to think: that the Western experiment, the experiment that [has] gone on since the seventeenth century in both natural science and political science, [has been] a mistake'.[7] Those who have taken the time to read Grant's *Lament for a Nation* are taught and told, in the most unmistakable way, that ideas that emerged in the sixteenth and seventeenth centuries have done much hurt and harm to one and all.

Grant, like Lewis, therefore, turned back of the Reformation, to the much older catholic and humanist Christian tradition for insight and assistance on his all too human journey. Grant, of course, gave himself much more to the Classical Platonic Anglican way (with its abiding commitment to contemplation and politics), and Lewis offered up the Medieval way as an answer. But, both men, as Classical Tory Anglicans, were deeply suspicious of the modern project which they argued began with the Reformation. It is this much older Anglican tradition, deeply grounded in the catholic way, that synthesized the very best of the Jewish, Greek and Roman ways into a coherent and lively Christian mind and vision, and it was to such a source that Lewis and Grant turned.

It is interesting to note, at this juncture, that both Lewis and Grant, for different reasons, were quite involved in the renewal of 'the Great Books' tradition in education. Lewis became an important figure, alongside Thomas Aquinas, for the renaissance of Medieval thought at such Roman Catholic institutions as Fordham University in New York. Neo-Thomism was very much in vogue, and it was argued that Aquinas, in contrast to the fragmentation in modern education, sought to synthesize and unify thought in one great and grand Christian system. Needless to say, this was much of the argument Lewis put forward about the Medieval tradition being concerned about organizing, codifying and building an intellectual system. The University of Chicago, of course, under the leadership of Richard McKeon, Robert Hutchins and Mortimer Adler was at the forefront of 'the Great Books' tradition. Cantor summed up the relevance of Lewis for the Roman Catholic and 'the Great Books' traditions when he said, 'Lewis's phenomenal popularity in America in the 1940s and 1950s [mostly in the Roman Catholic ethos] stemmed partly from the compatibility of his perception of medieval culture with neo-Thomist principles'.[8] This insight by Cantor very much reflects why Lewis, as Houston noted above, had many Anglo-Catholic and Catholic friends and colleagues. Lewis was, and this must be emphasized, adopted by Roman Catholics of the 1940s-1950s before the American Evangelicals made him one of their own in the 1960s-1970s. Lewis's catholicity cannot be doubted; Roman Catholics saw this, and they were drawn to him.

What, though, did Grant have to do with the renewal of Classical education, 'the Great Books' tradition or the University of Chicago? When George Grant had his confrontation with Professor Long at the University of Toronto about whether he could and would teach Plato and Christianity rather than Long's text in the philosophy department at the fledgling York University, Long won the day and Grant resigned from York in 1960. Grant had no job at the time, and Mortimer Adler was just compiling *The Great Ideas Today* series book for 1961. Grant had written an enthusiastic review of Hutchins' *The Higher Learning in America* in 1938, when he was nineteen and completing his BA at Queen's University.[9] So, even at an early age, Grant had an interest in 'the Great Books' tradition and their relevance for education. Grant worked with Adler and Hutchins in 1960-1961 and wrote a twenty-five-thousand-word article for them.[10] Grant had some affinities with 'the Great Books' tradition, but within a few years, he turned aside from them and hiked another path. Grant found Adler, Hutchins and tribe much too committed to Aristotle (and their dialectical and pluralist reading of the tradition) rather than the transcendent mysticism and political philosophy of Plato. Much, of course, hinges on whether one turns to Plato or Aristotle when the turn is made to the Classical tradition as the place of the good, true and beautiful.

I think it would be fair to say that both Lewis and Grant had some affinities with 'the Great Books' tradition but there came a point where both parted company with how the Great Tradition should be read and interpreted. The American reading, use and appropriation of the Classical and Medieval past, as interpreted by 'the Great Books' clan was something both Lewis and Grant had some questions about.

Tory Tendencies: The Magisterial Way

The second mark of a Tory can be found in his or her commitment to the public sphere whether in the area of culture, education or politics; in short, this is the classical Magisterial way. The Christian Tory does not retreat into some sort of religious ghetto, some purist enclave and toss negative stones at the public institutions. The Tory enters the public square with a certain understanding of what culture, education and politics should and ought to be. Needless to say, such a vision emerges from a deep religious source (and the institutions that carry and embody such a vision), but more of this later.

C. S. Lewis spent all of his mature life teaching at Oxford and Cambridge. Lewis emerged as one of the finest Christian scholars and apologists of his generation, but he learned his trade and ability to speak to his time by being in the thick of the battle. Sheila Grant (who with George avidly attended the Socratic Club and lectures by Tolkien) once told me, 'C. S. Lewis was a fine and competent literary scholar who was a Christian, also, and this was rare at Oxford at the time'.[11]

Lewis, after his conversion to Christianity (so well recounted in *The Pilgrim's Regress* and *Surprised by Joy*) gave himself to defending Christianity in the lion's den of the modern world. The Socratic Club was very much a place in which one and all were invited to face the big and challenging issues of the time. There was no doubt at the time that scientific empiricism and relativism were very much in vogue amongst the avant-garde, so Lewis invited the best and the brightest from such perspectives to state their case. Lewis, as I mentioned above, did not retreat into a religious ghetto and lament the passing away of Christianity. He knew what it was like to feel the sneers of his peers and fellows at Oxford and Cambridge for doing popular Christian apologetics, science fiction and stories for children. This did not seem to fit the scholar's role, but Lewis was determined to speak the Christian message to his time in a way that made the Christian message appealing and insightful.

Education, in the public realm, for Lewis, was about growing in wisdom, insight and moral depth; it was not just about facts, techne and information. The reason both teacher and student turned to the past was that the past still had much to teach about the human soul, desires, longings and the proper end and destination of such desires. This is why, for example, Lewis argued in both *Mere Christianity* and *The Abolition of Man* that there is an order in the universe, and it is the high calling and vocation of each and all to both know such an order and attune ourselves to it. Such an order, of course, was very much understood and articulated by the ancients and called natural law. It was to such 'permanent things' as natural law and the classical understanding of the virtues and vices that Lewis pointed the way. Lewis argued, in *The Abolition of Man*, that such ideas could be found in all the great religions of the world; Lewis, in the 'Appendix',[12] called this the *Tao*. Sheila Grant told me that the 'Appendix' to *The Abolition of Man* had meant a great deal to her, George and many others when it was published.[13] It is this notion of a natural law or the *Tao* that Grant was to use and make much of in his writings. It was these permanent things that drew, wooed and won the soul that Lewis and Grant held high in an age that sought to dismiss, censure or privatize. It was these permanent things that could be found in the best of all the religions of the world, and Lewis and Grant were quick and keen to acknowledge this.

George Grant, like C. S. Lewis, was deeply suspicious about the way reason had become the handmaiden and errand boy of both science and technology. Both men knew that the classical notion of reason as both a contemplative and receptive faculty and organ was quite different from the notions of reason that emerged at the Reformation, the Baconian empirical methodology of the sixteenth century and modern technical–instrumental reason. Such a classical notion of intellect was much more spacious, much more open to the eternal and the moving image of eternity, than the rather reductionistic notion of reason that was found in the dominant view of empirical science at the time. The classical notion of reason, as a contemplative faculty, immersed in the good, true and beautiful of the eternal, infused the moral order with a deeper significance.

Grant, like Lewis, argued that we either see order or liberty as the guiding star, and if we choose liberty, we often use it to violate the very order that gives meaning, happiness and fulfilment. It is by being open to such an order and attuning ourselves to it, that we are truly free. Grant's argument in *Philosophy in the Mass Age* is, in many ways, a fuller amplification of the arguments of Lewis in *Mere*

Christianity and *The Abolition of Man*. Both men clearly argue that there is a moral order in the cosmos, and to the degree we know and attune ourselves to such an order, we will live good lives. Such a notion and commitment ran very much against the grain, in modern culture, of the argument that all thought is merely opinion, perspective, subjective, private truth, pluralist and relative to place and time. Both Lewis and Grant knew where the modern liberal world stood and why, and both men went into the public realm to face the challenges. These men, as I mentioned above, did not retreat from public education, culture and politics; they, as older Tories, knew they had to live their faith in the public place and space.

Louis Greenspan, a student of Grant in the 1950s at Dalhousie, said, 'In an age where artists paint for artists, writers write for other writers and philosophers philosophize for other philosophers, George Grant steadfastly addressed the public realm'.[14] George and Sheila Grant, in many ways, continued the notion of the Socratic Club when they were in Dalhousie; their home became for many a student an intellectual salon of sorts. Grant made it very clear that it was the Socratic Club of Lewis that did much to shape and form him in his twenties. Grant said, 'You know, Lewis was a wonderful human being, and again, enormously articulate. His writing is very simple and clear, and his speech was like that as well. He looked like a great big English butcher, who might be selling meat behind a counter, and he spoke like a butcher, just direct, clear, lucid stuff. This was a wonderful part of my education. It just helped me enormously'.[15]

In short, both Lewis and Grant did not retreat from the public fray, celebrate a cloistered virtue, circle the religious wagons and rail against the world. They loved the world enough to engage it, to enter the public realm with a moral and religious vision and argue such a vision. Lewis did this at Oxford and Cambridge and his influence spread across England and much of the world. George Grant did this at Dalhousie and McMaster, and his influence has been felt in Canada (through the Canadian Broadcasting Corporation) and is, at the present time, having a growing impact outside of Canada.

I think it can be fairly argued that Grant was much more political in his thinking and actions than Lewis. Grant's High Tory approach to politics was framed in distinct contrast to American republican thought, and Grant never shied away from turning his Canadian Toryism on the United States. The Canadian High Tory tradition can be compared, in England, to what the late Margaret Thatcher called 'wet Tories', or to, in the United States, what Irving Kristol had called 'paleo-conservatives'. George Grant argued that it was the American way that most and best embodied the Puritan–Modern– Liberal spirit of history as progress, liberty, individualism, equality, free enterprise, the market economy, suspicion of the state, a turning of the back on the accumulated wisdom of tradition and the Calvinist work ethic. He made it most clear, in short, that the United States was formed and shaped on the anvil of liberal principles. Such principles were deeply part of the English liberal way of Locke, Hobbes, Hume and Paine who had broken, consciously so, from an older Tory way with its concern for the commonweal and the organic nature of society and the state. It was the Puritans, we must remember, that were suspicious of and broke from both the established church and the English state, and it is from such a tradition that notions of a lighter state, pluralism, schism and much of the modern world were birthed.

Grant's older Toryism, with its respect for order, the commonweal and the role of the federal government in bringing about a just nation had much affinity with the student Left of the 1960s. Grant was a darling of the New Left in the 1960s when he stood for a strong Canadian nationalism, with his opposition to corporate capitalism, his pacifism, his 'no' to C. W. Mills's power elite and the American military-industrial complex and his protests against the American invasion of Vietnam. But, Grant was also critical of the New Left. When George and Sheila dared to write against abortion and euthanasia in the 1980s, when Grant dared to hold high the importance of family and religion, the New Left (very much motivated by such liberal principles as liberty, equality and individualism) turned their backs on the Grants. Grant's brand of indigenous Canadian High Tory thought cannot easily be taken captive by the political right or left. We see George Grant, therefore, as extending his magisterial and moral vision to the world of politics and economics in a way Lewis, perhaps, never did. Lewis, for the most part, focused his religious and moral insights in the direction of literature and culture, philosophy and theology and a broad analysis of the modern liberal mood and temper. It is not totally true that Lewis avoided political issues as John West suggests in his essay in *Permanent Things: Towards the Recovery of a More Human Scale at the End of the Twentieth Century*, but Lewis never went as far nor was he as thorough as Grant was in the areas of politics and economics.

It might be timely to pause here for a few moments to yet further reflect on Lewis and Grant and the larger questions of political philosophy and economics. There is no doubt that Lewis and tribe (Tolkien, Sayers, Williams, Barfield, Chesterton, MacDonald) have become *ikons*, mentors and tutors to the Roman Catholic and Evangelical clans in North America. We might ask, why? There is no doubt that 'the Seven' (as they are affectionately called) were literary types with a certain fondness for the Medieval model. The shire and parish were held high, political ideas such as an elevation of society and suspiciousness of the state were smiled on. This meant civil society, the social principle, spheres of influence and subsidiarity were more welcome than the welfare state and a strong central government that created and maintained the commonweal or common good. In fact, Lewis wrote against the welfare state, in such essays as 'Is Progress Possible? Willing Slaves of the Welfare State'.[16]

John West makes clear in 'Finding the Permanent in the Political: C. S. Lewis as a Political Thinker',[17] that Lewis either had little to say about political policy or, when he addressed the political realm, he remained at the level of principles. When Lewis translated such principles into prudential practical guidance, the republican perspective won the day. It is significant to note that a more recent article by James Christie in *Pilgrimage*, 'Jack in the World: The Social Vision of C. S. Lewis', never really dips or dives into the world of Lewis as a serious political or economic thinker. Christie does say, though, 'If Lewis was reticent to endorse large causes either personally or financially, he was confident that nothing relieves the Christian from undertaking the charitable act when it was clearly presented before one'.[18] Such a notion of charity, philanthropy or simple human kindness, of course, plays quite nicely into the anti-statist tendencies of liberal republican thought. But Christie goes further than this: 'Lewis extends his thinking on these issues into the field of practical and party politics. He had, as do many of our contemporaries, a somewhat jaundiced view of politics'.[19] Lewis, also, in 'First and Second Things'[20] and 'The World's Last Night'[21] makes it clear that the first and most important things are God, the eternal and that which is ultimate. It is this way of thinking that panders to a thin approach to politics and a weak and limited approach to the penultimate and antepenultimate questions of political and economic life.

Lewis often retreats into a cynical, jaundiced view of politics, does not link the ultimate and penultimate world close enough, offers principles but moves away from political policies and activism and is quick to offer a kind hand to the needy—and, this all plays nicely into liberal republican thought. We need to ask why Lewis never seriously extended his thinking into the more economic and political spheres, or, when he did, why the turn to society rather than the state as an equal means of dealing with the common good? It is Lewis's lack of balance here that is quite worrisome. When society is pitted against the state (the former being idealized and elevated and the latter demonized and subordinated), there is reason for worry and concern. It is these republican tendencies in Lewis and the Seven that make them most acceptable to those of the American republican tradition. Lewis, of course, other than articulating philosophical principles, as I mentioned above, never really ventured forth into the economic and political arena. In short, it is virtually impossible to ever think the political Left and Lewis would have much in common. I realize, in saying this, Lewis can surprise us, though, and, even more so, shock those who try and convert him into a dutiful republican. There is a most interesting passage in *Mere Christianity* that can come as a surprise to those who attempt to stuff Lewis only and altogether into the Procrustean bed of republican political thought and action. Lewis states in the section on 'Social Morality', and I quote at length:

> All the same, the New Testament, without going into details, gives us a pretty clear hint of what a fully Christian society would be like. Perhaps it gives us more than we can take. It tells us there are to be no passengers or parasites: if a man does not work, he ought not to eat. Every one is to work with his own hands, and what is more, every one's work is to produce something good: there will be no manufacture of silly luxuries and then of sillier advertisements to persuade us to buy them. And there is to be no 'swank' or 'side', no putting on airs. To that extent a Christian society would be what we now call Leftist.[22]

Lewis also goes on to say further in this section:

> If there is such a society in existence and you or I visited it, I think we should come away with a curious impression. We

should feel that its economic life was very socialistic and, in that sense, 'advanced', but that its family life and code of manners were rather old-fashioned—perhaps even ceremonious and aristocratic.[23]

But, there are even more juicy morsels to chew on in 'Social Morality':

Now another point. There is one bit of advice given to us by the ancient heathen Greeks, and by the Jews in the Old Testament, and by the great teachers of the Middle Ages, which the modern economic system has completely disobeyed. All these people told us not to lend money at interest: and lending at interest—what we call investment—is the basis of our whole system.[24]

Lewis, in this section of 'Social Morality', yet further unpacks and unravels the dangers and dilemmas created by those who flaunt the social morality, insight and wisdom of tradition and build an economic civilization on interest or usury.

It seems to me we need a much closer reading of 'Social Morality' if we are ever going to get a fix and feel for Lewis's thought in a more nuanced way. This short chapter highlights the fact that Christian social morality might appear on the right wing of the spectrum, at times, and on the left wing of the political spectrum, at other times. The problem is this: the right and left selectively milk what suits their agenda and ideology and conveniently ignore what does not fit the equation and formula. Christian social morality, according to Lewis, therefore, will transcend the ethical tribalism of the left and right.

The vision Lewis articulates, about the ideal Christian society, is very close to that of Thomas More's *Utopia*, and it is interesting to note that More was deeply catholic, fully humanist and a true fan and supporter of the Renaissance in England that Lewis was such a booster of. *Utopia*, in many ways, anticipates 'Social Morality'. It is some of these ideas that both Lewis and his many acolytes never unpack that can come as a bit of a check to those who only interpret Lewis in a republican manner. Let us hear them again: a Christian society, in the economic sphere, would oppose the use of interest and be more Left and socialist when it comes to such ideas as a sharing of the common purse. We can see how Lewis and More have much in common, and it is important to note that More was a most important thinker for Grant. I wonder what would have happened if Lewis had followed some of these tantalizing hints, these appetizing morsels of sorts down a fuller political trail both in thought and deed. He never did, of course, and much of his thinking on politics, when he does think this way (which is not often), does not follow up this lead. I think, though, if Lewis had unpacked his insights on a Christian society in more depth and detail, we might find some affinity between the Toryism of Grant and Lewis. We might say, therefore, what is merely a hint, a suggestion, a faint thought, a minimal pointing of the finger, an implicit tendency in Lewis becomes much more developed, much more explicit in Grant. Grant, in many ways, within the Canadian context, fleshed out Lewis's 'Social Morality' essay in a way Lewis never did in his English context. This is what makes Grant such an interesting person—he will, at times, appear right-of-centre on issues such as abortion, euthanasia, gay rights, traditional family and religion; he will, at other times, appear left-of-centre when he goes after militarism, multinational corporations, the American empire and the military-industrial complex. It is, therefore, appropriate, I think, to argue that Grant unravels and unpacks a political tradition of the commonweal that is much more fully thought out than that of Lewis. Grant had a much more organic sense of the close relationship between the state and society than Lewis, and he articulated in a more regular manner a consistent life ethic. This is what makes Grant much more of a High, Red or Radical Tory than Lewis.

Grant's insights on the relationship of faith and politics, therefore, are quite different from Lewis's. Lewis never really unravelled his comments in 'Social Morality' in *Mere Christianity*, and it might be interesting to ask, why? Grant did, though, travel down the trail to which such hints pointed and this places him in a very different spot on the political map than Lewis. The Classical Anglo-Canadian tradition Grant draws from that includes, primarily, Plato in the Greek tradition, More, Hooker, Swift, Coleridge, Southey and Disraeli in the English tradition, and Simcoe, Macdonald, Leacock, Bennett, Diefenbaker and Creighton in the Canadian tradition, has a much greater respect for the role of the state in bringing about the common good. Grant, therefore, can never be confused or equated with the republican way as can Lewis and clan. In fact, Grant walked the extra mile, again and again, to distance and distinguish his understanding of conservatism and Toryism from American republicanism (which is really a blend of Puritanism and Lockean liberalism). We need not read too far in *Lament for a Nation* to realize Grant had little interest in American conservative republicanism which, as I mentioned above, Grant saw as a form of and the finest incarnation of the modern liberal work ethic, the *vita activa* and the entrepreneurial spirit. The Reformation, for Grant, was as much an economic reformation as a theological reformation, and Tawney's *Religion and the Rise of Capitalism* had taught Grant to read the sixteenth and seventeenth centuries in a more critical rather than hagiographical manner. In short, Grant's Toryism has more affinity with the political Left (even though he charts a different course on many issues) than that of Lewis.

The fact that Grant published, in 1961, 'An Ethic of Community', in *Social Purpose for Canada*,[25] speaks much about Grant's understanding of the commonweal and how it is to be brought about. Most of the authors of *Social Purpose for Canada* were committed social liberals or in the Co-operative Commonwealth Federation fold (about to become the New Democratic Party). It is Grant's turn to and interpretation of the Great Tradition, grounded in a different reading of the Classical-English-Canadian tradition, that makes him quite different from Lewis. Lewis, in many ways, is a modern liberal in a way Grant is not. Why do I say this? The liberalism of Locke, for example, tended to place culture and religion in a sphere that did not really engage economics and politics. There is a sense in which Lewis bought into this fragmentation in a way Grant never did. I think it can be argued that Grant has a more holistic, consistent and organic understanding of faith (and the relationship between the state and society) than do Lewis and tribe. There is a thinning out, a domesticating, a retreat from the economic and political sphere in Lewis and clan that cannot be found in the Canadian Tory tradition of which Grant thought and lived from. It is in this sense that Lewis and clan have a more aesthetic approach to faith and the world than does Grant. But, when the older, more organic understanding of the relationship and partnership between society and the state is forgotten, then the American conservative tradition comes to define the Canadian heritage. Grant's genius is in the way he retrieved the indigenous Canadian Loyalist–Tory tradition, and such a path does cover different turf and soil than the Lewis republican trail (and those who follow it). I do think, though, a paper yet needs to be done on Lewis and his comments on how, if the Christian tradition was more deeply understood, there are Leftist and Socialist dimensions to it. Such a paper could open up a more nuanced approach to Lewis, and it is from such a perspective that we can see why and how Grant took the path he did.

I think it is important to note and mention here that when we turn our gaze too steadfastly on Lewis and clan and ignore such fine Canadians as Grant and Leacock, we merely encourage a colonized mind. It is as we open ourselves to the best of Canadian thought rather than turning to the English or American imperial contexts that we step into a post-colonial way of seeing and being. Grant did this for many Canadians, and, in doing so, he takes us, as Canadians, much further along the path than Lewis and the Seven ever can. Lewis, in short, never did nor can address the Canadian context the way Canadians can, and to the degree we turn to England as our great and good place, our elsewhere community, we will not really know how to integrate our faith in the nation, home and culture we live in and inhabit in the True North. Grant, therefore, has both a greater breadth than Lewis and, as a Canadian, he can walk us out of a colonial mindset into a post-colonial way of thinking and living the Christian faith in Canada—Lewis never can.

It is perhaps significant to note here that Stephen Leacock (an important Canadian political economist, Tory, novelist and educator) met G. K. Chesterton on his tour of England in 1921. Both men spent a lively and animated afternoon together discussing literature and politics. Leacock had published, in 1920, *The Unsolved Riddle of Social Justice*, in which he argued for an important place for both an interventionist state (in the areas of education, health care and other areas) and a need to respect and honour the role of unions and labour. There is a direct line of continuity between the Canadian Toryism of Leacock and Grant. In fact, Grant's mother and sister studied with Leacock at McGill University, and Grant went to school at Upper Canada College with Leacock's son, Stevie. Chesterton, on the other hand, grounded as he was in an idealized and romanticized notion of the Medieval world, held high the importance of the local guild, of community, of society, of the parish and a certain suspicion of the growing importance of the state. We can, in short, see much in common, when we deal with the political, economic and social spheres, between Chesterton and Lewis, on the one hand, and

Leacock and Grant, on the other hand. It is in these differences that we can detect distinct ways of understanding how principles and ideas are to be applied in the world of state and society. It is in these differences we can see important ways of understanding how the Magisterial way is to be interpreted in the world of politics and economics. The conservatism of Lewis and clan, in many ways, could not be more different than the Toryism of Grant; the sources they draw from speak much. Grant had much affinity with the High Romanticism of Coleridge, Southey and Wordsworth, and such a tradition is summed up nicely by Christopher Dawson, in *The Spirit of the Oxford Movement*:

> In so far as the Oxford Movement was Tory, its Toryism was not that of the defenders of vested interests, the 'Conservatives' who aroused Hurrell Froude's scorn, but that of Southey and Coleridge and the young Disraeli who were among the first to denounce the injustices of the Industrial Revolution and the new Poor Law, and the evils of the factory system'.[26]

The integrated Toryism of the High Romantics, the blending of literature, education, politics, economics, religion and social concerns was something Grant had much affinity with. A line and lineage can easily be drawn, for Grant (and it was drawn) from Coleridge to Swift to Hooker to More to the Patristics to Plato's passion for justice. Grant, then, moved such thinking forward in time to the Canadian context. Grant would stand on the front lines and protest the Vietnam War, stand outside Litton in Toronto, protesting the way they made guidance systems for cruise missiles and was quite vocal about corporations. It is hard to imagine Lewis doing any of the above. Can we imagine, for example, Lewis, if he had lived a few years later, at Greenham Common? I don't think so. Lewis, in his compelling science fiction, *That Hideous Strength*, could depict an end time, apocalyptic scenario, but such visions do little to assist the activist and thinker to work within political parties for the common good within the world we live in. In fact, such novels create a sort of cynicism and apathy towards the political process or a retreat into small groups and anarchist opposition to such a hideous strength.

Grant's work and affinity with the CCF in his King's days, and his willingness to canvas for the NDP in the early 1960s places him in a very different spot on the political map than Lewis. It is difficult, for example, to think of Lewis as being open and willing to work with the Labour Party in England much less be out on the streets canvassing for them at election time. Lewis, in short, tended to veer away from such things, and, as I mentioned above, his way of doing justice would be much more focussed on the local, the guild, the parish and community. There are hints in Lewis, as I mentioned above, if followed up, that have some rather radical implications. There are few who have done this, hence Lewis has tended, almost by default, to be read in a republican manner. But, Lewis also points in such a republican direction in many of his writings. This older republican model is drawn from Aristotle and is basic to some aspects of the Medieval ethos. In short, given the fact that the thinking of Lewis had much affinity with the Medieval guild model, and, in some ways, the Puritan tradition drew from this tradition, his thinking, even though opposed to Puritanism in some ways, has much affinity with the Puritan model of the relationship between society and state. It is this way of thinking that has made Lewis popular within the republican tradition where there is concern for the 'permanent things' and also suspicion of the state in holding near and dear such permanent things. In short, the more organic and activist Toryism of Grant that held together a high role of the state and society was not knit together as well in Lewis, and this makes him more of a darling of the religious republicans. This old debate, of course, takes us back to the subtle differences and distinctions between Plato and Aristotle when they thought about political theory. Plato had a higher view of the role of the state than Aristotle; Grant tends to turn more to Plato, and Lewis to Aristotle. This same debate can be found in Jewish political thought between those who wanted a monarch (and more power in the monarch) and those who were more decentralized and tribal in outlook. I have, some might think, lingered too long on these distinctions between Lewis and Grant (and other ways of reading Lewis), but I have done this for the simple reason that there are differences, the differences do have consequences, and the distinctions have not really been duly noted or realized at this point.

Both Grant and Lewis would agree, though, that if virtue does not win the day, and vice sits on the throne, the form and means that are used to bring about the just and good commonweal and state can go awry. Both men, therefore, agreed, that politics must be grounded and rooted in certain immutable principles, but they differed and disagreed about how such principles could best be fleshed out in the actual world of political life and praxis. Issues such as national security, foreign aid, health care, education, culture, pensions and employment insurance all raise important questions about the role and responsibilities of the state and society, national standards and local (town, family, community) concerns. Lewis tended to lean towards a more decentralized, republican tradition with these questions, whereas Grant had a respect for both the state and society in fulfilling their due roles. Grant would see a greater role for an interventionist state than Lewis (although Lewis can be pressed further in this direction than he has been), and this is what makes Grant (like Leacock before him) a Red, High or Radical Tory.

It must be admitted, though, that Lewis and Grant, in their different ways, entered the public square with a flair and gusto that cannot be denied. The older Tory vision that animated them touched on such areas as literature, culture, philosophy, theology, social issues, economics and politics. It is this much older humanist, catholic and Tory vision that thinks in an integrated, interdisciplinary way and has a passion for the things public that Lewis and Grant embodied (even though they understood the nature of the integration in different ways). Both men insisted that we cannot forget the permanent things that make us truly human and humane. If we forget who we are, Grant often argued, we will live with 'intimations of deprival'. It is such intimations that point to a higher and better way. In sum, Lewis and Grant, as Tories, entered the public square (refusing to reduce religion to a private thing), they carried a certain moral vision that they applied to the areas of education, culture, theology, philosophy, ethics, economics and politics. Both men were most convinced that it was a religious imperative to work within the public institutions (and attempt to reform them) rather than turning against them. This meant, of course, there would be all sorts of tensions and challenges, given the dominance of liberalism, but both Lewis and Grant stayed the course.

Tory Tendencies: The Anglican Tradition

The third and final point that Lewis and Grant shared was their commitment to the Anglican tradition, but such a commitment was to the essence (*esse*) of the tradition. Both Lewis and Grant were much more interested in 'mere Christianity' rather than parties or clans within the Anglican way. The Anglican tradition can, when it is not careful, slip into High (Anglo-Catholic), Broad (Liberal) and Low (Reformed–Evangelical) tribes, and each clan tends to think it reflects, in the finest and fittest manner, the way, truth and life. Lewis and Grant were committed to the classical Christian tradition, but neither men doffed or genuflected before any of the clans. It is this ancient way of mere Christianity that is wisely, through time, built into the genetic code and DNA of Anglicanism that wooed, wed and held Lewis and Grant.

There is no doubt that the Anglican tradition can move slow, is not as nimble as smaller sects or denominations, but the institution does carry a broad and full vision of the Christian faith. Grant would often ask his students, when they turned against the older institutions, this simple question: 'Have you worn the robes?' Those, in short, who turn their backs on the ancient and time-tried institutions without really taking the time to understand what they are and why (usually in the name of renewal, revival or some arbitrary notion of openness to the Spirit) reflect the liberal notions of liberty and individualism. Those who know what it truly means to wear the robes of the ancient way of faith (and the responsibility of wearing such robes) do not caricature, distort or demean the institutions and communities (at a parish level) that bear the fullness of the Christian memory and the unity that such a memory points towards. This does not mean that Lewis and Grant did not dare to criticize the Anglican way. Both men were most critical of certain liberal tendencies in the church, and they spoke out loud and clear about their concerns. But, unlike the schismatic protestant tradition, Lewis and Grant would not leave the church. Grant, near the end of his days, was much more in despair about the Trojan horse of liberalism in the Anglican camp, but he never left the church.

The Anglican tradition of Lewis and Grant, also, never pitted, in a naive and foolish way, the Bible (*sola scriptura*) against tradition. Lewis and Grant, as good and faithful Tory Anglicans, were quick to see the wisdom of God in the pre-Christian era (and in other religions), the fullness of faith in Christ and 'the one, holy, catholic and apostolic church' and the unfolding of such a vision in the Christian tradition. In short, for Lewis and Grant, there was an organic notion of faith that unfolded through the centuries, and it was the Reformation that ruptured and destroyed such a lush garden and forest. It is this Anglican notion of theology fulfilling the longings and questions of philosophy, grace crowning nature, faith fulfilling culture, love delighting wisdom and God and the Church fulfilling the hunger for justice that Lewis and Grant hold out to and for us. This is the older catholic, humanist and Anglican way that so held Lewis and Grant. This is the world of Plato and Aristotle, Seneca and Cicero, Augustine and Bonventura, More and Hooker, Coleridge and Wordsworth. This is the world of the permanent things that we ignore to our personal, economic, political, educational and religious peril. This is the older Tory Anglican way that continues to shine even though the modern liberal eclipse seems to have thrown everything into shadows and darkness for a season.

Conclusion

I have suggested in this chapter that both C. S. Lewis and George Grant embody the best of the older Tory Anglican tradition. I have highlighted how this is the case in three ways; there are other paths I could have gone. Let me briefly review what has been said. First, both men argued that the past has still much to teach us, and it is only as we go back of the Reformation that we will retrieve the wisdom of the elders. It is the liberal way, originating in the Reformation, accelerated in the Enlightenment and dominating the modern landscape that is the problem. Second, both men viewed their faith in a public way; it is this Magisterial tradition that assumes faith must engage culture, education and politics that is very much a Tory vision. But, such an engagement is thick with a moral vision of what things might be—ought to be—if we have but eyes to see and ears to hear. Neither Lewis nor Grant retreated from the fray into a private religious world; both men worked and gave their lives to the very institutions that embodied the modern mood and temper. In short, it is the Magisterial Tory way not to retreat but to both preserve and seek to reform the public institutions that carry cultural memories. Third, both men worked out of, in a thoughtful and critical manner, the Anglican tradition. Anglicans have been called 'Tories at prayer', and Lewis and Grant, I suspect, embody what this means at its best. The Anglican respect for Bible–tradition, the Anglican notion of an organic unfolding between the Classical world and the Church, a grace-crowning-nature theology and a commitment to the institution that carries the insights of those who have gone before us are all part and parcel of the High Tory Anglicanism of Lewis and Grant. It is this older Anglican way, a way both fully catholic and deeply humanist, that Lewis and Grant, like sages and prophets call us to remember and retrieve.

CHAPTER THIRTEEN

STEPHEN LEACOCK AND GEORGE GRANT: TORY AFFINITIES

Leacock was a friend of the [Grant] family who had also taught Maude [Grant's mother] and later George's sister Margaret at McGill. Leacock was in and out of the house a lot when George was young. George recalled that his father used to try to provoke Leacock into swearing to annoy Maude. Later, when Maude was working at McGill after William's death, Leacock helped to sort out difficulties concerning her pension. George recalled him as 'a sweet man' and very loyal to his friends. — William Christian.[1]

A Journey

I have, over the years, been interested in the Tory affinities between Stephen Butler Leacock and George Parkin Grant. Many is the Leacock scholar and fan who devotes much time to the life and writings of Leacock. Many is the Grant scholar and fan who commits much time and energy to unpacking and unravelling Grant's thought and life. But, rare indeed is the article or book that draws together the Tory affinities of both Leacock and Grant. This is rather surprising given the fact that Leacock was closely connected to the Grant family, and Grant's mother and sister studied with Leacock at McGill University. Leacock taught at Upper Canada College in the 1890s, and Grant's grandfather George Parkin was principal of the school in Leacock's final years there. It was probably Parkin who encouraged Leacock to go to the University of Chicago to do his PhD, and Parkin's involvement in the Imperial Federation League would have done much to nudge Leacock's budding nationalism. Leacock's son, Stevie Leacock, was at Upper Canada College when George Grant was a student there, and both George Grant and Stevie Leacock belonged to the same 'religious discussion group'.[2] It is these educational, political, familial and religious connections that open up the possibilities of a study on the Tory affinities of Leacock and Grant.

The publication of *Radical Tories: The Conservative Tradition in Canada* in 1982 did much for me to bring into focus, in an elementary sort of way, the affinities between Leacock and Grant. Taylor, in *Radical Tories*, has separate chapters on both Leacock and Grant, and he places them within a tradition of Canadian Toryism that cannot be equated with that of the Blue Tories in the Conservative Party. Taylor's chapters 'A Special Destiny: Leacock, Sandwell and Deacon'[3] and 'Threnody: George Grant'[4] clearly demonstrate there is more to Canadian Toryism than we might think, and both Leacock and Grant belong to that much older tradition that is in danger of being forgotten, ignored and erased from the Canadian experience. The rest of this chapter will thread together the Tory affinities of Leacock and Grant, and, by doing so, highlight an older Canadian political tradition that is in danger of being written out of our communal memory and journey.

Most of us who grew up in Ontario a few decades back took in Leacock's many books of humour with our mother's milk. Laughter did, indeed, hold both its sides when Leacock was read, and Leacock was seen (both within and outside Canada) as our national court jester. The publication of *Literary Lapses* in 1910 launched a literary career that ended, thirty-five books later, with *Last Leaves*, at Leacock's death in 1944. But there was more to Leacock than his stellar and sterling career as a writer of humour, a literary critic and biographer of such humourists as Dickens and Twain. In fact, Leacock published more than thirty-five books. Leacock published, in total, sixty-one books in such fields as literature (thirty-five), literary criticism (five), political science (six), economics (two), history (nine), biography (three) and education (one). Leacock also published eighty-eight articles that spanned a variety of disciplines, and he published both in serious academic journals and in a more popular and accessible style. As an academic, Leacock began teaching in the political science department at McGill University in 1900, and, with the defence of his PhD thesis, 'The Doctrine of Laissez Faire' in 1903,[5] he was promoted to a full-time position at McGill; he retired from the political science department (amidst some protest) in 1936. But there is even more to Leacock than the political theorist and humourist. Leacock was also an Anglican, and many scholars have tended to ignore this aspect of his story. It is impossible to understand Leacock, the High Tory, without seeing the world through his Anglican soul and eyes.

George Grant, like Leacock, cannot be reduced to a specialist in one academic discipline. Grant was interested in theology, philosophy, literature, politics, education and law, and he too was an Anglican. Grant did his PhD in theology—his dissertation of 1950 was entitled 'The Concept of Nature and Supernature in the Theology of John Oman'[6]—he did much work for the Canadian Association for Adult Education between 1943 and 1945, and he appeared regularly on the CBC. Grant's primary interests were theology and philosophy, unlike Leacock's, which were more in the areas of political economy, political science and literature, but both men crossed disciplinary boundaries with much ease and brought forth many insights as a result of their interdisciplinary approach. Grant had an interest in law, education, politics and hot-button social issues such as abortion and euthanasia, and in each of these areas, he made probing, illuminating contributions.

We cannot, in short, reduce either Leacock or Grant to one area of interest or thought. Both men emerged from an older humanist tradition, a tradition rooted and grounded in the classics with an abiding concern for both the meaning of citizenship and how such a notion could be thought through and lived forth in an age of scientific dominance, technology and the emergence of corporate power. Indeed, both Leacock and Grant were cut from an older cloth. Both were grounded and rooted in the fullness of the Western tradition, and both sought to make sense of such a tradition in a world and ethos that was becoming more liberal, progressive, modern, and ironically, more reductionistic all the time.

The Tory affinities between Leacock and Grant have not been noted before, and, for the remainder of this chapter, I will touch on three areas: 1) public education: techne (knowing in the service of making, a defining characteristic of the technological age) or *paideia*?, 2) Tory politics: right or left?, and 3) religion: spirituality or church? Each of these themes will highlight important points of convergence between Leacock and Grant, and, equally so, clarify the place of historic Toryism in their thought.

Public Education: Techne or Paideia?

It is a rather simple and obvious truism, for those who have spent many years in university life, that the humanities have been under siege for a long time. The excessive fascination with an empirical methodology, a form of knowing that sets the other as an object over against the detached observer, and a squirrel-like attention to a gathering of ever more facts, have taken their toll. The tendency to measure students' skills by their ability to gather and spit forth such facts for exams, combined with a bending of the knee by those in power in the university to corporations, has had its impact on the meaning and significance of the academic curriculum and life. Leacock and Grant, in their different ways, saw the writing on the wall, protested against it and offered up an older notion of education. Both men raised strong objections to an educational culture that genuflected to techne as a way of knowing and a way of being. Both men realized this approach would never slake the human thirst for meaning even though such an approach might produce a well-trained hive of bees or well-disciplined worker ants. How, though, did such men protest against the imperial and colonizing nature of techne, and how could *paideia*—the older tradition of humanist education—be the resistance and counter-cultural force they turned to in their fight to decolonize the merchants of knowledge from the central place they had taken in the academy?

An intense battle had been waged in the nineteenth century at the university and cultural level. Science, with its empirical methodology had ascended the throne and the humanities were under siege. Knowledge that could not be colonized, controlled, mastered, verified and falsified by a certain type of science was seen as suspect. Matthew Arnold's *Culture and Anarchy* and the equally important *The Idea of a University* by John Henry Newman spoke to the dilemma of Victorian culture and offered a more balanced way. Stephen Leacock was well aware of the shift, at universities, from the humanities to the social sciences and the hard sciences. The turn, of course, had a purpose, or *telos*. The institution of education was now meant, above all else, to train students for jobs, for the workforce. And, who were the mandarins of this new reality? They were the chief executive officers of the corporations. And so, if the task of universities was to train incoming students for jobs, university authorities had to work hand in hand with the corporate sector and the university curriculum had to be tailored accordingly. This close connection and cooperation between business and the universities was not totally wrong, but the increasing dominance of this model did not bode well for the future of the humanities. Leacock saw this, as did Grant. Of course, Leacock perceived the trend much earlier, and he wrote with much concern about it.

Leacock's first full foray into this area can be found in his novel *Arcadian Adventures with the Idle Rich*, which was published in 1914. Most Canadians know Leacock through his earlier novel, *Sunshine Sketches of a Little Town*, published in 1912, but *Sunshine Sketches* and *Arcadian Adventures* need to be read together; they very much complement one another. Leacock makes it unmistakably clear in *Arcadian Adventures* what he sees as the educational problem. The move from the small-town Ontario of Mariposa in *Sunshine Sketches* to the big city in *Arcadian Adventures* moves the discussion, for Leacock, to the world of wealth and poverty, big business as education, and education as business or character formation. The link between *Sunshine Sketches* and *Arcadian Adventures* is the Mausoleum Club (the name speaks much). Mariposa is held up as an imperfect yet desirable ideal in *Sunshine Sketches* (even Dean Drone of the Anglican parish turns again and again to the Greek classics). The bridge between these two novels, though, is the final chapter in *Sunshine Sketches of a Little Town*. The chapter is called 'L'Envoi: The Train to Mariposa',[7] and in this final section of the book, two worlds are brought into an interactive place. The city and the country meet and greet, and those who have been a success in the city ponder what they have lost by being a success.

In *Arcadian Adventures*, the town of Plutoria, and more particularly the university of the same name, is seen as the death knell to the human spirit and life. It is from Plutoria that the president of the university, Dr. Boomer, broadcasts his ambitious aims for the university. The university will be a thriving business in which all subjects can and will be taught, and the university, in doing such a thing, will be like any other marketplace. Those who can advertise and sell their products the best will thrive and prosper, while those who cannot compete in the marketplace of ideas will wither on the vine. The aim, or *telos*, of all this is wealth, and the university exists to prepare people to make such wealth. Relationships rise or fall on who has the wealth, who might have it, and who is losing it. Plutoria University, Leacock argued in this novel, had very much lost its educational way. Leacock, in short, as a traditional Tory, knew in his bones that learning had something to do with wisdom, something to do with insight, something to do with character formation, something to do with hearing and heeding the wisdom of the past, but what was happening in Plutoria and at Dr.

Boomer's Plutoria University had nothing to do with such ideals, goals and aims.

Leacock begins and ends *Arcadian Adventures* with a long hard look at slum dwellers, servants of the 'idle rich', and the working poor. This is a Tory with a conscience, and his conscience would not be muted or cauterized. Leacock, in *Arcadian Adventures*, tends to juxtapose two approaches to learning. There was the crude, money-making, business approach of Dr. Boomer, then there was the quieter and more seasoned way of learning of Concordia College. Leacock sought, as a true classicist and Tory, to hold together both wisdom and justice, and he did not think Plutoria University was heeding either cairn from the past. Leacock does hold up, in *Arcadian Adventures*, an alternate view of reality that contests and opposes the idle rich, Plutoria, Plutoria University and the Mausoleum Club. It is to this alternate view—of the Duke, the Little Girl in Green, the Tomlinsons, Concordia College and the deeper core of religion as embodied in the life and teachings of the Reverend McTeague—that Leacock and the older tory tradition turn to for educational insight.

Arcadian Adventures was not the only book of Leacock's that fixed and focussed on the drift and direction of public education— *Essays and Literary Studies*, published in 1916, goes after the same topic yet again. Three essays in *Essays and Literary Studies* stand out in the clearest way and manner. 'The Apology of a Professor',[8] 'The Devil and the Deep Sea'[9] and 'The Lot of the Schoolmaster'[10] pull no punches and, without flinching, raise some of the hard and probing questions about the role of education, the meaning of teaching and the deterioration of ethics in an age when foundation stones were being dismantled. Leacock, in these probing essays, saw a close connection between the captains of industry redefining the curriculum, the loss and eclipse of the humanities and the erosion of ethical discourse. Leacock, for much of his life, attempted through public education, what Gerald Lynch has called 'a kind of memory-mining for the true gold of human community'.[11] It is not that Leacock saw no good in technical training, and, in a limited aspect, the desire to know and master things. But, there was a worm in the rose, a serpent in the tree. Leacock saw technical training as a lower good, and the humanities as offering a higher, more human and humane good. The technical approach to knowing had two aspects: a way of knowing that was reductionistic and that which was produced from such a way of knowing.

Leacock's final book of short stories, *Last Leaves*, clings to many of the same concerns that animated *Arcadian Adventures* and *Essays and Literary Studies*. Essays such as 'What Can Izaak Walton Teach Us?',[12] 'The School Is the Lever',[13] 'Rebuilding the Cities',[14] 'Commonsense and the Universe',[15] 'A Lecture on Walking'[16] and 'Good-Bye, Motor Car!'[17] take us into a contemplative and moral way of seeing the universe and being educated that forms a link between the early and the later Leacock. It is this more contemplative approach, this slower-paced and listening attitude, this inner receptivity that needed to be recalled and retrieved. Leacock saw this all so clearly in his early academic career, and his final essays in *Last Leaves* point in this direction again. Leacock did argue, though, that the humanities had played a significant role in bringing about their own demise. If, he argued, in the areas of theology, philosophy, ethics, political theory and economics, the centre and ground could not hold, and all was a matter of subjectivism and relativism, then it made some sense that those in search of some sort of certainty and order would turn to the hard sciences and the assured results of what techne could offer. If, in short, the humanities could do nothing but waffle on important ethical and social questions, the vacuum could and would be filled by those who did not forever vacillate and offer only cynicism and scepticism by day's end. Leacock sought to find a middle way between a form of cynicism that led to paralysis and a form of certainty that tended to distort the deeper and fuller mystery of life. It was this *via media* that tended to shape Leacock's approach to public education. But, much deeper than the middle way between absolutism and scepticism is Leacock's notion of human nature, and the purpose and end (*telos*) of such a nature. It is one thing to protest the dominance of techne as a way of knowing and being, and use the educational language of *paideia* as the alternate way. It is quite another thing to define and decide what is meant by *paideia*. If the purpose of learning is to speak to the human condition, what then is the human condition and human nature that such learning must speak to?

Is the turn to the classical tradition merely meant as a means to compare and contrast alternate ways of being and seeing, or is the turn to the classics a turn to the truth of being itself? It is these sorts of questions (when answered) that separate and differentiate the Tory approach to *paideia* from the more liberal approach. Leacock and

Grant tended to stand within the more classical and Tory tradition of *paideia*, and it is this approach that distinguishes, for example, the Leacock–Grant–Bloom turn to 'the Great Tradition' from the dialectical approach of the *Great Books* series of Mortimer Adler (for whom Grant once worked between 1959 and 1961).

George Grant, like Leacock, had a distrust of education as techne. *The George Grant Reader*, published in 1998, threaded together some of Grant's best insights on education and the relationship between a contemplative way of knowing and a more technical way of knowing. The essays in *The George Grant Reader*, 'Philosophy (1951)',[18] 'The Paradox of Democratic Education (1955)',[19] 'Letter of Resignation (1960)',[20] 'The University Curriculum (1975)'[21] and 'The Battle between Teaching and Research (1980)'[22] speak volumes about Grant's attitude and approach to public education. In 'Philosophy (1951)', Grant offended the philosophic Sanhedrin in Canada by daring to suggest and argue that philosophy was about the quest for meaning, for wisdom, for justice, rather than about dissecting the meaning of words and following the scientific path down the road of logical positivism and linguistic analysis. Grant took the position that philosophy was about openness to the perfection and goodness of God, and, as such, this contemplative way of knowing came as a criticism of the one-dimensional and single-vision approach of science. The tension between the two goes back to the differences between Plato and Aristotle, and the Medieval clash between the monastic and scholastic ways of knowing so well articulated by J. Leclercq in his classic missive *The Love of Learning and the Desire for God*. The rationalist–romantic debate and dialogue of the Enlightenment, the 'two cultures' of C. P. Snow, and Hans-Georg Gadamer's grappling with the dominance of the scholastic–rationalist method in *Truth and Method* speak to this dilemma. Both these different ways of knowing have a long tradition and pedigree, and there are serious consequences to face for saluting the one and either subordinating or banishing the other. Both traditions tend to yield different results, and the wise recognize the strengths of each. The dilemma, for those like Leacock and Grant, was this: the empirical, scholastic, rationalist, scientific, mastering way had come to dominate the world of thought and university life to such an extent that the contemplative, meditative, receptive, listening, romantic and attentive way of knowing had been exiled or reduced to the private and subjective. This, of course, has serious implications for religion, ethics, culture and politics. This is why Grant, again and again, returned to the issue of the ends, or *telos*, of human nature and public education. Grant, in this debate between different ways of knowing, traced and tracked the clash back to Plato and Aristotle. Grant was indebted to Erich Frank's article, 'The Fundamental Opposition between Plato and Aristotle'[23] for his analysis of the situation. It was this fundamental clash, built into the beginnings of Western intellectual life, between Plato and Aristotle, that Grant thought prepared the stage for the modern dominance of the Aristotelian way of knowing and being.

If the purpose of public education, in the classical sense, was to open the mind and imagination to the overtures of the divine, but modern education had turned against anything that could not be mastered and controlled, then was it possible for public education to truly educate anymore? If the ethos of public education banished any thought of God to the private sphere, to arbitrary subjectivity or reduced the study of religion to an object like any other object to be studied at university, then the real life and fire of authentic religion would be put out. Grant saw the modern approach to knowing as the death knell to a serious and substantive approach to education. It is in this sense that Grant stands very much in the line and lineage of an older notion of the purpose of education. It is this very difference that led Grant to do battle in 1960 with York University, and, when he left McMaster University in 1980, he fleshed out his arguments in his article 'The Battle between Teaching and Research (1980)'.[24]

As I mentioned above, this debate about the hegemony of techne as a way of knowing and being, and countering such a way of knowing and being with *paideia* raises substantive questions. What do we mean by *paideia*, is there a nature and *telos* towards which humans can and should be formed, informed and shaped or is human nature an open-ended project? The turn to 'the Great Books' tradition raised questions for Grant. How were 'the Great Books' to be studied, and who defined what books were to be canonized? Grant, as I mentioned above, had been quite involved with Mortimer Adler and 'the Great Books' series between 1959 and 1961, and when he was a student at Queen's University, he wrote a review of Robert Maynard Hutchins' *The Higher Learning in America*.[25] Grant found himself a dissident within the liberal ranks of 'the Great Books' clan. Adler tended to see a study of 'the Great Books' as a way of opening up a student to a vast array of choices. Exposure to the classics was a way into a wider and fuller horizon, but Adler (being the good Aristotelian he was) was rather shy about suggesting the purpose of studying the classics was that such a commitment led to a knowing of the truth. Adler's essay in *Freedom in the Modern World: Jacques Maritain, Yves R. Simon, Mortimer J. Adler*, 'Great Books, Democracy and Truth',[26] clarifies his difference with Allan Bloom in this regard, and Grant was closer to Bloom than Adler. Adler argued, in his article, that a 'dialectical' approach rather than a 'dogmatic' approach was the best way to study 'the Great Books'. It does not take too much reflection to realize what is at stake in this debate. Is there such a thing as truth? Can it be known or are we just left with a pondering of ponderous insights, perspectives and positions from the past? The answer to these sorts of questions shapes, therefore, how the turn to *paideia* will be taken as a corrective to the dominance of techne.

Grant, like Leacock, tried to find a middle way between intellectual cynicism–scepticism and a simplistic certainty– absolutism. Both men held high and priorized the contemplative and meditative way of knowing, a way of knowing that personally connects the reading of classical texts with inner formation and transformation of the inner–outer life in opposition to a way of knowing that was merely for technical information or the reduction of learning to a 'museum culture'. Both men thought there was such a thing as an innate human nature that, through education, could be drawn forth, and in the drawing forth, the wisdom and presence of the past could still teach much. Both Leacock and Grant emerge from the same culture. Both were Tories of an older ilk, and, as such, both men had viewed the role of public education in a more human and humane way. Both men knew they were battling against a methodological liberalism that genuflected, on substantive issues, to both the empirical way of knowing and corporate power. Both men held high a contemplative way of knowing, an openness to the wisdom of the humanities and shared a desire to see the public institution of education as a means to raise the more important questions of wisdom, justice, citizenship and the longing for God.

It is this older Tory attitude about education that very much informed and shaped the educational vision of Leacock and Grant, and it is the loss of this form and approach to education that has been well tracked and traced by Philip Massolin in his informative book, *Canadian Intellectuals, the Tory Tradition, and the Challenge of*

Modernity: 1939–1970. Although *Canadian Intellectuals* tends to confuse, at some important points, the classical Tory and liberal approaches to education (hence the meaning of *paideia*), there is much in this book that highlights both the intellectual and institutional problems that Leacock and Grant faced as they engaged the direction of public education.

Tory Politics: Right or Left?

We have seen, in Canada, in the last few decades, the language of conservatism take on a different meaning than it once had. The more Canada has veered away from her English moorings and come within the gravitational pull of the United States, the more our understanding of conservatism has come to echo and ape the American republican way of interpreting conservatism. The American republican tradition seeks to conserve the first generation of liberal political thought. This is the world of Locke, Smith, Hobbes and Hume. This is also the ethos of Burke who accepted the fiscal and economic liberalism of Locke and Smith while resisting and opposing their middle class social liberalism. C. B. Macpherson, in both *The Political Theory of Possessive Individualism: Hobbes to Locke* and *Burke*, has highlighted what he calls an 'underlying unity' in the liberal tradition, and this is its possessive individualism. Similarly, Grant recognizes many of the liberal political theorists listed above as philosophers of greed.[27] In fact, Grant, like Macpherson, tends to place Burke in the same family and tribe as Locke, Hobbes, Smith, Kant and Hume. In *English-Speaking Justice*, he makes the point poignantly and succinctly:

In that bourgeois dominance the notes of comfort, utility and mastery could alone ring fully in the public realm. Among those who wrote political philosophy since Hobbes and Locke, there has been little more than the working out in detail of variations on utilitarianism and contractualism, their possible conflicts and their possible internal unclarities. What do Bentham or J. S. Mill or Russell add to Locke at the level of fundamental political theory? Indeed it is better to put the question: what has been lost in them of his comprehensiveness, subtlety and depth? The confidence of that Whig dominance is illustrated by the way that Burke has been interpreted since his day. He has been taken as our chief 'conservative' in contradistinction of our 'liberals'. In fact he was in practice a Rockingham Whig, and did not depart from Locke in fundamental matters, except to surround liberalism with a touch of romanticism. That touch of the historical sense makes him in fact more modern than the pure milk of bourgeois liberalism. Such figures as Swift and Johnson and Coleridge, who attempted (in descending order of power) to think of politics outside the contractarian or utilitarian contexts, were simply taken as oddities dominated by nostalgia for a dying Anglicanism, and having no significance for the practical world.[28]

Grant makes it plain in this passage that, in the area of political philosophy, there is a clear distinction between the Liberal and the Tory family tree and lineage. Grant agrees with Macpherson that Burke is very much a liberal, and must be seen as such. Those like Swift, Johnson and Coleridge belong to an older tradition that is rooted in the Anglican ethos and, as such, have a different political vision to offer than the Liberal tradition. Grant and Macpherson (who was identified with the political left in Canada) agree on the deeper underlying unity of liberalism, but Grant turns to an older Toryism that is embodied in Swift, Johnson and Coleridge. It is this tradition that Grant holds high, at the level of philosophic principle, and that he uses to question and interrogate the hegemony of liberalism in the modern world.

It is this early or first generation form of liberalism that tends to be somewhat suspicious of the state (except for support of the military and police), wary of increased taxation for state activities in distributing wealth and social welfare and, of course, keen on the market economy and free trade. The elevation of the protestant work ethic, the responsibilities of the individual, the equality of each and all and the ideal of liberty tend to dominate this liberal way of thinking. It is this type of liberalism that American republicans seek to conserve. Such underlying principles as liberty, individualism, equality, will to power (progress and technology) serve, therefore, to define and shape views of religion, economics, education, culture and politics within the American republican tradition.

But, is this notion of conservatism (as first generation liberalism) true and faithful to the Anglo-Canadian tradition of conservatism?

Has the 'Tory touch' within Canada nudged us to understand conservatism in a different way and manner? The Canadian tradition has tended, at its best, to hold in tension the commonweal and the individual, order and liberty, the good and power, reason and will and an organic nature of society (with obvious differences and gifts) with equality. We have had a higher respect for Swift, Johnson and Coleridge in Canada than is to be found in the United States. Conservatism in Canada has never been as opposed to the use of the federal state to create and bring into being the common good as has American conservatism. If, as I have mentioned above, Canadian Toryism is, in some ways, the polar opposite of American conservatism, do Leacock and Grant reflect this tendency and truism? Just as we saw that Leacock and Grant had many of the same concerns about the drift and direction of education (hence their Tory affinities), we will see, in the area of politics, both Leacock and Grant shared many of the older Tory notions of the commonweal, and it was such notions that also gave them a certain affinity with the political left. Let us briefly see how this was the case.

Leacock, in the preface to *Sunshine Sketches of a Little Town*, said, 'In Canada, I belong to the Conservative party'.[29] Leacock's understanding of what such a statement meant is in stark contrast to the view that tends to define conservatism today. Leacock completed his PhD on 'The Doctrine of Laissez Faire' at the University of Chicago.[30] The thesis was hardly an unqualified defence of hands off in the marketplace. Leacock, in his thesis, tracked and traced, in a historical way, the doctrine of *laissez-faire* and raised some telling questions about such a dogma. Such a stance would hardly endear Leacock to contemporary conservatives. In 1907, Leacock's *Greater Canada: An Appeal*, clarion-like, called for a form of Canadian nationalism that would not and could not be taken captive by American or English imperialism. Again, this sort of position would hardly earn Leacock the blessings of our modern conservatives. The publications of *Arcadian Adventures with the Idle Rich* and *The Unsolved Riddle of Social Justice* in 1914 and 1920 made it clear that Leacock sought to find a middle road between socialism and capitalism. Leacock was as critical of the excesses and abuses of capitalism as he was of socialism. His nimble and subtle economic and political mind would not and could not be taken captive by the ideologues of the right and left.

Leacock began, as I mentioned above, teaching at McGill University as a sessional in 1900 and by 1903 he was hired on a permanent basis. Leacock was chair of the department of political economy–science until he was forced to retire in 1936. It is important to note that McGill was a hotbed of leftist thought and radicalism at the time, and many of the students and staff who were front and centre in the ferment and activism of the time were either Leacock's students, former students, staff he hired or staff he defended when pressure came from the board and president to encourage and nudge such dissidents to go to other places. It was Leacock who suggested to Frank Scott, Leon Edel and A. J. M. Smith that a new magazine was needed at McGill to ask some of the hard questions that beset Canada in the first two decades of the twentieth century. Scott, Edel and Smith founded *The McGill Fortnightly Review* (published from 1925 to 1927), and Leacock helped fund the magazine and contributed to it. Leacock hired the controversial Eugene Forsey as a sessional in 1929, and when J. King Gordon and Eugene Forsey dared to defend some of the more positive aspects of the Soviet experiment, many at McGill suggested Leacock let Forsey go. Leacock refused to bend to corporate pressure, and he kept Forsey on staff. Leonard Marsh was hired in the economics department in 1930, and in 1931 it was Leacock who suggested Marsh should be given a tenured position. Marsh served as the national president of the League for Social Reconstruction from 1937 to 1939, and it was the 'Marsh Report' that called Canada to bring into being a solid and sound social policy.[31] Leonard Marsh, Eugene Forsey, J. King Gordon, Frank Scott and David Lewis to name but a few were all involved in the leftist thinking of the 1920s-1930s, and Leacock did not turn against them as many did. In fact, he often came to their aid and assistance. This is hardly the type of conservatism that dominates the stage today.

Leacock died in 1944, but before he died, he had four manuscripts ready to go to the press. Two of these books, *While There Is Time: The Case against Social Catastrophe* and *Last Leaves* walk the extra mile to highlight Leacock's abiding passion for the commonweal, the role of the state and society in bringing about such a good and the need for Canada to take leadership in both war and post-war thought and political action. It is significant to note that Leacock wrote a telling introduction to R. B. Bennett's (1870–1947) *The Premier Speaks to the People*, published in 1935,[32] and both Leacock's introduction and Bennett's five addresses argue, quite clearly, that the state must be more interventionist on a variety of social and economic issues. This is hardly the type of conservatism that dominates the political landscape these days. Leacock had, also, done a tour of western Canada in the mid-1930s, and he was alarmed by the position of the Social Credit Party in Alberta. His book, *My Discovery of the West: A Discussion of East and West in Canada*, published in 1937, makes plain what he thinks of the Social Credit Party, and, more to the point, the economic philosophy that undergirded and justified it. Leacock's understanding of conservatism was grounded and rooted in a much older notion of conservatism, and it was this older approach—with its concern for the common good and the role of both the state and society in bringing about such a good—that gave Leacock some affinities with the political left.

It is interesting to note that an important music festival that began in 1961 (that drew many of the protest activists of the counter-culture) was called the Mariposa Festival. This festival was held in Orillia, but because of opposition from some in the town, it was moved to Centre Island in Toronto. Mariposa, of course, was the name of Leacock's town in *Sunshine Sketches of a Little Town*. Nicholas Jennings, in *Before the Gold Rush: Flashbacks to the Dawn of the Canadian Sound*, sums this up when he said, 'The founding manifesto [of the Mariposa Festival] stated that an annual festival could help folk singers make a career in Canada instead of having first to be recognized in the States. The mission statement added earnestly: We also want to make the people of Canada familiar with their own folk songs. All that was left was to select a name. They chose Stephen Leacock's fictional name for Orillia—Mariposa'.[33] Leacock's brand of conservatism lived on into the 1960s as the activists of the time noticed an affinity between what Leacock said and did in his time and what they were attempting to do in theirs. In short, conservatism and the left are not necessarily opposed in the Canadian conservative and Tory tradition.

George Grant, like Leacock, did not see a stark and unbridgeable opposition between conservatism and the political left. In fact, Grant, like Leacock, realized there was much in common between these two traditions. Grant's 1945 book *The Empire: Yes or No?*[34] sounds much like what Leacock was doing in *Greater Canada: An Appeal* and many of the essays in *Last Leaves*. The CBC lectures in the late

1950s that became *Philosophy in the Mass Age* highlighted, all so clearly, Grant's suspicion of individualistic liberalism and his openness to some of the finer aspects of Marxism. Marxism, unlike some variants of liberalism, still tended to think of the community, the common good, the fact we are social beings and the need for the state to protect such a good against the corrosive impact and influence of technology and the will to power of powerful individuals who had no sense of restraint, limitation or the common good.

The publication in 1961 of 'An Ethic of Community' in *Social Purpose for Canada*[35] clearly aligned Grant with the political left and the emerging vision of the NDP, although Grant did have some serious philosophic concerns about some of the deeper principles of the New Left. When the NDP and the Liberals voted to bring down the government of John Diefenbaker in 1963, Grant was appalled. Grant saw in Diefenbaker, flawed and fallen though he was, a man who was willing to stand and fall by noble principles, a man who would be willing to stand against the wealthy elite and the military-industrial complex of the United States, a man who would stake his political future on such a decision. There was something heroic for Grant about Diefenbaker—and, perhaps, more to the point, his defence minister, Howard Green—and Grant, never blind to Diefenbaker's follies and foibles, saw the good that Diefenbaker stood for. *Lament for a Nation* was both a political and philosophic tract for the times that held high an older conservative vision that was, even at the time, being eroded by Goldwater-type republicanism in Canada. *Lament for a Nation* stirred and woke a new generation of leftist political activists. Horowitz called Grant a 'Red Tory' and others saw him as a member of the protest left of the 1960s. Many of Grant's students and friends such as Dennis Lee, Matt Cohen, James Laxer, Bob and Art Davis and Gad Horowitz were involved with many of the hot-button issues of the time. Lee and Cohen were active in the controversial Rochdale College (as were some of Grant's children) and Laxer and Horowitz were keenly committed to the NDP at the time. Laxer was at the forefront of the Waffle controversy in the NDP in the late 1960s and early 1970s that attempted to unseat and overthrow the Lewis dynasty in the party and move it in a more decidedly leftist and nationalist direction. Grant wrote a generous foreword to Laxer and Laxer's *The Liberal Idea of Canada: Pierre Trudeau and the Question of Canada's Survival* published in 1977.[36]

It is important to note that just as Leacock, in his final days, left manuscripts ready to go to the press that articulated his more compassionate Toryism, so Grant made it clear in his final days in 1988 that he stood by the side of John Turner against Brian Mulroney in the forthcoming federal election. Turner was against free trade and more in tune and touch with a Canadian nationalistic perspective, while Mulroney not only supported free trade with the United States, but was also a committed fan of Ronald Reagan. Grant's High Tory nationalism was not, in short, bound to any party. Turner, in the 1988 election, stood closer to historic Tory thought, and Mulroney was much more the dutiful liberal. This blend of Diefenbaker-type conservatism and leftist thought was central to Grant's brand of Toryism. The fact that students in the 1960s asked Grant to speak at the 'teach-ins' spoke much about his affinity with the Left. But Grant, like Leacock, although an admirer of the Left, did have his questions—Grant's 'Protest and Technology'[37] and 'The Value of Protest'[38] speak much about his ability to deftly see the good in the Left but also its Achilles heel. *Lament for a Nation* very much emerges, politically and philosophically, from a classical perspective, a perspective that is grounded in the Western intellectual and political journey but a perspective that is also applied to the twentieth century Canadian and American setting and context.

Grant's brand of Canadian conservatism, with its concern for justice, the good, the proper and due end and purpose of the human journey and the disturbing fact that all this was being forgotten, erased and eclipsed by modernity and liberalism meant that a voice had to be raised in protest. Grant did turn to the classical tradition of Plato (as interpreted by Simone Weil and Iris Murdoch), to the English High Tory tradition of Richard Hooker, Jonathan Swift and Samuel Taylor Coleridge, and to the Canadian Tory tradition of John A. Macdonald, R. B. Bennett and John Diefenbaker. It was this older tradition as applied, interpreted and made sense of in the Canadian journey that drew and held Grant, just as it did Leacock. It was this form of conservatism that was embodied in Benjamin Disraeli that interested Grant—in a review of the first two volumes of *Benjamin Disraeli Letters*, Grant states, quite clearly, the connections between the visions of Disraeli and Macdonald: 'To take a small influence: one cannot understand the conservatism of Canada (Macdonald, Whitney, Borden, Ferguson, Bennett, Diefenbaker) without thinking of Disraeli.'[39] The literary and political conservatism of Disraeli, as

Grant was obviously aware, was about a concern for the poor and marginalized, and the use of the state and society to minimize glaring social injustices. It is this form of conservatism that antedates Disraeli, of course, that Grant turned to in his understanding of conservatism. It is this form of conservatism that has little in common with the Blue Tory tradition in the Conservative Party, and it is this form of toryism that both Leacock and Grant shared that define them as conservatives of a much older stock and variety. It is classical conservatism, in short, that has some affinities with the political left rather than the political right and that sets the Canadian tradition apart from the American experiment.

I think it can be argued that just as Leacock and Grant, in the area of public education, sought to find a middle way between *paideia* and techne (while elevating the former and subordinating the latter in opposition to the trends of the time), so in the area of politics both Leacock and Grant sought to find a middle way between capitalism and socialism, hence their High Toryism. Both Leacock and Grant were committed to the older classical form of education, and this meant, in the area of public education wisdom took precedence over knowledge, and, in the area of public politics, justice and idealism took precedence over realism and pragmatism.

Religion: Spirituality or the Church?

Charles Taylor's *Varieties of Religion Today: William James Revisited*, published in 2002, speaks volumes about contemporary spiritual quests. Taylor points out in this missive that William James, in his *The Varieties of Religious Experience*, was a bridge between the romantic perspective of the eighteenth and nineteenth centuries and postmodern spirituality. This Jamesian form of spirituality pits experience against tradition, individualism against community, feelings against dogma and contemplation against the institutions that bear and carry the tradition and doctrines of the historic community. Experience, individualism, feelings and contemplation are held high and idealized, whereas tradition, community, dogma and institutions are seen as the problem, as the very thing that inhibits and represses an authentic and genuine quest to know the meaning and core of the faith journey. It is this stark and obvious contrast between spirituality and religion (the former idealized, the latter subordinated or demonized) that Leacock and Grant, as Tories grounded in an ancient way, would find both short-sighted and, sadly and tragically so, quite reductionistic and reactionary. Taylor, of course, finds these contrasts rather simplistic and silly, but he does note the power of them for many. The romantic–Jamesian–postmodern approach to spirituality has won the day for many.

Stephen Leacock, like George Grant, was committed to both spirituality and religion, experience and the institutions that carry the truths of the past from one generation to the next. Their organic view of religion and society, also, recognized the close relationship between faith and justice, spirituality and the politics of the commonweal. This organic connection between spirituality and dogma, the church and public–political life was part and parcel of the way Leacock and Grant understood their faith journey. Leacock, like Grant, was a member of the Anglican Church of Canada, but both men were critical loyalists of such a two-thousand-year-old line and lineage. Just as Erasmus in his *Colloquies* and *The Praise of Folly* could lampoon much theology and religious practices in his day yet remain a faithful Roman Catholic, and just as Chaucer could do the same in *The Canterbury Tales*, so Leacock and Grant could and would go after the Anglican tradition yet remain faithful to its inner core and essence. Many have assumed Leacock was a sceptic who had no real interest in religion other than as an organization and way of life to mock and make sport of, but there is more to Leacock than this. It is true, of course, that Leacock takes to task the follies and aberrations of religion in *Sunshine Sketches of a Little Town* and *Arcadian Adventures with the Idle Rich*, but within the pages of these missives he also demonstrates a certain fondness for those who live their lives with integrity. Dean Drone does have his vicar-like appeal as does the Reverend McTeague. Carl Spadoni has, rightly so, in his annotated edition of *Sunshine Sketches of a Little Town* looked at Leacock's more nuanced understanding of the role of religion and the Anglican tradition. In Leacock's final book, *While There Is Time,* he holds high comments by the Archbishop of Canterbury on the Beatitudes, and when he died in the spring of 1944, the Archbishop of Canada, Derwyn Owen (a friend of Leacock) travelled north to Sibbald Point to lead the funeral service at St. George's parish. In short, the High Toryism of Leacock was quick and nimble to point out folly and foolishness when seen, but, when day was done, Leacock knew what he held to and why. Leacock was aware of the danger of being too certain on religious matters, but he was also alert to the dangers of being too sceptical—his essay, 'A Rehabilitation of Charles II'[40] makes this point most clear and plain. It is within this classical Anglican middle way (or *via media*) between scepticism and certainty, between socialism and capitalism, between knowing and not knowing, between wisdom and knowledge, between spirituality and religion that Leacock can be placed. It is in placing him here that we can see his Toryism in the best possible perspective. In fact, the place where Leacock is buried is the resting place of many of the finest Anglican Tories of the nineteenth and twentieth centuries. Susan Sibbald (a good friend of Bishop John Strachan) is buried at St. George's, as are Mazo de la Roche and Caroline Clement. In short, although Leacock did not write a great deal about theology and philosophy, there is little doubt that his faith was a central part of his being and was deeply rooted and grounded in the Anglican way and tradition.

Leacock tended to be more interested in the sociology of religion and the political implications of religion than in probing the intricate philosophical and minute theological depths of religion. George Grant, on the other hand, tended to have a greater interest in the philosophical and theological aspects of the faith journey. The fact that Leacock's doctoral dissertation was in the area of political economy and Grant's was in the area of philosophical theology speaks much about their different leanings and tendencies. But, both men had an abiding concern for the larger questions of faith and religion.

George Grant, unlike Leacock, was not a cradle Anglican. Grant was a Presbyterian by birth, and his wife, Sheila, was raised Roman Catholic, but she had left her Roman Catholic upbringing by the time she had met Grant. The genius of the Church of England has been the way it is both catholic but not Roman Catholic and reformed but not schismatic. It is this middle way between Roman Catholicism and protestantism that defines the Church of England and the Anglican way and ethos. It is this tradition that is always on the alert for the best in various perspectives but is also quite willing to see the dangers of excesses and extremes. George and Sheila Grant became Anglicans in 1956 while George was teaching philosophy at Dalhousie University, and although Grant, like Leacock, could never be seen as an orthodox churchman, both men lived and thought forth their faith from an Anglican genetic code and DNA. Grant read and thought the thoughts of Hooker, the Caroline Divines, Swift, the

English High Romantics, and he and Sheila participated in C. S. Lewis's Socratic Club while they were at Oxford. Grant had an abiding respect for Lewis, and at Oxford he was quite taken, too, with Austin Farrer. When the Grants were in Halifax, they had much connection with the University of King's College (the oldest University in Canada and a bastion of High Church Anglicanism). Grant, in 1955, published his article 'Adult Education in an Expanding Economy' in *The Anglican Outlook*.[41]

When the Grant family moved to the Hamilton area, Grant was involved in a variety of issues in his diocese. George and Sheila Grant were active in the 1960s-1970s in nominating and supporting a conservative bishop (Joe Fricker), and both opposed the new Sunday school curriculum and jointly wrote an alternate one for their parish. George and Sheila, by the mid-1970s, saw the direction the Anglican Church of Canada was going on abortion and euthanasia, and they wrote much about such a drift and direction. The Grants' essay 'Abortion and Rights: The Value of Political Freedom', in *The Right to Birth: Some Christian Views on Abortion*, stated George and Sheila's views quite clearly.[42] It is important to note that this book was published by the Anglican Book Centre (ABC), and was edited by the well-known Anglo-Catholic Anglican, and professor at Trinity College, Eugene Fairweather. By the late 1970s, Grant had become increasingly disgruntled with the liberal drift of the Anglican Church of Canada. He would often speak at Low Church parishes, and when Grant was given an honourary doctorate at Thorneloe University in 1979, he gave a stirring, powerful and never-to-be-forgotten homily at the Church of the Epiphany on justice and righteousness.[43]

It is essential that Grant's understanding of 'the Good' and God be seen together, and his interpretation of the Good–God could not be taken captive by the culture wars of either his time or ours. Grant could and would speak against the ills and evils of abortion, euthanasia, the breakdown of the family, and for the importance of historic and institutional religion (which seemed to put him on the political right), but, at the same time, Grant's commitment to the commonweal, his pacifism, his opposition to the Vietnam War, his stinging criticisms of the American imperial way, his opposition to corporate wealth and his support of the Canadian state as a means of bringing into being the common good seemed to place him on the political left. Grant, in short, deftly eludes the ethical tribalism that so dominates the landscape of the political right and left and points to a third way that cannot be easily netted by political ideologues.

Grant would often ask those who turned against the more formal, institutional side of religion this simple question: 'Have you worn the robes?' Those who have not taken the time to truly wear such robes (in thought, word and deed) often caricature and dismiss that which they know little about. It is in the willingness (never easy) to wear such robes that Leacock and Grant part company with those who would, in glib and reactionary ways, sever and separate spirituality from the church. When this is done, sadly so, spirituality becomes thinned out, reductionistic and somewhat narcissistic. It seems to me that the prophetic nature of Leacock and Grant is best understood in the way they lived from the tradition yet were critical of it. In short, Grant did dare to raise all the hard questions within the Anglican Church of Canada—he was no churchman in the classical sense of the term, but as a loyal-yet-troubled layman and parishioner, he entered the fray and fought the good fight. It is interesting to note that although Leacock and Grant played substantive and public roles in Canada, and did so as Anglicans, most histories of Anglicanism in Canada have ignored them. This omission is somewhat disturbing given the fact that Leacock and Grant have had a higher profile than most Anglicans, and they were, probably, the finest Anglicans at work in the areas of political economy, literature, culture, public education, theology and philosophy in Canada in the twentieth century.

Grant was also a theologian and philosopher of some note, and this needs to be unpacked in more detail by way of conclusion. Grant's thinking always turned to the mystery at the heart of things, and the God of love who we could sense but never fully know. It was this blending of the *via positiva* (cataphatic) and the *via negativa* (apophatic) that drew Grant to the riches and bounty of the Orthodox tradition near the end of his life. Needless to say, there has been much interaction between Orthodoxy and Anglicanism, hence the transition was not hard for Grant. Grant's reading of Sherrard's *The Greek East and the Latin West* confirmed for him, as did his reading of the Christian Platonist Simone Weil, that unless the intellect (*nous*) was illuminated by the mystery of love, much would remain hidden and obscure. The Greek Orthodox tradition has argued that God's essence is beyond any categories, although his energies can be known by analogies. It is this essence–energy distinction in the areas of both theology and philosophy that drew Grant in his latter years. Grant also wanted to make it quite clear that talk of God had to be equated with the classical notion of 'the Good'. George and Sheila Grant spent time with Iris Murdoch and her husband, John Bayley, while at Oxford, and Murdoch emphasized, quite clearly, that God and 'the Good' were one and the same. This is, I might add, Simone Weil's position also. Simone Weil connected faith and charity and faith and justice in a way that turned the tables on the usual discussion of faith and metaphysics. Much of theology at the time was more concerned, in the area of apologetics, with the relationship of faith and what the mind and imagination could and could not know. It was this way of doing theology and philosophy that Grant had problems with. It is this connection and unity between faith, God and 'the Good' (hence the Platonic concern for justice) that separates Grant–Murdoch–Weil from Martin Heidegger. Murdoch, like Grant, had strong Church of England connections, and her affinities were with the High Church party.

It seems to me if we are ever going to understand Grant as a theologian we need to hold, in tension, three areas of his thought. There was, as I have mentioned, his interest in the Orthodox way. The Orthodox tradition, when day is done, holds high the sheer mystery and unknowability of God. Hence, the human journey is one of ever-greater openness to the divine love that can only be received as a mystery and gift. Second, there was, also, Grant's commitment to seeing God and 'the Good' as one and the same. Grant would not and could not sever and separate the God of mystery, love and 'the Good'. This meant, therefore, that the mystery of God's love was not so unknowable that silence about the ultimate was the final position. God was, is, and always will be the God of goodness and justice, hence ethical and political decisions can be made, theologically, about injustice in the world. And, third, there was the theology of the cross. Grant sought to make sense of Luther's theology of the cross and theology of glory in a way that led him straight into the mystery and redemptive nature of the cross and suffering. Perhaps this synthesis is not, in the end, that difficult to reconcile.

Plato's notion of 'the Good' identified God as sheer goodness, but this was a mystery that we could only know through a glass darkly. The journey to 'the Good' is fraught with many a peril, and those who elevate the triumphalistic theology of glory while sidestepping the theology of the cross misunderstand the nature of 'the Good'. Christ, on the cross, illuminates for us the divine nature of 'the

Good'. God becomes the servant, dies for us, so that we may live the divine life. God, as the embodiment of 'the Good' and love comes not as victorious warlord and conqueror but as a suffering servant, entering the sadness and tragedy of human affliction and suffering. The cross, in this sense, demonstrates the real nature of God, 'the Good' and divine love. 'The Good' is incarnated in time and history, and on the cross we come to see the real nature of 'the Good' as suffering love, a letting go. This dying God, in Christ, demonstrates and illuminates for us that divine love and goodness are one and the same. It is in seeing the theology of the cross as the door into the resurrection and the theology of glory that we come to see that divine love and goodness are about suffering with others so each and all might live the abundant life. The true divine mystery is that goodness is about a God who seeks, through suffering alongside us, to draw each and all back into the unity of love. The longings and hunger of Plato find their embodied fulfilment in the Christ of the cross. Plato, Orthodoxy and the Roman Catholic–Protestant traditions (Paul–Augustine–Luther–Calvin) are brought together. Grant drew from these various and varied wells, and the bucket he returned with carried waters from many places. Grant, in many ways, was one of the most articulate and probing theologians Canada has produced, and as more of his previously unpublished manuscripts are read, we will come to see why, I think Grant, as an Anglican, has a theological vision with all sorts of ecumenical possibilities. Grant has gone further than most in synthesizing the best of the Protestant, Roman Catholic and Orthodox traditions, and, in this sense, he is very Anglican. Grant is not systematic in his thinking, and there is a reason for this. The danger of techne, of mastering, of controlling, of demanding of the other its reasons (in thought and deed), is the great temptation of the West. Grant points, probes, tosses out flares, and, in doing so, like Simone Weil, he begs us to be attentive and alert to what might speak to us if we have contemplative and meditative ears to hear. Those who use the Baconian and Cartesian mind might see some things, but the deeper illumination of divine love is missed. Grant points us to what we miss in our modern approach to knowing and being, and he asks of us that we heed such 'intimations of deprival'.

Grant spent half of his academic life (the initial and latter part) in Halifax, and while at Dalhousie University, as pointed out earlier, he had much involvement with the High Church Anglican university, the University of King's College. At the heart of King's is the commitment to carry forth and hold high the classical Anglican tradition of faith and the classics. King's stands as an academic bulwark against the corrosive nature of modernity and liberalism. Although Grant would not have been drawn to the High Church liturgical tradition of King's, he certainly was on the same page with them when it came to their passion for the ancient way in opposition to the modern way. Much more work needs to be done on Grant and the High Church King's College tradition to get a firmer feel for Grant's deeper Anglican way and how it informed many of the issues he engaged in. Near the end of his life, for example, he published 'Nietzsche and the Ancients: Philosophy and Scholarship' in *Dionysius*[44] and contributed 'Abortion and Rights: The Value of Political Freedom' to the 1986 Atlantic Theological Conference, Holy Living: Christian Morality Today, the papers from which were published by St. Peter Publications.[45] Both *Dionysius* and St. Peter Publications are closely connected to the High Church Anglican tradition of King's College. It is also significant to note that Grant's tombstone has these words on it: 'Out of the Shadows and Imaginings into the Truth'.[46] These words have been attributed to J. H. Newman, and such insights could also be much at home with the Platonic Anglicanism that Grant welcomed and sought to understand and live out in his life. It is only as we have a firm feel for the above that we will come to understand Grant's opposition to Hegel, and, to the theological and philosophical vision of James Doull (who dominated much of educational life at Dalhousie–King's for many decades). A book is yet to be written on the Grant–Doull debate and its significance for both Anglican and Canadian theological, philosophical and political thought and action.

Conclusion

I began this chapter with the argument that nothing of a comparative nature has been done on Stephen Leacock and George Grant. This is a rather disturbing fact given the reality that both men have important Tory affinities. These Tory affinities can be best seen in their approach to public education, political theory and the relationship between spirituality and the church. Both men, in a critical, ongoing and active way, were committed to calling the public institutions of their time (in education, political parties and the Anglican Church of Canada) back to the core and founding vision of these institutions. In this sense, both men were reformers and prophets. The Tory affinities that Leacock and Grant share are deserving of much more research, and this chapter is but a dipping of the toes in the water. The much larger swim and deep dive to find the pearls is yet to be done.

CHAPTER FOURTEEN

GEORGE GRANT, CLARK PINNOCK
AND POLITICAL THEOLOGY:
HIGH TORY NATIONALIST MEETS COMPRADOR

George Grant 'has been called Canada's greatest political philosopher',[1] and Clark Pinnock has been called 'perhaps the most significant evangelical theologian of the last half of the twentieth century.'[2] George Grant was also a philosopher and theologian just as Clark Pinnock was a political philosopher. Both men are Canadians, both men taught in Hamilton at McMaster (University and Divinity School), and both men have been seen as conservatives. But, Grant's understanding of conservatism is quite different from Pinnock's understanding of conservatism.

George Grant's political theology is deeply rooted and grounded in the subtle synthesis of Classical thought as fed through the English High Tory tradition of Hooker, Swift, and Coleridge and applied to the Canadian nationalist context, whereas Clark Pinnock's political theology is, in principle, Biblical, but, in interpretive fact, a form of Lockean–Smithean liberalism and, consequently, American republicanism. Grant is, consciously so, an Anglo-Canadian High Tory nationalist whereas Pinnock is, consciously so, a liberal Anglo-American republican. Grant was an Anglican, whereas Pinnock was a Baptist. How is it that both men can be seen as conservative and yet their understanding of conservatism is, almost, at polar opposite ends of the political spectrum? Grant never writes about Pinnock, and yet they were both in the Hamilton area for many years, and Pinnock is silent on Grant. Why is it that 'Canada's greatest political philosopher' and 'the most significant evangelical theologian of the last half of the twentieth century' never really met and engaged in serious dialogue? Or, were the premises, prejudices, worldviews and presuppositions they were starting from so different that their understandings of political theology could never be reconciled?

There are, obviously, points of affinity between George Grant and Clark Pinnock, and these should be noted at the outset. There are five areas in which Grant and Pinnock could, in some ways, agree and shake hands.

First, Pinnock had, in his courageous life, attempted to think outside the box of a constrictive theological rationalism. Pinnock, to his credit, attempted to live in the needful tension between God's abundant grace and human responsibility. This has offended many in the evangelical Calvinist Sanhedrin. Pinnock tried, wisely so, to blend Calvin and Wesley, Augustine and Pelagius; he should be applauded rather than maligned for doing so. Grant was raised as a Presbyterian (English Calvinist), but he turned to the Anglican way for the simple reason that he saw more to theology than a servile attachment to Calvin. Pinnock and Grant stand with an understanding of the Christian tradition that does not sever grace from human responsibility.

Second, Pinnock's notion of 'open theism' has raised the dander of many within the broader evangelical tribe, and his idea that God does not know the future and is generous and gracious to the end does conflict with notions such as election and double election, predestination and is a more open-ended view of history. Pinnock is willing, also, like C. S. Lewis (who taught him much) to see that there are seeds of insight and wisdom in religious and philosophic traditions other than Christianity. In short, theology does crown philosophy just as grace fulfils the longings of nature. We can find in George Grant much the same thing. He turned to those like the Fathers of the Church in the East and West, just as he deeply admired the life and writings of Simone Weil. Both the Fathers of the Patristic era (who held a high view of the contemplative theology of Plato) and Simone Weil were quick to acknowledge that the Greeks, Romans and Eastern traditions had much insight Christians could learn from to their gain and profit. Indeed, Athens had much to teach Jerusalem just as Jerusalem had much to teach Athens. This need not be an either–or clash. Pinnock and Grant had much in common in this area—Grant was a Platonic Anglican (this is an ancient line and lineage) and Pinnock thought certain theological wars need not be fought, and he sought to declare a peace between such tribes and clans.

Third, both take the Bible and the Christian tradition seriously, but they did differ on how the Bible should be interpreted and what part of the tradition should be more of an authority than another part. Grant was, as I mentioned above, Anglican, and Pinnock was Baptist, and at core and centre such traditions do begin and end in different places. There are, in short, deeper interpretive principles at work in these two traditions that predefine how both the Bible and the tradition should be interpreted. The Baptist tradition emerges from within the protestant liberal tradition of liberty, equality, conscience and individualism, whereas the Classical Anglican tradition is more about the commonweal, the role of state and society in providing for such a common good, order and good government. The Bible and tradition might, in a formal sense, be held high, but the deeper interpretive principles are the real authority. Anglicans are magisterial and deeply catholic, Baptists and evangelicals tend to be anti-statist and liberty-loving liberals in the areas of the marketplace, their fear of the state and the question of their rights to interpret the Bible and worship as conscience dictates.

Fourth, Pinnock and Grant are, in many ways, social conservatives. Both, for different reasons, hold high the importance of family, question the pro-choice movement, doubt a too eager drift to euthanasia and call into question the problems of our secular and relativistic society. Both men hold high standards that cannot be reduced to values. This stance by Grant and Pinnock on these social issues seems to place both men more on the political right.

Fifth, both men affirm the notion that theology and spirituality must be worked out within the context of the life of the church— Grant and Pinnock butted horns with both their Anglican and Baptist–Evangelical Sanhedrins, and such clashes have not been easy to think through and live with, but loyalty and criticism have, prophetic-like, been lived and held in tension.

These five points seem to bring Grant and Pinnock together and define them as conservatives. But, it is in their stark differences that their views of conservatism take them down different paths. How, then, are Grant and Pinnock different as political theologians? There are five areas (there are others, of course) to note and flag here.

First, Pinnock's liberty-loving ways meant, in his political journey, he turned to both the American anarchist left and republican right for his north star. American anti-statist models of the political left and right have tended to dominate his political theology. Pinnock rarely turns to indigenous Anglo-Canadian intellectual history for his north star. The Bible is interpreted through distinctly liberal–Baptist–republican eyes and lenses. Grant, on the other hand, has a high view of the state, and the role of the Canadian state in bringing about the commonweal. This does not mean the state should not and cannot be criticized; it should be when it violates its high calling—but abuse does not prohibit use. Pinnock tends to lean more in the direction of society for bringing in the common good, whereas Grant recognizes both the state and society can and do err, and it is crucial to hold both together in a living tension. Grant was very much welcomed by the political left for his more statist thinking, whereas the statist left has never applauded Pinnock.

Second, Pinnock tended, as I have mentioned above, to see the American empire (although imperfect, flawed and finite) as the best of the political worst. It was the United States, was it not, that ended the rule and reign of communism, and it is the United States that best embodies the values of liberty and democracy. Grant has, for the most part, seen the United States as an empire like Rome, and he consistently argued that Canada was built on different foundation stones than the empire to the south. This, of course, is the irony of Pinnock and Grant. Pinnock seems to be anti-statist yet he becomes most statist when it comes to supporting the American empire in many ways. In a sense, Christian American republicanism is just a form of neo-Constantinianism. Grant saw serious and fatal flaws in the American theological, philosophic and political tradition, and he never would have turned to it as a guide and model in the same way Pinnock did in his political journey.

Third, Pinnock had a tendency to applaud the market economy as the best way to bring about a just and equitable world, and to minimize the state. The idea that the state has a role to distribute wealth and intervene and manage the economy did not sit well with Pinnock. This smacked of socialism to Pinnock, and socialism we must avoid and spurn at all costs. Grant, on the other hand, argued that the Canadian state needs to be strong to protect Canadian citizens, and assure them of justice and keep the Americans at bay. It is hard to imagine Pinnock as a Canadian nationalist: Grant was certainly one. Pinnock was, in many ways, an apologist for American nationalism. This turn, as a Canadian, to the United States for political models makes Pinnock a Canadian comprador theologian and liberal colonial, whereas George Grant was very much an Anglo-Canadian High Tory nationalist. It is quite easy, of course, to see the roots of Pinnock's political theology in those like Ernest and Preston Manning and Stephen Harper (Alberta being our most American of Canadian provinces), whereas the High Toryism of George Grant is more indebted to those like Stephen Leacock, John Diefenbaker and Sir John A. Macdonald. We see little of this family tree in Clark Pinnock.

Fourth, it is easy to see how Pinnock stands very much within the ideological liberal and republican right both within the classical English liberal tradition and the American and Canadian republican traditions. All the ducks are lined up and in perfect and predictable order. George Grant, on the other hand, seems to be on the political right when it comes to social questions, but when it comes to larger economic, military, environmental and statist questions, he seems to be more on the political left. The New Left was quite drawn to Grant in the 1950s-1960s-1970s just as the New Right was drawn to Grant's social position in the 1970s-1980s. Grant defies political categorization in a way that Pinnock does not. Pinnock is a liberal republican that seeks to conserve such a liberal republican way, whereas Grant seeks to conserve a tradition much older than the protestant and liberal way of either the English or American traditions. Grant goes back to Plato and the politics of the Patristics, he holds high the political theology of More and Hooker, Swift and Coleridge, Disraeli and Macdonald, Diefenbaker and Leacock. This is not Pinnock's family tree. In short, Grant seeks to conserve a tradition that is much older than the synthesis of the Bible and Smith–Locke. Grant found in such a synthesis the true compromising and assimilation of the Christian faith to and into American liberal and imperial aims and ambitions.

Fifth, Grant and Pinnock were both deeply shaped and influenced by the life and writings of the prominent Anglican C. S. Lewis, but Grant and Pinnock interpreted Lewis in quite different ways. There has been a worrisome tendency amongst American republicans to read and interpret Lewis to serve and suit American right-of-centre politics. Lewis was much too profound and nimble a thinker to be co-opted by such an ideology. But, Pinnock tends to stand within such a tradition. Grant read Lewis in more of a Classical High Tory way, and his read of Lewis in such a manner did much to shape his understanding of a more consistent approach to social, economic and political issues. Grant, of course, walked much further than Lewis down the political path and trail, but there is little doubt he and Pinnock read Lewis in a different way and manner.

In sum, Grant takes us to a way of doing political theology that Pinnock does not—Grant opens up for both Christians and Canadians a way of doing theology and politics that allows us to think outside the matrix of American liberalism and imperialism. Grant offers Canadians a way of doing political theology that is neither ideologically on the left or right. He knows how to think outside of the matrix of liberalism within which Pinnock is enmeshed. Grant was very much a political prophet on both empire and liberalism in a way Pinnock never was, and this is why it is both right and accurate to see Grant as 'Canada's greatest political philosopher', and, I might add, greatest political theologian. Grant does political theology in a way that is profoundly prophetic, whereas the political theology of Pinnock is much more ideological. Pinnock, 'the most significant evangelical theologian of the last half of the twentieth century' could have learned much from 'Canada's greatest political theologian'. Canada does not need more comprador and colonial theologians that turn to the United States as their polaris and north star.

Pinnock does this, and this is his fault and failing. Grant does not do this, and this is where he shines as a distinctly Canadian prophetic political theologian. We are in desperate need for more George Grants in Canada at this time of a distorted understanding of Harperite conservatism in Canada. May the hard work of Grant bear much counter-culture fruit in the future of the True North. The politics of the anarchist left and republican right will not do, no more than the ideology of the right, left and sensible centre. Grant points the way beyond these tendencies and trends and we do well to see where he points and why.

CHAPTER FIFTEEN

GEORGE GRANT AND ROBERT CROUSE: PROPHETIC TORIES

Robert D. Crouse represents that paradigm of those most catholic of scholars, whose investigations of the Christian tradition have consistently shown courageous sensitivity to its complex origins and trajectories from late antiquity to our present.
— Robert Dodaro, OSA, Institutum Patristicum Augustinianum[1]

George Grant has been called Canada's greatest political philosopher. To this day, his work continues to stimulate, challenge, and inspire Canadians to think more deeply about matters of social justice and individual responsibility.
— *Athens and Jerusalem*[2]

Introduction

There can be little doubt that George Grant and Robert Crouse (1930–2011), for different reasons, were two of the most significant Canadian Anglican intellectuals of the latter half of the twentieth and first decade of the twenty-first centuries. Grant was a public intellectual in a way Crouse never was, but Crouse had a depth to him (in his many probes into the Patristic–Medieval ethos) that Grant did not. Grant challenged the ideological nature of liberal modernity at a philosophical and political level in a way Crouse never did, but Crouse, in a detailed and meticulous manner, articulated and enucleated the complex nature of the Patristic–Medieval vision in a way Grant did not. Both men were deeply concerned about the passing away of a more classical vision of the soul, church and society and both attempted to retrieve the discarded image. Crouse was much more of an Anglican churchman than Grant, but Grant engaged the larger public square in a way Crouse never did.

I have been fortunate, over the last few decades, to do in-depth work on George Grant and I have many a letter from Sheila Grant (George's wife) on life at Dalhousie–King's (where George began and ended his academic life). I also have many a letter from Robert

Crouse, many a fond memory of visits with Robert (some fine photos also) when in Nova Scotia or when Robert visited the west coast (Robert bunked in at our home). My interest, therefore, in the Anglican life and writings of George Grant and Robert Crouse is both of some academic interest but also of a personal nature—hopefully, this chapter will embody and reflect this in its approach.

Professor–Student

The Anglican theologian that most impressed Grant was undoubtedly Austin Farrer. — Robert Crouse[3]

Austin Farrer taught Grant a lot when they were at Oxford, more than C. S. Lewis. — Sheila Grant[4]

George Grant began his academic life (after completing a PhD at Oxford) in the late 1940s at Dalhousie University in the philosophy department. It would be somewhat remiss to ignore the fact that Austin Farrer (certainly one of the most important Anglican theologians of the twentieth century) had a significant role to play in Grant's faith journey. Grant's PhD, in many ways, bridged the often contentious divide between theology and philosophy, and his friendship with James Doull (professor of classics at Dalhousie) introduced Grant to a much deeper and fuller read of Plato. The complex combination, in Grant's journey, of Farrer and Doull (the lasting impact of Farrer would go deeper and endure longer than Doull) did much to shape and inform Grant's budding faith pilgrimage. It is significant, and rightly so, that, in recent years, more and more attention is being paid to Farrer (who was also a close friend of C. S. Lewis—Lewis had quite an impact on Grant, also). Grant did, though, in the late 1940s-early 1950s, in many ways, recognize Doull as his guide into Classical philosophy. The fact that they parted paths on how to read the ancients did mean two of the most significant Canadian philosophers of the twentieth century did point to different places to understand and define the faith journey. Robert Crouse, as a student of Grant and Doull, had to decide, in time, where he would turn and why.

The young Robert Crouse attended Dalhousie University–King's College and graduated with a BA (with distinction) in 1951—not many finish their BA with distinction when only twenty-one years of age—Crouse was, obviously, a gifted young man. Crouse continued his studies at King's (divinity) and Dalhousie (philosophy) from 1951 to 1952—George Grant and Robert Crouse did many a class together between 1947 and 1952, Grant the aspiring professor (in his thirties) and Crouse the gifted and eager student (in his twenties). The fact that Grant via Doull was deepening his understanding of philosophy from a classical perspective meant that his notion of philosophy (unlike the more scientistic attitude of logical positivism that he had encountered at Oxford) was, increasingly so, contemplative philosophy (and, by extension, contemplative theology). The publication in 1951 of Grant's 'Philosophy' in the much-heralded Massey Commission seriously vexed the philosophic Sanhedrin in Canada.[5] Grant suggested in 'Philosophy' that much of modern philosophy, by turning against the depth and wisdom of the past, had seriously distorted the meaning and purpose of philosophy (in the realm of experience, thought and life). It was Grant's immersion in the thinking of Plato and Aristotle that took him to such places. Fulton Anderson led the armada contra Grant, and in the 1952 gathering of the philosophic elders in Canada, Grant was the target of their fury—the ancients and the moderns were very much on a collision course. The young Robert Crouse certainly leaned in Grant's direction. The ancients, in short, had still much to teach if we had but the ears to hear and souls to welcome.

In 1956 George and Sheila Grant became, formally, Anglicans (Sheila from a Roman Catholic, and George from a United-Presbyterian background). Bishop William Davis brought them into the life of the Anglican Church of Canada (ACC), and both, in their different ways, were to challenge the drift and direction of a type of liberal ideology that was about to dominate the Anglican Church of Canada. Robert Crouse was at Harvard University in the mid-1950s (he once told me that Grant had suggested he study at Harvard after leaving King's–Dalhousie—there was a significant renewal of Patristics studies there in the 1950s). The fact that Werner Jaeger was at Harvard in the 1950s (and at the cutting edge of classical–patristic studies) does need to be noted. Doull studied with Jaeger, but, in time, Doull would part paths with Jaeger's read of the ancients. Grant and Crouse (Crouse more than Grant) would argue that the classical tradition (Greek–Patristic synthesis) embodied a depth and perennial relevance we ignore to the peril of soul, church and society, whereas Doull would suggest that the classical phase of human thought and culture (following Hegel) anticipated but did not adequately or fully embody the modern liberal ethos in which we live, move and have our being.

Grant emerged in Canadian life in the 1950s as one of the most prominent public intellectuals—he was becoming well published and a regular participant, speaker and lecturer on the CBC circuit. Crouse was still feeling his way, and Doull, certainly, did not have the public profile that Grant did in the 1950s (in fact, Doull never did have the public persona that Grant had). Grant took a sabbatical in England in 1956-1957, and a variety of diverse ideas were at work in his research. Much of his work, in a broader way, was delivered on the CBC in 1959. The book from the lectures became Grant's first significant public philosophic missive that engaged the issue of the ancients and moderns. '*Philosophy in the Mass Age* was Grant's first book, and it drew together much of the thought of the Dalhousie years'.[6] A read of *Philosophy in the Mass Age* makes it abundantly clear why Grant thought the ancients were superior to the Hegelian moderns (as this becomes, in time, played out in American and Canadian thought, life and public culture).

Robert Crouse was attending Trinity College (a High Church Anglican college with emerging post-World War II liberal tendencies) at the time Grant was waxing in a mature way about the co-opting of thought and public life by liberalism. The Low Church Anglican college across the street was Wycliffe College. It was quite natural that Crouse would attend Trinity rather than Wycliffe given his catholic Anglican commitments and studies. Crouse finished his studies at Trinity with a MTh in 1957 (first class honours) with a thesis on 'St. Augustine's Doctrine of Justitia'. The probes that Crouse was making into the deeper dimensions of Christian Patristic theology pointed in vocational directions that he would mature in as the years unfolded—Grant never went in such a direction. Much of Crouse's work presupposed the validity of the Christian vision and its ongoing relevance and significance. Grant's life was lived out at a public university in which Christendom was over, various forms of science, rationalism and secularism dominated and religion (when studied) was viewed in an empirical, sociological and pluralistic manner. Grant's task, unlike Crouse's, was to highlight the worrisome side of ideological liberalism and point the way to alternate ways of being and thinking—Crouse's work was to walk the interested and committed further down the path that Grant pointed to. There must, in short, be some curiosity and interest in the Christian tradition if an in-depth study is going to be made of it. Those who have no interest in Christianity are not likely to give their time, attention, energy and finances to learning more about classical–patristic–medieval–early modern thought (or Anglicanism which is part of such a narrative). In short, Crouse's role is significant for those who see the issues for what they are. Grant's task was to illuminate, for the unwary and uncritical, how they were enfolded in liberal ideology, what such enfolding meant when unfolded and options to the inadequacies of liberal modernity in the church and world.

When Robert Crouse was at Trinity College in the 1950s, he would have studied with Eugene Fairweather ('Mr. Theological Canada'). Fairweather was, without much doubt, one of the most learned catholic Anglicans in North America at the time (and, like Crouse, of Nova Scotia loyalist stock and breeding). Crouse would, when at Trinity, contribute an article to Fairweather's 1956 book, *A Scholastic Miscellany: Anselm to Ockham*. The publication of Fairweather's *The Oxford Movement* in 1964 established Fairweather as a prominent catholic Anglican at the time, but the definition and meaning of catholicity was about to be challenged and redefined in many ways. The worldview and ideological shifts that were taking place in the larger world were, naturally, going to work themselves out in seminaries, church and parish life, though. The emerging liberal paradigm was, in time, going to redefine catholic Anglicanism, and the tensions and clashes between Fairweather and Crouse bring substantive differences, at the core and centre, into the crosshairs. Robert Crouse was, like Grant, very much moving in a classical catholic direction—Fairweather was heading in a liberal catholic direction from which, in time, the notion of catholicity would become shaped and defined by the prejudices of liberalism. These tensions were in seed form when Crouse studied with Fairweather in the 1950s at Trinity College. The reality of the Hegelian liberal tradition in Canada and the Anglican Church of Canada would bud, blossom and bear much fruit in the ensuing decades. But, the Farrer–Grant–Crouse counter-culture and fifth column opposition to the emerging liberal establishment (which Eugene Fairweather and James Doull would embody) was very much just under the soil in the 1950s.

The fact Crouse taught at Trinity College from 1954 to 1957 (he spent the summer term of 1955 at the University of Tubingen) meant he and Fairweather had plenty of interaction. Fairweather, like Grant and Doull, were Crouse's elders by about a decade or more. Much was occurring at Trinity College in the 1950s that would have a substantive impact on the Anglican Church of Canada and Robert Crouse was in the thick of the fray. Crouse did go to Harvard again from 1957 to 1960, and in those years, his interest and commitment to the Patristic ethos (and its impact on Medieval Christendom—which, in time, became Crouse's focus) was clarified and sharpened. Grant was about to make a serious change in his academic journey by 1960 that would have a substantive impact on his life and the larger Canadian intellectual public discourse.

The Anglican Church of Canada was going in one direction— Grant and Crouse in another direction.

Grant and Crouse: Voices to the Times

George Grant always claimed that *Lament for a Nation* had been misunderstood. — Sheila Grant[7]

I'm not sure I disagree with Grant's conservatism, except that I think it needs the nutriment of a fuller historical understanding (e.g. Grant pretty much skipped from Plato to S. Weil, with a passing nod to St. Augustine) and a deeper institutional commitment than he seemed to consider necessary. — Robert Crouse[8]

When Robert Crouse left Harvard in 1960, he was offered the position of Assistant Professor of Church History and Patristics at Bishop's University (where he taught from 1960 to 1963). Bishop's had been an English-speaking Anglican college in Quebec and, to some degree, the Anglican respect for church history and patristics still lingered on—Crouse was the bearer of such a line and lineage—his training at Dalhousie–King's in Halifax, Trinity College in Toronto and Harvard (where a Patristic revival was afoot) prepared Crouse well for his position at Bishop's. Grant had left Dalhousie by 1960, was temporarily hired as the first professor in philosophy at the newly established York University in Toronto, but a clash with his old philosophical nemesis, Fulton Anderson (University of Toronto) led to his resignation at York.

Grant, unlike Crouse, entered the lion's den where science, rationalism and secularism reigned and did battle. Grant saw, all too clearly, that new gods had come to dominate the cultural and educational scene and if such gods were not challenged, interest in Christian thought, life and culture would become an irrelevant and fading reality, significant only for a shrinking minority—the Anglican Church, would, as part of the passing of the Christian ethos, go the way of all flesh.

As Crouse was settling in at Bishop's, Grant through the assistance, ironically enough, of two leading liberal Anglicans, Michael Creal and William Kilbourn (who taught history at McMaster), was offered the position as founding chair of religious studies at McMaster University in Hamilton, Ontario.

The implicit premises of liberalism that were scarcely under the soil in the 1950s burst forth with rapid growth, in an explicit way, in society and the church in the 1960s, and the Anglican Church of Canada was front and centre in such a historic reality. In 1963 the General Board of Religious Education of the Anglican Church of Canada invited (via Ernest Harrison) a significant Canadian journalist, Pierre Berton, to write a book on faith, the church and Canadian life. The book was published in 1965 as *The Comfortable Pew*—the book was an immediate bestseller (more than 150,000 printed and sold in the first few years). *The Comfortable Pew* was unabashedly a defence of the liberal agenda and a justification for why the church should assimilate into the spirit of the age. Needless to say, reactions were intense (pro–contra). The Anglican Church of Canada replied to Berton's book in a more nuanced and moderate way with *The Restless Church: A Response to the Comfortable Pew* in 1966—William Kilbourn was the editor of the many essays—Michael Creal was also involved as was Eugene Fairweather. Kilbourn, Creal and Fairweather did not go as far as Berton in their embrace of liberal modernity, but they were on the same path. Ernest Harrison, who initiated the invitation to Berton, published *A Church without God* in 1967. There could be no doubt that Harrison was going further down the secular liberal path than Berton, but one and all were on the same trajectory at some of the highest levels of the Anglican Church of Canada.

It is apt and significant to note that Grant's *Lament for a Nation: The Defeat of Canadian Nationalism* was published in 1965. Grant, like Daniel before him, saw the writing on the wall, and, like Jeremiah, lamented the passing away of the grandeur of the Christian ethos and vision. Sheila Grant rightly noted that most readers of *Lament for a Nation* misunderstood the deeper intent and content of the political missive and manifesto. The store front of *Lament* was the defeat of Prime Minister John Diefenbaker by Lester Pearson in the 1963 federal election. Pearson was a keener on President Kennedy (and the United States as the great good place)—both were liberals at a variety of worrisome levels. Diefenbaker (although imperfect and flawed— Grant does note this) stood for an older Tory way. Grant was, therefore, not only lamenting the defeat of the Progressive Conservative Party by the Liberals—he was lamenting the passing away of a way of seeing, thinking and living a more substantive Tory worldview and way of life. Grant saw more than most in the 1960s (both in the world and the church) that the liberal ideology was becoming hegemonic and imperial—those who dared to differ with such an agenda would be marginalized—Harrison, Berton, Creal, Fairweather and many other Anglicans had uncritically bought into such an agenda. Grant lamented both the uncritical attitude of the church towards liberalism and the lack of understanding of an older Toryism among the *cause du jour* liberals.

Lament for a Nation turned to Hooker's oft quoted comment in *Of the Laws of Ecclesiastical Polity* that was directed at the puritans of his time: 'Posterity may know we have not loosely through silence permitted things to pass away as in a dream'.[9] The puritans of Hooker's day were, at a deeper philosophic level, not much different than the liberals of Grant's day—Grant connected the dots well and wisely. Grant, of course, had little or no patience for Berton's triteness and trivia in *The Comfortable Pew*, he thought Harrison to be a silly reactionary and he did not contribute to *The Restless Church* (although an essay by Grant might have been of some worth). *Lament for a Nation* and *The Comfortable Pew* pointed in different directions—the former an in-depth articulation of a classical Tory tradition, the latter a genuflecting to liberalism at a variety of ethical and religious levels. The Anglican Church of Canada heeded Berton, and decades later, the implication of such a heeding, led to the splitting of the Anglican Church of Canada with the emergence of the Anglican Network in Canada (ANiC) and the larger and more conservative North American opposition to the dominance of a liberal ideology in both the Anglican Church of Canada and the Episcopal Church in the United States.

The Anglican Church of North America (ACNA), although conservative in tone and texture, certainly lacks the deeper Toryism that Grant understood and articulated so well in *Lament for a Nation*. It is significant to note that Robert Crouse (considered by most as *abba* of the Canadian Book of Common Prayer–Prayer Book Society way) had more affinities with Grant's High Tory form of politics than many within the Prayer Book Society that lean in a more Blue Tory or American conservative and republican direction—this does need to be noted, and, in many important ways, it links Crouse and Grant with another fan of the Book of Common Prayer: Eugene Forsey. Forsey, Grant and Crouse were Tories of a more classical political sense—somewhat suspicious of the captains of industry, pro-state as a means of bringing about an imperfect common good and wary of American imperial ambitions (the New Romans).

It is somewhat essential to realize, also, that the catholic Book of Common Prayer–Prayer Book Society (BCP–PBS) vision of Crouse and followers would be much less inclined to split from the Anglican Church of Canada and join the Anglican Network in Canada—their catholic commitment to the unity of the church in a spiritual, formal and material way did mean a parting of the paths with the Anglican Network in Canada–Anglican Church of North America. This did create quite a clash within Canadian classical catholic Anglicanism over how, in an ecclesial sense, same-sex blessing and, earlier, the ordination of female priests, would be handled. The differences between Bishop Don Harvey (thoroughly catholic in life and commitment, and first bishop of the Anglican Network in Canada) and Robert Crouse could not be more stark and revealing on this issue—Harvey led the schism charge, Crouse opposed it.

The publication of *Lament* in 1965 further consolidated Grant's position in Canada as a leading public intellectual. Robert Crouse left Bishop's by 1963 and returned to Dalhousie (where he was an assistant professor of classics from 1963 to 1967). Crouse would remain at Dalhousie for the rest of his academic life while also teaching at King's. The Maritime Anglican tradition at Dalhousie–King's still had much of the older Tory touch in its blood and bones and Crouse became a model and mentor for many on how to understand the best of the time-tried Anglican way in the church, university and public realm. The fact that Crouse was becoming an established Patristic scholar by the 1960s-1970s-1980s (and publications were multiplying aplenty) meant he attracted the attention of Roman Catholics. Crouse was invited to be Visiting Professor of Patrology at the Institutum Patristicum Augustinianum at the Pontifical Lateran University in Rome in 1991, 1995 and 1998. It is virtually impossible to imagine Grant being offered such a prestigious position. Crouse had also, in 1986, published his insightful book, *Images of Pilgrimage: Paradise and Wilderness in Christian Spirituality* through St. Peter Publications (an Anglican conservative publishing house in Charlottetown, Prince Edward Island).

There can be no doubt that Robert Crouse had emerged as a classical catholic within the Anglican Church of Canada in the latter decades of the twentieth century. He was deeply respected for his piety, pastoral compassion and learning. The fact he was a founder of the annual Atlantic Theological Conference that began in 1981 (as an attempt to clearly articulate the historic theological and liturgical meaning of the Anglican heritage) meant Crouse was seen as an elder within the Anglican family who could articulate, in a thoughtful, measured, reasonable and historic way why and how the Anglican Church was losing its way by genuflecting uncritically to the liberal agenda. Crouse's many contributions to the Atlantic Theological Conferences (and his insights offered) have been ably tracked by Wayne Hankey (one of Crouse's earlier disciples of sorts) in his superb paper, 'Visio: The Method of Robert Crouse's Philosophical Theology'.[10] Hankey's paper is one of the finest introductions and overviews of Crouse's multilayered thinking—a must read for those interested in the importance and significance of Crouse for Canadian Anglican thought and life in the latter half of the twentieth century (when the culture wars were waged with much intensity within the world and church).

When George and Sheila Grant (and growing family) left Dalhousie in Halifax, they eventually settled in Dundas (on the outskirts of Hamilton where McMaster University is located). The Grant family attended St. James' parish in Dundas throughout most of the 1960s-1970s (before returning to Halifax in the early 1980s). The three rectors at St. James' when the Grant family attended were front and centre in moving the Anglican Church of Canada (both in their diocese and at the national level) more and more into the liberal fold: John Bothwell, from 1960 to 1965, Joachim Fricker, from 1965 to 1973, and Philip Jefferson, from 1973 to 1984. George and Sheila did, in time, after the initial honeymoon phase at St. James' was over, come to differ, on essential philosophical points, with Bothwell, Fricker and Jefferson. Robert Crouse is right, of course, in his critique of Grant. The more the Anglican Church came to embrace the liberal agenda, the more Grant withdrew from parish, diocesan and national church life. Sheila was more faithful to parish life, but even she, in time, stepped out of the troubling fray. The publication of *New Life: Addressing Change in the Church—St. James' Dundas Sesquicentennial 1838–1988* in 1989 could not be more poignant. Most of the contributors were either moderately or uncritically changing with the times at the levels of principle, theory and practice. The essay by George and Sheila dealt with the controversial issue of abortion and the too easy way the Anglican Church of Canada, with reservations, approved of a pro-choice agenda.

Robert Crouse, unlike Grant, remained in the struggles and, unlike Grant, dug deeper and deeper into the subtle and mother lode depths of the Christian tradition—Grant lacked the nuance and depth of Crouse. The paper by Hankey, mentioned above, highlights in sensitive detail, Crouse's commitment to the Prayer Book, the Fathers' impact on Medieval Christian thought and the ongoing relevance of the Great Tradition for the modern and postmodern ethos. The publication (a *festschrift* of sorts for Robert Crouse), *Divine Creation in Ancient, Medieval and Early Modern Thought: Essays Presented to the Rev'd Dr Robert D. Crouse*, is most telling. Each of the essays is an in-depth probe of the fullness of the classical past and the implications (by being ignored, banished or discarded) for the present. Much of Robert Crouse's own pastoral and academic writing continues to be available through St. Peter Publications.

George Grant and Robert Crouse both, though in different ways, continue to speak in a prophet-like manner to those who would change, without deeper question or critique, to conform to the demands of the mood and ethos of the times.

SECTION IV

TORY TRADITIONS MEETING A NEW WORLD

CHAPTER SIXTEEN

THE MATRIX OF LIBERALISM: A SEVEN-ACT DRAMA

Liberalism was, in origin, criticism of the old established order. Today, it is the voice of the establishment. — George Grant[1]

I have found from many observations that sometimes our liberal is incapable of granting anyone else his own convictions and immediately answers his opponent with abuse or something worse. — Fyodor Dostoevsky[2]

The Matrix of Liberalism

All of us, whether we are consciously aware of it or not, think from a core of philosophic principles. It is from these seed thoughts, principles or ideas, that the fruit of various and varied ethical positions grows. We live in a period of time in which many ethical positions are embraced, contested and questioned in our culture wars. Many is the hot-button issue that, when articulated and argued in the public places, creates many a reaction. Ethical tribes and clans (and chieftains aplenty) have emerged to beat the drums for ethical positions on the political 'right', 'sensible centre' and political 'left'.

If we are ever going to come to a serious and substantive dialogue about both the roots and fruits of ethical positions, we do need to nudge the discussion to a much deeper level. It does little good to argue the case pro–contra of abortion, euthanasia, death penalty, traditional family values, militarism, market economy, globalization, environmental concerns, gay rights, drugs, stronger state–lighter state, religious pluralism and many other issues if we do not understand the principles that animate and predefine the positions taken before they are taken.

We do need to turn, therefore, to the question of principles, prejudices, presuppositions, and ideas before we venture into the controversial hot-button ethical issues. Just as an acorn becomes an oak tree, a sunflower seed becomes a sunflower plant, a colt a horse, a calf a cow, a baby a teen and adult, so, in seed form, it is principles that bud, blossom and bear fruit in the area of ethical issues.

We all know that taking a lawnmower over a field of dandelions does not get rid of the dandelions. The mower will cut off the yellow heads of the dandelions, but, a few weeks later, the roots will produce yet another yellow field of dandelions. It is from the roots that the flower is produced, and if we are not pleased with the blossom (be it weed or flower), we must take the time to dig up the roots. The same analogy could be applied to fruit on a tree. A tree might produce good, bad or mediocre fruit. It is rather pointless, though, to think that by throwing away bad fruit on a tree (or blaming the fruit that is produced) that the tree will then produce a harvest of fine fruit. If the fruit is bad, then it is important to check out the soil, the inner life of the tree, the sap and deeper roots.

There is no doubt we live in an age dominated by liberalism. The principles, prejudices and premises of liberalism are the creed and dogma of the time. It is virtually impossible in our age and time to think outside of the matrix of liberal ideas. The hot-button issues in the culture wars often favour those who are apologists of the liberal way and sway. If we, for the most part, are born and bred in the liberal matrix, what is the nature of this matrix, and how does it shape, socialize and predefine how we should think on a variety of ethical and metaphysical questions? And, more importantly, is it possible to think outside of this intellectual matrix? If not, have we not set ourselves up for a benign form of totalitarianism or soft despotism? It is ironic that many liberals hold a high view of reason and critical thinking, but they seem incapable of being critical of the principles of liberalism.

We are very much in the matrix of liberalism at the present time, and we do need, if we are ever going to be minimally thoughtful and critical, to ask ourselves this rather simple and elementary question: what is the appeal and limitation of liberalism? If we are only boosters or knockers of the liberal project, we become reactionaries and ideologues. If and when we ponder the *sic et non* (yes and no) of the liberal agenda, we can open our minds to examine a fuller way of thinking and living.

The Principles of Liberalism

The matrix of liberalism, as I mentioned above, is founded and grounded on certain principles, ideas, worldviews, prejudices, and presuppositions. These principles are not new, but they do dominate, define and enframe most of the modern dialogue on ethical issues. What are these principles, what are the historic roots of such principles, and what is both the appeal (strength) and limitation (dark sides) of such ideas? Richard Weaver had a book published in 1948 called *Ideas Have Consequences*. Whether we agree with all of Weaver's arguments is not the point here, but Weaver is right when he argues that ideas do have consequences. Ideas (or principles) do lead to decisions, and decisions have consequences in both a personal and public way. Therefore, it is to the level of ideas (principles) we must turn to make sense of how the oak tree of ethical issues is but the consequence of the small acorn of certain philosophical principles.

What, then, are the principles from which the liberal project emerges? There is little doubt that liberalism tends to accept and embrace the principles of liberty (freedom), individualism, equality, fraternity (solidarity), conscience, historicism and the quest for meaning, happiness or authenticity. These principles, of course, can be priorized in different ways, and as they are priorized in a different way, different forms and types of liberalism will emerge. Those who priorize liberty will be suspicious of any form of state or community interference with individual longings and desires in either the social or economic sphere. Those who priorize fraternity (solidarity) will attempt to curtail some individual rights so that all may have their liberty enhanced. The liberal project, as a way of knowing, can elevate reason and critical thinking over and against intuition and imagination or imagination in opposition to reason. It is this debate that has defined and shaped the rationalist–romantic dialogue within the liberal clan and family.

The actual content of what is known and ethical positions taken in the liberal project are quite secondary to the principles that are accepted by faith and are the dominant creed and dogma of liberalism. Liberal principles are like a sacred and time-tried vase and container that will be protected at all costs. The actual liquid that is poured into the vase is not of primary importance. It is more important that liberty, individuality and equality are protected than defining how liberty, equality and individuality are to be defined. Each and all, within the liberal ideal, should and can use such principles as they see fit to serve and suit their own journey for meaning and happiness, and, of course, these terms are open to be defined by the individual.

If liberal principles can be seen, in some sense, as the trunk that steadies and does much to produce the fruit of liberal ethical issues, the deeper and more demanding roots of the liberal way take us to the liberal notion of human nature. Human nature, within the liberal tradition, tends to be open and weak on boundaries and limitations. Human nature is a project in which we make ourselves. Just as a painter creates a work of art on a blank canvas, a poet creates a poem on an empty piece of paper, the liberal notion of human nature tends to see the human journey as open ended. There is no doubt we have desires, longings, hopes and dreams, passions and hungers, but the way we direct, form, shape and heed such longings is as open as there are possibilities to experiment with. We are products of time and history (historicism), and who is to say what is the best way to live?

It is this liberal notion of human nature coupled with the liberal notion of historicism that is the deeper roots of the liberal tradition and creed. The matrix of liberalism, when probed at the level of human nature and historicism, takes us to the heart, core and centre of the liberal project. Where did such ideas come from that so dominate our age and ethos, and can they be questioned? In fact, dare they be questioned? More worrisome, though, what happens when we dare not question such principles and ideas? But, let us turn to the historic roots of the liberal way. Ideas often take centuries to fully work and play themselves out, and this is just as true of liberalism as any other ideological and intellectual system.

The Historical Drama of Liberalism: A Seven-Act Play

Many has been the debate about the historical beginnings of liberalism. There are those who are keen on taking the dialogue about the origins of liberalism back to the Classical era. Plato and Aristotle are pitted against one another, and Plato is seen as the conservative and Aristotle is viewed as the liberal. There were, obviously, differences between Plato and Aristotle, but both men did participate within the Classical understanding of what it means to be human. Both men viewed contemplation as higher than action, and both men were grounded in the notion of natural law, and the idea that all things have a proper purpose and end (*telos*), and to the degree all things moved towards such an end, the good life would be realized and actualized. The virtues–vices played an important role in giving shape and form to such an end, and a person was only free to the degree they lived within such a form and structure. There is no doubt that Plato had a greater interest in metaphysics and dialogue as a way of knowing, but he was also most concerned about politics and economics. Aristotle lingered longer on questions of logic, science and the inductive way (which Plato saw as a lower way of knowing and being), but both men accepted the fact that there was an order in the cosmos, and to the degree each and all knew such an order and attuned and aligned themselves with it, they would be free. It is only in a suggestive sense that we can argue that the origins of liberalism can be found in Aristotle, but many is the American and European republican that will attempt to track and trace the liberal republican way back to Aristotle, Seneca and Cicero.

The painting by Raphael, *The School of Athens*, depicting Plato and Aristotle entering a large room, and Plato pointing to the heights and Aristotle to the firm earth below distorts the insights of both men. Plato and Aristotle sought to integrate both eternity and time, metaphysics and ethics in their way of thinking. The Medieval era tended to be more indebted to Plato than Aristotle, but by the High Middle Ages, Aristotle began to make a return. The beginning of liberalism, I think, can be tracked to the latter half of the Middle Ages.

The shift in philosophy from an interest in universals to particulars signalled this beginning. This is Act One in the West of liberalism. With the rise of nominalism, we begin to see more emphasis on the individual, on the particular. This was but a seed tossed into the soil of thought, but seeds, in time, do break through their constrictive skins and produce trees and orchards of thought. William of Occam and Duns Scotus were key thinkers in this early phase of liberalism. Occam and Duns Scotus had a great respect for the senses (and what could be known through them), and they had a certain cynicism about what the mind could know. The nominalist tradition did put forward the importance of individual things and the uniqueness of the particular. It was this philosophic tradition (good in its time as an important corrective to the collective and transcendent) that opens up the drama of liberalism. It is important to note, at this point, that the Anglican movement of Radical Orthodoxy holds firmly to this axial point. John Milbank's *Theology and Social Theory* and Catherine Pickstock's *After Writing: On the Liturgical Consummation of Philosophy* argue that the roots of modernity and the liberal ethos can be found in the Late Medieval world. The Radical Orthodox movement, interestingly enough, has some affinities with the perspective of C. S. Lewis. Lewis thought that with the coming of the Reformation (that was heralded by certain Late Medieval intellectuals), Western thought had a decisive and significant turn on the human journey.

If William of Occam, Duns Scotus and nominalism can be seen as an Act One in the liberal drama, then the Reformation takes us to Act Two. The ideas and notions that were in the air in the Late Medieval era took a more formal and material form in the Reformation period. There is little doubt that many important theologians and activists in the sixteenth century appealed to liberty, equality and individual conscience for their authority in contrast to the church, institutions and tradition. It was this appeal to these principles (even though the Bible was used as an external form of authority) that truly sets the liberal tradition in motion. Those like Luther, Calvin and the Anabaptists turned against the historic Roman Catholic Church, and even though they justified their actions in reference to the Bible, the deeper principles that animated their decisions were conscience, liberty and individualism. If it was simply a matter of returning to the Bible as the source and fount of authority to solve the problems of the Roman Catholic Church, then the Reformers should have agreed on things. But the fact that the Reformers soon disagreed on how to interpret the Bible meant that some other authority was at work. And this new authority was the primacy of the individual, in conscience, choosing what he or she thought was the best interpretation of scripture. As each and all applied such implicit and liberal principles to the religious life, it was just a matter of time, of course, before the church would splinter and fragment in many different directions. It is in this sense that the Reformation embodies Act Two of the liberal drama. The fragmentation of the church in the sixteenth and seventeenth centuries is the beginning of pluralism and multiculturalism, and the politics of identity that underwrite both pluralism and multiculturalism are the liberal principles of equality, liberty, conscience and individuality.

It was just a matter of time before the Bible and the Church waned as matters of primary interest in Western thought and civilization, but the principles initiated by the Reformers came to dominate the landscape of the time. Act Three in the liberal drama emerged in the latter half of the seventeenth century. The English Civil War and the Thirty Years' War in Europe raised two important issues. Those who often claimed to have absolute knowledge differed on who had it, and each and all who claimed to have such knowledge could be quite vicious and violent with those who differed with them. Many thinkers at the time came to the conclusion that knowledge was just a matter of perspective (both knowledge in the area of science and knowledge about human nature), so it was much saner and wiser to accept this fact and avoid absolute claims. Human nature was now seen as a blank piece of paper waiting to be written on or a wet and sticky piece of wax awaiting an imprint and seal. The Bible and the Church might fulfil some private and subjective needs, but the real authority was the individual and their right to life, liberty and estates. The human journey was an open-ended project, and there were little or no boundaries or precedents to tell a person how to live such a journey or what trail and path to hike. The principles, though, of individuality, liberty, equality and conscience had become the new dogma and creed. The content of such principles could be decided as each individual saw fit. This hands-off approach in the areas of religion, economics and the arts moved the liberal drama to yet its new scene and act.

The Enlightenment of the eighteenth century yet further consolidated the liberal way and franchise. Act Four was well under way, the crowds were riveted in their seats, and most applauded the drift and direction of things. Those who had argued for liberalism in the sixteenth and seventeenth centuries were mostly of the emerging middle class. It was this class that longed to exert their liberty and individuality over and against the upper classes, the monarchy and the lower classes. The Christian denominations that arose in the sixteenth and seventeenth centuries appealed to liberty, conscience, equality and individualism to oppose and distance themselves from the historic forms of Christianity such as the Roman Catholic and Church of England traditions. The Puritans on the Continent, in England and in America all turned to the liberal principles of conscience, liberty and the rights of the individual in good conscience to choose and live the good and holy life. This is why it is important to see Puritanism as the parent of liberalism. Many think that Puritanism and liberalism are at odds and enemies. Nothing could be further from the truth. The very principles that Puritans appealed to are the founding principles of liberalism. The Enlightenment of the eighteenth century used the principles that were claimed by many of the Reformers and the Puritans to undermine the religious zeal and commitment of the Reformers and Puritans. The Enlightenment in England, France and America (and other places for that matter) argued that each and all should have the freedom to question both Christianity and the Middle Class. If the Reformers and Puritans used the principles of liberty, conscience, equality and individuality to deconstruct and undermine the historic church, then the Enlightenment used the same principles to undermine the Reformers, the Puritans and Christianity. Why should not each and all have the freedom to choose the faith of their choice? What made Christianity any better than any other religious tradition? Truth is just a matter of perspective and relative (is this not what the Reformers and Puritans had essentially created with their fragmented church and different interpretations of the Bible?). The Enlightenment further argued that freedom should also be for the working and lower classes, the peasants and the people. Freedom should be for one and all both in a religious and political sense, and no one should have the right to oppose or resist such a noble and ennobling idea. The roots of liberalism were going deep, and the tree was growing a strong cultural trunk and spread out many a tenacious branch. It now had become, for most, the only perspective to adopt and bow before. Who could possibly stand against this mighty force? Surely only reactionaries and those nostalgic for an idealized past could say 'no' to such a progressive and forward way of looking at life.

The Victorian era opened up Act Five in the Western drama. The idea of progress and evolution were very much the air breathed by many at the time. The past was the dark ages, and the new was the best and better. This notion of history as progress and the idea of historicism dwelt in a symbiotic relationship. If the past was a backward time, and we were all products of our time, and the only real way to live in time was to exercise our liberty in the best way possible, then there were little or no restraints to define how we were to use such freedom. The Victorian era lingers for some as the last vestiges of the dying Puritan ethos, but, in fact, the Victorian era in England, and the Romantic movement on the Continent drove forward the language of liberty and individuality to new heights and with a greater passion. The Bible, the Church and the Middle Class (who had initiated the liberal way) were being bypassed. A new generation of liberals were emerging who were, in a religious sense, open to all faiths (and no faiths) and, in a political sense, urging and arguing for liberty of the lower classes. Workers of the world unite—

you have nothing to lose but your chains. The content of liberty, equality and fraternity was changing, and those appropriating it changing, but the principles set forth by William of Occam, the Reformers, the Puritans and the Middle Class remained the same. Ideas do have consequences, and it often takes centuries to fully play such ideas out, but the fully grown plant is in the seed. The end is in the beginning. The drama does move ever forward and onward. The actors and actresses are more sure of their parts as one scene opens and unfolds into another scene.

The twentieth century ushered us into Act Six in this drama. The principles of liberty and equality, individualism and conscience still shaped how the play was to be directed and the actors and actresses were to act their predictable parts. Women used such liberal notions to fight for the vote, and many urged the state to get involved so one and all would have, at least, equality of condition and opportunity. The more sensitive artists probed the nature of conscious, unconscious and subconscious life, and human nature was seen as a mysterious and questionable project. Impressionism in painting and a literary stream of consciousness came to dominate the day. Each and all were expected to dive deep and probe the mysteries of the inner depths. The turn to the inner life was part of the search for the authentic, real and genuine self as opposed to the fictions and conventional ego that many were content to live with and from. Just as the Puritans of old had used the language of conscience and liberty to interpret the Bible and live a life of holiness, the modern twentieth century liberal used the language of conscience and liberty to interpret the text of the soul and live a life of authenticity. The principles remained the same even though the texts used were different and the content of things found went in different directions. And, just as the Reformers and Puritans differed on how to interpret the Bible, and created different churches and traditions to reflect this reality, so the modern liberal differed on how to interpret the needs and longings of the soul, and different tribes, clans and the media worked together to create holy sites for such seekers to turn to in their search for meaning and purpose.

The latter half of the twentieth century and the early part of the twenty-first century have been called the postmodern era, a period that has brought to an end the meta-narratives, foundational and structural thinking. This, in many ways, brings us into Act Seven in the liberal drama. This is a period of time in which human nature and human identity is defined in a variety of ways. Many argue that we should have the right to make ourselves into anything we wish, just as we should have the right to pick any food from the shopping mall or wear any clothes we wish. We can change our image of ourselves and our identity as we change clothes, and who is to say which garment is the best to wear. All is a matter of opinion and perspective, is it not? The culture wars that take place between many liberals and conservatives these days are often not so much about the underlying principles that have defined and shaped these traditions. They are more about how and where these principles are applied and the new water poured into such vessels. Even though the language of postmodernism is really just an extension and variant of liberalism, conservatives and liberals do clash on what form liberalism should take and why. We do need to remember that Occam, Duns Scotus and nominalism, the Reformers and the Puritans, the Middle Class revolution and Marxism were about extending the franchise of freedom in new areas. The Reformers and the Puritans wanted the freedom to think and worship as they pleased in opposition to the historic church, and they were for a market economy in opposition to mercantilism. But the principles appealed to were liberty and conscience. The church was fragmented, a hands-off approach to the economy was held high. Holiness and the godly life were at the core of this position. Our postmodern liberals appeal to the same principles, and rather than holiness, happiness and authenticity are their ends and goals. Liberty is now extended to such areas as gay rights, abortion, feminism, alternate family values, spirituality and the right to create identity as each and all see fit. Ideas do have consequences, a seed does, in time, produce a fully grown plant, and the ideas and principles of Occam, nominalism, the Reformers, the Puritans, Locke, Smith, Paine, Mill and many others have come home to roost. Act Seven in the liberal drama is playing itself out in a predictable way and manner, and the language of rights, diversity, process, tolerance, pluralism and openness is very much the sacred speech, script and shibboleth of the liberal drama.

We do need to ask ourselves, though, this simple question. What is the good in liberalism and what are its limitations? If we cannot question the liberal drama and play, what sort of literary critics are we? If we do not know how to raise critical questions, have we not been taken in by the matrix of liberalism? Liberals often lament the way propaganda works to seduce and numb the mind and imagination, but how many liberals are aware of how liberal propaganda might do the same thing? Is it possible to think outside of the matrix, and, if so, how is this to be done? There are those like Francis Fukuyama who have argued that we have come to the end of history, and it is the liberal principles that have brought us thus far. It is these principles, Fukuyama argued, that now shape what is good, true and acceptable in our global village. All must conform to these principles if they ever hope to get a hearing in the courts, public places and universities. The task, now that we live at the end of history (in terms of an intellectual journey) is just to apply these sacred principles in the world of history. The text has now been settled on. We just need to apply it to the practical sphere of life. But, are we at the end of history, and, is it possible to challenge the creed and dogma of liberalism?

The End of Liberalism and the End of History: Philosophical Probes

Charles Taylor is very much a leading apologist of the Liberal Enlightenment project. Taylor has walked the extra mile, to define and defend liberalism, against its postmodern aberrations on the one hand, and, in opposition to the Classical tradition, on the other hand. Taylor, at his sensitive, insightful and incisive best, does offer the reader the most nuanced and most attractive versions of liberalism. It is then to Taylor we will turn to send out some philosophical probes about the problems and weak chinks in the liberal agenda.

Taylor's *Sources of the Self: The Making of the Modern Identity*, and his smaller and more popular missive on the same subject, *The Malaise of Modernity*, do much to articulate both the most attractive and compelling arguments for the liberal way, and some of the frets and worries of a thoughtful liberal. *Sources of the Self* is a rich read in the historical Western journey, and the way those within this journey have attempted to understand and define the self. Taylor does, regrettably so, distort and caricature the Classical tradition somewhat, but this is a predictable tendency of most liberals. They do need to justify their principles, prejudices and ideas in opposition to what went before them, so they often do so by doing a questionable read of such a tradition. Hans-Georg Gadamer, Alasdair MacIntyre or Werner Jaeger are much better and more dependable guides into the Classical ethos. *Sources of the Self* is divided into five sections: 1) Identity and the Good, 2) Inwardness, 3) The Affirmation of Ordinary Life, 4) The Voice of Nature, and 5) Subtler Languages. In each of these sections, Taylor probes and inches ever nearer and closer to the core of the liberal tradition. It is important to note, both by way of conclusion in *Sources of the Self* and throughout *The Malaise of Modernity*, that Taylor does have concerns about the way liberalism can be used, abused and misused. He comes as a critic of those who abuse and misuse the liberal agenda, but he also, in a limited sort of way, comes as a probing critic of those who are uncritical fans and boosters of liberalism.

There are many knockers of liberalism at the present time. Taylor is not one of them. There are many uncritical defenders of liberalism. Taylor is not merely one of them. Taylor, in fact, concludes *Sources of the Self* with 'The Conflicts of Modernity'. The liberal tradition both within itself and in the contest between conservatism and liberalism does have its problems, and these must be faced. What, then, are some of the conflicts within the modern liberal agenda? There are six we will briefly touch on.

First, liberalism emerged in history in response to and as a reaction to a certain read and interpretation of conservatism. Liberals often know what they want to be free from, but when it comes to defining what they want to be free for, the content of such choices tends to be a rather open-ended project. It is true, of course, that liberalism did put forward as its leading principles such notions as liberty, choice, equality, reason–imagination, the rights of the individual and the quest for meaning and happiness as guiding ideas. But, such principles when disconnected from the good can come to be defined in a variety of ways. This, then, is the first dilemma of liberalism, and it is this dilemma that sets it apart from the Classical way. Liberalism tends to be quite shy and hesitant about suggesting that there is a good (in both a metaphysical and ethical sense) that one and all can know. When notions such as the good, the true and the beautiful are both privatized and relativized, then they can be defined as each and all see fit. It is this liberal fear and suspicion of saying much about the ultimate (or reducing it to a mystery that each and all perceive and define in their own way) that makes liberalism a chameleon-like agenda that can become whatever an age wants or wishes it to be.

Second, the liberal notion of the self, identity or nature tends to lack boundaries that could give focus and direction to the self. Liberals have tended to argue that the self is a project in the making, that we begin as blank pieces of paper, and what is written on us and what we write on the page of our emerging journey is the self. This is why the language of process, pilgrimage, dialogue, diversity and many other terms is the *lingua franca* of this tradition. The strength of liberalism is its openness, but its limitation is its lack of boundaries. The Classical notion of order, rooted and grounded in the good, comes as an affront to the Liberal emphasis on liberty and freedom. Liberalism has a difficult time in understanding boundaries for the self for the simple reason, for most liberals, the very notion of boundaries and limitations are the problem. Liberty often stands in stark contrast to the repressive nature of boundaries and limitations. Liberty is seen as the good (regardless of the content of liberty), and order is seen as the enemy of liberty. It is this overemphasis on liberty, and this tendency to see order as the problem that is a problem in liberalism as it seeks to interpret the self and articulate some sort of ethical position.

Third, the liberal principles of liberty, choice, equality, individualism, fraternity (solidarity) and the role of reason–intuition as a means of knowing do raise some troubling questions. The collision, for example, between the rights of the individual in their longing for liberty and the rights of the community and the common good often collide. There are the principles of liberalism; then there is the priorizing of such principles. There have been, since the birth of liberalism, these tensions, conflicts and collisions within the liberal family. The leftist tradition will tend to priorize the communal and fraternal side of liberalism, and the rightist tradition will play up and priorize the liberty aspects of liberalism. The problem for liberalism is this: given the principles that define liberalism, what criteria does the liberal use to priorize such principles and why? These deeper criteria go to the very unresolved heart and core of the liberal way. Liberalism itself cannot and does not have the resources to resolve such a dilemma, and this is why liberalism (in its right, left and centrist traditions) lives in such unresolved conflict.

Fourth, and this is a telling point, liberals long to be open to one and all, seek to be understanding and honour perspectives and different ways of being. This approach, of course, often takes a person to the place in which listening, hearing and respect for the other is held high, but such a position makes it difficult to state and argue that there are rights and wrongs, goods we should desire and things we should avoid. The more we argue that there are standards one and all should heed, hear and abide by, the more we take a position that there are limits to hearing, listening and dialogue. This dilemma has been worked out, in an interesting way, in Taylor's life and thought. Taylor was most active in the 1950s and 1960s as a guiding light of the New Left in both England and Canada. In fact, Taylor was the president of the NDP in the 1960s. Taylor's *The Pattern of Politics*, published in 1970, was a blistering attack and assault on Trudeau and Trudeau's brand of liberalism. Taylor was, in short, committed to the New Left liberal standards of fraternity (solidarity) as a guiding principle and light from which liberty would emerge. All must be free so that each may be free. Taylor, at this point in his life and journey, did not suggest that all philosophical and political perspectives (and the parties that embodied them) were just a matter of where a person stood, how they saw things. Taylor thought and acted as if certain things were better than others, and, as such, it was important to act and live from such realities. As the 1970s and 1980s took their toll on Taylor, he moved, increasingly so, into the area of hermeneutical suspicion. This means that much is just a matter of how we see, and how we see and perceive things is conditioned by where we stand. This new stance by Taylor means that he does not have quite the same passion he once had for firmer political positions. His new position is one of suspicion about those who take positions of firmness and clarity. This dilemma for Taylor is well articulated by Ronald Beiner in *Philosophy in a Time of Lost Spirit: Essays on Contemporary Theory*. Beiner did his PhD with Taylor, and in a chapter in the book, 'Hermeneutical Generosity and Social Criticism', Beiner probes this dilemma in Taylor.[3] Taylor, the social critic in the 1950s-1960s became Taylor the political fence sitter in the 1970s-1980s-1990s as he moved into the area of hermeneutical generosity.

The more all is seen as a matter of perspective, the more difficult it is to be committed about much other than perspectives. The more a person is committed to what is perceived as the better or the good, the less inclined they are to reduce most things to an equal level of perspectives. Liberalism does dwell in this intellectual dilemma. The agnosticism built into its very fibre does, when day is done, make it difficult to take anything, other than diversity and pluralism, agnosticism and perspectives with much seriousness. It is this dilemma that often confounds the liberal. There is the human desire to know and believe some things are better than others, but the liberal undercuts and undermines taking such commitments with too much seriousness. This then leads to a sort of sitting on the fence and a paralysis when it comes to committed action. We purchase tolerance at the price of relativizing all things. When this occurs, much is dumbed down to the trivial and silly. Taylor would have his questions about this, but, at a higher level, most liberals are very much trapped in Taylor's dilemma.

Fifth, liberals hold high certain principles that I have mentioned above, but what is most interesting (given the commitment to critical thinking) is that many liberals simply do not question the principles themselves. If asked about the limitations of liberty, equality, choice, individualism, identity as task-in-the-making, most liberals go mute and silent. Many liberals are quick and hasty when it comes to exposing the limitation of conservatism, but they tend to be slow off the mark in unmasking the principles of liberalism. This is called the mote and beam syndrome: it is one thing to see the mote in the eye of the other—it is much more difficult to see the beam in one's own eye.[4] The fact that liberals often can, and do not, do this should raise some questions in the mind of the thoughtful. A good question that each and all should, in a regular way, pose to liberals is this: what are the weakness and limitations of the liberal way (both at the level of principle and practice)? If this question cannot be adequately raised or answered, then liberalism is no different than the conservatism or fundamentalism it often differs with. It is often this inability of liberals to critique themselves that is most illiberal.

Sixth, Liberalism is often weak and wanting when it comes to offering any sort of content to the principles of liberalism. It is this silence on questions of content (or this openness to any sort of content poured into such vessels) that does need to be probed. If, at the level of liberal principles, questions need to be raised, it is equally important to ask the liberal, what criteria are used to decide the content to be poured into principles of liberty, choice and equality? It is these criteria, again, that do raise some troubling questions for the thoughtful liberal.

In sum, if we dare to send some philosophic probes the liberal way at the end of history, we do need to question the dogmatic commitment to certain principles, the problems of how such principles should be priorized and why, and questions about the sources of the self, the tension of thinking there is a good yet being agnostic about the good and the need to articulate some positive content and grounding for the use of freedom need to be asked.

The End of Liberalism: Contemplative Probes

The liberal notion of the self, as I mentioned above, tends to lack a certain depth and inner structure. The self, within such a tradition, can and has been seen as a blend of the rational and conscious life, a deeper subconscious and unconscious mythic life. Needless to say, the life of the body and its many needs and wants are part and parcel of this bundle of needs, longings, wants and hungers for meaning and purpose. Liberals tend to shy away from positing anything foundational, structural and of knowable meta-truth. This, it is often argued, limits freedom and leads to repression. The will to be free, and to define freedom in whatever way is in the interests of he or she who longs for such freedom is the code of the liberal way.

The contemplative traditions in most of the major and minor religions of the world do differ with the liberal project in this regards, and this is why many who have come to the end of the liberal way often turn to the contemplative traditions in either the West or East in search of greater depths. The Orient posits the notion that there is a moral law in the cosmos, and to the degree this law is heeded and attuned to, the good life can be known and lived. The Indian tradition calls this *dharma* and the Chinese tradition calls this the *Tao*. *The Abolition of Man*, by C. S. Lewis, walks the extra mile to highlight how many of the major religions share a common ethical core. The Western tradition holds high the idea of natural law, the Decalogue and the Beatitudes. Each of these traditions points to a deeper moral, metaphysical and ontological order in the universe, and they, as one, warn one and all that those who fail to heed and respond to such an order will do hurt and harm to all and one. What is this order, and how does it relate to an understanding of the self?

The Western tradition, from its origins and beginnings, has argued that humans live in a divided self. Plato compared this to the dark and white horse that the chariot rider must keep under control. Augustine distinguished between *caritas* (the good within which is love and leads towards unity) and *cupiditas* (the dark and shadow side within which leads towards fragmentation and disunity). The Fathers of the Church made a distinction between the image of God within each person (that could not be eradicated and was good) and the likeness of God within each person (that had been tarnished and distorted what humans were meant to be). The Greek philosophers made the distinction between *eros* (that force within that moved all things to the fullness of being) and *thanatos* (that death instinct and power within all things which sought to thwart and negate the longings of *eros*, and drove those who heeded the dark side to non-being). Rousseau made the distinction between healthy self-love (*amour de soi*) and unhealthy self-love (*amour propre*). Thomas Merton summed up these differences quite well when he said, 'Contemplation is precisely the awareness that this "I" is really "not I" and the awakening of the unknown "I" that is beyond observation and reflection and is incapable of commenting upon itself', and 'Our external, superficial ego is not spiritual. Far from it, the ego is doomed to disappear as completely as smoke from a chimney. It is utterly frail and evanescent'.[5]

This distinction between the ego that is forever restless, forever hungry, forever consuming a variety of things to fill and fulfil its nagging emptiness and restlessness has no substance. Unfortunately, for many liberals, the ego is the alpha and omega of identity. The flux and stream of consciousness of the ego, the random and many thoughts and images that jump to and fro within each person, like so many monkeys on a tree is often the material liberals work with to forge and form the self. But, the contemplative tradition argues that if human identity is sought at this level, restlessness and inner turmoil and suffering will be the result.

The Indian and Chinese traditions take this issue to the same level. What are *dharma* and the *Tao*? Such ideas are surely more than a sweet moral code of nice and pleasant behaviour that boy scouts and girl guides might doff their dutiful caps to. Both of these traditions argue and insist, and demonstrate through a variety of practical spiritual disciplines, that the ego is empty, and until we see it as such, we doom ourselves to a frantic search for meaning. It is by seeing the emptiness of the ego, it is by seeing all as *maya* and *sunyata* that a new fullness emerges. But, and this is the key, the ego must die, must be let go of, must disappear, must be detached from for the deeper reality to be known and experienced. The liberal tradition tends to have a weak and limited understanding of anything deeper than the ego, and this is its weakness and limitation. Liberalism was formed and forged on the anvil of the ego, and it has tried, century after century, to set free the ego, through the principles of liberty, equality, choice and individualism. But, the very means used work against the deeper ends that the liberal seeks to attain. *Dharma* and the *Tao* will not accept those who come with the pack of their ego full. All must be let go of if and when insight and wisdom are to be found. John of the Cross insisted that until the nothingness (*nada*) of the ego was seen for what it is, the fullness (*todo*) of real life would never be known. There is an instructive Zen parable that nicely sums up this issue. Nan-in, a Zen master, had a university professor visit him. Nan-in served the professor tea, and he kept filling the cup until the tea spilled over the rim. The startled professor watched until he could no longer contain himself. 'Can't you see that the tea is spilling all over me?' he cried out. Nan-in stopped pouring, then he said, 'You are like this cup. You are so full of your knowledge, opinions, speculations. How can I show you real Zen and your true self unless you first empty the cup of the stale water of your ego?'

It is at the point when liberalism has come to the end of its tether on the question of ego, the self and identity, it could despair or continue to run round and round on the treadmill but go nowhere. There came a point for many liberals in which the liberal quest for the self had to go to deeper levels. It was in this frustration with the limited understanding of the liberal notion of the self that there emerged, in its most recent phase, the turn to the East. The 1950s signalled a significant season in the most recent turn by many liberals to the East for a deeper spiritual source. What makes this such a liberal turn is that most of the major liberal themes are at work, but the themes appear at a deeper level. The deeper level, as I mentioned above, tends to focus on the self beyond the ego. Much must die, much must be left behind, many an addiction and attachment must be bid adieu to. But, at the far end of the ego, what sort of self do we find? Are all religions saying much the same thing at this juncture? This is where the liberal Enlightenment project kicks back in yet again.

Those such as Huston Smith, Ram Dass, Robert Aitken, Philip Whalen, Gary Snyder, Allen Ginsberg and many other dissatisfied liberals that turned East in the 1950s, and remain teachers to many today, are pluralists. Thich Nhat Hanh, the Dalai Lama, and in a lesser and lighter way, Bishop Michael Ingham's *Mansions of the Spirit*, are gurus for many, and their appearances and books are bestsellers. Why is this? They very much play into the Western liberal commitment to religious pluralism. This has become the new shrine that many bow at, and not to bow at such an altar is to be banished from the liberal Sanhedrin. The argument is fairly simple, and it goes like this. True and authentic religion is about spirituality, contemplation and mysticism. Mystics are all of one accord, so this argument goes, that we must all die to live. The ego and shadow side must be faced and not allowed to dominate the inner life. What, though, is on the far side of the ego? Do all mystics and contemplatives agree about the nature and substance of the new being, and do they all agree that mystics agree about this? The establishment liberal mystics all tend to see each and all religion as being different and diverse on an exoteric level, but on the inner, esoteric and mystical level, each and all sit side by side and agree. But, do all mystics agree about what the self is like beyond the ego, and what the nature of union with God (if there even is a God to be united with) is like? A serious study of the mystics both within each tradition and between traditions indicates this is not the case. Such a statement comes as an affront to those who argue, whether through the Parliament of the World's Religions such as Wayne Teasdale in *The Mystic Heart: Discovering a Universal Spirituality in the World's Religions* or Phil Cousineau's edited conversations with Huston Smith, *The Way Things Are: Conversations with Huston Smith on the Spiritual Life* that this is the case. Liberals are back in the game again. Just when we think they have left, they return with Enlightenment mystical pluralism and syncretism well in hand. We only need to read Lessing's *Nathan the Wise* to get a sense of deja vu.

Many a thoughtful and engaged Christian has attempted to heed and hear the best from the contemplative and mystical East. The dialogue between Thich Nhat Hanh and Daniel Berrigan in *The Raft Is Not the Shore: Conversations toward a Buddhist–Christian Awareness*, the Thomas Merton and D. T. Suzuki dialogue in *Zen and the Birds of Appetite, Speaking of Silence: Christians and Buddhists on the Contemplative Way* (edited by Susan Walker) and the more recent dialogue between Robert Aitken and David Steindl-Rast, *The Ground We Share: Everyday Practice, Buddhist and Christian* tend to point the way to points of concord, convergence and commonality within and between these contemplative traditions. Bede Griffiths remains a guru to many Christians, also, for the way he has done much the same thing for Christian–Hindu contemplative dialogue. Books such as *The Marriage of East and West* and *Return to the*

Center do tell their own compelling tale. This approach, of course, works very well within the liberal agenda. But, we might want to ask this rather simple question: do these traditions (and the mystics and contemplatives that live from within them), at the deepest level, agree on what lies on the far side of the ego? Is there a self after the letting go of the ego? What are the contours and horizons of this self? Is there even a self to speak of, or is this not yet another illusion we need to rid ourselves from?

Griffiths, Berrigan, Merton and Steindl-Rast have walked a generous and gracious distance to find the points of commonality with contemplatives and mystics in other religious traditions. The approach used is popular for the simple reason it is the child of the Enlightenment pluralist creed of the time. Dare liberals, though, question such a dogma, and what is the fate of those who do? Do all mystics agree that at the centre and core all is one and the same? This is just not the case. We do not need to read too far or deeply into the writings of mystics both within and between traditions to discover that their notions of the self beyond the ego are quite different. It takes only a cursory read of Geoffrey Parrinder's *Mysticism in the World's Religions*, R. C. Zaehner's *Concordant Discord: The Interdependence of Faiths* or Frederick Copleston's *Religion and the One: Philosophies East and West* to discover this elementary truth. Parrinder, Zaehner and Copleston had the contemplative sensitivity of Berrigan, Merton and Steindl-Rast, but they, also, were quite willing to ask questions about points of discord and divergence between the major religions at a deeper contemplative level. Needless to say, Parrinder, Zaehner and Copleston are not popular within the liberal pluralist ethos in the same way that the Dalai Lama, Thich Nhat Hanh, Huston Smith, Robert Aitken, D. T. Suzuki, Gary Snyder, Allen Ginsberg, Wayne Teasdale or David Novak are. The latter group speaks to the pluralist spirit of the age, and the former group dares to challenge such a perspective. It seems to me prophets and saints do not exist to baptize and bless the status quo. They come to question and critique such dominant ideologies.

Liberalism (in either its crude or more sophisticated mystical form) is very much the establishment creed of the age. Establishment thought can be equated with Constantinianism. Those who uncritically bow before the pluralist shrine of liberalism are like those, in the early church, who sought to see the interests of the state and the church as one and the same. It was the Christian mystics and prophets who challenged such a union and synthesis. Dare they do less today?

Let us wrap up this rather lengthy chapter. It is almost impossible to avoid the matrix of liberalism these days. It shapes and defines, it enframes and conditions virtually all ethical, political, religious, educational, cultural and social thought. If we have not learned to think outside this matrix, we probably have not yet learned to truly think. It is considered quite unspeakable to question liberals about the weaknesses of liberalism, but it is such raids on such unspeakable things we must do if we are ever going to be minimally alert and alive.

CHAPTER SEVENTEEN

CHARLES TAYLOR AND THE HEGELIAN EDEN TREE: CANADIAN COMPRADORISM

the tree was good for food ... it was pleasant to the eyes, and a tree to be desired to make one wise — Genesis 3:6

The fact that the well-known Canadian philosopher, Charles Taylor, won the enviable Templeton Prize for Progress toward Research or Discoveries about Spiritual Realities in 2007 has been noted and noticed by many. There are few that have won this prestigious award, and fewer Canadians have taken the trophy home. Taylor did so, and did so in a way that has made many a Canadian proud of their native-born boy. But, philosophy is about asking critical questions, and critical questions keep us from slipping into hagiography. Why did Taylor win the Templeton Prize, what questions need to be asked of Taylor, what intellectual agenda does he serve and are there other Canadians of equal worth and merit that might have won the Templeton Prize but did not?

Most Canadians that study philosophy in any serious way often learn of Plato and Aristotle—if they are fortunate, of the Patristic contemplative way (many know little of this), Medieval thought, the fragmentation of thought in the Reformation, then the journey into the modern and postmodern mood and ethos. I suspect, if most Canadians (or non-Canadians) that study philosophy were asked about Canadian philosophy and philosophers a blank and confused stare would come across their bewildered faces and baffled minds. Surely, there is no such thing as a distinct Canadian philosophical tradition and Canadian philosophers that embody such a tradition. Such is the colonial mind. Nothing good can emerge from within the womb of Canada, hence the turn most Canadians make to a variety of elsewhere communities (past and present) in their study of philosophy.

Is there, though, a distinctive Canadian tradition of philosophy, and, if so, what is it? And, if there is such a tradition, where does Charles Taylor stand in relation to such a heritage, line and lineage? The answer to these questions might assist us in understanding why Taylor won the Templeton Prize.

There is little doubt that *The Faces of Reason: Philosophy in English Canada, 1850–1950*, by Leslie Armour and Elizabeth Trott, did much to highlight the obstinate fact that there is a distinct philosophical tradition in English Canada. Armour and Trott ignored French Canada, and this is a limitation in their approach, but *The Faces of Reason* made it clear that between 1850 and 1950 a distinct form and way of doing philosophy had emerged in Canada. Canadian philosophy and philosophers saw things differently and thought in a different way, in a general sort of way, than those in the United Kingdom and the United States. Leslie Armour, more than any Canadian philosopher, has walked the extra mile to highlight the fact that there is a distinctive Canadian way of doing philosophy. Armour's faithful and conscientious work means that he has opened up a path for many to see. This is why, and rightly so, a *festschrift* was written and dedicated to Armour. *Idealism, Metaphysics and Community* has many a fine essay dedicated to Armour, and most of his publications are listed in a well-pondered bibliography. But, what has Armour to do with Taylor other than the fact that both are Canadians and both are philosophers? Taylor won the Templeton Prize and Armour did not. Why linger much longer on the work of Leslie Armour?

The Faces of Reason makes it most clear that the Canadian tradition of philosophy that is nearest and dearest to the Canadian soul and psyche is a form of Hegelian idealism. This fact, and its historic reality, was made even clearer in a recent book on George Grant—there are three essays in *Athens and Jerusalem: George Grant's Theology, Philosophy, and Politics* that deal with Grant's questioning of the Hegelian tradition in both Hegel and the Canadian appropriation of Hegel. Robert C. Sibley's 'Grant, Hegel, and the "Impossibility of Canada"',[1] Alexander Duff's 'Response to the Strauss–Kojeve Debate: George Grant's Turn from Hegel to Christian Platonism'[2] and Neil Robertson's 'Freedom and the Tradition: George Grant, James Doull, and the Character of Modernity'[3] all tell, in different ways and for different reasons, why Grant parted company with Hegel and his modern disciples and followers in Canada. Interestingly enough, in *Athens and Jerusalem*, there were no articles on Grant and Taylor. This should be noted given the fact that such an essay would have brought the debate between the ancients and moderns, Grant and Taylor into the Canadian context. Grant and Doull (a modern Canadian Hegelian) squared off on the Classics–Modern debate, and there is no doubt Grant engaged Canadian liberal Hegelianism in many forms in Canada, but the Grant–Taylor differences were left untouched in *Athens and Jerusalem*. What has been the nature of Charles Taylor's journey, what role has Hegel played in such a journey, why can Canadian Hegelianism be a form of colonialism and compradorism and how can George Grant come as a distinct critic of Hegel, Hegelianism, Taylor and the modern project? Let us begin with Hegel, then move ever onward and forward to Hegel in Canada and Taylor's appropriation of Hegel. There is no doubt that Charles Taylor stands within a certain philosophical tradition, and it is best to know what such a tradition is and why.

There is little doubt that Hegel is the grand magus of the modern liberal ethos. He has, more than most, articulated why liberalism is and should be the reigning ideology of our age, and why it is foolish to resist and oppose such an intellectual system. Hegel argued that all of human history (guided by the *Weltgeist*–World Spirit) is about our increasing consciousness of the meaning of liberty and freedom. The seeds of such a way of being were planted in the Classical past, emerged with some maturity in the Roman Catholic civilization of Patristic and Medieval Europe, bore yet greater fruit in the Protestant forms of Christianity, found a certain beauty and fragrance in various religions of the world, and in the Enlightenment bore abundant fruit. Each generation, in such an organic unfolding, in a dialectical way, builds on the previous generation. Liberty and freedom is the key to such a fuller awakening, and to oppose or question such a fundamental reality is to dare to question the spirit of the age that ever seeks to stir and enliven one and all, souls and civilizations with an ever more profound alertness to the meaning of liberty. Those who are out of step with such movement of history are out of touch with the meaning and forward march of history. There are left wing Hegelians (Marx and clan), centrist Hegelians (social democrats and democratic socialists) and right wing Hegelians (liberty-loving Americans), but each and all (left, centre and right) hold high the flag of liberty. The differences within the Hegelian clan are not about liberty and freedom (this is the creed and what the high council has decreed), but about how such a reality can be best delivered. This is why there are those that have argued that we have come to the end of history. Most now agree that liberty is the foundation that none can doubt or question. The debates, as I mentioned above, are more about how liberty and freedom can be best delivered and practiced not whether the premises of freedom dared be challenged. The modern world is, in essence, Hegelian, and it is virtually impossible, in the liberal modern ethos to question such a position and perspective. Where does Charles Taylor fit into such a tradition? Taylor studied at McGill University from 1948 to 1952, then he was off to England to do graduate and doctoral studies. When Taylor was in England, he was a founder of *Universities and Left Review* that became, in time, *New Left Review*. Taylor also headed the World University Services in Vienna. It does not take too much reflection to realize where Taylor tipped his intellectual and political hat. Taylor returned to Canada in 1961, and he began teaching at McGill. The 1960s were an interesting period of time for Taylor. He taught, but he was also at the centre of NDP activism. Taylor ran four times as an NDP candidate at a federal level, and he ran against Pierre Trudeau in the 1965 election. Trudeau had supported Taylor in the 1963 federal election. We could say that Taylor was a soft left Hegelian in the 1960s, although his writings on Hegel were minimal. Taylor's more committed NDP activism began to wane in the 1970s, but before such a turn occurred, he published *The Pattern of Politics* in 1970. This is a small book, and a tract for the times just like Grant's *Lament for a Nation*. The interesting thing to note, though, in *The Pattern of Politics* is that the intense nationalism of Grant is missing, but there is no doubt that Taylor is attempting, within a Canadian context, to determine how freedom and liberty can best be accomplished for each and all. Taylor is certainly aware, in *The Pattern of Politics*, that the United States and corporate wealth inhibit a fuller liberty for Canadians, and he warns Canadians of being 'a miniature replica'[4] of the United States and of being mired in the 'quicksands of dependence'.[5] It is important to note, though, that Taylor's concerns with the colonization of Canadian culture and economics never brought him to the point of being as committed to nationalism and socialism as was the Waffle movement in the late 1960s-early 1970s in the NDP. The goal is liberty, but liberty for Canadians must not be pushed too hard or too far. It is not easy to reconcile Canadian nationalism and American imperialism. The means is a left-of-centre approach, but a left-of-centre approach that was cautious and wary of offending at a certain level of discourse and action. George Grant and Robin Mathews would have their doubts about Taylor's rather assimilationist Hegelianism in *The Pattern of Politics*. Hegel is the silent sage through the 1960s for Taylor, though.

It was just a matter of time before the silent sage would move from his hidden throne room and be summoned forth to appear. Taylor had to recognize his master. It was in the 1970s that Hegel, the magus, appeared on the stage for all to see. Taylor did the introductions well. *Hegel*, published in 1975, and *Hegel and Modern Society*, published in 1977, established Taylor as a leading Hegelian scholar, and such an explicit doffing of the intellectual and political cap placed Taylor in the mainstream and establishment tradition of Canadian Hegelianism. Much of Taylor's work since the 1970s has been merely a fleshing out, within the Canadian context and beyond, of the essential rightness of Hegel (past, present, and future).

What is the genius of Hegel and why has Taylor drawn so deeply from the well of Hegel? Hegel emphasized that the Enlightenment tradition was superior to the Classical tradition, but the Enlightenment had a tendency to fragment in three directions. There was the rationalist wing of the Enlightenment that turned to science, reason and the empirical way as the yellow brick road into the future. There were the romantics that dared to differ with the rationalists, and the romantics held high the way of poetry, the arts and intuition. Then, there were the humanists. It was the humanists that attempted to see the best in the romantics and rationalists yet question their limited approaches to knowing and being. It was the humanists within the Enlightenment that attempted to synthesize the best of the rationalist and romantic traditions and raise both to a higher level through such a synthesis.

Charles Taylor, like Hegel, stands very much within the humanist wing of the Enlightenment. Both see the Classical past as limited and partial, and both see the notion of liberty and freedom as best expressed in the humanist vision of the Enlightenment. Poetry and science need not be enemies. Religion and reason need not oppose one another. Individualism and community need not butt horns. There is a place for a higher synthesis of the best elements of both approaches to life and society. Both the soul and civilizations falter and weaken when any extreme dominates the day. The goal of both Hegel and Taylor is the reconciliation, through struggle and opposition, to an ever-higher level of the liberal goal of the consciousness of freedom.

There are those, of course, that would disagree with Hegel's four epochs of human history (Oriental, Greek, Roman and Christian Germanic), but Hegel's underlying thesis of liberty lives on. The modern and postmodern carry the tale of freedom ever forward. It is at this point, though, where Taylor breaks with the postmodern. He argues that postmodernity has broken the dialectic. Individualism has run rampant to the exclusion or marginalization of community and the state. Hegel's vision of the humanist liberal vision was that the freedom of each could only be actualized within the whole, and the public was as important (if not more so) than the private and the individual.

There are right wing Hegelians that insist that the liberty of the individual trumps the good of the community, there are centrist Hegelians that hold the freedom of community, state, nation and individual in tension, then there are committed leftist Hegelians that insist that the freedom of the state takes precedence over the freedom of nation, community and individual. Taylor very much stands within the centrist social democratic stream of Hegelianism within the Canadian context.

The larger philosophic and political questions beg a deeper question. What does it mean to be human? Are liberty and freedom a form of faith that cannot be questioned? If such premises cannot be questioned, has not liberalism lost its critical edge? If an ideological leftist theory held Taylor in the 1950s, and Taylor's leftist activism preoccupied him in the 1960s, a turn occurred in the 1970s. Taylor began to take his theory deeper. Taylor's two books in the 1970s on Hegel placed him on front stage in the world of Hegelian scholarship. The 1980s nudged Taylor to greater depths on the questions of human nature and the self—*Sources of the Self: The Making of the Modern Identity* was published in 1989. The ideology of the 1950s had waned, the activism of the 1960s thinned out, Hegel had been probed in the 1970s. The time had come to examine the roots and sources of the self. *Sources of the Self* is an exquisite and compelling apologia for the modern notion of the self, the sources of such a self and the conflicts within the modern liberal project. Taylor tends, as ever, to caricature or ignore the classical tradition when he needs to dive deeper. But, this is part of his commitment to Hegelian liberalism. The past is merely a preparation for the present as the present is an unfolding preparation, of ever-increasing goodness, for the future. The cunning of reason will make it so. All, in the end, is about progress to a higher understanding of liberty.

The larger issues of political theory and activism had given way to questions of the self in the 1980s for Taylor. *Sources of the Self* was such a convincing and compelling defence of modern liberalism that Taylor was asked to do the CBC Massey Lectures for 1991—*The Malaise of Modernity* is a reader's digest version of *Sources of the Self*.[6] Those who have followed Taylor's journey from the 1950s to the 1990s cannot help but sense that political theory and political activism have lost their lustre by the 1980s, and Taylor's project through the 1980s and 1990s is a defence of Hegelian liberalism. This means much work must be done on unpacking the sources of the self and the varied ways of defining identity. Pluralism and multiculturalism become the buzz words, and dialogue and dialectic ever continues. The more substantive questions of Canadian nationalism and American imperialism simply don't exist, in a serious way, for Taylor. He has become, in many ways, the quintessential bourgeois and humanist liberal, defending the liberal status quo in a thoughtful and sophisticated way and manner.

There are, in short, some serious shifts and alterations in thought and action between the younger Taylor and the elder Taylor. These shifts have been aptly noted and painstakingly probed in Ronald Beiner's essay 'Hermeneutical Generosity and Social Criticism' in *Philosophy in a Time of Lost Spirit: Essays on Contemporary Theory. Philosophy in a Time of Lost Spirit*,[7] like Beiner's earlier book, *What's the Matter with Liberalism?*, dares to interrogate the ideology of liberalism. 'Hermeneutical Generosity and Social Criticism' points out that Taylor cannot have it both ways. It's impossible to have a foot on the dock and another foot on the boat as the boat is leaving the dock. Those who turn more and more to a generous interpretive approach to the self, society and politics find it increasingly difficult to raise hard critical questions about politics, society and the self for the simple reason that positions and perspectives, dialogue, process and dialectic is the new ideology. Procedural liberalism wins the day. But, when social criticism comes to the fore, notions such as right and wrong, good, better and best, bad, worse and worst take front stage. There is no doubt that Taylor tended, in the last two decades of the twentieth century, to marginalize social criticism (the younger Taylor) while holding high hermeneutical generosity. The feet of the soul need to be either on the dock or the boat. A thinker or activist cannot have it both ways. Hermeneutical generosity tends to lead to a paralysis of action on substantive issues while social critics tend to be weak on accepting as equal the truth claims and insights of most perspectives.

There is no doubt that Charles Taylor is one of the most important defenders of the modern liberal project. He does not summon forth its deeper premises and question them. He accepts them as the best for this ethos that we live in. Taylor is quite willing to question some of the aberrations of liberalism but not the core and centre of liberalism. The Classical and the Postmodern will not do for Taylor. It is the Hegelian liberal project, for good or ill, that must be defended. Such a project, in a distorted way, exists in the United States, and, in a deeper more leftist form, exists in Canada. The fact that Taylor turned more to questions of the self and hermeneutical generosity means he has less and less to say on larger questions of Canadian nationalism and American imperialism. Taylor has, increasingly so, become preoccupied with the liberal agenda of pluralism, deeper diversity, French nationhood recognition and some of the dilemmas that modernity raises for those committed to it as the reigning ideology of the age.

A problem exists when we marginalize the larger questions and become preoccupied with the secondary questions. This has happened, I fear, with Taylor. This is a more subtle way of being colonized. We just don't discuss the large issues. We become overly concerned with the self and community. The meaning of nationhood gets lost in the shuffle. We accept the status quo. The New Romans win not by might or force, arms or tanks but by the simple fact that important philosophers just don't ask the questions about imperialism (and its consequences for many on this fragile earth, our island home). This is, perhaps, why Taylor won the Templeton Prize for Progress toward Research or Discoveries about Spiritual Realities. Taylor has given himself to progress as defined by Hegel and accepted by the power elite and ruling mandarin class in Canada and the United States. He was offered his laurels for serving the spirit of the age, and the Sanhedrin that guard such a *weltgeist*.

Just as Hegel thought the spirit of the age had settled best and in the most mature way in his culture, so Taylor has accepted and defended the dominant ideology of our age. Religion must genuflect, also, to modernity if it expects to be heard and have a voice. Taylor knows this, his understanding of religion, like all else, plays into the liberal agenda of pluralism, hence the Templeton Prize. We do not need to read too far into Taylor's *A Catholic Modernity?* or *Varieties of Religion Today: William James Revisited,* published in 1999 and 2002, to get a feel for Taylor's thinned out and rather tame Roman Catholic thinking and perspective. Is Taylor more of a liberal catholic or catholic liberal? He is, certainly, not a classical catholic in his thinking. Those who serve the age cannot be so. Grant saw clearly, and told those who would hear, the way in which pluralism is the monism of our time.[8] Taylor could learn much from Grant.

It does seem rather odd that, on the one hand, philosophy is supposed to be about critical thinking, yet, on the other hand, a philosopher like Charles Taylor is not very critical of the reigning ideology of his day. It is a rather sad day when a liberal lacks the ability to critique liberalism. But, to question liberalism would be to question the air breathed by most intellectuals. The New Romans would not be pleased; neither would the senators that insist that liberalism is the only way to think.

Taylor has seen, taken and tasted from the Hegelian liberal Eden tree. Such a tree is good to see, better to taste and offers a sort of pleasing wisdom. But, as Taylor himself rightly notices, there is a malaise within modernity that is produced by modernity. It is the toxins coming from the core alerting us to the fact that something is not right in Denmark. George Grant often spoke about the 'intimations of deprival' that the most sensitive feel that have tasted the fruit from the Hegelian Eden tree. It is such symptoms, felt and articulated, by the best and brightest, that should warn us about the deeper problems at the heart and core of the liberal project. Most of the battles in the culture wars are more about the type and form of liberalism to be defended rather than a questioning of the foundations of liberalism itself.

The political and cultural left, centre and right merely tap into various aspects of Hegelian liberalism. There are few that have summoned forth the magus from his hidden chambers and dared to both challenge and break the spell of such a centuries old wizard. George Grant was one of the few in Canada to do this. Charles Taylor does not, and he is the dutiful and faithful servant of the magus. The future of Canada and our attitude to the New Romans hinges on who we hear and why.

CHAPTER EIGHTEEN

GEORGE GRANT AND GAD HOROWITZ: THE RED TORY DIALOGUE

Since the tory and socialist minds have some crucial assumptions, orientations, and values in common, there is a positive affinity between them. From certain angles they may appear not as enemies, but as two different expressions of the same basic ideological outlook. This helps to explain the Canadian phenomenon of the *red tory*. At the simplest level, he is a tory who prefers the socialists to the liberals, or a socialist who prefers the tories to the liberals, without really knowing why. At a higher level, he is a conscious ideological tory with some 'odd' socialist notions (R. B. Bennett, Alvin Hamilton) or a conscious ideological socialist with some 'odd' tory notions (Eugene Forsey). At the very highest level, he is a philosopher who combines elements of socialism and toryism so thoroughly in a single integrated *Weltanschauung* that it is impossible to say that he is a proponent of either one or the other. Such a red tory is George Grant of McMaster University, author of *Lament for a Nation: The Defeat of Canadian Nationalism* [1965]. — Gad Horowitz[1]

Yet what is socialism, if it is not the use of the government to restrain greed in the name of the social good? In actual practice, socialism has always had to advocate inhibition in this respect. In doing so, was it not appealing to the conservative idea of social order against the liberal idea of freedom? — George Grant[2]

It is virtually impossible to walk the streets in the political public square without, sooner or later, hearing the language of Red Toryism. The language of Red Toryism is often toyed and played with by various journalists, political pundits and activists without much understanding of its source and shades of meaning. When did the language of Red Toryism enter the political vocabulary of Canadians and what are the points, in principle and content, of concord and discord between Red Toryism and socialism?

The Language of Red Toryism entered the political discourse of Canadians in 1965 when Gad Horowitz responded to George Grant's *Lament for a Nation* published in that year. Grant and Horowitz continued their dialogue from 1965 to 1970. This chapter will, all too briefly, discuss the nature of this dialogue and, by doing so, hopefully, clarify some points of misunderstanding.

Grant, in *Lament for a Nation*, never used the language of 'Red Tory', and he was always somewhat wary of how such a term was applied to him. But, there is no doubt that *Lament for a Nation* opens itself to such a dialogue. *Lament for a Nation* mourns how liberalism has become the dominant political philosophy in much of North America. This political tradition privileges the individual and subordinates the common good. The historic theorists of the tradition are the Puritans, Locke, Smith and clan. The American republic was founded on the inspiration and insight of these men, and this is what many Americans seek to conserve and what they call conservatism. Grant had argued this point in his 1957 CBC lectures that became *Philosophy in the Mass Age*.[3] *Lament for a Nation*, therefore, continued Grant's argument with and against liberalism and its notion of the autonomous individual. Grant appealed to an older political tradition that antedated and ran alongside liberalism. It is this older tradition that we call toryism, but Grant's toryism moved in a somewhat different direction than that of many conservatives. Grant appealed to the 'judicious Hooker', the feisty and satiric Swift and S. T. Coleridge as his guides and teachers in the fight against liberalism. Hooker, Swift and Coleridge, also, pointed back to the insights of Plato, Aristotle, Augustine and Aquinas. The worldview of such Classical, Patristic and Medieval political philosophers had little in common with that of the autonomous individual with little or no notion of boundaries. The self, in short, as a blank piece of paper and project that is made up as the journey goes along has little resonance with the tory tradition even though it is the creed and unquestioned dogma of liberalism. Grant argued, in *Lament for a Nation*, that Canada had absorbed and internalized an older English and French toryism, and, in doing so, it elevated the good of the whole over and against the rights of the individual. The Conservative Party from Macdonald to Diefenbaker held high these ideals, hence they, unlike the Liberals, resisted American attempts to colonize Canada and protected their unique way of life in the True North.

It was arguments like this, by Grant, that drew the ire of American-style Goldwater conservatives, but such an argument fascinated and attracted many within the New Left in Canada. Grant was appealing to an older political tradition that seemed to have many affinities with most of the concerns of the New Left. This was all most confusing for many. Most thought that socialism and liberalism had much more in common than conservatism and socialism. After all, didn't both liberalism and socialism share the principle of equality? But, the tale and drama is more complex the deeper the intellectual spade goes. Conservatism and socialism, even though they differ on the equality principle, both share the notion that the commonweal or the collective is more important than liberty and the holding high of such notions as individual rights. The older tory notion, in fact, like socialism, resists the liberal notion of the autonomous individual and liberty as an unquestioned and unquestionable good. It is these distinctions that drew Gad Horowitz to the dialogue. It is essential to note at this period in Canadian history that C. B. Macpherson had, a few years earlier, in 1962, published *The Political Theory of Possessive Individualism.* Macpherson had, in this important work of English political theory, made it quite clear that liberalism had, from Hobbes, the Levellers, Harrington and Locke, an 'underlying unity'. This unity, as the title of the book suggests, is the possessive, competitive, accumulating, market-driven, autonomous and atomistic individual. Macpherson's book had a pronounced impact on young scholars like Horowitz. It is equally interesting to note that one of the main inspirations for Macpherson was R. H. Tawney, who wrote *Religion and the Rise of Capitalism.* Tawney, like Grant, lamented what had happened with the coming of 'economic man' in the sixteenth and seventeenth centuries. So, there was much more in common between Tawney, Macpherson, Grant and Horowitz that needed to be probed and explored at the time within the Canadian context. The meaning and significance of Red Toryism hinged on such a dialogue.

Lament for a Nation was published in the winter of 1965. It did not take too long for Gad Horowitz to reply to Grant's controversial tract for the times. Grant, as I mentioned above, had never mentioned the term Red Tory in his missive. But, in May-June 1965, Horowitz had an article published in *Canadian Dimension.* Horowitz was teaching in the political science department at McGill University at the time, and he called his response 'Tories, Socialists and the

Demise of Canada'.[4] The burden of this article, for the most part, was to laud Grant's argument. Horowitz, in this timely essay, introduced the language of Red Toryism to the Canadian public. The term, obviously, was meant to do two things: it highlighted that there are two types of tories (red and blue), and, it sought to clarify what such a distinction meant. Horowitz argued that 'George Grant is also a socialist, a radical critic of the power elite of corporate capitalism, who would replace this society of competition and inequality with the co-operative commonwealth.'[5] There is little doubt that Horowitz, in his article, had a tendency to interpret Grant as a Red Tory, then he went on, almost to equate Red Toryism with socialism. This move, of course, Grant would never make. Horowitz, though, to be fair, ends the article by saying, 'a tory past contains the seeds of a socialist future.'[6] Horowitz, in this article, is doing some interesting things; he is arguing that socialists have, in many ways, more in common with red tories than with liberals, hence socialists should spend more time with Grantian type red tories than with liberals. Grant, though, might reply that socialists are crypto-tories, and the more socialists veer away from tory principles the more liberal and modern they become. In short, the content poured into such compelling slogans as liberty, equality and fraternity (solidarity) can mean very different things for a red tory, socialist, blue tory and liberal. In fact, for most tories, such principles do not pilot the ship of political discourse even though, in a nuanced way, they are factored into the dialogue.

Horowitz, in 1966, built up his argument in a most sophisticated manner. 'Conservatism, Liberalism, and Socialism in Canada: An Interpretation'[7] is now a must read for most students interested in the history of Canadian political theory. There are, obviously, many who agree and disagree with the argument, but it is essential to absorb and internalize if one ever hopes to understand why and how Canada is different from the Americans even though we, obviously, have much in common. Horowitz argued that since Canada did not break away from England in the same revolutionary way the Americans did, we still have a tory touch to us. It is true that both liberalism and conservatism emanated from England, but our nation, as its founding vision congealed, maintained a tension with toryism–conservatism in a way that the United States did not. It is in this tension that we, as Canadians, are quite different, but, as we become more American and liberal, this tory touch and this Red Toryism is dissolving like a cloud. Horowitz, then, like Grant, is interpreting Canadian history in a way that clearly highlights how and why we are different from the empire to the south of us and why we need to remember from whence we have come. If we forget our epic tale and drama, we will just be absorbed into the melting pot to the south.

The publication, in 1970, of William Kilbourn's *Canada: A Guide to the Peaceable Kingdom* again sought to interpret what it means to be a Canadian. Horowitz's article 'Red Tory'[8] and Grant's 'To Be a Citizen in North America' opened up some of the emerging points of divergence between Grant, Horowitz and the New Left. Grant walked the extra mile to affirm the best of the New Left, but he, also, argued that their idealism often did not take account of the sheer power of liberalism and technology. This did not mean, Grant argued, that cynicism, apathy and a retreat from politics should be the order of the day. Grant said:

> I am not advocating inaction or cynicism. I do not deny for one moment the nobility of protest or that justice is good and that injustice is evil and that it is required of human beings to know the difference between the two. To live with courage in the world is always better than retreat or disillusion. Human beings are less than themselves when they are cut off from being citizens. Indeed one of the finest things about the present protest movements in North America is that they try to give meaning to citizenship in a society which by its enormity and impersonality cuts people off from the public world.[9]

Canadian Dimension published 'Horowitz and Grant Talk' in 1969-1970.[10] Both men agreed on many things. Both men clarified in more depth and detail what they felt was the aggressive, will to power and dehumanizing nature of much technology. Both men clarified, in more depth and detail, distinctions to be made within the New Left. Grant critiqued the way the New Left tended to be both utopian and naive about such notions as progress; in this sense, they were very much insulated and late nineteenth century liberals.

Grant never shared, like Marcuse and other American Marxists, the credo that technology, when properly applied, would take us into a better world. In fact, technology imprisons us. Grant insisted that 'Marxism is, after all, a part of the modern experiment, and what I'm questioning is the whole of the modern experiment.'[11] Horowitz, of course, was keener on Marcuse and much of the hopes and dreams of the New Left in a way that Grant's older view of things would not allow. Grant, of course, spotted the deeper attitudinal liberalism in Horowitz, and he refused to walk the path of liberal hope and progress. Grant used the sword of Nietzsche to parry and thrust with Marcuse. Grant, in doing so, was making a turn to a much older conservative worldview. Horowitz was not quite sure he could or would follow the aristocratic radicalism of Nietzsche. Grant, of course, would not only hike down this path, but he would engage Nietzsche, Heidegger, think through their strengths–limitations and emerge a much deeper tory as a result of it.

Grant's toryism was most nuanced and complex; he was a philosopher of a high order. Horowitz was right, it seems to me, when he recognized that toryism and socialism have much in common, but the tory notion of natural law and the classical virtues makes it clear that equality of opportunity and condition are important as a start, but much effort, work and discipline are needed for noble deeds to be done, and often, the heroic and epic individual acts like the prophet and gadfly to the people. Grant's turn to religion—his involvement in the Anglican Church and interest in the Orthodox tradition—sets him apart from many socialists who are more secularist. Grant would not see either the state or politics as the final and ultimate end of what it means to be human. The turn to the role of thinking, the contemplative way and life in the parish all play a significant role in distinguishing the toryism of Grant from Horowitz's socialism. Socialism, it must be clear, participates deeply in the modern project, and, as Grant argued above, he comes as a critic, root and branch of liberal modernity. The fact that Grant turned to the English tory heritage as a guide meant that such principles as liberty, equality, and fraternity needed to be interrogated and brought before the dock. Is there more to human nature, its purposes and ends than is given us in the liberal modern project? Interestingly enough, these sorts of questions sounded in Charles Taylor's article, at the time, 'The Agony of Economic Man'.[12]

The Grant–Horowitz Red Tory dialogue continues to go on. There are many such as Janet Ajzenstat and David Warren (former editor of *The Idler*) who think Horowitz has misinterpreted Grant to serve his socialist impulses and interests; methinks they protest too loud.[13] Ajzenstat and Warren, obviously, interpret what they prefer in Grant to serve their agenda. Grant, of course, is a much grander and fuller human being than those tribalists who would use him to serve their interests. If Horowitz is right in arguing that Grant is a Red Tory, even though Grant was hesitant about using such a term, it is important that we further clarify what Red Toryism is in principle and content, and how such a notion is different from blue toryism, socialism and liberalism. The dialogue between Horowitz and Grant from 1965 to 1970 opened up the issue; we now need, as we have moved into the next century, to further clarify what such distinctions mean and the consequences of such distinctions in the hurly-burly of political activism. We do need, though, to be grateful to Gad Horowitz for introducing the language of Red Toryism to us, for engaging with George Grant on such a topical and timely issue and for highlighting some important points of convergence between Red Toryism and socialism. The future of the dialogue will hinge on what we mean when we speak the language of tory (red and blue), liberal and socialist. We can, of course, play fast and loose with such language, but, when push comes to shove on the stage of serious political choices, clarity is essential. When there is a lack of clarity, much misunderstanding often occurs and many inflated expectations deflate into vanishing dreams and disappearing hopes—this is the last thing that is needed if we ever hope to educate Canadians about what it means to be an active citizen in the public place.

CHAPTER NINETEEN

THE ANGLICAN TRADITION AND THE RED TORY WAY

I have tried to think through the usage of the terms 'Tory' and 'Conservative' in an absolute sense, because I am often vexed by the casual use of them. I think we should agree to something like these definitions: 1) Toryism is the political expression of a religious view of life. 2) Conservatism is an attempt to maintain Toryism after you have lost your faith. 3) Progressive Conservatism is an attempt to maintain conservatism after you have lost your memory, too. Put another way, conservatism is just Toryism after a haemorrhage; or Toryism in a passive, modest, self-conscious, unsatisfying and self-defeating form. — David Warren[1]

The Anglican tradition is, almost, two thousand years old, hence it has had much time to think clearly and fully about the relationship of religion and politics. Anglicans have often been called Tories at prayer, and this comment has often been made in a biting manner. But, there might be much more to this comment than we suspect. If we ever hope to understand the Red–Blue Tory distinctions and the historical reasons for such distinctions, we need to understand the Anglican tradition. What can it mean and what has it meant to suggest that Anglicans are Tories at prayer?

There are three ways in which the Anglicans as Tories at prayer can be interpreted. First, Tories can mean the upper class, the landed aristocracy, those who have been born to privilege, rank, title and family pedigree; such people tend to see themselves as the natural rulers with a noble obligation to one and all, to protect, in short, the common good of the nation. When most people think of Toryism, this is what comes to mind. Needless to say, such an attitude and its outworkings has had many a distortion and abuse, but the seeds of Red Toryism linger within this tradition.

The second understanding of Toryism is more connected to the Reformation, the Puritans, the Glorious Revolution of 1688 of William and Mary, Locke, the liberals and Burke. It is important to note that the seeds of Blue Toryism can be found in this newer tradition. The second interpretation of Toryism is much more about the ascendency of the middle class. The middle class sought to support such notions as the work ethic and vocation, a market economy, the rights of the individual to choose their way in religion and economics as they saw fit. Religion and capitalism, with some qualifications, were much more compatible within such a framework of thinking. This second interpretation is much closer to what we might call conservatism within the American tradition. It is, probably, helpful to distinguish between Tories and Conservatives, and the ideas listed above just might assist in such a process. C. B. Macpherson's *The Political Theory of Possessive Individualism* is a foundational and must-read book for those interested in the historic Blue Tory liberal way on such contentious issues as the market, competition, the state and property–possessions.

There is, though, a third understanding of what it means to be a Tory that is often missed. Tories have a great respect for history and tradition, but the question soon becomes whose interpretation of history will be the canonized and accepted one? We need to follow further this track. It is in this third understanding of what it means to be a Tory that the Red Tory lineage can be found. The English tradition has seen, time and time again, revolts and dissidence from within the labouring, working and peasant class. It would be foolish, of course, to idealize or slip into a simplistic class analysis, but, at the heart of the many of these uprisings, has been a cry and plea for justice for the commonweal and the role and responsibility of the state and church in ensuring such a reality exists for one and all. It is important to note that within such a radical reading of Toryism the role of leadership is not based on wealth, land, entrepreneurial abilities, possessions or property; it is rooted in those fitted by nature or God to bring about the just kingdom.

When, then, we hear that the Anglican tradition can be likened to Tories at prayer, we need to ask ourselves what interpretation of Toryism will we accept and why? It will be my contention, in the remainder of this chapter, to argue that it is in this more radical reading that we can find the source, fount and roots of Red Toryism; such a position can be found, and its economic, political and social outworking can be spaciously discovered, within the Anglican tradition (past and present).

If then, we hear the comment that Anglicans are Tories at prayer, we need to ask what kind of Tories? Let me, all too briefly, skim the waters of English history to highlight my point. It should be noted, though, that the Anglican tradition has been very much part of the establishment within English history. This does not mean, though, that there has not been constant friction between monarchs and archbishops, squires and bishops, tax collectors and priests, the wealthy and the people. It has often been the role and responsibility of the Anglican tradition to speak up for the people when the state would drive a deeper wedge between the wealthy and the poor.

We could start our reading of Anglican history earlier, but 1381 is a good place to begin; this was the year the Peasants Revolt took place. The Peasants Revolt was led by many clergy who, only too clearly, saw the tale of two cities growing ever worse and wider. The Peasants Revolt, unlike Tyndale and the Lollards, never sought to overthrow the historic institutions of church and state; they sought to purge them of their injustices. Langland's *Piers Ploughman*, also, stood by the side of the ploughman but in such a way that avoided the temptation of the emerging protestant way. It is true that significant elements of state and church opposed such movements, but the fact that such movements rose and spoke forth speaks about another way of interpreting and reading what it might mean to be a Tory. More's *Utopia* in the sixteenth century tells its own compelling tale just as Swift's Toryism had little patience for the emerging middle class with their captains of industry and philistine values. Coleridge, Southey and Wordsworth turned to the inspiration of the Peasants Revolt in the late eighteenth century when they penned their inspirational tracts for the times. The Tory tradition in the nineteenth century, inevitably so, faced the challenges of Marxism and socialism, and it is significant to note that many radical Anglo-Catholics were most drawn to various elements of such a challenge. The Marxist–socialist emphasis on economics, the commongood, changing rather than merely interpreting history and making a state that responded to the people was basic to the radical Anglo-Catholic agenda of Ludlow, Headlam, Noel, Marson, Dolling and many others. The nineteenth and twentieth centuries saw the Anglican tradition, in a significant way, heed the older Catholic way about the commonweal and the role of the church and state in protecting such a good. The forming of the Jubilee Network in 1974 continued such a vision; Margaret Thatcher viewed such an Anglican group as the most dangerous in all of England. 'The Red Dean of Canterbury' carried on an old tradition in which the radical or Red Tory way had much support.

It is as we turn to two leading Anglo-Catholic theologians of the twentieth century, Eric Mascall and Archbishop Ramsey, that we can see how and why such thinkers and activists did not turn against the older English notion of the commongood and commonweal. Both Mascall and Ramsey were most supportive and involved with groups in England such as the Church Socialist League, the League of the Kingdom of God and the lively publication *Christendom*. The oft quoted comment by Bishop Frank Weston remained a banner for such people: 'You cannot claim to worship Jesus in the Tabernacle, if you do not pity Jesus in the slum'.[2] Men like Mascall, Ramsey, Reckitt and many other Anglo-Catholics were at the forefront of much political activism in their day, and, in many ways, they continued the radical perspective of Ludlow, Headlam, Dearmer and Noel. Mascall and Ramsey, also, were at the forefront of dialogue with the Orthodox tradition; such a dialogue opened up thinking to the best of Greek and Russian Christianity; it is from within such a tradition that such notions as mystical theology and nationalism find a fit focus. It is interesting to note at this point that George Grant was drawn via Simone Weil to the good in Greek Christianity. Grant, as a Canadian Anglican, in many ways, carried on the work of Mascall and Ramsey within the Canadian context. Grant's article 'In Defence of Simone Weil'[3] and Lawrence Schmidt's article, 'George Grant on Simone Weil as Saint and Thinker'[4] take us into the centre and heartland of why the more radical Greek reading of Christianity might just give us a better understanding of the relationship of spirituality and politics, nationalism and justice. Canadians, such as Grant, then drew both deeply from the English tradition and much of the Greek tradition that many Anglo-Catholics such as Mascall and Ramsey were so fond of supporting. Therefore, the more we probe the English tradition, the more we are taken inevitably back to the classical tradition of Plato–Aristotle and the Patristics. This is the path that George Grant, guided by the wise hand of Simone Weil would have us walk. It is significant to note in all this that it is an Orthodox Archbishop (Archbishop Lazar of the Orthodox Church in America) that has played such an important role in furthering the Red Tory cause in Canada; Grant would be most pleased with all the connections made both in thought and deed.

It is this English–Anglican tradition, with its different interpretations of what it means to be a Tory, that has had such an impact on the Canadian heritage. We, as Canadians, did not break from the fullness of the English way as did the empire to the south. We have, in fact, a DNA or genetic code within us that is much more concerned about the good of the nation, the organic relationship between the citizen, society and the state, the limitations of the market and protecting our own. There is little doubt that there was a nationalist bent within the English heritage, and the church and state worked together to protect the identity of such a heritage. We, in Canada, need not do the English thing, but there are elements within the English Tory tradition that transcend the English ethos.

It needs to be noted, though, that a great break took place in the West between AD 1400 and AD 1700. This did much to shape and redefine what it meant to be a Tory and Anglican. The fact that Canada did not emerge, formally, as a nation until 1867 meant that we were tugged and pulled in different directions. The Blue Tory way of thinking, obviously, made many inroads into the fledgling state. But, the much older notion of Toryism did not vanish. In fact, it continued to work its way into the fabric of this country. We can see this most clearly in many decisions taken by the historic Conservative Party from Macdonald to Diefenbaker.

The fact that the English tradition has had such a substantive impact on most of Canadian political, economic, social, religious and cultural history means that we cannot avoid the Tory touch. The fact that the Anglican tradition is intimately interconnected with the English Tory way cannot be ignored. The fact that both have shaped the Canadian way of life needs to be probed much deeper and further. If, Anglicans are Tories at prayer, what kind of Tories do we mean? Who are some of the Canadians who have drawn deeply from the English Tory tradition and made sense of it in the True North? We must, of course, be clear that the Red and Blue traditions have had their contentious points of difference, and these points of difference have shaped both the Conservative Party and the Anglican tradition within Canada.

The fact that the more entrepreneurial Blue Tory tradition began and matured between AD 1400 and AD 1700 meant that Canada could not help but be shaped by this tradition. I would suggest, and I think as a general statement there is much truth to it, that Low Church Anglicans (Reformed–Evangelical) tend to be more Blue Tory and the High Church Anglicans (Catholic) tend to be more Red Tory. The Broad Church (liberals) tend to waffle in different directions. The fact that the High Church tradition begins with what we share in common, our need to protect such a shared inheritance and the role of church and state in doing so means that the individual, the marketplace and possessions–property are not privileged. Also, the ascetic tradition within the High Church way comes as a radical critique of the accumulation of property.

This High Church–Red Tory, Low Church–Blue Tory distinction is played out quite clearly in two examples on the west coast. Leon Ladner and the Ladner family played a significant role in building up British Columbia and the Progressive Conservative Party. Many within the Ladner family were Anglicans, but they were Anglicans of a Blue Tory bent. Those who have attended the University of British Columbia are quite familiar with the Ladner Tower that reminds us of the march of time; it is positioned and poised between the two libraries. Leon Ladner's book *The Ladners of Ladner: By Covered Wagon to the Welfare State* tells its own interpretive tale about what it means to be a Blue Tory. The active and enterprising Ladners are held high as models of good Canadian citizens. It is important to note that the Ladner family were good friends with a significant and most controversial Anglican clergyman, Edward Cridge. Cridge was the chaplain to the Hudson Bay Company, and he locked horns so firmly and strenuously with his bishop, George Hills (1816–1895), that he left the Anglican Church to start his own schismatic Anglican community. The Ladners and Cridge very much represent the Blue Tory tradition whereas Hills stood within the more High Church Catholic way. I raised this point, and there are many other illustrations I could use to point out that when we think of Anglicans as Tories at prayer, we need to know whether we are meaning, high, low or broad church Anglicans; the differences do reflect different attitudes towards the individual, the market, business, the state and property–possessions. Those who have been breastfed and nourished from both within the Anglican and Conservative Party are only too aware of these distinctions and the different paths such distinctions take one down.

The impact on Canada of the Red–Blue Tory way both within the Anglican tradition and the Conservative Party has been immense; everything hangs on how AD 1400–1700 is interpreted. The Anglican Red Tory way finds fit and firm expression, in Canada, in the life and writings of Stephen Leacock, George Grant, Donald Creighton, W. L. Morton (1908–1980), Robert Stanfield (1914–2003) and William Christian (b. 1945); these men, and many others, have sought to maintain some of the religious-political principles that take Canada down a different path than the Blue Tory tradition. When we hear that Anglicans are Tories at prayer, we need not jump to too hasty a conclusion; there is much more both to what it means to be a Tory and Anglican than at first appears. The open-minded and curious will find a mother lode if they have the courage to follow the nuggets along the stream bed to the source.

CHAPTER TWENTY

STEPHEN LEACOCK AND T. S. ELIOT: A MEETING OF MINDS

Stephen Leacock is known, by most Canadians, as an important literary humourist (with a gentle Swiftian bite) and as a political economist. Most do not realize that Leacock wrote some fine books on Canadian history and literary criticism. Many know T. S. Eliot as an incisive and demanding poet, literary critic and dramatist. Both Leacock and Eliot, though, were grounded in a classical High Tory Anglican way (this is often conveniently ignored by most). It was from such deeper historic places that there was a meeting of minds. Both men had an affinity for the best that had been thought, said and done in the past and the ongoing relevance of such permanent things to the malaise and ethos of their times.

Leacock brought together a collection of timely essays on education, literature, politics, morality and history in 1916—the book, *Essays and Literary Studies*, sold well, and, true to form, went after the strange gods of the era. *Essays and Literary Studies* was neatly divided into nine inviting and charming chapters: 1) The Apology of a Professor, 2) The Devil and the Deep Sea, 3) Literature and Education in America, 4) American Humour, 5) The Woman Question, 6) The Lot of the Schoolmaster, 7) Fiction and Reality, 8) The Amazing Genius of O. Henry, and 9) A Rehabilitation of Charles II.

Each of the essays brims with gracious yet insightful criticisms of the emerging liberalism at the turn of the twentieth century and the consequences of uncritically doffing the cap to such a creed and dogma. In each of the chapters, Leacock probes and plies his literary and historical trade, doing what he can to find a centre that can and will hold. A Tory is, above all, in search of the solid, permanent and sound things and the application of such principles to the fleeting world of time and history. *Essays and Literary Studies* is on a quest to find a worthy ship to sail across the turbulent and oft uncharted waters of time. Leacock has, true to form, an uncanny and puckish habit of making us see by coaxing us into laughter. The moral and metaphysical quest, in short, is always served up on the plate of good stories and laughter holding both its sides. Leacock, in this sense, has much affinity with Chaucer's *The Canterbury Tales* and Erasmus's *The Praise of Folly*.

T. S. Eliot (1888–1965) was a younger contemporary of Leacock (1869–1944), but he was drawn to Leacock. Peter Ackroyd, in his biography, *T. S. Eliot: A Life*, said, '1915 was the year which marked the beginning of his career as a poet'.[1] Eliot saw into and through the wasteland of the modern world, and he was ever in search, like Leacock, of something that would and could slake the thirst for meaning. Much of Eliot's early poetry and prose both exposes the emptiness and mirages of modern thought and culture, and, equally so, points the way to the places of soul rest and refreshment on our short and all too human journey. *Essays and Literary Studies*, as I mentioned above, was published in 1916, and it was at this time that Eliot was doing a book review for *The New Statesman*—Leacock was forty-seven at the time and Eliot was twenty-eight. Eliot turned to Leacock's *Essays and Literary Studies* with much interest and delight, and, in many ways, he found in Leacock an elder Tory brother and kindred spirit.

The New Statesman has a review by Eliot of Leacock's *Essays and Literary Studies*. The review is positive and supportive, and there is nary a critical word written. Eliot saw in Leacock someone who was further down the path and who spoke what needed to be said to a culture that was losing its way, compass and north star. In fact, Eliot thought that Leacock was one of the few writers and activists in North America that still embodied an older and deeper grasp of the important things. Eliot says in the review, 'There are few writers in America who share Mr. Leacock's views'.[2] Both Leacock and Eliot were aware that what they stood for was passing away, was being clear-cut like the ancient forests, and they knew that serious cultural, social, economic and political problems would arise when the forests of old had been slashed and burned. Both men stood like sentinels and guardians of a way of life, thinking and education that was about to be destroyed by the juggernaut of an ideological liberalism.

Leacock and Eliot have often, in the more popular understanding, been reduced to literary critics or writers of poems, plays or novels. Both men were much more than such a limited understanding of them. Both men, for different reasons, lived from the depth and fullness of the Anglican way. Such a tradition (as a magisterial way), at its noblest and best, is committed to the commonweal of the people and the role of state and society in bringing into being such a commonwealth. Leacock taught in the department of political economy all his teaching life at McGill University, and he was an unflagging conscience of the Conservative Party when it veered to the blue tory right-of-centre on the political spectrum. Eliot was no different. Eliot served on a variety of committees after he moved to England that articulated how and why church, state and society should work together, in an organic way, for the good of the country. Just as Leacock lauded Archbishop William Temple's political vision in one of his final books, *While There Is Time: The Case against Social Catastrophe*, Eliot worked closely with Archbishop Temple's political and economic insights (largely inspired by R. H. Tawney[3]) after World War II. Leacock and Eliot, therefore, never separated their interests in literature, culture and religion from the pressing social, economic and political issues of their time. The connections between Leacock and Eliot have often been ignored, but their High Tory Anglican affinities cannot be denied, and Eliot's review of *Essays and Literary Studies* offers us hints and pointers about a meeting of minds.

Leacock and Eliot, like prophets of old, spoke against the thinness and errant ways of the ethos of their day and pointed the way to a fuller clearing. Eliot, by disposition, was more sober and serious than Leacock (although even he had his puckish side). Leacock saw the darkness much as Eliot did but humour was his weapon to ward it off. The perennial twinkle in Leacock's eyes spoke both sunshine and sadness and neither dominated the day (although they often competed to do so). Eliot scholars rarely if ever compare Leacock and Eliot. Leacock scholars simply never discuss the affinities between Leacock and Eliot. There is little doubt that Leacock's *Essays and Literary Studies* and Eliot's review of the book in *The New Statesman* is a good place to begin. Such a meeting of minds can and will tell us much about a Tory way of being that we ignore to our cultural, intellectual and political peril. It was the passing away of such a time-tried vision that George Grant lamented in *Lament for a Nation*. Those who sense what Grant called 'intimations of deprival' or what Charles Taylor called the 'malaise of modernity' can find much insight and wisdom in searching out such issues in the writings of Leacock, Eliot and Grant.

SECTION V

THE ANGLICAN CHURCH: TORIES AT PRAYER

CHAPTER TWENTY-ONE

THE CANADIAN HIGH TORY ANGLICAN TRADITION: BISHOP JOHN STRACHAN, STEPHEN LEACOCK, GEORGE GRANT

But there are remnants left around me … very strange remnants … in this case the Anglican Church which has in it some of the ancient truth and therefore I will live within it. — George Grant[1]

Introduction

There has been a regrettable tendency within the authorized reading of Canadian history (to quote Donald Creighton) to demean, caricature and distort the unique and distinctive Canadian High Tory way and idealize and uncritically genuflect to the liberal interpretation of the origins, development and contemporary ethos of Canadian life. Such an approach to understanding the Canadian tradition censors out the significant contributions of High Toryism to Canadian religion and public life.

There are those who, when studying the Anglican heritage, focus on Anglican spirituality, theology, exegesis, ecclesiology, liturgy, literature, pastoral responsibilities, clerical–lay–parish life, sacraments, significant documents–landmark texts, councils–creeds and ecumenical and interfaith commitments. This approach to understanding the Anglican tradition is a necessary but insufficient way of entering the fullness of the Anglican fold. There is a comprehensiveness to the time-tried Anglican path that engages the larger cultural, political and public spheres, hence the magisterial–kingdom aspect of Anglicanism—if this element of Anglicanism is ignored or marginalized, a serious domesticating and thinning out of the Anglican heritage occurs.

There is also the danger when telling the Anglican tale to overdo the English roots and virtually miss the obvious fact that different states and jurisdictions have their own unique histories. The drama of Canadian High Tory Anglicanism has often been omitted from many books on Canadian Anglicanism, and this chapter will attempt to fill in some of the obvious gaps and blind spots.

I will, in this chapter, begin with Bishop John Strachan, move onto Stephen Leacock, then conclude with George Grant. There have been many misreads of Strachan from the liberal authorized historians in Canada who curtly dismiss Strachan and the Family Compact as irrelevant and regressive—such an approach misses Strachan's deeper insights about the drift in American thought and the impact of American thought and life on Canadian public life. Strachan was a High Tory nationalist who understood, all too clearly, the dangers to Canadian public life and society if the American republican way came to dominate. Bishop John Strachan often visited Susan Sibbald and the Sibbald family at Eildon Hall at Jackson's Point at the southern shore of Lake Simcoe in Ontario— Susan Sibbald wrote about such visits in her vivacious and insightful *Memoirs*. Susan Sibbald played a significant role in the building of St. George's Anglican parish in the Eildon Hall area in 1838.

Stephen Leacock grew up in the Sutton and Sibbald Point environs, and his mother knew the Sibbald family quite well (as did Leacock). Both Susan Sibbald and Leacock's mother formed a bridge between the era of Bishop John Strachan and the next phase of Anglican High Toryism in Canada. Leacock attended Upper Canada College (an Anglican school in Toronto), became head boy for a time and did his PhD on 'The Doctrine of Laissez Faire' at the University of Chicago.[2] Leacock taught in the political economy department at McGill University from 1901 to 1936, he was one of the foremost humourists and political theorists in Canada, his Anglicanism cannot be missed in his writings and he is buried at St. George's Anglican parish—the Archbishop of Canada (Derwyn Owen) took Leacock's funeral in 1944. Leacock Hall at McGill University was named after Stephen Leacock for his contributions to Canadian educational, literary, political, economic and religious life.

George Grant, like Stephen Leacock, did his early schooling at Upper Canada College (where his father was the principal). Grant continued his studies at Queen's University (where his grandfather was once the president). Grant emerged in the latter half of the twentieth century as one of the most prominent public intellectuals in Canada—he also founded the religious studies department at McMaster University (Hamilton, Ontario) which has become one of the largest undergraduate and graduate departments of religious studies in North America. Grant (and his wife Sheila) was active in his local parish in Dundas (near Hamilton) and Grant wrote often about larger issues of modern secularism and the need to recover the sacred. Grant was, without much doubt, the most important Anglican in Canada in his lifetime, and when he did his PhD at Oxford, he was quite active with the Socratic Club of which C. S. Lewis (another Anglican) was the leading light.

The trilogy of Bishop John Strachan, Stephen Leacock and George Grant stands within, in many ways, a distinctive and unique Canadian High Tory Anglican way, and for the rest of this chapter, I will highlight how this is the case.

Bishop John Strachan

John Strachan was born in 1778 in Scotland to a working class family. The fact that his earliest religious upbringing was Scottish Presbyterian meant he began his faith journey within the fold of Calvinism. Such a position did not hold him as he aged and matured, but Calvinist theology and Presbyterian ecclesiology was the first form of Christianity Strachan encountered as a young man. Strachan had a definite interest in being educated and being an educator and this was evident when still in Scotland. Strachan in his later teens became a tutor to younger students, and in 1799 at the age of twenty-one moved to Upper Canada.

Strachan's move to Kingston in Upper Canada put him in immediate touch with the emerging British Loyalist leadership in the area that came to be known as the Family Compact. Again, Strachan was a tutor to many of the children of the Loyalists and his commitment to education brought him to the forefront in Kingston and Cornwall. The fact that many of the Loyalists that were part of the Family Compact were also Anglican meant that Strachan began in a shift in his thinking at both theological and ecclesial levels. It was this significant transition that was, in time, to position him as one of the most significant Anglican churchmen, educators and public leaders in the fledging years of pre-Confederation life in Canada.

Strachan was ordained as an Anglican priest in 1803 when twenty-five years of age and his commitment to both his parish and the broader educational and public life in Kingston–Cornwall and beyond began to wax in significance. The increasing impact of republicanism across the fragile border (and its ripple effect in Upper–Lower Canada) was something that Strachan and the Family

Compact were concerned about. The deeper concerns, though, were theological, philosophical and the outworking of both in the areas of politics and public life. Strachan, like many Family Compact Anglicans, saw in the fractious disputes to the south a form of liberty and individualism that would lead, just as the Protestant Reformation had done, to fragmentation, conflict and violence. The class clashes and tragic loss of life of the French and American revolutions could not be missed and Strachan lived closer than most to the reality of such warlike ways of solving differences. Strachan was committed to a more ordered and stable way of challenging the path the French and Americans had taken in bringing change.

The War of 1812 was a crossroads period in Strachan's life. The invasion from the south confirmed the worst fears of the Loyalists, Family Compact and Strachan. The ideas of republicanism that had emerged within Puritan Calvinism were now taking an aggressive and military form in Upper Canada. Many in Upper Canada saw in the War of 1812 the coming to be of the French and American revolutions in what was to become Canada. The point to note here, and that is often missed, is that Strachan was defending a classical tory tradition (or a form of tory nationalism) in opposing a revolutionary way of bringing a just political order into being. Again, it was the principles of liberal republicanism and the military means of actualizing such principles that Strachan and the Family Compact opposed. We can see in such an approach to change the historic Canadian moderate way of peace, order and good government.

Strachan realized, only too keenly, that education was essential to raising up a new generation of leaders who would be committed to life in the church and politics. The highly integrated and holistic position of Strachan in the areas of education, politics and church life was opposed by those who were more inclined to keep the church out of politics, the sacred far from the profane and secular. Strachan thought that such a move would distort, tame and domesticate the fuller vision of what the faith journey was meant to be.

The outbreak of cholera in 1832 and 1834 that killed almost one-twelfth of the population in Upper Canada again drew forth Strachan's leadership abilities—it was Strachan at his compassionate and kindly best. Strachan worked tirelessly to aid the victims of the epidemic and his founding of the Society for the Relief of the Orphan, Widow and Fatherless provided aid and support for many in dire need.

The rise of the Anglo-Catholic movement in England in 1832, led by Pusey, Keble and Newman drew and held Strachan. There was an Anglo-Canadian form of catholic Anglicanism that Strachan played a significant role in heralding and leading. The Anglican middle way between Roman Catholicism and various types of Methodist and protestant schismatic types was the position that Strachan attempted to chart and plot forward for Canadian Anglicans. This meant, to some degree, offended Low Church Anglicans that had some affinity with their reformed, evangelical and charismatic brothers and sisters. There was, in a sense, something quite Laudian about Strachan—he was, in many ways, the Canadian William Laud in an era and ethos in which the classical Anglican catholic and tory way was waning. The overwhelming ideology of liberalism had taken hold in North America and an older way of understanding and living the faith was being systematically clear-cut. Strachan saw, only too clearly, what was occurring and more significantly, what would occur, as such an agenda unfolded.

The disagreement between two religious and political ideologies came to a stark clash in the 1837 Upper Canada Rebellion—it was, in many ways, the arch-tory Strachan going head to head with the arch-liberal, William Lyon Mackenzie. Again, Strachan knew only too well what was at stake. Would Upper–Lower Canada (and other parts of the young nation) become an appendage to the ideals that dominated the south or could the north embody a more stable and peaceful way of bringing into being the common good? There can be no doubt the fiery Mackenzie was the flag bearer of American republican values (and the implications of them) just as Strachan stood for a more complex and complicated way in which Tory and Liberal, stability and change dwelt together in a mature tension. The Upper Canada Rebellion was put down and a form of responsible government emerged that was neither fully committed to Strachan nor Mackenzie.

John Strachan became the first bishop of Toronto in 1839 and his work as a churchman, educator and public figure continued. Strachan founded Trinity College in 1852 (after seeing what was to become the University of Toronto founded on more secular and pluralist principles). The life and ecclesial vision of Bishop John Strachan had much to do with St. James' parish and cathedral and for those interested in a thoughtful understanding of Strachan's often turbulent journey, *The Parish and Cathedral Church of St. James', Toronto 1797–1997* is amply worth the read.

Stephen Leacock

Bishop John Strachan spent many a fond hour at Eildon Hall located in what is now Sibbald Point Provincial Park. Sibbald Point Provincial Park was named after Susan Sibbald and the Sibbald family. The final chapter in Sibbald's must-read *The Memoirs of Susan Sibbald* has many a tender and touching comment on Bishop John Strachan.[3] Stephen Leacock grew up in the Sibbald Point area, his mother knew Susan Sibbald well and many a pleasant day was spent at Eildon Hall. Leacock is buried (interestingly enough) across from Mazo de la Roche (one of Canada's finest novelists—best known as the author of the *Jalna* series–*Whiteoak Chronicles*) in St. George's parish graveyard that was financed by Susan Sibbald. There is, therefore, a direct High Tory Anglican connection from Bishop John Strachan, to Susan Sibbald to Stephen Leacock.

I mentioned above that Archbishop Derwyn Owen (Primate of Canada from 1934 to 1947) took Stephen Leacock's funeral in 1944. My grandmother lived with the Owen family in the Archbishop's manse in Toronto in the 1940s until Derwyn Owen's death in 1947. We, as a family, also spent some summers in the Sibbald–Jackson Point areas—such splendid places. Mordecai Richler once said, 'Man cannot live by Leacock alone'.[4] The comment obviously reflects the significance of Leacock as a Canadian, political–literary humourist, educator, public figure and Anglican. Leacock was, in many ways, a softer and more moderate version of Strachan. Leacock (his grandfather on his mother's side was an Anglican priest) grew up in the High Tory ethos of Toronto–Sibbald Point, and he was acutely aware of both its appeal and limitations. Much of his life was an attempt to chart a thoughtful and engaged Tory Anglican way.

There has been an unfortunate tendency when reading and writing about Stephen Leacock to separate and fragment Leacock into various bits and pieces—there is Leacock the political economist who taught at McGill University from 1901 to 1936—there is Leacock the Canadian historian and political theorist—there is Leacock the humourist and literary critic—there is the Leacock who inspired the young T. S. Eliot (yet another Anglican). And, much to the surprise of many who reduce Leacock to a political economist and philosopher or literary humourist and critic, there is Leacock the Anglican (he is much more than merely a religious critic and sceptic, as some suggest). The deeper Anglican ethos runs like a subterranean stream through most of Leacock's writings and this has been missed by his many interpreters.

Leacock definitely established himself as an academic political economist with the publication of *Elements of Political Science* in 1906, but it was the publication of *Literary Lapses* and *Sunshine Sketches of a Little Town* in 1910 and 1912 that brought Leacock to the broader public stage. The humour and politics met and intermingled in these two books that won the hearts and minds of many in North America and England. Leacock had become a potent mix of Mark Twain and Charles Dickens, but there was also the probing Anglicanism of Leacock well at work in both *Sunshine Sketches of a Little Town* and its must-read companion novel, published in 1914, *Arcadian Adventures with the Idle Rich*. Leacock was, without much doubt, a Tory Anglican, but his brand of conservatism, like Strachan's, had a tender conscience towards the suffering and those on the margins, and he thought the state, church and society had to work together to relieve and end such injustices. It was this High Tory Anglicanism that deepened and broadened, softened and moderated Strachan's, at times, more reactionary Tory Anglicanism.

Leacock had a long line and lineage in the Anglican fold (he even encountered through his parents' few years in South Africa the controversial Bishop Colenso). The fact Leacock spent most of his formative years at Upper Canada College (with its strong Anglican presence) meant he had internalized the Anglican tradition (and its complex nature) in a way few laymen had done in as thoughtful or measured a manner.

The vision, public profile and ongoing presence of Leacock in Canadian educational, political, literary and religious life did much to shape and define the Canadian identity. When the depression occurred in the 1930s, it was Leacock, once again, who stood on front stage, prophetic-like, calling on the Canadian people and state to work together for the eradication of such a crisis and disproportion of wealth, poverty and power. Leacock's graphic writings on this period of North American history have been ably and wisely collected and published by Alan Bowker in *On the Front Line of*

Life: Stephen Leacock: Memories and Reflections, 1935–1944. Again, we can see in Leacock the High Tory Anglican conservative a passion for the people, a concern for the common good and the role of church, state and society in bringing to an end the tragic reality of the depression.

World War II brought to an end the depression of the 1930s, and Leacock was forced to retire from McGill University in 1936. The ever-creative and ever-engaged Leacock continued to ponder in his last few years the social reality that would emerge after World War II. The Archbishop of Canterbury from 1942 to 1944 was William Temple, and Temple's political position before, throughout and after World War II had a profound impact on Anglican thought and life, Leacock and the Primate of Canada at the time (Derwyn Owen). In fact, one of Leacock's final books, published after his death, *While There Is Time: The Case against Social Catastrophe* draws explicitly from the writings of Archbishop William Temple—'The Gathering Crises' in *While There Is Time,*[5] word for word in places, highlights the principles Temple had articulated, from an Anglican perspective, that should inform public life—the Beatitudes played the core ethical role in such an ecclesial commitment. In short, Leacock, Archbishop Temple and Archbishop Owen were all on the same page. It is quite understandable, therefore, why, when Leacock died, Owen presided over the funeral.

It is obvious why Leacock is buried at St. George's parish graveyard at the southern end of Lake Simcoe—his summer home was at the northern end of Lake Simcoe in Orillia. I have been, for many years, the political science advisor to the Leacock home and museum, in Orillia. I have, many times, driven the route from St. George's at Sibbald Point to Orillia and back. Leacock, as I mentioned above, knew well the High Tory Anglicanism of Bishop John Strachan and Susan Sibbald, but Leacock was less willing than the previous generation to castigate all things liberal and republican—there was nuance and subtleness in Leacock's Tory Anglicanism often missing in leaders of the Tory Anglicanism of the nineteenth century.

George Grant

When George Grant's father, William Lawson Grant, died in 1935, it was Stephen Leacock who assisted Maude Grant (George Grant's mother) in getting the position of warden of at Royal Victoria College, McGill University from 1937 to 1940. Leacock had been a student of William Lawson Grant when he taught at Upper Canada College from 1898 to 1904 (William Grant was the headmaster at Upper Canada College from 1917 to 1935). George Grant's mother (Maude) and sister (Margaret) studied with Stephen Leacock when they were at McGill also. There is an obvious line and lineage between Leacock and the Grant family and the deeper affinity has much to do with their Tory Anglicanism.

George Grant, when young, studied at Upper Canada College where his father was headmaster. Upper Canada College had, in its origins, a strong influence from Bishop Strachan—the Anglican presence and ethos could not be denied. Grant did his undergraduate degree at Queen's University (which his grandfather, as principal, had played a significant role in making a leading public university). Grant, like Strachan, began as a Presbyterian, but by 1956 Grant and his wife, Sheila, became Anglicans—Grant was teaching philosophy at the time at Dalhousie University in Halifax.

There can be little doubt that George Grant became, in the middle to latter half of the twentieth century, the most prominent Tory Anglican in Canada—his lectures on the Canadian Broadcasting Corporation in the 1950s (Northrop Frye was also emerging at this time as Canada's leading literary critic and was often on the Canadian Broadcasting Corporation) positioned Grant as the voice of a thoughtful conservative. The publication of *Philosophy in the Mass Age* in 1959 solidified Grant's reputation as a leading public intellectual in Canada, although many of his previous writings in the 1950s had dealt with theology, education and politics post-World War II. Grant's article on 'Adult Education in an Expanding Economy' was published in *The Anglican Outlook* in 1955[6]—the threading together of faith, education and public responsibility was something that Strachan, Leacock and Grant shared as Tory Anglicans—Leacock and Grant did this as laymen—Strachan as a bishop and churchman.

George Grant was initially hired as the first professor of the philosophy department at the fledgling York University in the early 1960s, but an ongoing clash with the chair of philosophy at the University of Toronto, Fulton Anderson, that had begun in the late 1940s when Grant dared to challenge Anderson led to Grant's resignation from York—Anderson had insisted that Grant use texts that undermined both Plato and Christianity. Grant was asked, shortly thereafter, to start the religious studies department at McMaster University.

The Grant family were quite active in the local Anglican parish when at McMaster and at larger diocesan and national levels. The fact that Grant had a decided High Tory leaning meant that he had ongoing concerns about the trendy drift within the Anglican Church of Canada towards an uncritical attitude about liberalism. When the General Board of Religious Education (GBRE) of the Anglican Church of Canada asked Pierre Berton (a lapsed Anglican and much-respected Canadian journalist) to do an assessment of the Anglican Church of Canada in 1963, few expected the publication of his book in 1965, *The Comfortable Pew: A Critical Look at Christianity and the Religious Establishment in the New Age*, would evoke such strong reactions. *The Comfortable Pew* was very much an apologia for the incoming trendy liberalism of the 1960s both in society and the church. It is significant that George Grant's *Lament for a Nation: The Defeat of Canadian Nationalism* was also published in 1965. There is an intellectual depth and breadth in *Lament for a Nation* decidedly lacking in *The Comfortable Pew*. Grant calls forth the pedigree of Hooker, Swift, Johnson and Coleridge (who stand on the shoulders of many who went before them) to buttress a notion of the Anglo-Canadian intellectual and political heritage that Berton has little understanding of. We can see, in a most obvious way, how the differences between Berton and Grant embody and reflect two paths (liberal and High Tory) the Anglican Church of Canada could have taken—Berton tended to be heeded more faithfully, and the Anglican Church of Canada has had to deal with the consequences of ignoring the more prophetic Grant.

It is somewhat telling that in Grant's review of a book on the history of St. James' Anglican parish in Dundas (where the Grant family attended), Grant holds high the role and significance of Bishop John Strachan in the building up and consolidating of the Anglican way in Ontario in the nineteenth century.[7] Strachan, like Grant, feared that the corrosive impact of liberalism would erode and undermine the richness and fullness of the Anglican tradition— Strachan faced the problem in its infant form in the nineteenth century—Grant confronted the fully grown and dominant adult form in the twentieth century.

There is so much more that could be said about George Grant as theologian, Biblical exegete, philosopher, educator, writer–lecturer, public intellectual and troubled thinker as an Anglican (who saw all too clearly and wisely how Canadian Anglicanism was being co-opted by an ideological liberalism at all levels of church and seminary life). Grant was, probably, the pre-eminent Canadian prophet in both church and society in the middle to latter years of the twentieth century.

Conclusion

Philip Carrington did much spade work in the late 1950s-early 1960s on unearthing the Canadian Anglican way: *The Anglican Church in Canada: A History* was published in 1963 to coincide with the large gathering of the Anglican Communion in Toronto for the Anglican Congress—Strachan is given, tentatively, his due and a nod—Leacock and Grant are absent. The more recent biography of Archbishop Ted Scott, *Radical Compassion: The Life and Times of Archbishop Ted Scott,* published in 2004, ignores Grant even though Grant thought that Scott was a good-hearted but unthinking devotee of *cause du jour* liberalism. The recent history of the Anglican Church of Canada, *Seeds Scattered and Sown: Studies in the History of Canadian Anglicanism,* published in 2008, tends to tip a wary hat to Strachan (most liberals within the church, academy and society view Strachan as a relic of a past Canadians need to bid adieu to)—Leacock and Grant are virtually absent from *Seeds Scattered and Sown.* We do need to ask, by way of conclusion, why such a read of Canadian and Anglican history dominates the way it predictably does. Why are three of the most prominent Canadians (better known than most Anglicans in church and public life) absent from the telling of the Anglican tale? The answer, in many ways, is most obvious—the liberal paradigm so dominates the day that an older High Tory tradition is submerged and marginalized. It is such a tradition, though, that can come as a prophetic corrective to the Liberal heritage that often silences other voices. The more a sane and wise read of Bishop John Strachan, Stephen Leacock and George Grant comes to the fore again, the more a mature understanding of the two-thousand-year-old Anglican Church will fully reveal itself.

CHAPTER TWENTY-TWO

GEORGE GRANT
AND THE ANGLICAN CHURCH OF CANADA:
A TWENTIETH CENTURY PROPHET

George Grant was Canada's most significant public philosopher, meaning that his public was Canadian. — Graeme Nicholson [1]

They are foolish and ill-educated men who don't recognize that, when they get into bed with liberalism, it won't be they who do the impregnating—but that they will be utterly seduced. — George Grant [2]

The inside flap on the recent book about George Grant, *Athens and Jerusalem: George Grant's Theology, Philosophy, and Politics*, says this: 'George Grant (1918–1988) has been called Canada's greatest political philosopher. To this day, his work continues to stimulate, challenge, and inspire Canadians to think more deeply about matters of social justice and individual responsibility. However, while there has been considerable discussion of Grant's political theories, relatively little attention has been paid to their theological and philosophical underpinnings.' [3] There is little doubt, in short, that Grant was the most important Christian public intellectual in Canada in the latter half of the twentieth century, and for those who take their faith with some intellectual seriousness, much can be learned from George Grant the prophet, theologian, philosopher and engaged thinker.

Athens and Jerusalem walks the extra mile to highlight the deep theological well where Grant turned to slake a thirsty and parched soul. There is more to Grant, though, than the theological and philosophical underpinnings for his public vision. George Grant was an Anglican, and, sadly so, his Anglicanism has often been ignored. In the midst of the culture wars in the Anglican Church of Canada, Grant can offer us a way through and beyond the theological and ethical tribalism of left and right, liberal and conservative that so besets and divides us these days.

There is a form of Christianity, well lived and articulated by Grant, that might be called the Classical Christian tradition. Such a read of the Christian drama can come as a corrective to the liberal, conservative and fundamentalist versions of Christianity that often compete for dominance in the house of faith today. Grant's classical understanding of the Christian and Anglican way can still teach us much about the *esse* of what we need to conserve.

The fact that Grant attended Upper Canada College (with Anglican roots and history), and the equally important reality that his father was principal of the school meant that Grant was exposed, when young, to the Anglican heritage from a variety of educational and liturgical levels. Grant did his BA at Queen's University in Kingston (a strong Anglican and historic Loyalist stronghold) and he was offered a Rhodes Scholarship to study at Oxford. It was at Oxford that Grant met Sheila, his future wife (who had taken courses with J. R. R. Tolkien). George and Sheila moved to Halifax, Nova Scotia after World War II where Grant was offered a position in the philosophy department at Dalhousie University.

George and Sheila Grant became Anglicans in 1956 while Grant was teaching in the philosophy department at Dalhousie. Bishop William Davis brought the Grant family into the Anglican Church, and it is significant that it was Bishop Davis's son, Arthur Davis, that edited (along with Henry Roper and Peter C. Emberley) the four volume *Collected Works of George Grant*. It was also Arthur Davis that edited *George Grant and the Subversion of Modernity: Art, Philosophy, Politics, Religion, and Education*.

The turn by George and Sheila Grant to the Anglican tradition was preceded and formed somewhat by Grant's PhD studies when at Oxford—his thesis was one thing, his interaction with the Socratic Club that C. S. Lewis guided so wisely and informatively was even more important. Sheila Grant once told me that it was the publication of C. S. Lewis's *The Abolition of Man*, when George and Sheila were at Oxford, that did much to deepen and confirm Grant's commitment to Christianity and the Anglican way. Grant was also profoundly impacted by another Anglican divine, Austin Farrer, when at Oxford, and Farrer was one of Grant's examiners for his PhD thesis. It would be remiss when pondering Grant's indebtedness to Anglican divines and poets to ignore George Herbert and Herbert's classic poem 'Love'.[4] Herbert was a poetic mentor and guide to Grant in many ways, and it was Herbert's compressed theology in poetry that so 'enraptured' Grant.

George Grant completed his PhD thesis at Oxford in 1950 on 'The Concept of Nature and Supernature in the Theology of John Oman',[5] and in 1951, his article in the Massey Commission, 'Philosophy', stirred a hornet's nest in the philosophic Sanhedrin in Canada. Grant began the essay with these words: 'The study of philosophy is the analysis of the traditions of our society and the judgment of those traditions against our varying intuitions of the Perfection of God.'[6] He also argued that authentic philosophy was about contemplation of God rather than an analysis and description of God. Grant was decades ahead of his time in this suggestion. Such challenging words about the 'Perfection of God' and contemplative philosophy and theology did not please those who were neither interested in perfection, contemplation nor God. In fact, Grant's essay on philosophy so irritated and annoyed the philosophic Sanhedrin in Canada that, in 1952, the annual meeting of the tribe met to debunk Grant's older notion of the purpose and meaning of philosophy—*Philosophy in Canada: A Symposium* sums up the Sanhedrin's response with Fulton Anderson (Grant's nemesis) writing the 'Introduction'. The battle for the books at the level of public education was heating up and Grant was at the forefront with a more classical notion of the purpose of learning and philosophy that was being lost and forgotten.

In 1953, Grant delivered a paper, 'Two Theological Languages', to the Presbyterian and United Church clergy.[7] The original paper and various additions are basic to Grant's approach to doing theology in a post-Christian world. There is no doubt, though, that Grant was very much grappling with the relationship between theology and philosophy in this timely and telling essay. Grant sought to discern, in 'Two Theological Languages', the differences between the language of revelation and the language of reason. The language of revelation is appropriate within the life of the church, but, within the larger public world, it is the language of reason that dominates.

What is reason, though, and how are Christians in a post-Christian world to address their culture in a way that their culture understands? It is of little use, in short, to use the language of revelation in a culture that does not accept revelation as a form of authority. Grant was, in short, calling Christians to be fully bilingual; they had to know how to speak both the language of revelation and the language of reason if they were ever to communicate meaningfully to the church and the world. But, much hinged, of course, on what is meant by reason. It is this issue that led Grant to Plato and Heidegger. Their views of reason were quite different from the scholastic, empirical and Cartesian notions of reason that had so thinned out the older and deeper classical notions of reason as a contemplative and mystical faculty and organ at the seat of the heart and soul.

Grant's lectures for CBC, *Philosophy in the Mass Age*, were published in 1959.[8] It is obvious in these compelling lectures that Grant was grappling with the tensions between Plato and Hegel. Plato had argued there is an eternal order that we attune ourselves to, whereas Hegel argued that history is about the unfolding of our consciousness of liberty. Hegel is the grandmaster of emerging liberalism, and Plato of the 'moving image of eternity'. Grant saw where the thinking of Hegel led, and he came to side with Plato, and the tensions between Plato and Christianity, Socrates and Christ.

I have mentioned Hegel for an important reason. Grant was raised in a thoughtful educational context in which Hegelian thought permeated and defined his upbringing. The dialectical idealism of Hegel that so defines the modern liberal project was what Grant took in with his upbringing. Hegelian thought, in many ways, has come to define the broader Canadian philosophical and political ethos, also. *The Faces of Reason: An Essay on Philosophy and Culture in English Canada, 1850–1950*, published in 1981, and *Northern Spirits: John Watson, George Grant, and Charles Taylor: Appropriations of Hegelian Political Thought* and *The Undiscovered Country: Essays in Canadian Intellectual Culture*, published in 2008 and 2013, all make it abundantly clear that Hegelian liberal modernity has played a significant role in shaping and forming Canadian theological, philosophical, educational and political life.

Grant had internalized, when young, such a Hegelian way, but, as he matured, he came to see the cracks and fault lines in the Hegelian liberal agenda. It was this seeing and seeing through Hegel that turned Grant to Plato and Platonic Anglicanism. Much hinges, of course, on whether Hegel or Plato, Plato or Hegel is held high as the north star and polaris on the journey. Grant came to oppose, in the clearest terms, Hegel's misread of the ancients and Plato. It was, in short, Grant's rereading of Plato's insights as the 'moving image of eternity' that brought him into conflict with Hegel and Canadian Hegelians.

James Doull was, in many ways, Grant's philosophic mentor when at Dalhousie University in the 1950s. Doull taught in classics, Grant in philosophy. There came a point, though, when Grant came to question Doull's Hegelian read of Plato and the classics. It was this break from Doull that created many a problem, but such a break set Grant on a course that took him to an older and more classical Anglican read of Plato—a form of contemplative theology and philosophy that was both mystical and political, a synthesis of Athens and Jerusalem—there was yet a thoughtful classical Greek vision to be mined that could speak to the hyper-rationalist and hyper-driven Western culture and ethos. Hegel, in short, erred and misread Plato and the implications were momentous for church and society. Plato and Hegel, Grant and Doull were on a collision course. It was just a matter of time before Grant would leave Dalhousie in Halifax for York University in Toronto.

I should mention the important mentoring and tutoring role Grant played for many when at Dalhousie. One of the men he encouraged and affirmed was Robert Crouse (who became a significant theologian and scholar within the Anglican Church of Canada). Robert often stayed at our place when on the west coast (he lived in his later years in Crousetown outside Halifax) and we exchanged many a fine letter. Robert often mentioned to me that his interest in the Fathers of the Church was inspired, as a young man, by classes with George Grant at Dalhousie—the Anglican King's College in Halifax remains, to this day, a bastion and stronghold of a much older Anglican theological heritage—Robert Crouse was very much an elder and father to many when he taught at King's (and classics at Dalhousie). Robert, at the height of the theological battles in the Anglican Church of Canada in the last twenty years, was on the Primate's Theological Commission—in short, Grant lived on through his representative Robert Crouse who, in time, became a mentor to many up-and-coming Anglican priests and theologians.

The fact that Grant had come to question Hegel's dominance in Canadian life and the equally important publication of *Philosophy in the Mass Age* meant that Grant, by the late 1950s, had become, in Canada, a preeminent public intellectual—he often spoke on the publically funded Canadian Broadcasting Corporation on issues of significant import. 'Christ, What a Planet' was delivered in 1959 on CBC, and in this provocative reflection, Grant ponders the previous year and the future of the globe.[9] He pulls no punches about the injustices in the world, but Grant's understanding of the reasons for global injustice and a healing of such tragedies is quite different than that of the liberal tradition.

Grant was one of the first professors to be hired at York University, and he was the first to resign in 1960 for the simple reason that Plato and Christianity could not be taught in a positive manner (Grant's conflict with Fulton Anderson was at the core of the battle—this time it was Francis Bacon, whom Anderson held high, or Plato whom Grant gave the nod to—the philosophic wars were indeed intense). Grant was invited by St. John's Anglican College in Winnipeg to give the convocation address in November 1960.[10] It is impossible to miss in the convocation address Grant's passion for Christianity and the dark clouds he sees on the educational, religious and political horizon. Grant saw in the 1950s-1960s many of the dilemmas Anglicans struggle with today, and he thought through the issues in a way that can still instruct and teach us.

After Grant left York, he was hired at McMaster University. Grant came to be hired at McMaster largely through the work of another prominent Anglican at the time, William Kilbourn (who taught in the history department at McMaster, and then became dean of humanities at York University). The Grant family attended the local parish in Dundas near Hamilton, and George and Sheila were active in parish life. George was fondly called 'the bishop' in the area, and his review of a book on the parish, *Fountain Come Forth: The Anglican Church and the Valley Town of Dundas, 1784–1963*, speaks much about Grant's interest and grounding in the Anglican way.[11]

Grant addressed the McMaster Divinity School in October 1961 on Jesus and Pilate, and by the late 1960s, after publishing his controversial *Lament for a Nation*, he pondered the meaning of the Eucharist in 'Qui Tollit: Reflections on the Eucharist'.[12]

Grant began a most engaging correspondence with Derek Bedson in 1956 (when he became an Anglican), and between 1956 and 1984, twenty-seven letters were written by Grant to Bedson. Bedson, like Grant, was an Anglican, and in these letters Grant pondered the meaning of Anglicanism in the Anglican Church of Canada.[13] Grant was fond of the Swiftian distinction in 'Battle of the Books' between the spider and bee.[14] The spider creates and spins out webs of reality from its womb, whereas the bee goes from flower to flower, drawing forth the pollen and taking it to the hive—sweet honey is the result. Grant and Swift saw in the spider the inner reality of liberalism—a convergence of liberty, making and power—no reality other than what we spin out of our minds, imaginations and wills. The bee, on the other hand, merely draws from the finest of what existed (the best that had been thought, said and done within the Great Tradition) and sweet honey is the product.

The General Board of Religious Education of the Anglican Church of Canada, in the early 1960s, asked Pierre Berton (an up-and-coming former Anglican), to write a book on the issues the church had to face in the 1960s and afterwards—the book was a popular form of trendy Hegelianism. Grant found Pierre Berton's *The Comfortable Pew* a shallow and thin book—it is significant that *Lament for a Nation: The Defeat of Canadian Nationalism* (that was dedicated to Derek Bedson and Judith Robinson) and *The Comfortable Pew: A Critical Look at the Church in the New Age* were both published in 1965. Much hinges on whether Grant or Berton would be followed for the Anglican path after these two missives were published. Grant points the way in *Lament* to a deeper and older conservatism, and Berton points the way in *The Comfortable Pew* to a trendy and ideological liberalism—the bee and spider are very much at the forefront in the different worldviews in these two important Canadian and Anglican classics of the 1960s. Much of the Anglican Church of Canada has followed Berton's lead, and, sadly so, most conservatives who see themselves as orthodox, have ignored Grant—Anglican High Toryism cannot be easily pressed into the service of either an uncritical liberalism or a reactionary conservatism—High Tories are much more judicious than to be true believers of either tribe.

The Anglican Church of Canada published a reply to Berton's *The Comfortable Pew*—Grant was asked to contribute to the reply book edited by William Kilbourn, *The Restless Church: A Response to the Comfortable Pew*, but Grant thought the book so foolish, it was not worth a reply. The fact that the General Board of Religious Education of the Anglican Church of Canada would pander to such trendy and *cause du jour* liberalism made Grant question whether the Anglican Church of Canada was seriously losing its exegetical, theological and intellectual way at a variety of ecclesial, synodical and seminary levels. Grant, as a classical High Tory, saw clearly what was going on at a deeper level in a way few did. It is significant that Grant ends chapter one of *Lament for a Nation* with these words from Richard Hooker's *Of the Laws of Ecclesiastical Polity:* 'Posterity may know we have not loosely through silence permitted things to pass away as in a dream'.[15] Grant saw much passing away via the dominance of a form of liberalism-as-progress ideology and he would not be silent. *Lament for a Nation* is much more, of course, than merely a Jeremiah-like lament for the defeat of the Progressive Conservative Party by the Liberal-led party of Lester Pearson (and his fawning before President J. F. Kennedy)—it's much more a lament for the passing away of an older vision of faith and society, an ethos of sorts that is quite different from the various forms of liberalism that were coming to dominate church and society.

Michael Creal, William Kilbourn and Ernest Harrison played significant roles in both encouraging and supporting Berton's *The Comfortable Pew* and *The Restless Church*. Harrison's growing scepticism about both Christian theology and the church was worked out in a variety of books, but *A Church without God*, published in 1967, convinced Grant that significant leadership in the Anglican Church of Canada was losing all bearings and sense of direction.

This was also a period of time when the Anglican Church of Canada was seriously pondering the decision to create a formal union with the United Church of Canada—this, for Grant, would be disastrous— Grant even thought of leaving the Anglican Church if this occurred— the United Church of Canada embodied, for Grant, the co-opting of the church by liberalism—in short, the United Church had been impregnated by liberalism and most of her children were trendy liberals. Grant feared that the same fate would occur to the Anglican Church of Canada if such a marriage took place. The fact that Berton and Harrison had worked together at the highest levels in the Anglican Church of Canada to pander and capitulate to liberal modernity meant that serious problems were afoot. Michael Creal and William Kilbourn did not go as far down the sceptical pathway as Berton and Harrison, but Grant became, in time, suspicious of their more benign liberalism, also. I received the following correspondence from Michael Creal more than a decade ago regarding Grant, Berton and liberalism—it is important to note that Creal, Kilbourn and Harrison worked together to support Berton's *The Comfortable Pew*—Creal's reply:

George Grant's Anglicanism is not all that easy (for me) to describe. He was certainly not a liberal. He refused to contribute to 'The Restless Church' because it was a response to Pierre Berton's book (even though he—George Grant—was a friend of Bill Kilbourn's and mine). The underlying liberal position of Berton was not something he felt the Church should waste its time on.[16]

Indeed, Grant, prophetic-like, stood against the drift and direction of liberalism in both society and the church—the sheer fragmentation and relativism that were the children of such principles let loose meant nothing could be held together—divisiveness had come to replace unity, liberal ideology silenced and marginalized opposition—Grant saw this in the clearest and starkest terms and the implications of it for human nature, human identity, relationships, church life, social life and politics.

Grant dedicated, as I mentioned above, *Lament for a Nation* to Derek Bedson (a catholic Anglican) and Judith Robinson. Judith Robinson was a fiery Canadian nationalist who often had John Farthing in her home to discuss the larger issues of toryism and liberalism. Judith Robinson's nephew, Harry Robinson, sat in on many of those fireside chats when a young man. The combination of Judith Robinson and John Farthing was a heady mix for the young Harry Robinson. Harry, in time, became an Anglican priest, and when Harry was rector of a parish in Toronto (Harry ended his days at St. John's in Vancouver), Grant gave many a homily in Harry's parish. Harry was much shaped and influenced by Judith Robinson, John Farthing and George Grant's form of tory Anglicanism, and when the culture wars in the Anglican Church of Canada heated up in the 1990s, Harry was front and centre in the fray. I asked Harry to write a memorial reflection on Grant's life and impact on him ten years after Grant's death, in 1998, and Harry's article was timely and touching—again, Grant's impact rippled forth in a variety of directions. It is interesting to note that Harry was much more committed to a more moderate low church Anglican way (evangelical and reformed), but Grant was wise enough to see the good in such a time-tried party within the larger Anglican family—an interesting convergence, in some ways, between the catholic Anglicanism of Robert Crouse and the reformed–evangelical Anglicanism of Harry Robinson—both, in some ways, children of George Grant.

It is pertinent to note that in June 1966, Adrienne Clarkson (another Anglican and future Governor General of Canada) interviewed Grant for the *First Person* series. Grant makes it quite clear in this interview that he thinks Western Christianity, for the most part, is near the end. Most forms of schismatic and fragmentary protestantism have been totally co-opted by modernity, but the 'Anglican Church ... has in it some of the ancient truth and therefore I live within it.'[17] Grant saw in the time-tried Anglican way 'strange remnants' of an older, deeper way that was much closer to the heart of Christianity. It was this 'ancient truth' and 'strange remnants' that drew and held Grant.

When Ted Scott became the tenth Primate of Canada (from 1971 to 1986), Grant saw the writing on the wall. Scott, in many ways, merely fleshed out Berton's shallow liberalism. There is no doubt that Scott was a compassionate man, but the intellectual underpinnings of his thought were thin and meagre. Scott, in many ways, moved the Anglican Church of Canada further down the liberal path and trail. Grant was quick to see in Scott and tribe an uncritical attitude in the Anglican Church towards liberalism, and he also saw the consequences in the ethical and political realms of this attitude. Grant not only saw it, but he analysed the problem at the core and foundation levels: none were doing this at the time. Grant was, indeed, preoccupied by what Canadian church and society were 'enfolded' within and the 'unfolding' of such principles in social and church life. Grant also saw his task as one of the 'enucleating' of what, at a deeper level, predetermined how we approached ethical, economic and religious issues—if these deeper premises, presuppositions and prejudices were not examined, our approach would be enframed in uncritical ways and means.

Most conservatives in the reign of Ted Scott were reacting to issues and symptoms but not probing the deeper philosophic roots that produced the worrisome fruit on the tree of the church. Much was masked and hidden, often, by Scott's seeming compassion and desire for dialogue (which often masked a lack of a foundation, core or centre). Grant saw through all this, and called it for what it was. Ideas do have consequences, and Grant perceived, clearer than most, decades ahead of most, the corrosive nature of liberalism.

It is not very liberal of a liberal not to question liberalism, but the ideological liberalism of Grant's day (and ours) had to be doubted and interrogated. Grant did this both in the Anglican Church of Canada and the much broader Canadian culture. He was often a lone voice, but he was a prophetic voice to the Anglican Church, Christianity and Canadian culture.

One of the finest Canadian painters of the twentieth century was Alex Colville. Grant and Colville were close friends. Colville designed the 1967 Centennial coins—one of the coins is a lone wolf howling against the winds of the day. Colville told Grant that the lone wolf coin was dedicated to him—Grant, often, the lone wolf and prophet—many more need to know Grant and know him well.

CHAPTER TWENTY-THREE

THE ORTHODOX TRADITION AND CANADA'S MOST SIGNIFICANT PUBLIC PHILOSOPHER: GEORGE GRANT

George Grant has been called one of the most important public intellectuals in Canada in the latter half of the twentieth century. In his article in *Athens and Jerusalem: George Grant's Theology, Philosophy and Politics*, Graeme Nicholson called him 'Canada's most significant public philosopher'.[1] George Parkin Grant had a wide-ranging mind and imagination that covered and touched most aspects of the Western and Eastern traditions. Grant was a Christian renaissance humanist in the best sense of that compelling term. The fact that Grant was drawn to the best of the Western theological, philosophical and political tradition meant that he encountered the riches of Orthodoxy in his many probes. This chapter will touch on Grant's encounter with Orthodoxy. I will ponder his encounter and engagement with the Orthodox tradition in five unfolding phases.

First, George Grant's initial encounter with Orthodoxy was through the marriage of his sister, Alison Grant, to George Ignatieff. Grant had studied with George Ignatieff's brother, Nicholas Ignatieff, who taught history at Upper Canada College in the 1930s. But the meeting of George Ignatieff and Alison Grant, and their marriage in November 1945 brought George Grant into the centre of the Russian Orthodox way as it was embodied in England and Canada in the World War II period. George Ignatieff had this to say about his Russian Orthodox heritage in his classic book, *The Making of a Peacemonger: The Memoirs of George Ignatieff*:

The Orthodox Church gave me a sense of belonging, of being in touch with my roots, of safety and stability in an otherwise confusing world. Even in early childhood I derived great comfort from prayer and from the familiar Orthodox liturgy, and I have remained a devoted member of the church ever since.[2]

Ignatieff had this, also, to say about the unusual nature of the wedding:

We were married in Montreal, in the United Church in deference to Alison's family and in the Russian Orthodox Cathedral for the sake of mine.[3]

The Ignatieff family was well known in Russia, but they had to flee the country when the communists came to power. George's father (Count Paul Ignatieff) was the last minister of education in Russia under Czar Nicolas II, and even though he was at the forefront of reforming the educational system in Russia before the revolution, he saw the writing on the wall in 1917. The Ignatieff clan, initially, moved to England, then to Canada. George Ignatieff became a prominent civil servant in Canada, and he worked closely in the 1940s-1950s-1960s with Lester B. Pearson.

Ignatieff's book, *The Making of a Peacemonger: The Memoirs of George Ignatieff* tells the tale well of the journey of the Ignatieff clan from Russia to England to Canada. There is little doubt that Grant, as a young man, would have been exposed to Russian Orthodoxy through his friendship with Nicholas Ignatieff and the fact his sister was married to George Ignatieff.

The son of George Ignatieff and Alison Grant is Michael Ignatieff (former leader of the Liberal Party in Canada), and Michael has written about the Ignatieff–Grant family connection in *True Patriot Love: Four Generations in Search of Canada*. There emerged in the 1950s-1960s serious tensions between George Grant and George Ignatieff. Grant felt that the Pearson–Ignatieff duo had become fawning servants of the emerging American empire, and this difference fragmented the family. Grant thought that there was an indigenous form of Canadian nationalism that had to be affirmed to resist and oppose the liberal Canadian drift into the embracing arms of imperial America. Grant's argument for this position is clearly articulated in his classic political missive, *Lament for a Nation: The Defeat of Canadian Nationalism*. It is essential to remember President Kennedy was quite involved in backing Pearson in the 1963 election, and Grant was astutely aware what this meant for the future of historic Canadian Toryism.

It is somewhat interesting to note that George Ignatieff never mentioned George Grant (his well-known brother-in-law) in *The*

Making of a Peacemonger. It seems the two men had quite different understandings about what it meant to be a peacemonger. But, there is no doubt that George Grant's exposure to Orthodoxy came through the Ignatieff family. It is too bad we do not have any serious records of conversations that took place between George Grant and George or Nicholas Ignatieff on Orthodoxy.

It is significant to note that after George Ignatieff had finished his more active role as one of the more prominent Canadian diplomats of the 1950s-1960s, he was offered the position of provost of Trinity College (the leading High Church Anglican College of the time in Canada) in 1972. There was an implicit convergence of the Orthodox tradition and catholic Anglicanism via George Ignatieff, and the Ignatieff–Grant family connections facilitated this pioneering Orthodox–Anglican dialogue within the Canadian ethos. In some important ways, the Orthodox–Anglican ethos as embodied in the Ignatieff and Grant families had some affinities with the English St. Alban–St. Sergius convergence of Anglicanism and Russian Orthodoxy.[4]

George Grant did have his differences with George Ignatieff, but he was quite miffed, though, when Prime Minster Pierre Trudeau bypassed George Ignatieff for the role of governor general in 1979.[5] I do see in Ignatieff's close relationship with Pearson, and Pearson's close alliance with Kennedy contra Diefenbaker, Ignatieff's explicit merging of church, Canadian politics and American empire. Ignatieff was, at the time, a member of St. Thomas's parish (Anglo-Catholic) in Toronto, but his implicit Russian Orthodox understanding of church and state still lingered. The Americans were the major opponents of Russian communism, Canadian–American relations formed the North American phalanx against Russian communism, therefore Pearsonian Liberalism and Kennedy's Democrats made for a heady opposition to the communism Ignatieff so opposed. It was this Constantinian synthesis that Grant so saw through and opposed in *Lament for a Nation*. The historic High Tory Canadian tradition could offer a third way beyond the Cold War dualism and ideology, and Grant was at the forefront of suggesting such a vision.

Second, when Grant became chair of the religious studies department at McMaster University in 1961, he was quite keen to check the drift of liberalism by bringing to the university those forms of Christianity that embodied the more classical Christian way.[6] It is important to note at this juncture that Grant's more catholic form of

Anglicanism made for many an affinity with the Orthodox way, and in England at the time much work was being done on Anglican–Orthodox dialogue (the Fellowship of St. Alban and St. Sergius was on the cutting edge of this deeper ecumenism).

Grant would have imbibed the Anglican–Orthodox dialogue that was going on in England in the 1930s-1940s, and this made him eager to bring the dialogue to the Canadian context. Grant had been active in C. S. Lewis's Socratic Club when at Oxford, and the outside reader for his PhD thesis was Austin Farrer (both men had decidedly classical and mystical leanings). George Ignatieff, as a young man, had attended the well-known Anglican Trinity College (High Church) in Toronto in the 1930s, and George and Alison had an affinity with the High Church Anglican–Orthodox way that was unfolding in Toronto.

The personal letters of George Grant (*George Grant: Selected Letters*) make it clear that Grant was drawn to what he identified as some of the sounder and more stable aspects of the Roman Catholic and Orthodox ways in opposition to the way he thought that the Anglican tradition was capitulating to liberal modernity. There is no doubt, therefore, by the early 1960s Grant had a growing interest in Orthodoxy, and he was keen to get Orthodox theologians lecturing at McMaster University.

Third, when Grant was doing research on Simone Weil in the 1960s, he read Philip Sherrard's *The Greek East and the Latin West*.[7] Sherrard's read and interpretation of Orthodoxy had a profound impact on Grant for a variety of reasons. Sherrard had suggested in *The Greek East and the Latin West* that the clash between the East and West hinged on the way the West had accepted at the Third Council of Toledo in AD 589, and ratified such a position in 1014, that the Holy Spirit proceeded from the Son (Jesus) and the Father. This move by the Roman Catholic West is called the '*filioque* clause' which deeply offended the Greek Orthodox Church. What is the issue at the core of the dilemma, and why was Grant drawn to Sherrard's read of the clash and its implications? There is no doubt that the conflict separated the Eastern Orthodox from the Western Roman Catholics, and Grant took the side of the Orthodox on this issue. Does it really matter whether the Holy Spirit proceeds from the Father alone or the Father and the Son? Why bother quibbling about such details? But, details can make a difference, and this is what interested the Orthodox Sherrard and the Anglican Grant.

For Grant, the distinction is important for the simple reason that the West attempted to too clearly define God, God's being and God's energies (economy), whereas the Orthodox tradition was more willing to dwell in the mystery and essence of God, Father, Son and Holy Spirit. The fact that the Roman Catholic Church attempted to be too sure about the economy and operation of God by the inclusion of the '*filioque* clause' (the relationship between Father, Son, Spirit and Son and Spirit) worried Grant. It was this Western need to sharpen, clarify and fully understand that blinded the West to that which could not be comprehended. Grant thought that Aristotle was back of the Western Roman Catholic–Protestant way, and Plato informed the more mystical and contemplative Orthodox way.[8]

Fourth, Grant had a real fondness for Tolstoy and Dostoevsky, but he was more drawn to the Russian Orthodox vision of Dostoevsky than Tolstoy.[9] Grant's lecture in 1959 on Dostoevsky on CBC for *Architects of Modern Thought* walked the attentive listener and reader into the centre and core of Dostoevsky's painful probes of the human condition.[10] Grant drew from Dostoevsky's novels to highlight the depths to which humans can sink and the heights to which the saints can rise. Where but in such Russian classics so grounded in the Orthodox way could such a tantalizing vision be articulated and lived? There is no doubt, also, that Dostoevsky was a profound critic of the way Russia and the Russian Orthodox Church had become Westernized and modern, and he attempted to reverse this capitulation to liberal modernity.

Grant was very much with Dostoevsky in the clash between the ancients and the moderns, and he thought the ancient and time-tried way of Orthodoxy was absolutely needed and necessary to question the progressive liberal drift of the modern world. Grant gave a series of lectures in 1976 to graduate students on Platonic Christianity, and in the final lecture, he dealt with 'Dostoevsky's Christianity'.[11] The lecture went deeper and further than his 1959 CBC lecture on Dostoevsky, and in the span of the presentation he pondered Dostoevsky's understanding of the relationship of suffering and freedom, and more to the point, how the Grand Inquisitor in *The Brothers Karamazov* embodied, in the most beguiling and seductive way, the temptation of the West and Western Christianity.

The Jesus of *The Brothers Karamazov* confronts the Western Christian church. The Roman Catholic Church had become the Judas figure in many ways. Jesus's reply to the Grand Inquisitor is a kiss on the cheek. Such a kiss speaks volumes. There is no doubt where Grant stood in all this. The Orthodox vision of Jesus in *The Brothers Karamazov* comes as an affront and challenge to the Judas-like church of Western Christianity. Grant had by 1976, in many ways, fused the theological Greek–Russian Orthodox traditions with the literary Russian Orthodox tradition in his reflections on Sherrard and Dostoevsky.

Fifth, a good teacher is often indebted to those that have gone before, and such wise teachers and their students pass on, like a torch, the noblest that has been given them—Grant is no exception to this truth and reality. What, though, has this to do with Grant and Orthodoxy? Grant was a member of the Socratic Club at Oxford that C. S. Lewis started and developed. Grant had a high view of Lewis—Lewis was a Classical–Medieval–Renaissance scholar, and Grant walked the extra mile to hold high the 'discarded image' of such an ancient way of thinking and being. The fact that Lewis was so grounded in the classical tradition meant that both the Orthodox and Roman Catholic traditions have often seen Lewis as a convincing embodiment of their heritages. The well-known English Orthodox bishop and theologian Kallistos Ware, for example, has written quite fondly of Lewis in his touching and timely article, 'God of the Fathers: C. S. Lewis and Eastern Christianity'. Ware has called Lewis an 'anonymous Orthodox'.[12]

Grant was held by Lewis, and Lewis's rooting in the classics (and by implication Orthodoxy) was something that Grant would understand. Grant also passed on his interest in the Russian Orthodox and Classical way to his students. Bruce Ward did his MA and PhD with Grant at McMaster University, and Ward's two books on Dostoevsky are Canadian classics on this seminal Russian writer. *Dostoevsky's Critique of the West: The Quest for the Earthly Paradise* is Ward's doctoral thesis completed under Grant turned into a book, and his *Remembering the End: Dostoevsky as Prophet to Modernity* (with P. Travis Kroeker) turns once again to the insights of Dostoevsky as a prophet to the failings of the liberal West.

Spencer Estabrooks, another student of Grant's at McMaster, is now an Orthodox priest, and is front and centre in the running of the St. Arseny Institute (Orthodox) in Winnipeg. Archbishop Lazar of Ottawa, unlike Bruce Ward and Spencer Estabrooks, never studied with George Grant, but as one of the most prominent Orthodox theologians in Canada and the United States, Lazar has a high regard for George Grant, and the way Grant attempted to integrate the often fragmented realities of spirituality and politics. It is significant to note, also, that David Goa (yet another prominent Orthodox intellectual in Canada) has tipped his cap often to George Grant. Goa's *A Regard for Creation: Collected Essays*, from an Orthodox perspective, is a Canadian first on Orthodoxy and ecology, and Goa is quick to acknowledge in the missive his interest in Grant. It is obvious that Grant has passed on the Orthodox way to both Ward and Estabrooks, and both men have taken Grant's lead further and deeper. Grant has, also, had an impact on important Orthodox thinkers and activists in Canada such as Archbishop Lazar and David Goa.

Grant's commitment to recovering the discarded image of the ancients meant he had affinities with those classical forms of Christianity that were rooted and grounded in the Great Tradition. Orthodoxy is very much immersed in such an ancient and time-tried way, and this is why Grant and Orthodoxy have much in common. There is, indeed, a sense in which Grant is a probing pioneer in Canada of both Anglican–Orthodox dialogue and an approach to Orthodoxy that is not enmeshed with American imperial politics. Grant can, in many ways, offer North American Orthodoxy a way beyond its often worrisome legacy of Orthodoxy being the unquestioning chaplain to the state. Grant can, also, when read aright, offer a way to challenge the present trend of a common ground between Evangelicals, Roman Catholics and Orthodox in degenerating into a reductionistic and republican read of these *ad fontes* and 'ressourcement' traditions.

CHAPTER TWENTY-FOUR

THE TORY ANGLICAN WAY
AND THE ANGLICAN CHURCH OF CANADA

The Anglican way did not begin (as some wrongly assume) with King Henry's overactive glands. It began nearly two thousand years ago with the coming of Christian missionaries to the Celts in Albion (England). The Anglican tradition, since then, has been deeply Celtic, firmly Catholic, thoroughly Reformed, generously Liberal, eagerly Evangelical and openly Charismatic. Many will wonder how such a motley combination of theological perspectives can live together under the same tent and in the same cathedral. Needless to say, many a tension is involved in holding together such seemingly disparate ways of interpreting the Christian faith, but such is the genius of the Anglican way. It is not, primarily, an English thing. It is much more than that. It is a way of understanding the faith journey that claims to embody and reflect the very nature of reality. It is a way that holds high diversity but not divisiveness. It is a way that, true to Augustine and Baxter, attempts to be unified on the essentials, grants gracious freedom in the non-essentials and attempts to be charitable in all things. Needless to say, this is not always lived forth, but this is the ideal that such living forth seeks to embody.

What is the Anglican way, then, and what are some of the tensions and struggles that take us into the very core and centre of the Anglican way at this point in history? Each moment and period of history has its own unique challenges, and when the church is true to herself, she rises to the occasion, wearing well the thick robes of wisdom and insight that only time can stitch and sew on such colourful vestments. Our time is no different than any other, and, as such, it is right and fitting that the Anglican tradition should be struggling and grappling with many a hot-button issue in the culture wars.

What is the Anglican way, then? There are eleven foundation stones in the Anglican tradition, and it is from these rock firm stones, cemented and held tight together, that the edifice and fine roof of the Anglican cathedral is supported.

First, the Anglican way is committed to the wisdom of tradition. Such a stone-quarried way avoids the dangers of Biblicism, on the one hand, and traditionalism, on the other hand. The language of tradition clearly distinguished between the *esse* (essentials of the tradition), the *bene esse* (that which points to and illustrates the essence of the tradition) and the *adiaphora* (that which is conventional, an accretion and quite unnecessary within the tradition). It is by keeping these distinctions in mind that important reforming decisions for the life of the church can be made.

Second, the Bible is a basic document that informs and shapes the life of the church, but the Bible, within the Anglican tradition, is part of a tradition and must be interpreted by tradition. The Anglican way has lived long enough and seen enough in its two-thousand-year history to know the Bible can be and has been used to justify some of the most foolish and silly things imaginable. This is why the interpretive wisdom of two thousand years must be used to weigh and reflect upon new and novel interpretations of the Bible. The Anglican way both thinks from history and community, hence the role of the creative individual is important, but when such an individual ignores or turns their back on both history and community (often in the name of being a prophet), the Anglican tradition has serious questions to ask.

Third, the Anglican way assumes that experience, spirituality, mysticism and the contemplative way are a vital and living part of the journey, but it is cautious and critical of those who pit spirituality against religion, mysticism against creeds and contemplation against community. Such a reactionary and one-dimensional way of understanding the religious journey tends to be quite trendy in our time, but the more integrated Anglican way refuses to say 'yes' to those who idealize spirituality while demonizing or placing religion on a lower rung of the ladder. Most of the Anglican mystics have been deeply committed and devoted to both the tradition and the living church.

Fourth, the Anglican tradition is a magisterial tradition. This means that to be an Anglican the large political, economic and social issues must be faced. Anglicans do engage the magistrates and those in power. Anglicans do not retreat from the fray into pietistic ghettoes. They are also not lackeys and lapdogs for political or economic power. There is a startling prophetic dimension to the Anglican magisterial way that hikes a never easy tightrope between pietism and Constantinianism. It is this magisterial and prophetic way that places Anglicans (who truly know their tradition) at the forefront of all the hot-button issues in the culture wars, but does it in such a way that the prophets cannot and will not be taken captive by the ideologues of the political right, left or sensible centre. The Anglican tradition, within Canada, has been at the forefront of opposing American republican ideas and American imperialism. It is this High Anglican–High Tory Anglican way that has faced the stare of the American way and not backed down. Bishops Inglis and Strachan both opposed the attempt by the United States to take over and colonize Canada. The telling of the tale of nineteenth century attitudes and actions by High Tory Anglican Canadians towards the United States is fitly recounted in S. F. Wise's *God's Peculiar Peoples: Essays on Political Culture in Nineteenth-Century Canada*. It is, also, the Anglican High Tory way (with its concern for the commonweal–commonwealth) that played a significant role in establishing in Canada a form of federalism that priorizes the good of the nation in opposition to the individual. It is from such a political perspective that nationalism emerges from the political Anglican way. Anglican political theology is both concerned with the common good of Canada and Canadians (hence nationalist and federalist) and stands on constant guard against American republican ideas and American imperialism. Anglican political theology, therefore, within Canada is post-colonial (not English), nationalist (the common good of Canadians is held high and both the state and society have important roles to play in bringing about such a good) and American imperialism is seen for what it is.

Fifth, the Anglican tradition holds high the role and importance of the arts and culture. The aesthetic dimension of being human cannot and should not be denied or censured. The good, true and the beautiful are means of grace, and must be seen as such. This is why, within the Anglican tradition, poetry, literature and art have flourished. Church buildings (both interior and exterior) are constructed in such a way that a geography of the inner life is revealed, and religious services embody a liturgical and dialogical drama. All the sights, sounds and colours that are used within the Anglican way both appeal to our physical and sensual side and are meant to evoke a deeper aesthetic response. Beauty, though, within such a heritage is never disconnected from other aspects of life. Justice and truth always find their way and place within the artist's journey and the art produced.

Sixth, the Anglican way has a profound respect for nature as a good. This is why Anglicans have played a leadership role in the environmental movement. God made this world and said it was good, and even though much has happened since then, nature still has much goodness in it. It is true that we do live east of Eden, and we are ever hiking towards the New Jerusalem, but in this in between phase, God's grace is ever present, and nature is where God can be often found. Nature is not God, of course, nor should nature be confused or equated with God, but it is an *ikon* that can reveal to us much about God and the wisdom of God. Those who turn from nature as a source of revelatory insight or those who treat nature as an object to be used, abused and manipulated are blind to much, and will not see deeply nor live fully. Those who care for, tend and seek to honour nature are very much doing the work and will of God. If Anglican political thought leans towards a Red–High Tory perspective, the Anglican attitude towards nature points the way, predictably so, towards a form of Green Toryism.

Seventh, the Anglican view of the church attempts to find a middle way and path between a centralized and magisterial way as embodied in the Roman Catholic tradition and a more schismatic way as embodied in the protestant tradition. Anglicans are both catholic and reformed, and this is one of many tensions they consciously live in. It is in the living of these tensions that the genius of the Anglican way can be found and celebrated. It is the Anglican way to see the good in much, but not to run off with one aspect of truth to the exclusion of others. It is in this balancing and middle way that Anglicanism has much appeal. There are many other tensions that Anglicanism holds together, also, but the way the catholic and reformed perspectives are respected does say much about an understanding of the church that attempts to be both unified (in a spiritual and material way) but honour and respect the insights of other perspectives within the Christian vision.

Eighth, education is held high within the Anglican tradition, and, at her best, the Anglican tradition has sought to make education available to one and all. Our minds, like our imaginations, are gifts of God, and should be seen as such. Reason can be distorted and slip into rationalism, and the imagination can lose its way in phantasy, but, at their best and noblest, mind and imagination are lovers and dancing partners. It is this basic truth that has been the reason why Anglicans have built many of the best universities in the world, and

Anglicans have never feared learning and the challenges learning does bring. Milton said, 'I cannot praise a fugitive and cloistered virtue, unexercised and unbreathed, that never sallies out'.[1] The purpose of teaching one and all to think and ponder the big and substantive questions is so that they will sally forth and not retreat into a cloistered virtue. The mind, though, within the Anglican mystical and contemplative way, goes much deeper than the Cartesian mind. It goes much deeper than the logical, empirical, inductive and deductive ways of knowing. The Greek word *nous* best sums up such a notion of the mind. Mind or intellect in the 'noetic tradition' is a contemplative and receptive faculty at the very core and centre of the human person. It is a head in the heart, a heart in the head integration. It is this more centred way of knowing that waits and listens, that is attentive and still, that is basic to the Anglican way. Such a way of knowing is indebted to the Fathers and Mothers of the Church (both West and East), and when the Church has been true to such sources, she has lived with depth and vigour.

Ninth, Anglicans have refused (and rightly so) to accept the split between the sacred and the profane, between the inner and the outer journey, between the private and the public aspects of life, between spirituality and politics, between the cult and justice. It is this much more integrated way of life that is more whole, holy and healthy. All of life can be an *ikon* and sacrament if we have but the eyes to see, the ears to hear and the inner attention and alertness to be awake to the signals being sent our way.

Tenth, Anglicans live in the tension of the conservative and the liberal way. Anglicans are nimble enough of thought to realize that neither the past nor the present are perfect in thought, word or deed. But, there is much wisdom in the past and the old ways we ignore to our hurt, harm and peril. We must ever be wary, as C. S. Lewis has reminded us, of 'chronological snobbery'. Each age is a mix of wheat and tares, gold and dross. Those who only see good in the modern, liberal ethos lack a certain critical depth. Those who only see good in an idealized past lack a certain critical depth. Both Conservatives and Liberals see, but they see through a glass darkly. Both Liberals and Conservatives need one another. They are the two eyes of the church, and when they turn on one another, all lose, falter and fail. Liberals need to see the beam in their own eye just as Conservatives do. Jesus made it quite clear, when he told the parable of the Pharisee and the publican in the temple, where he saw the problem. When either side in the culture wars dares to say, 'Thank God I am not as them', all is lost. It is in this ongoing dialogue between Liberals and Conservatives that health and healing in the Anglican tradition will best be found and restored. When Liberal clans and Conservative tribes arise that turn on one another, all suffer.

Eleven, the parish is basic to the Anglican way. We live in an age in which there is much flitting from place to place in search of some religious setting that will slake the thirst of the individual pilgrim. When one place ceases to fill a need, there is a moving to another place. Religion has become, for many, just another commodity and product, and he or she who puts the best show on in town and sells the best product gets the customers. This notion and attitude to religion (very much a product of a capitalist society) runs contrary to the meaning and significance of the parish. The parish in the Anglican tradition signifies both place and people. The word parish comes from a Latin and Greek word that means the larger and more extended family. Just as in a blood family, each and all must learn to live with those who see life differently yet care and love one another through many a storm and tempest; the parish is the place where the larger faith family works out how to live together. This does not mean all will go well and smooth, and life in the parish (as in family) can be like a hair shirt at times, but it is by being loyal and committed that the deeper life emerges. It is in the context of parish family life that differences and conflicts will emerge, and if people disappear whenever the hard battles come to the fore, there will always be a thinness in the spiritual journey. This is why a commitment to the parish family life is a form of communal spiritual discipline. The parish is the place where each and all are forced to face their dark and shadow side, and this is never easy to do. This is a more common (rather than esoteric and detached) way to live the faith journey. It is also at the level of the parish that global things can be thought through, but life is lived locally. The role of both society and the state come together when the Anglican distinctions between parish, deanery, diocese and national church emerge. The parish not only cares for the concerns of the local congregation but also for the issues of the community.

The centrality of communal parish life in the Anglican tradition as a place and form of spiritual formation has been nicely summarized and articulated by S. T. Coleridge. In 'The Rime of the Ancient

Mariner', the Mariner kills the albatross. This takes both the Mariner and the sailing crew into a dark night of the soul. It is only when the Mariner has the courage to apologize for his violent and brutal deed that his soul begins to heal. The there-and-back-again journey ends with these telling lines:

> O sweeter than the marriage-feast,
> 'T is sweeter far to me,
> To walk together to the kirk
> With a goodly company!—
>
> To walk together to the kirk,
> And all together pray,
> While each to his great Father bends,
> Old men, and babes, and loving friends
> And youths and maidens gay![2]

Many have argued that Coleridge was far from the Anglican tradition when 'The Rime of the Ancient Mariner' was written, but in the passage mentioned above it is impossible to miss the connection between the life of faith and 'the kirk'. Coleridge explored this idea yet further in his *Biographia Literaria*. He said, in this important literary and religious treatise, 'that to every parish throughout the kingdom there is transplanted a germ of civilization; that in the remotest villages there is a nucleus, round which the capabilities of the place may crystallize and brighten; a model sufficiently superior to excite, yet sufficiently near to encourage and facilitate imitation.'[3] I have mentioned Coleridge, 'The Rime of the Ancient Mariner' and *Biographia Literaria* for a rather simple reason. Stephen Leacock and Mazo de la Roche are both buried in St. George's graveyard at Sibbald Point in Ontario. The stained glass window on the left as a person enters St. George's was dedicated to Mazo de la Roche. The stained glass window has the lines from Coleridge's 'The Rime of the Ancient Mariner' on it. The connection across time cannot be missed. The parish and the kirk are both the anvil on which the soul is shaped and formed and the place of kindness and goodly company.

The eleven points I have listed above are like the anatomical structure of the Anglican way. It is when this anatomy is strong and healthy that the Anglican tradition is true to herself. What, though, has this to do with the Anglican Church of Canada? Much is going on in the Anglican Church of Canada and the Anglican Communion at the present time. There is, in short, much sifting and sorting, much heart searching and purifying, and, all this is needed. The publication of the 2004 biography of Archbishop Ted Scott, *Radical Compassion: The Life and Times of Archbishop Ted Scott, Tenth Primate of the Anglican Church of Canada (1971–1986)* has filled in many a detail for us. The leadership, though, of the Anglican Church of Canada in the last few decades has been dominated by Liberals, and this has been a cause of concern.

It is significant to note that when the Anglican Church of Canada asked Pierre Berton to write a book about the state of the Anglican Church (and other historic forms of Christianity), he wrote and spoke in a rather convincing manner. *The Comfortable Pew: A Critical Look at the Church in the New Age*, published in 1965, was a bumper-crop seller, and it articulated and anticipated the Liberal agenda to which society was going (and to which the church was expected to go). Most of the ideas put forward in *The Comfortable Pew* are what we just take for granted today. Much of the Anglican Church of Canada (in the Scott and Peers regime and reign of power) has followed Berton's lead and guidance. It is, though, this lack of critical reflection on Berton's Liberal agenda that has caused a reaction in the Anglican Church of Canada. *The Comfortable Pew* was the work of a journalist, hence it was written in a more popular way. But, the issues raised were written about and pondered in a deeper and more demanding way. The publication of *The Future of Anglican Theology* in 1984 did reflect some of the deeper cleavages and divisions in the Anglican theological way. It was in the 1980s that the tensions (at an intellectual, activist and organizational level) began to emerge and become more obvious. Many of the Conservatives, in a fragmented and disorganized sort of way, began to emerge from their places of hiding and contest the dominance of Liberalism in the church. Groups such as the Prayer Book Society, the Evangelicals and the Charismatics began to find their feet and footing. The primate, at the time, Michael Peers, tended to ignore these groups as on the fringe and not really reflecting the thoughts of most in the pew.

It was just a matter of time before what was small, untried and unsure grew, matured and stood tall and firm. The 1980s, inevitably so, turned to the 1990s, and in 1993, the Prayer Book Society, Evangelical and Charismatic Anglicans linked arms and decided to put on a large conference. The Liberals, so the Conservatives argued, had turned from the essentials of the Great Tradition, and there was need to call the Anglican Church back to the essentials. A conference was planned for Montreal in 1994, and it focused on the essentials of the Anglican way. It was a step of faith, and most were unclear and unsure how many would turn up for the event. Many crossed the country to attend the Essentials I conference in 1994, and it sent a signal to those in the Anglican Church of Canada that something was afoot. A book was published as a result of the Essentials I conference, *Anglican Essentials: Reclaiming Faith within the Anglican Church of Canada*. Most of the presentations of the conference were included in the book, and the 'Montreal Declaration' was also included. The Essentials I conference and the publication of *Anglican Essentials* made it clear that a renaissance and reforming movement was at work in the Anglican Church of Canada, and this movement could no more be ignored. The Liberals began to muster their forces, and with the publication of *The Challenge of Tradition: Discerning the Future of Anglicanism* in 1997 a volley of shots was fired across the Conservative bow. Unfortunately, *The Challenge of Tradition* lacked a serious and sustained criticism of *Anglican Essentials*, and it was not taken with much seriousness by most.

Lines were being drawn in the sand, though, and the next battle was about to erupt and emerge. The Bishop of New Westminster, Michael Ingham, had a book published in 1997 that created an even greater stir and reaction. *Mansions of the Spirit* argued that most of the world's religions, at their finest and best, at their mystical and contemplative core, were saying much the same thing. Needless to say, there was a direct line to be drawn from Berton to Ingham. Ingham had written an earlier book, *Rites for a New Age: Understanding the Book of Alternative Services* in 1986. This book very much positioned Ingham in the liberal camp. He came as an uncritical fan, booster and advocate of the Book of Alternative Services in contrast to the more dated Book of Common Prayer. The Liberal tendencies of *Rites for a New Age* took their next and more worrisome step with *Mansions of the Spirit*. It was just a matter of time before the liberal way of thinking that was initiated in liturgical questions would be applied to interfaith and ethical questions. There is a predictable consistency in Ingham's thought. The reply to *Mansions of the Spirit* from within the Anglican fold was *In a*

Pluralist World in 1998. *In a Pluralist World* argued that there were serious flaws in the way Ingham interpreted the mystical traditions both within Christianity and other religions. Mystics do not all agree, and this must be acknowledged and recognized. Things were heating up, though, and it was just a matter of time before the Diocese of New Westminster would take its next step down the liberal path and trail.

The Conservatives organized an Essentials II conference. This was held at Trinity Western University in the summer of 2002. More turned out at the Essentials II conference than had attended the Essentials I conference in 1994 in Montreal. The question of same-sex blessing was on the minds of many. Needless to say, at a deeper level, this was not the real issue. This was more of the presenting problem. The real issue was the way both the broader liberal culture (and those in the church that reflected such a culture) lacked any sense of self-criticism. Such liberal notions as a more open-ended notion of human nature and sexuality fed and fuelled by such liberal principles as liberty, individualism, equality, choice, will and authenticity had become the new interpretive grid for many in the church. It was to this level of principles that Conservatives sought to take the dialogue and discussion. The hot-button liturgical, ethical, political, economic and metaphysical issues were but so many symptoms and fruit on the tree. The publication, by Regent College, of *The Future Shape of Anglican Ministry* in 2004 does much to clarify, yet further, the Conservative position in opposition to the Liberals. Unfortunately, many of the Conservatives within the Anglican Church of Canada either retreat from the world of politics into a pietistic cocoon or they come forward and support an American right-of-centre republican way on the hot-button issues in the culture wars. It is in this sense that the Conservative reaction to the Liberals in the Anglican tradition in Canada is not very conservative. The Canadian High Tory Anglican way is not well represented or understood by self-styled Conservatives within the Anglican Church of Canada, and it is this lack of understanding that has created two tribes that seem incapable of hearing and heeding one another. A course in basic Canadian Anglican history would go a long way to cure both Conservatives and Liberals of some rather basic misconceptions of the tradition. Unfortunately, the Conservatives still often doff and bow their caps to England all the time (they are still theological colonials) and the Liberals genuflect to whatever is trendy and the issue *du jour* in the larger liberal society. Liberals, also, have a weak understanding of the High Tory Anglican way in Canada, and their many caricatures of it are thin and tiresome.

It is to this area of history and principles, prejudices, presuppositions, premises and notions of human nature and identity that the real discussion must go. Those who live, think and have their being from within the matrix of liberalism often lack the ability to see outside of the creed and dogma that so dominates, shapes and controls their thinking. It is in this sense that the Conservatives come as thoughtful critics of the time. Our age and ethos is dominated by liberalism, and the church must be wary of being uncritically wooed, wed and bed by liberalism. Those who marry the spirit of their age become widows when such an age dies is an adage that liberals within the church do well to heed and hear. Liberals who can only be critical of Conservatives are not very liberal. Each and all need to see and face the beam in their own eye, and until they can do this not much of thought and insight will be accomplished in the church or society. The Conservatives need to do some hard reflective work, also. They have, rightly so, raised some good questions about the trendy and uncritical nature of liberalism. What, though, are the dark sides and shadows in the Conservative way? The Anglican Church of Canada will never go forward in a serious and substantive way until both Liberals and Conservatives become more self-critical.

We have an indigenous High Tory Anglican tradition in Canada that most are either unaware of or simply ignore. If Anglicans in Canada keep turning to England as their great and good place, they remain committed to a colonial worldview. Much good has happened in the last few centuries in Canada, and many an Anglican has come forward to articulate a view of God, Church and the World that has much to commend it. The Anglican Church of Canada is still one of the largest forms of Christianity in Canada. There is no doubt it is going through many a test and trial at the present time, but this is not new. The church has gone through such tense and refining moments in the past, and she will do so in the future. It is by going through such struggles that wheat and chaff are separated, gold and dross go in different ways.

The Canadian High Tory Anglican tradition, if line and lineage are traced and tracked, goes back to the Fathers and Mothers of the Patristic era (Latin West and Greek East). It is from this well and source (*ad fontes*) that the water is deepest and purest. The Classical tradition dug the wells deep, and it was from such places that those like the Victorians, John Scotus Eriugena and Bonaventura turned for refreshment when all seemed parched and dry. The Oxford Humanists and Reformers (Colet, More, Erasmus) refound the paths to the ancient wells when most pointed to other paths and destinations. Richard Hooker, the Caroline Divines and Jonathan Swift reminded one and all that those who drink from foreign wells will not slake their thirst at the deepest levels. The English High Romantics (Coleridge, Wordsworth, Southey) relit the torches when all was going dark and the old paths seemed overgrown with much shrub and alder. They pointed the way to the ancient paths and the wells at journey's end. It was this Classical Patristic tradition, as interpreted and carried on by the English Humanists and High Romantics that did much to define and offer guidance to the Canadian High Tory tradition. The Canadian High Tory Anglican way as articulated and lived forth by those like Bishops John Strachan, Charles Inglis and Robert Machray (1831–1904) was indebted to those who had gone before. They did stand, knowingly so, on the shoulders of giants. George Denison, Stephen Leacock, George Grant, Catherine Parr Traill, Mazo de la Roche and John Farthing (1897–1954) saw the ancient wells and pointed with much fervour to them. Donald Creighton, Eugene Forsey, and Marya Fiamengo (1926–2013) reminded one and all that those who forgot the ancient markings were doomed, like Cain, to wander the face of the earth, ever restless and never finding. It is not that the eternal wells go dry. It is more a case that we forget where they are, the paths to them become overgrown, and we then search for things to replace them. But the thirst for the eternal waters within will never abate, and the places that buckets can be dropped deep will never disappear. We, though, can forget where such places are located, and it is the role of the High Tories, High Romantics, Humanists and Mothers and Fathers of the Church to remind us where to turn when we have tried everything and found it wanting and waning.

The home and native land of the Anglican Church of Canada is, obviously, Canada. This is the place in which this ancient and time-clad lady lives, moves and has her being. Her eyes, in an ultimate sense, are fixed on eternity and that which will never change nor alter. She also lives in time, and this means she must deal with the challenges of penultimate and antepenultimate questions and issues.

Indeed, the home and native land of the Anglican Church of Canada is beyond, yet in, time. The place to which the grand lady points is the far shore where all is green and bright, and to which we all must go when the ships from the far shore come to take us across the water to our true home. The task, as this fair lady well knows, is to evoke and kindle within the soul and heart, mind and imagination, of one and all, a desire for that country of deepest longings and most intense desires. And, it is towards such an end that all must be focused and fixed.

There is, therefore, by way of conclusion a third way that needs to be heard and heeded in the Anglican Church of Canada at the present time. This third way might be called the Humanist, the High Romantic or the High Tory way. It is this path and trail that comes as a critic and alternate to the rather dated and reactionary Conservative and Liberal dead ends and cul-de-sacs we now so sadly and tragically find ourselves in. It is only when we come to the point of seeing that the Conservatives and Liberals can only take us so far that we will be open to this Humanist and High Tory way. Until this occurs, much energy and time will be wasted flailing about in a dense and thick forest without ever finding the clearing and the spacious cathedral in it. We are in desperate need of a theology that is nimble enough to elude and evade the Conservative and Liberal Sanhedrins (our modern Sadducees and Pharisees) and point the way to an older, yet ever-new, path to the snow-capped peaks.

CHAPTER TWENTY-FIVE

ANGLICANISM AND ORTHODOXY

the centre cannot hold—mere anarchy is loosed upon the world
— W. B. Yeats[1]

that they may be one, even as we are one — Jesus[2]

My theological journey, as a young man in my early twenties, took me to L'Abri in Switzerland from 1973 to 1974. I was quite taken by Francis Schaeffer, but I was never fully convinced by his brand of an updated version of Calvin and the Calvinist tradition. In short, I was never held by the Reformed tradition. The Reformation is the womb of modernity, and much of the fragmentation we face today is the consequence of the Reformation. The children are out of the womb, now adults and each doing what is right in the sight of their own eyes (and few agree on what the right is).

I had been reading a great deal of C. S. Lewis in the late 1960s and early 1970s, and I was quite aware that Lewis and Schaeffer dwelt in different environs. Lewis was grounded in the classical way, a Medieval–Renaissance scholar, a catholic Anglican—he had serious doubts about both the Reformation tradition and puritan Calvinism. Schaeffer was a true believer in the Reformed read of the Reformation, and its implications for the church and society. Lewis could argue the case for mere Christianity, but there comes a point in the trail when Schaeffer and Lewis part paths for substantive theological, ecclesial and cultural reasons.

Lewis, as I mentioned above, was a catholic Anglican (meaning his thinking was deeply rooted in the Bible–Patristics–Medieval–Renaissance thought), and I found the breadth and depth of such an approach to the Western way most appealing. The fact that many evangelicals have co-opted, thinned out, distorted and misunderstood Lewis should not deter the curious and committed from following the leads of Lewis to the 'discarded image' he sought to reclaim and refind in opposition to the modern liberal project.

The fact that Lewis had a deep respect for the Patristic era meant that he dwelt in a period of time that the Orthodox, Roman Catholics and Anglicans hold high as a significant moment of church history. Lewis was, in fact, part of the catholic renaissance of the 1930s-1940s-1950s that attempted to restore the classics to the life of soul formation, formal education and the church. This was why, for example, Lewis wrote the introduction to St. Athanasius's *On the Incarnation* (*De incarnation verbi Dei*) that was eventually published by St. Vladimir's Orthodox Theological Seminary, although Lewis's introduction to *On the Incarnation* had been published much earlier.

I did a BA at the University of Lethbridge from 1977 to 1979, and as I neared the end of my studies, taken as I was by the insights of Lewis and Thomas Merton, I seriously considered doing graduate studies at the Pontifical Institute of Medieval Studies (PIMS) in Toronto. I was convinced it was in the synthesis of the Patristic–Medieval way, when engaged with the Modern, that a way forward could be found. The Classic Christian, if nothing else, highlights and priorizes unity within the body of Christ, whereas the modern protestant way has ushered in an unprecedented era of fragmentation within the church.

I decided against studying at the Pontifical Institute of Medieval Studies and went to Regent College where I focused on both the Desert tradition and the Patristic era. I did an MA thesis on John Cassian (whom Merton used a great deal), then I went to the University of British Columbia and did an MA on Origen and Anthony. I was, in brief, thoroughly immersed in the leading *ammas*, *abbas* and mystical theologians of the Patristic period. I was a student and teaching assistant of James Houston's when I was at Regent College, and Jim suggested, given my obvious commitment to the Patristic tradition, that I seriously think of becoming an Anglican priest. Jim, when in England, worked closely with many Orthodox and Anglicans. My wife and I pondered such a suggestion on a long walk by the ocean in Vancouver, and we decided, like C. S. Lewis and T. S. Eliot, Samuel Taylor Coleridge, Stephen Leacock and George Grant, my vocation was that of an informed layperson, and my task was to work more in the world than in the church. I remember, with much fondness, my many conversations with Jim Houston.

Regent College had obvious reformed and evangelical institutional leanings and commitments, but Jim Houston, again and again, led the interested and spiritually hungry to the classics of the Christian mystical and contemplative way. When I was at Regent from 1979 to 1981, Francis Schaeffer and Malcolm Muggeridge had both spoken, at different times, at the college. Jim mentioned how disappointed many were with Schaeffer's reactionary reformed ways and how taken many were by Muggeridge's informed catholicity.

I was also reading a great deal of Vladimir Lossky at the time, and I had thoughts of either attending St. Vladimir's Seminary (Orthodox) or Nashota House (High Church Anglican). So, I had a great affinity for both Orthodoxy and High Church Anglicanism by the 1980s, and I was somewhat gratified to know that the future Archbishop of Canterbury (Rowan Williams) did his doctoral dissertation on Lossky when at Oxford. A. M. Allchin's *The Kingdom of Love and Knowledge: The Encounter between Orthodoxy and the West* brought this into sharp relief for me. *The Kingdom of Love and Knowledge* was dedicated to Lossky, and there is a fine chapter on Lossky and Williams in the alluring book.

Rowan Williams was just emerging as a significant English theologian in the 1980s (he had visited St. Vladimir's in 1974), and the publication of *The Wound of Knowledge: Christian Spirituality from the New Testament to St. John of the Cross* in 1979 placed Williams at the forefront of Anglican–Orthodox relations. The publication of Andrew Louth's *The Origins of the Christian Mystical Tradition: From Plato to Denys* in 1981 was also a significant crossroads book for me as I was thinking through the Patristic–Orthodox–Anglican dialogue.

Needless to say, the world of High Church Anglicanism and Orthodoxy had taken me a long distance from Schaeffer and L'Abri by the 1980s.

I mention the above for the simple reason that St. Vladimir's Orthodox Seminary invited Archbishop Rowan Williams to give the twenty-seventh annual Father Alexander Schmemann Memorial Lecture on 30 January 2010. Williams' lecture was called 'Theology and the Contemplative Calling: The Image of Humanity in the Philokalia'. I had, when doing my studies at Regent College and the University of British Columbia, spent a great deal of time in the *Philokalia* and many of the short yet pithy Desert wisdom sayings, and I did a course when at the University of British Columbia, in which I translated and read Gregory of Nyssa's *Life of Moses*. I was fortunate, for a few years, to study regularly the *Philokalia* with Archbishop Lazar Puhalo at the Orthodox monastery in the Fraser

Valley. St. Vladimir's also gave Archbishop Rowan Williams an honorary doctorate when he gave his lecture on the *Philokalia*. Indeed, the Anglican and Orthodox ways have many a meaningful affinity.

Rowan Williams is part of a High Church Anglican tradition that has attempted to discern the relationship between spirituality, the church and prophetic politics. I was quite drawn to the radical Anglo-Catholic way that those like Williams, Kenneth Leech and others have articulated. I was fortunate to spend time with Kenneth Leech in East London, and his earlier book, *Soul Friend*, played a significant role in my inner–outer growth just as his missive, *Subversive Orthodoxy*, congealed much for me. *Subversive Orthodoxy* was a series of lectures given at Trinity College in Toronto in 1991 and published by the Anglican Book Centre. Needless to say, both Williams and Leech are quite fond of Thomas Merton.

There is much more that I could say about the Anglican–Orthodox dialogue. My leanings are High Church (Anglo-Catholic) Anglican, and I have been quite fortunate to work with many Orthodox over the years. In fact, a few years ago, in 2008, I was in Eagle River, Alaska to celebrate the fortieth anniversary of the last final retreat that Thomas Merton gave before he traveled to Asia. The area where Merton gave the retreat is now an Orthodox cathedral, and the Orthodox community was most receptive to my visit. In fact, I stayed in the Merton room, and when there, gave a lecture to the Orthodox on Merton and Orthodoxy. The recent book, *Sophia: The Hidden Christ of Thomas Merton*, makes abundantly clear Merton's many affinities with Orthodoxy. Merton, in his final retreat in Eagle River, turned to Lossky as a serious entry point to Orthodoxy.

Some of my concerns about the recent convergence that is the Orthodox, Roman Catholic, Anglican and Evangelical linking-of-arms in affectionate familial bonds have much to do with how theology is translated into the public realm. Sadly so, much of the concord between those turning to 'the Great Tradition' often translates into a form of republican politics in the public square. I don't think that the richness and fullness of the Christian tradition can be reduced to a right-of-centre ethical stance in the culture wars. Most of the finest thinkers and activists in 'the Great Tradition' would surely question the tribalism of the right, left and sensible centre. It is one thing, therefore, to hear the clarion call to return to the ancient ways—it is quite another thing to restrict the prophetic-like dynamism of the tradition to a plaything and dancing bear of republican–conservative politics. I'm all for a return to 'the Great Tradition', but I question whether the tradition can be merely interpreted, in the present tense, to serve the agenda of the political right-of-centre (whether in a sophisticated, popular or crude manner).

There is a form of conciliar Roman Catholic thought as embodied in those like Thomas Merton, and a form of High Church Anglicanism as incarnated by Rowan Williams and Kenneth Leech that has a great deal of affinity with an Orthodox tradition that has dug deeply into the peace and justice way. The future of the church hinges on how these classical and ancient types of faith are interpreted and work together. The ecclesial journey into the future must surely oppose both the fragmentary forces at work in modern and postmodern forms of Christianity that erode, yet further, the centre and the increasing fragmentation that so defines and besets liberal modernity. Such a pilgrimage into the Great Tradition must be wary of any public agenda that reduces the political vision of the church to the ideology of the right, left or centre. It is by articulating a higher and more consistent ethical stance that the church is true to her prophetic calling, and within the Canadian context, there is no doubt that George Grant has pointed the way to such an ennobling place to live, move and have our being.

NOTES

CHAPTER 1—CANADIAN TORYISM AND AMERICAN CONSERVATISM

1. Walter Raleigh, ed., *The Complete Works of George Savile, First Marquess of Halifax*, Oxford, Clarendon Press, 1912, p. 246.
2. Charles Inglis, *The True Interest of America Impartially Stated: In Certain Strictures on a Pamphlet Entitled Common Sense*, 2nd edition, Philadelphia, Pennsylvania, James Humphreys, Jr., 1776.
3. William H. Nelson, *The American Tory*, Oxford, Clarendon Press, 1961, p. 186.

CHAPTER 2—JANUS, TERRORISM AND PEACEMAKING

1. Saint Augustine of Hippo, *Concerning the City of God against the Pagans*, trans. Henry Bettenson, Harmondsworth, Middlesex, Penguin Books, 1972, bk. 4, ch. 4, p. 139.
2. Sunera Thobani, 'It's Bloodthirsty Vengeance', speech delivered at Women's Resistance: From Victimization to Criminalization, Canadian Association of Elizabeth Fry Societies and Canadian Association of Sexual Assault Centres, Ottawa, 1 October 2001. Published as Sunera Thobani, '"It's Bloodthirsty Vengeance": Transcript of UBC Professor Sunera Thobani's Speech at the Women's Resistance Conference', *The Vancouver Sun*, 3 October 2001, p. A6.
3. Samuel P. Huntington, 'The Clash of Civilizations?', *Foreign Affairs*, Vol. 72, No. 3, Summer 1993, pp. 22–49.
4. Adam Curtis, dir., *The Power of Nightmares: The Rise of the Politics of Fear*, video documentary broadcast on BBC2, 20 October 2014–3 November 2014.
5. On the political influence of Leo Strauss, see Shadia B. Drury's *Leo Strauss and the American Right*, New York, St. Martin's Press, 1997.
6. Thomas Merton, *Peace in the Post-Christian Era*, Maryknoll, New York, Orbis Books, 2004, pp. 41–42.
7. Augustine, *Concerning the City of God against the Pagans*, bk. 4, ch. 4, p. 139.
8. Ronald G. Musto, *The Catholic Peace Tradition*, Maryknoll, New York, Orbis Books, 1986, p. 119.

CHAPTER 3—NOAM CHOMSKY AND THE CANADIAN WAY

1. John Newlove, 'America', in Margaret Atwood, ed., *The New Oxford Book of Canadian Verse*, Oxford, Oxford University Press, 1982, p. 344.

2. Noam Chomsky, 'Necessary Illusions: Thought Control in Democratic Societies', *CBC Massey Lectures*, radio broadcast on CBC Radio, 28 November 1988–2 December 1988. Published as Noam Chomsky, *Necessary Illusions: Thought Control in Democratic Societies*, Montreal, CBC Enterprises, 1989.
3. Mark Achbar and Peter Wintonick, dirs., *Manufacturing Consent: Noam Chomsky and the Media*, documentary film, Montreal, 1992.

CHAPTER 4—NOAM CHOMSKY MEETS ROBIN MATHEWS

1. Paul Robinson, 'The Chomsky Problem', *The New York Times*, 25 February 1979, pp. 3, 37, at p. 3.
2. James Lorimer, 'Robin's Egging Us on Again', *Books in Canada*, Vol. 6, No. 1, January 1977, p. 23.

CHAPTER 5—HOWL AND LAMENT FOR A NATION

1. John Suiter, *Poets on the Peaks: Gary Snyder, Philip Whalen & Jack Kerouac in the Cascades*, Washington, D. C., Counterpoint, 2002, p. 148.
2. See Kenneth Rexroth, *An Autobiographical Novel*, Garden City, New York, Doubleday and Co., 1966, ch. 30, pp. 277–294.
3. Allen Ginsberg, *Howl and Other Poems*, City Lights Books, San Francisco, California, 1956, twenty-first printing, April 1969, back cover.
4. Peter C. Emberley, 'Foreword', in George Grant, *Lament for a Nation: The Defeat of Canadian Nationalism*, 40th anniversary edition, Montreal, McGill-Queen's University Press, 2005, p. lxxviii. *Lament for a Nation* is reprinted in George Grant, *Collected Works of George Grant: Volume 3, 1960–1969*, ed. Arthur Davis and Henry Roper, Toronto, University of Toronto Press, 2005, pp. 271–367.
5. Darrol Bryant, 'The Barren Twilight: History and Faith in Grant', in Lawrence Schmidt, ed., *George Grant in Process: Essays and Conversations*, Toronto, House of Anansi, 1979, pp. 110–119, at p. 114.
6. Kenneth Rexroth testified during Allen Ginsberg's 1957 obscenity trial on the nature and theme of 'Howl' saying, 'Well, the simplest term for such writing is prophetic; it is easier to call it that than anything else because we have a large body of prophetic writing to refer to. These are the prophets of the Bible, which it greatly resembles in purpose and in language and in subject matter.' See trial transcript in Bill Morgan and Nancy J. Peters, eds., *Howl on Trial: The Battle for Free Expression*, San Francisco, California, City Lights Books, 2006, p. 165.
7. Ginsberg, *Howl and Other Poems*, p. 3.
8. Jack Kerouac, *Lonesome Traveler*, New York, McGraw-Hill, 1960, p. vi.
9. Grant, *Lament for a Nation*, p. vii.
10. Ginsberg, *Howl and Other Poems*, p. 9.
11. Ibid., p. 3.

CHAPTER 6—WHAT IS CANADIAN CONSERVATISM?

1. Stephen Leacock, *Greater Canada: An Appeal*, Montreal, Montreal News Co., c. 1907, p. 9.
2. Grant, *Lament for a Nation*, p. 5.

CHAPTER 7—LEACOCK AND THE CANADIAN TORY TRADITION

1. Alan Bowker, 'Introduction', in Stephen Leacock, *Social Criticism: The Unsolved Riddle of Social Justice and Other Essays*, ed. Alan Bowker, Toronto, University of Toronto Press, 1996, pp. ix–xlviii, at p. xxxvii.
2. Ian Ross Robertson, 'The Historical Leacock', in David Staines, ed., *Stephen Leacock: An Appraisal*, Ottawa, University of Ottawa Press, 1986, pp. 33–49, at pp. 47–48.
3. Alan Bowker, 'A Postscript', in Leacock, *Social Criticism*, pp. li–lix, at p. lvii.
4. See Horowitz's well-worn article, Gad Horowitz, 'Conservatism, Liberalism, and Socialism in Canada: An Interpretation', *Canadian Journal of Economics and Political Science*, Vol. 32, No. 2, May 1966, pp. 143–171, and his earlier trial-balloon article, Gad Horowitz, 'Tories, Socialists and the Demise of Canada', *Canadian Dimension*, Vol. 2, No. 4, May-June 1965, pp. 12–15.
5. Ibid.
6. James A. 'Pete' McGarvey, *The Old Brewery Bay: A Leacockian Tale*, Toronto, Dundurn Press, 1994, pp. 81–83.
7. Stephen Leacock, *Sunshine Sketches of a Little Town*, ed. Carl Spadoni, Peterborough, Ontario, Broadview Press, 2002, p. 4.
8. Published in Stephen Leacock, *My Recollection of Chicago and The Doctrine of Laissez Faire*, ed. Carl Spadoni, Toronto, University of Toronto Press, 1998.
9. Carl Spadoni, 'Editor's Introduction', in Leacock, *My Recollection of Chicago and The Doctrine of Laissez Faire*, pp. vii–xxxix, at p. xxiv.
10. Ian Ross Robertson, 'The Historical Leacock', in David Staines, ed., *Stephen Leacock: An Appraisal*, Ottawa, University of Ottawa Press, 1986, pp. 33–49, at p. 33.
11. This now well-rehearsed line, Stephen Leacock's 'John Bull', first appeared in the conclusion to his article 'After the Conference—John Bull and his Grown-up Sons' in the London *The Morning Post*, 17 May 1907, and took on a life of its own in the commentary of the magazines of the day. See John S. Ewart, 'A Perplexed Imperialist', *Queen's Quarterly Review*, Vol. 15, No. 2, October-November-December 1907, pp. 90–100, at p. 90; see also J. Castell Hopkins, *The Canadian Annual Review of Public Affairs: 1907*, Toronto, Annual Review Publishing Co., 1908, pp. 374–375.
12. William Peterson, as quoted in Leacock, *Social Criticism*, p. xiv.

13. Winston Churchill, as quoted in Ewart, 'A Perplexed Imperialist', p. 90.
14. Leacock, *Greater Canada: An Appeal*, p. 9.
15. Stephen Leacock, *Приключения в Плуториа-клубе*, Moscow, Огонек, 1929.
16. Stephen Leacock, 'The Great Fight for Clean Government', in *Arcadian Adventures with the Idle Rich*, Toronto, McClelland and Stewart, 1989, ch. 8, pp. 180–203.
17. Leacock, 'L'Envoi: The Train to Mariposa', in *Sunshine Sketches of a Little Town*, ch. 12, pp. 151–156.
18. Bowker, 'Introduction', in Leacock, *Social Criticism*, pp. ix–xlviii, at p. xix.
19. Ibid., at p. xxxviii.
20. Stephen Leacock, 'Foreword', in R. B. Bennett, *The Premier Speaks to the People: The Prime Minister's January Radio Broadcasts Issued in Book Form—The First Address*, Ottawa, Dominion Conservative Headquarters, 1935, pp. 5–7. These five radio broadcasts were issued in a series of five booklets, each having a foreword by a different author—Leacock introduced the initial issue, the first of the addresses.
21. Stephen Leacock, 'What Can Izaak Walton Teach Us?', in *Last Leaves*, Toronto, McClelland and Stewart, 1945, pp. 13–20.
22. Robertson Davies, 'Stephen Leacock', in Claude T. Bissell, ed., *Our Living Tradition: Seven Canadians*, Toronto, University of Toronto Press, 1957, pp. 128–149, at p. 147.

CHAPTER 8—DONALD CREIGHTON AND EUGENE FORSEY

1. Eugene Forsey, as quoted in Charles P. B. Taylor, *Radical Tories: The Conservative Tradition in Canada*, Toronto, House of Anansi, 1982, p. 97.
2. Taylor, *Radical Tories*, ch. 2, pp. 21–48.
3. Ibid., ch. 5, pp. 97–126.
4. Donald Grant Creighton, 'Eugene Forsey: Political Traditionalist, Social Radical', in *The Passionate Observer: Selected Writings*, Toronto, McClelland and Stewart, 1980, pp. 190–211, at p. 211.
5. Eugene Forsey, as quoted in Taylor, *Radical Tories*, p. 99.
6. Eugene Forsey, 'What Have These Reformers Wrought?', *The Machray Review*, No. 6, December 1997, pp. 34–39.

CHAPTER 9—THE TROJAN HORSE OF LIBERALISM

1. Robin Mathews, *The Canadian Intellectual Tradition: A Modern People and Its Community*, Burnaby, B. C., Simon Fraser University, 1990, p. 114.

CHAPTER 10—LAMENT FOR A NATION AND RED TORYISM

1. The Royal Commission on National Development in the Arts, Letters and

Sciences, 1949–1951.
2. George Grant, 'Philosophy', in Canada, *Royal Commission Studies: A Selection of Essays Prepared for the Royal Commission on National Development in the Arts, Letters and Sciences*, Ottawa, E. Cloutier, Printer to the King, 1951, pp. 119–133. Reprinted in George Grant, *Collected Works of George Grant: Volume 2, 1951–1959*, ed. Arthur Davis, Toronto, University of Toronto Press, 2002, pp. 3–21.
3. See George Grant, 'Tyranny and Wisdom: A Comment on the Controversy between Leo Strauss and Alexendre Kojeve', *Social Research*, Vol. 31, No. 1, Spring 1964, pp. 45–72. Reprinted in Grant, *Collected Works of George Grant: Volume 3, 1960–1969*, pp. 532–557.
4. See Denis Smith, *Rogue Tory: The Life and Legend of John G. Diefenbaker*, Toronto, MacFarlane Walter and Ross, 1995.
5. William Christian, *George Grant: A Biography*, Toronto, University of Toronto Press, 1993, p. 279.
6. Grant, *Lament for a Nation*, p. 3.
7. Ibid., p. 5.
8. Ibid., p. 7. See Richard Hooker, *The Works of Mr. Richard Hooker, Containing Eight Books of the Laws of Ecclesiastical Polity*, 2 vols., Oxford, J. Vincent for T. Tegg, 1839, p. 107.

CHAPTER 11—GEORGE GRANT AND RADICAL ORTHODOXY

1. John Milbank, letter to Ron Dart, 15 December 2014.
2. John Milbank, letter to Ron Dart, 2 January 2015.
3. See Jonathan Swift, 'A Full and True Account of the Battel Fought Last Friday, between the Antient and the Modern Books in St. James's Library', in *A Tale of a Tub*, London, J. Nutt, 1704, pp. 229–278.

CHAPTER 12—C. S. LEWIS AND GEORGE GRANT

1. George Grant, letter to David Llewellyn Dodds, 11 November 1986. Published as George Grant, '282', in *George Grant: Selected Letters*, ed. William Christian, Toronto, University of Toronto Press, 1996, p. 361.
2. Arthur Davis, 'Introduction to Volume 1: 1933–1950', in George Grant, *Collected Works of George Grant: Volume 1, 1933–1950*, Toronto, University of Toronto Press, 2000, pp. xxi–xxxviii, at p. xxx.
3. David Cayley and George Grant, *George Grant in Conversation*, Concord, Ontario, House of Anansi, 1995, pp. vii–viii.
4. Norman F. Cantor, *Inventing the Middle Ages: The Lives, Works, and Ideas of the Great Medievalists of the Twentieth Century*, New York, Quill–Morrow and Co., 1991, p. 218.
5. Jim Houston, 'Reminiscences of the Oxford Lewis', in David Graham, ed., *We Remember C. S. Lewis*, Nashville, Tennessee, Broadman and Holman Publishers, 2001, pp. 129–143, at p. 136.

6. Cayley and Grant, *George Grant in Conversation*, p. 9.
7. Ibid., p. 7.
8. Cantor, *Inventing the Middle Ages*, p. 216.
9. George Grant, review of *The Higher Learning in America* by Robert M. Hutchins, 'The Bookshelf', column in *Queen's University Journal*, 18 January 1938, p. 3. Reprinted in Grant, *Collected Works of George Grant: Volume 1, 1933–1950*, pp. 6–8.
10. George Grant, 'The Year's Developments in the Arts and Sciences: Philosophy and Religion', in Robert M. Hutchins and Mortimer J. Adler, eds., *The Great Ideas Today: 1961*, Chicago, Illinois, Encyclopaedia Britannica, 1961, pp. 336–376. Reprinted in Grant, *Collected Works of George Grant: Volume 3, 1960–1969*, pp. 66–108.
11. Sheila Grant, phone conversation with Ron Dart, 18 October 2001.
12. C. S. Lewis, 'Appendix: Illustrations of the Tao', in *The Abolition of Man; or, Reflections on Education with Special Reference to the Teaching of English in the Upper Forms of Schools*, New York, Touchstone Books, 1996, pp. 89–109.
13. Sheila Grant, phone conversation with Ron Dart, 25 October 2001.
14. Louis Greenspan, 'George Grant Remembered', in Wayne Whillier, ed., *Two Theological Languages by George Grant and Other Essays in Honour of His Work*, Queenston, Ontario, Edwin Mellen Press, 1990, pp. 1–5, at p. 1.
15. Cayley and Grant, *George Grant in Conversation*, p. 53.
16. C. S. Lewis, 'Is Progress Possible? Willing Slaves of the Welfare State', in *God in the Dock: Essays in Theology and Ethics*, ed. Walter Hooper, Grand Rapids, Michigan, W. B. Eerdmans, 1970, pp. 311–316.
17. John G. West, Jr., 'Finding the Permanent in the Political: C. S. Lewis as a Political Thinker', in *Permanent Things: Towards the Recovery of a More Human Scale at the End of the Twentieth Century*, ed. Andrew A. Tadie and Michael H. Macdonald, Grand Rapids, Michigan, W. B. Eerdmans, 1995, pp. 137–148.
18. James Christie, 'Jack in the World: The Social Vision of C. S. Lewis', *Pilgrimage: The Toronto C. S. Lewis Society Bulletin*, Vol. 9, No. 1, November 2001, pp. 1–16, at p. 3.
19. Ibid., at p. 9.
20. C. S. Lewis, 'First and Second Things', in *God in the Dock*, pp. 278–281.
21. C. S. Lewis, 'The World's Last Night', in *The World's Last Night and Other Essays*, New York, Harcourt Brace, 1960, pp. 93–113.
22. C. S. Lewis, 'Social Morality', in *Mere Christianity*, New York, HarperCollins, 2001, pp. 82–87, at p. 84.
23. Ibid.
24. Ibid., at p. 85.
25. George Grant, 'An Ethic of Community', in Michael Oliver, ed., *Social Purpose for Canada*, Toronto, University of Toronto Press, 1961, pp. 3–26. Reprinted in Grant, *Collected Works of George Grant: Volume 3, 1960–1969*, pp. 20–48.

26. Christopher Dawson, *The Spirit of the Oxford Movement*, New York, Sheed and Ward, 1933, p. xi.

CHAPTER 13—STEPHEN LEACOCK AND GEORGE GRANT

1. William Christian, *George Grant: A Biography*, p. 379.
2. Ibid., p. 30.
3. Taylor, 'A Special Destiny: Leacock, Sandwell and Deacon', in *Radical Tories*, ch. 1, pp. 9–20.
4. Taylor, 'Threnody: George Grant', in *Radical Tories*, ch. 6, pp. 127–157.
5. Published in Stephen Leacock, *My Recollection of Chicago and The Doctrine of Laissez Faire*, ed. Carl Spadoni, Toronto, University of Toronto Press, 1998.
6. Published as George Grant, 'DPhil Thesis: Oxford 1950 The Concept of Nature and Supernature in the Theology of John Oman', in *Collected Works of George Grant: Volume 1, 1933–1950*, ed. Arthur Davis and Peter Emberley, Toronto, University of Toronto Press, 2002, pp. 157–420.
7. Leacock, 'L'Envoi: The Train to Mariposa', in *Sunshine Sketches of a Little Town*, ch. 12, pp. 151–156.
8. Stephen Leacock, 'The Apology of a Professor', in *Essays and Literary Studies*, New York, John Lane, 1916, pp. 9–37.
9. Leacock, 'The Devil and the Deep Sea', in *Essays and Literary Studies*, pp. 39–61.
10. Leacock, 'The Lot of the Schoolmaster', in *Essays and Literary Studies*, pp. 161–189.
11. Gerald Lynch, 'Afterword', in Stephen Leacock, *Arcadian Adventures with the Idle Rich*, Toronto, McClelland and Stewart, 1989, pp. 205–211, at p. 211.
12. Leacock, 'What Can Izaak Walton Teach Us?', in *Last Leaves*, Toronto, McClelland and Stewart, 1945, pp. 13–20.
13. Leacock, 'The School Is the Lever', in *Last Leaves*, pp. 103–105.
14. Leacock, 'Rebuilding the Cities', in *Last Leaves*, pp. 83–87.
15. Leacock, 'Commonsense and the Universe', in *Last Leaves*, pp. 35–51.
16. Leacock, 'A Lecture on Walking', in *Last Leaves*, pp. 21–26.
17. Leacock, 'Good-Bye, Motor Car!', in *Last Leaves*, pp. 27–31.
18. George Grant, 'Philosophy (1951)', in *The George Grant Reader*, ed. William Christian and Sheila Grant, Toronto, University of Toronto Press, 1998, pp. 157–173. Originally published in Canada, *Royal Commission Studies: A Selection of Essays Prepared for the Royal Commission on National Development in the Arts, Letters and Sciences*, Ottawa, E. Cloutier, Printer to the King, 1951, pp. 119–133. Reprinted, also, in Grant, *Collected Works of George Grant: Volume 2, 1951–1959*, pp. 3–21.
19. Grant, 'The Paradox of Democratic Education (1955)', in *The George Grant Reader*, pp. 174–187. Reprinted, also, in Grant, *Collected Works of George Grant: Volume 2, 1951–1959*, pp. 166–181.

20. Grant, 'Letter of Resignation (1960)', in *The George Grant Reader*, pp. 188–190. Reprinted, also, in Grant, *Collected Works of George Grant: Volume 3, 1960–1969*, pp. 5–8.
21. Grant, 'The University Curriculum (1975)', in *The George Grant Reader*, pp. 191–200. An earlier version of this essay is published in Grant, *Collected Works of George Grant: Volume 3, 1960–1969*, pp. 558–576.
22. Grant, 'The Battle between Teaching and Research (1980)', in *The George Grant Reader*, pp. 200–203. Reprinted, also, in George Grant, *Collected Works of George Grant: Volume 4, 1970–1988*, ed. Arthur Davis and Henry Roper, Toronto, University of Toronto Press, 2009, pp. 421–425.
23. Erich Frank, 'The Fundamental Opposition between Plato and Aristotle', *The American Journal of Philology*, Vol. 61, No. 1, January 1940, pp. 34–53.
24. Grant, 'The Battle between Teaching and Research (1980)', in *The George Grant Reader*, pp. 200–203.
25. George Grant, review of *The Higher Learning in America* by Robert M. Hutchins, 'The Bookshelf', column in *Queen's University Journal*, 18 January 1938, p. 3. Reprinted in Grant, *Collected Works of George Grant: Volume 1, 1933–1950*, pp. 6–8.
26. Mortimer Adler, 'Great Books, Democracy and Truth', in Michael D. Torre, ed., *Freedom in the Modern World: Jacques Maritain, Yves R. Simon, Mortimer J. Adler*, Mishawaka, Indiana, University of Notre Dame Press, 1989, pp. 33–45.
27. 'These days when we are told in North America that capitalism is conservative, we should remember that capitalism was the great dissolvent of the traditional virtues and that its greatest philosophers, Hobbes and Locke, Smith and Hume, were Britishers. In the appeal to capitalism as the tradition it is forgotten that the capitalist philosophers dissolved all ideas of the sacred as standing in the way of the emancipation of greed.' George Grant, *Technology and Empire: Perspectives on North America*, Toronto, House of Anansi, 1969, p. 66. *Technology and Empire* is reprinted in Grant, *Collected Works of George Grant: Volume 3, 1960–1969*, pp. 473–594.
28. George Grant, *English-Speaking Justice*, Sackville, New Brunswick, Mount Allison University Press, 1974, pp. 49–50. *English-Speaking Justice* is reprinted in Grant, *Collected Works of George Grant: Volume 4, 1970–1988*, pp. 190–268.
29. Leacock, *Sunshine Sketches of a Little Town*, p. 4.
30. Published in Stephen Leacock, *My Recollection of Chicago and The Doctrine of Laissez Faire*, ed. Carl Spadoni, Toronto, University of Toronto Press, 1998.
31. Report on Social Security for Canada, Advisory Committee on Reconstruction, 1943. Published as Canada, *Report on Social Security for Canada*, prepared by L. C. Marsh for the Advisory Committee on Reconstruction, Ottawa, King's Printer, 1943.
32. Leacock, 'Foreword', in Bennett, *The Premier Speaks to the People—The First Address*, pp. 5–7.

33. Nicholas Jennings, *Before the Gold Rush: Flashbacks to the Dawn of the Canadian Sound*, Toronto, Viking, 1997, p. 33.

34. *The Empire: Yes or No?* is reprinted in Grant, *Collected Works of George Grant: Volume 1, 1933–1950*, pp. 97–126.

35. George Grant, 'An Ethic of Community', in Michael Oliver, ed., *Social Purpose for Canada*, Toronto, University of Toronto Press, 1961, pp. 3–26. Reprinted in Grant, *Collected Works of George Grant: Volume 3, 1960–1969*, pp. 20–48.

36. George Grant, 'Foreword', in James Laxer and Robert Laxer, *The Liberal Idea of Canada: Pierre Trudeau and the Question of Canada's Survival*, Toronto, James Lorimer and Co., 1977, pp. 9–12. Reprinted in Grant, *Collected Works of George Grant: Volume 4, 1970–1988*, pp. 330–334.

37. George Grant, 'Revolution, Responsibility, and Conservatism', address delivered at the Toronto International Teach-In, Varsity Arena, Toronto, held 8–10 October 1965. Published as George Grant, 'Realism in Political Protest', *Christian Outlook*, Vol. 21, No. 2, November 1965, pp. 3–6. Reprinted as George Grant, 'To Be a Citizen in North America', in William Kilbourn, ed., *Canada: A Guide to the Peaceable Kingdom*, Toronto, Macmillan of Canada, 1970, pp. 219–222. Reprinted, also, as Grant, 'Protest and Technology', in *Collected Works of George Grant: Volume 3, 1960–1969*, pp. 393–401.

38. George Grant, 'The Vietnam War: The Value of Protest', address delivered at a demonstration for peace in Vietnam, Toronto, 14 May 1966. Published as George Grant, 'The Value of Protest', in *The George Grant Reader*, ed. William Christian and Sheila Grant, Toronto, University of Toronto Press, 1998, pp. 90–94. Reprinted, also, in Grant, *Collected Works of George Grant: Volume 3, 1960–1969*, pp. 426–430.

39. George Grant, review of *Benjamin Disraeli Letters* by Benjamin Disraeli, first and second volumes, edited by J. A. W. Gunn et al., in *The Globe and Mail*, 8 May 1982, p. E15. Reprinted as Grant, 'Review of Benjamin Disraeli: Early Letters, Volume I and II, edited by J. A. W. Gunn, John Matthews, and Donald M. Schurman', in *Collected Works of George Grant: Volume 4, 1970–1988*, pp. 911–915, at p. 912.

40. Leacock, 'A Rehabilitation of Charles II', in *Essays and Literary Studies*, pp. 267–310.

41. George Grant, 'Adult Education in an Expanding Economy', *The Anglican Outlook*, Vol. 10, No. 7, May 1955, pp. 8–11. Reprinted in Grant, *Collected Works of George Grant: Volume 2, 1951–1959*, pp. 100–109.

42. Sheila Grant and George Grant, 'Abortion and Rights: The Value of Political Freedom', in Eugene Fairweather and Ian Gentles, eds., *The Right to Birth: Some Christian Views on Abortion*, Toronto, Anglican Book Centre, 1976, pp. 1–12.

43. Ted Heaven, phone conversation with Ron Dart, 3 June 2003.

44. George Grant, 'Nietzsche and the Ancients: Philosophy and Scholarship', *Dionysius*, Vol. 3, December 1979, pp. 5–16. Reprinted in Grant, *Collected Works of George Grant: Volume 4, 1970–1988*, pp. 639–651.

45. This article was republished as Sheila Grant and George Grant, 'Abortion and Rights: The Value of Political Freedom', in G. Richmond Bridge, ed., *Holy Living: Christian Morality Today—1986 Theological Conference*, Charlottetown, Prince Edward Island, St. Peter Publications, 1986, pp. 28–35.
46. George Grant is buried in the churchyard of St. Paul's parish, Terence Bay, Nova Scotia.

CHAPTER 14—GRANT, PINNOCK AND POLITICAL THEOLOGY

1. Ian H. Angus, Ron Dart, and Randy Peg Peters, eds., *Athens and Jerusalem: George Grant's Theology, Philosophy, and Politics*, Toronto, University of Toronto Press, 2006, inside flap.
2. Henry H. Knight III in Barry L. Callen, *Clark H. Pinnock: Journey towards Renewal*, Nappanee, Indiana, Evangel Press, 2000, back cover.

CHAPTER 15—GEORGE GRANT AND ROBERT CROUSE

1. Robert Dodaro, 'Preface', in Michael Treschow, Willemien Otten and Walter Hannam, eds., *Divine Creation in Ancient, Medieval and Early Modern Thought: Essays Presented to the Rev'd Dr Robert D. Crouse*, London, Brill, 2007, xi–xiii, at p. xi.
2. Angus et al., *Athens and Jerusalem: George Grant's Theology, Philosophy, and Politics*, inside flap.
3. Robert Crouse, letter to Ron Dart, 3 March 1997.
4. Sheila Grant, letter to Ron Dart, 18 August 1998.
5. George Grant, 'Philosophy', in Canada, *Royal Commission Studies: A Selection of Essays Prepared for the Royal Commission on National Development in the Arts, Letters and Sciences*, Ottawa, E. Cloutier, Printer to the King, 1951, pp. 119–133. Reprinted in Grant, *Collected Works of George Grant: Volume 2, 1951–1959*, pp. 3–21.
6. Arthur Davis, 'Introduction to Volume 2: 1951–1959', in Grant, *Collected Works of George Grant: Volume 2, 1951–1959*, pp. xvii–xxxvi, at p. xxxi.
7. Sheila Grant, 'Afterword', in Grant, *Lament for a Nation*, pp. 97–99, at p. 97.
8. Robert Crouse, letter to Ron Dart, 3 March 1997.
9. Grant, *Lament for a Nation*, p. 7. See Hooker, *The Works of Mr. Richard Hooker, Containing Eight Books of the Laws of Ecclesiastical Polity*, p. 107.
10. W. J. Hankey, 'Visio: the Method of Robert Crouse's Philosophical Theology', in Susan Harris and Nicholas Hatt, eds., *Recognizing the Sacred in the Modern Secular: How the Sacred Is to Be Discovered in Today's World*, Charlottetown, Prince Edward Island, St. Peter Publications, 2012, pp. 115–148.

CHAPTER 16—THE MATRIX OF LIBERALISM

1. Grant, *Lament for a Nation*, p. 91.
2. Fyodor Dostoevsky, *The Idiot*, trans. Henry Carlisle and Olga Carlisle, New York, New American Library, 1980, p. 313.
3. Ronald Beiner, 'Hermeneutical Generosity and Social Criticism', in *Philosophy in a Time of Lost Spirit: Essays on Contemporary Theory*, Toronto, University of Toronto Press, 1997, pp. 151–166.
4. Matthew 7:1–5.
5. Thomas Merton, *New Seeds of Contemplation*, New York, New Directions Books, 1961, p. 7.

CHAPTER 17—CHARLES TAYLOR AND THE HEGELIAN EDEN TREE

1. Robert C. Sibley, 'Grant, Hegel, and the "Impossibility of Canada"', in Ian H. Angus, Ron Dart, and Randy Peg Peters, eds., *Athens and Jerusalem: George Grant's Theology, Philosophy, and Politics*, Toronto, University of Toronto Press, 2006, pp. 93–107.
2. Alexander Duff, 'Response to the Strauss–Kojeve Debate: George Grant's Turn from Hegel to Christian Platonism', in Angus et al., *Athens and Jerusalem*, pp. 108–123.
3. Neil Robertson, 'Freedom and the Tradition: George Grant, James Doull, and the Character of Modernity', in Angus et al., *Athens and Jerusalem*, pp. 136–165.
4. Charles M. Taylor, *The Pattern of Politics*, Toronto, McClelland and Stewart, 1970, pp. 81.
5. Ibid., p. 85.
6. These lectures were published, in an expanded form, in conjunction with their November 1992 CBC Radio broadcast, as Charles M. Taylor, *The Malaise of Modernity*, Concord, Ontario, House of Anansi, 1991.
7. Beiner, 'Hermeneutical Generosity and Social Criticism', in *Philosophy in a Time of Lost Spirit*, pp. 151–166.
8. Grant summed up this reality well when he said, 'The rhetoric of pluralism simply legitimizes the monistic fact'. Grant, *Technology and Empire*, p. 119.

CHAPTER 18—THE RED TORY DIALOGUE

1. Gad Horowitz, 'Tories, Socialists and the Demise of Canada', in H. D. Forbes, ed., *Canadian Political Thought*, Toronto, Oxford University Press, 1985, pp. 352–359, at p. 354.
2. Grant, *Lament for a Nation*, p. 57.
3. See George Grant, *Philosophy in the Mass Age*, New York, Hill and Wang, 1960, chs. 6–7, pp. 80–110. *Philosophy in the Mass Age* is reprinted in

Grant, *Collected Works of George Grant: Volume 2, 1951–1959*, pp. 310–407.

4. Gad Horowitz, 'Tories, Socialists and the Demise of Canada', *Canadian Dimension*, Vol. 2, No. 4, May-June 1965, pp. 12–15. Reprinted in H. D. Forbes, ed., *Canadian Political Thought*, Toronto, Oxford University Press, 1985, pp. 352–359.

5. Horowitz, 'Tories, Socialists and the Demise of Canada', in Forbes, *Canadian Political Thought*, pp. 352–359, at p. 354.

6. Ibid., at p. 359.

7. Gad Horowitz, 'Conservatism, Liberalism, and Socialism in Canada: An Interpretation', *The Canadian Journal of Economics and Political Science*, Vol. 32, No. 2, May 1966, pp. 143–171.

8. Gad Horowitz, 'Red Tory', in William Kilbourn, ed., *Canada: A Guide to the Peaceable Kingdom*, Toronto, Macmillan of Canada, 1970, pp. 254–260.

9. George Grant, 'To Be a Citizen in North America', in William Kilbourn, ed., *Canada: A Guide to the Peaceable Kingdom*, Toronto, Macmillan of Canada, 1970, pp. 219–222, at pp. 220–221. Originally published, from a 1965 address entitled 'Revolution, Responsibility, and Conservatism', as George Grant, 'Realism in Political Protest', *Christian Outlook*, Vol. 21, No. 2, November 1965, pp. 3–6. Reprinted, also, as Grant, 'Protest and Technology', in *Collected Works of George Grant: Volume 3, 1960–1969*, pp. 393–401.

10. Gad Horowitz, interview with George Grant, 'Horowitz and Grant Talk', *Canadian Dimension*, Vol. 6, No. 6, December 1969-January 1970, pp. 18–20. Reprinted as Grant, '"Technology and Man": An Interview of George Grant by Gad Horowitz', in *Collected Works of George Grant: Volume 3, 1960–1969*, pp. 595–602.

11. Grant, '"Technology and Man": An Interview of George Grant by Gad Horowitz', in *Collected Works of George Grant: Volume 3, 1960–1969*, pp. 595–602, at p. 597.

12. Charles M. Taylor, 'The Agony of Economic Man', in Laurier LaPierre et al., eds., *Essays on the Left: Essays in Honour of T. C. Douglas*, Toronto, McClelland and Stewart, 1971, pp. 221–235.

13. David Warren, 'On George Grant's Nationalism', in Peter C. Emberley, ed., *By Loving Our Own: George Grant and the Legacy of Lament for a Nation*, Ottawa, Carleton University Press, 1990, pp. 59–73; Janet Ajzenstat, 'The Conservatism of the Canadian Founders', in William Gairdner, ed., *After Liberalism: Essays in Search of Freedom, Virtue, and Order*, Toronto, Stoddart Publishing, 1998, pp. 17–32.

CHAPTER 19—THE ANGLICAN TRADITION AND THE RED TORY WAY

1. David Warren, 'On George Grant's Nationalism', in Peter C. Emberley, ed., *By Loving Our Own: George Grant and the Legacy of Lament for a*

Nation, Ottawa, Carleton University Press, 1990, pp. 59–73, at p. 69.
2. Frank Weston, 'Our Present Duty', in Francis Underhill and Charles Scott Gillett, eds., *Report of the Anglo-Catholic Congress*, London, Society of SS. Peter and Paul, 1923, pp. 179–186, at p. 185.
3. George Grant, 'In Defence of Simone Weil', *The Idler*, No. 15, January-February 1988, pp. 36–40. Reprinted in Grant, *Collected Works of George Grant: Volume 4, 1970–1988*, pp. 855–866.
4. Lawrence Schmidt, 'George Grant on Simone Weil as Saint and Thinker', in Arthur Davis, ed., *George Grant and the Subversion of Modernity: Art, Philosophy, Politics, Religion, and Education*, Toronto, University of Toronto Press, 1996, pp. 263–281.

CHAPTER 20—STEPHEN LEACOCK AND T. S. ELIOT

1. Peter Ackroyd, *T. S. Eliot: A Life*, New York, Simon and Schuster, 1984, p. 61.
2. T. S. Eliot, 'Mr. Leacock Serious', review of *Essays and Literary Studies* by Stephen Leacock, in *New Statesman*, Vol. 7, No. 173, 29 July 1916, pp. 404–405, at p. 405.
3. See R. H. Tawney, *Religion and the Rise of Capitalism: A Historical Study*, Harmondsworth, Middlesex, Penguin Books, 1922, as but a primer to Tawney's emerging vision.

CHAPTER 21—THE CANADIAN HIGH TORY ANGLICAN TRADITION

1. Adrienne Clarkson, interview with George Grant, *First Person*, video broadcast on CBC Television, 2 June 1966. Published as George Grant, 'Individuality in Mass Society', in *Collected Works of George Grant: Volume 3, 1960–1969*, ed. Arthur Davis and Henry Roper, Toronto, University of Toronto Press, 2005, pp. 407–412, at p. 410.
2. Published in Stephen Leacock, *My Recollection of Chicago and The Doctrine of Laissez Faire*, ed. Carl Spadoni, Toronto, University of Toronto Press, 1998.
3. Susan Sibbald, 'Envoi—1856–1866: Canada', in *The Memoirs of Susan Sibbald (1783–1812)*, ed. Francis Paget Hett, London, John Lane, 1926, pp. 314–324.
4. Mordecai Richler in a letter to Jack McClelland, as quoted in Janet Beverly Friskney, *New Canadian Library: The Ross–McClelland Years, 1952–1978*, Toronto, University of Toronto Press, 2007, p. 101.
5. Stephen Leacock, 'The Gathering Crises', in *While There Is Time: The Case against Social Catastrophe*, Toronto, McClelland and Stewart, 1945, ch. 1, pp. 1–17.
6. George Grant, 'Adult Education in an Expanding Economy', *The Anglican Outlook*, Vol. 10, No. 7, May 1955, pp. 8–11. Reprinted in Grant, *Collected*

Works of George Grant: Volume 2, 1951–1959, pp. 100–109.

7. This review appears to have remained unpublished until it appeared as George Grant, 'Review of Fountain Come Forth: The Anglican Church and the Valley Town of Dundas, Prepared by R. B. Gilman', in *Collected Works of George Grant: Volume 3, 1960–1969*, ed. Arthur Davis and Henry Roper, Toronto, University of Toronto Press, pp. 221–223.

CHAPTER 22—GEORGE GRANT AND THE ANGLICAN CHURCH

1. Graeme Nicholson, 'Freedom and the Good', in Ian H. Angus, Ron Dart, and Randy Peg Peters, eds., *Athens and Jerusalem: George Grant's Theology, Philosophy and Politics*, Toronto, University of Toronto Press, 2006, pp. 323–340, at p. 323.
2. George Grant, letter to Derek Bedson, 21 September 1965. Published as George Grant, '163', in *George Grant: Selected Letters*, ed. William Christian, Toronto, University of Toronto Press, 1996, p. 233.
3. Angus et al., *Athens and Jerusalem*, inside flap.
4. George Herbert, 'Love', in *The Temple: Sacred Poems and Private Ejaculations*, Cambridge, T. Buck and R. Daniel, printers to the University of Cambridge, 1633, p. 183.
5. Published as George Grant, 'DPhil Thesis: Oxford 1950 The Concept of Nature and Supernature in the Theology of John Oman', in *Collected Works of George Grant: Volume 1, 1933–1950*, ed. Arthur Davis and Peter Emberley, Toronto, University of Toronto Press, 2002, pp. 157–420.
6. George Grant, 'Philosophy', in Canada, *Royal Commission Studies: A Selection of Essays Prepared for the Royal Commission on National Development in the Arts, Letters and Sciences*, Ottawa, E. Cloutier, Printer to the King, 1951, pp. 119–133. Reprinted in Grant, *Collected Works of George Grant: Volume 2, 1951–1959*, pp. 3–21, at p. 4.
7. George Grant, 'Two Theological Languages', in Wayne Whillier, ed., *Two Theological Languages by George Grant and Other Essays in Honour of His Work*, Queenston, Ontario, Edwin Mellen, 1990, pp. 7–15. Reprinted in Grant, *Collected Works of George Grant: Volume 2, 1951–1959*, pp. 49–65.
8. George Grant, *Philosophy in the Mass Age*, Vancouver, Copp Clark Publishing Co., 1959.
9. Published as George Grant, 'Christ, What a Planet', in *Collected Works of George Grant: Volume 2, 1951–1959*, ed. Arthur Davis, Toronto, University of Toronto Press, 2002, pp. 420–424.
10. Published as George Grant, 'Convocation Address Given at St John's College, Winnipeg', in *Collected Works of George Grant: Volume 3, 1960–1969*, ed. Arthur Davis and Henry Roper, Toronto, University of Toronto Press, 2005, pp. 9–19.
11. Published as George Grant, 'Review of Fountain Come Forth: The Anglican Church and the Valley Town of Dundas, Prepared by R. B. Gilman', in *Collected Works of George Grant: Volume 3, 1960–1969*, ed.

Arthur Davis and Henry Roper, Toronto, University of Toronto Press, 2005, pp. 221–223.

12. Published as George Grant, 'Qui Tollit: Reflections on the Eucharist', in *Collected Works of George Grant: Volume 3, 1960–1969*, ed. Arthur Davis and Henry Roper, Toronto, University of Toronto Press, 2005, pp. 470–472.

13. These letters were published in George Grant, *George Grant: Selected Letters*, ed. William Christian, Toronto, University of Toronto Press, 1996.

14. See Swift, 'A Full and True Account of the Battel Fought Last Friday, between the Antient and the Modern Books in St. James's Library', in *A Tale of a Tub*, pp. 229–278.

15. Hooker, *The Works of Mr. Richard Hooker, Containing Eight Books of the Laws of Ecclesiastical Polity*, p. 107.

16. Michael Creal, letter to Ron Dart, 20 March 1997.

17. Adrienne Clarkson, interview with George Grant, *First Person*, video broadcast on CBC Television, 2 June 1966. Published as George Grant, 'Individuality in Mass Society', in *Collected Works of George Grant: Volume 3, 1960–1969*, ed. Arthur Davis and Henry Roper, Toronto, University of Toronto Press, 2005, pp. 407–412, at p. 410.

CHAPTER 23—GEORGE GRANT AND THE ORTHODOX TRADITION

1. Graeme Nicholson, 'Freedom and the Good', in Ian H. Angus, Ron Dart, and Randy Peg Peters, eds., *Athens and Jerusalem: George Grant's Theology, Philosophy and Politics*, Toronto, University of Toronto Press, 2006, pp. 323–340, at p. 323.

2. George Ignatieff and Sonja Sinclair, *The Making of a Peacemonger: The Memoirs of George Ignatieff*, Toronto, University of Toronto Press, 1985, p. 33.

3. Ibid., p. 84.

4. The Fellowship of St. Alban and St. Sergius was founded by Russian Orthodox, who fled to England after the 1917 Russian Revolution, and High Church Anglicans. Nicholas Zernov was a founder of the Fellowship of St. Alban and St. Sergius, and his history of the organization up to 1979 with his wife, Militza, *The Fellowship of St. Alban and St. Sergius: A Historical Memoir*, tells the tale well of the origins and history of this Anglican–Orthodox *sobornost* organization up to 1979. The Fellowship continues to this day. I was quite fortunate when doing graduate studies at Regent College (Vancouver, British Columbia) from 1979 to 1981 to be the teaching assistant of Jim Houston (first principal of Regent College). Jim had lived with Nicholas Zernov in Oxford from 1947 to 1953, and both Zernov and Houston spent a great deal of time with C. S. Lewis. Lewis was also involved with the Fellowship. George and Sheila Grant, when at Oxford in the 1940s, were quite involved with C. S. Lewis.

5. Christian, *George Grant: A Biography*, p. 340.

6. Ibid., p. 235.
7. Ibid., pp. 232–233.
8. Ibid., pp. 232–237.
9. The extent of Dostoevsky's influence on George Grant was expressed by him in a letter to Alice Boissonneau written in the spring of 1946; see Grant, '80', in *George Grant: Selected Letters*, p. 128.
10. Published as 'Fyodor Dostoevsky', in *Architects of Modern Thought, Third and Fourth Series: Twelve Talks for CBC Radio*, Toronto, Canadian Broadcasting Corporation, 1959, pp. 71–83. Reprinted in Grant, *Collected Works of George Grant: Volume 2, 1951–1959*, pp. 408–419.
11. George Grant, 'Dostoevsky's Christianity', lecture delivered at McMaster University, Hamilton, Ontario, 1976. Published as the fifth lecture in George Grant, 'Five Lectures on Christianity', in Ian H. Angus, Ron Dart, and Randy Peg Peters, eds., *Athens and Jerusalem: George Grant's Theology, Philosophy and Politics*, Toronto, University of Toronto Press, 2006, pp. 233–237. Reprinted, also, in Grant, *Collected Works of George Grant: Volume 4, 1970–1988*, pp. 946–950.
12. Timothy Ware, 'God of the Fathers: C. S. Lewis and Eastern Christianity', in David Mills, ed., *The Pilgrim's Guide: C. S. Lewis and the Art of Witness*, Grand Rapids, Michigan, Eerdmans, 1998, pp. 53–69, at p. 69.

CHAPTER 24—THE TORY ANGLICAN WAY

1. John Milton, *Areopagitica*, ed., John E. Hales, Oxford, Clarendon Press, 1894, p. 18.
2. Samuel Taylor Coleridge, 'The Rime of the Ancyent Marinere', in Edward Dowden, ed., *Lyrical Ballads Reprinted from the First Edition (1798)*, London, David Nutt, 1891, p. 50.
3. Samuel Taylor Coleridge, *Biographia Literaria; or, Biographical Sketches of My Literary Life and Opinions*, London, William Clowes and Sons, 1817, pp. 110–111.

CHAPTER 25—ANGLICANISM AND ORTHODOXY

1. William Butler Yeats, 'The Second Coming', in *Later Poems*, London, Macmillan and Co., 1922, pp. 346–347.
2. John 17:22.

SELECTED BIBLIOGRAPHY

Achbar, Mark and Peter Wintonick, dirs., *Manufacturing Consent: Noam Chomsky and the Media*, documentary film, Montreal, 1992.

Ackroyd, Peter, *T. S. Eliot: A Life*, New York, Simon and Schuster, 1984.

Aitken, Robert and David Steindl-Rast, *The Ground We Share: Everyday Practice, Buddhist and Christian*, Boston, Massachusetts, Shambhala, 1996.

Ajzenstat, Janet and Peter J. Smith, *Canada's Origins: Liberal, Tory or Republican?*, Ottawa, Carleton University Press, 1995.

Alighieri, Dante, *The Inferno of Dante Alighieri*, trans. Henry Francis Cary, London, James Carpenter, 1805.

Allchin, A. M., *The Kingdom of Love and Knowledge: The Encounter between Orthodoxy and the West*, New York, Seabury Press, 1982.

Anglican Church of Canada, *The Book of Alternative Services of the Anglican Church of Canada*, Toronto, Anglican Book Centre, 1985.

Angus, Ian H., *The Undiscovered Country: Essays in Canadian Intellectual Culture*, Edmonton, Alberta, Athabasca University Press, 2013.

Angus, Ian H., Ron Dart and Randy Peg Peters, eds., *Athens and Jerusalem: George Grant's Theology, Philosophy, and Politics*, Toronto, University of Toronto Press, 2006.

Angus, Ian H. and Jerald Zaslove, *Anarcho-Modernism: Toward a New Critical Theory in Honour of Jerry Zaslove*, Vancouver, Talon Books, 2001.

Arendt, Hannah, *The Origins of Totalitarianism*, New York, Harcourt, Brace and Co., 1951.

———, *The Human Condition*, Chicago, Illinois, University of Chicago Press, 1958.

Armour, Leslie and Elizabeth Trott, *The Faces of Reason: An Essay on Philosophy and Culture in English Canada, 1850–1950*, Waterloo, Ontario, Wilfred Laurier University Press, 1981.

Arnold, Matthew, *Culture and Anarchy: An Essay in Political and Social Criticism*, London, Smith, Elder and Co., 1869.

Athanasius of Alexandria, Saint, *The Incarnation of the Word of God, Being the Treatise of St. Athanasius De incarnation verbi Dei*, trans. A Religious of C. S. M. V., intro. C. S. Lewis, London, Geoffrey Bles, 1944.

Atwood, Margaret, ed., *The New Oxford Book of Canadian Verse*, Oxford, Oxford University Press, 1982.

Augustine of Hippo, Saint, *En Habes optime lector absolutissimi doctoris Aurelij Augustini, opus absolutissimum, de Ciuitate Dei*, ed. Juan Luis Vives, Basel, J. Frobenium, 1522.

———, *Concerning the City of God against the Pagans*, trans. Henry Bettenson, Harmondsworth, Middlesex, Penguin Books, 1972.

Bacon, Francis, *Instauratio magna*, London, John Bill, 1620.

————, *New Atlantis; A Work Unfinished*, London, Thomas Newcomb, 1659.

Beiner, Ronald, *What's the Matter with Liberalism?*, Berkeley, California, University of California Press, 1992.

————, *Philosophy in a Time of Lost Spirit: Essays on Contemporary Theory*, Toronto, University of Toronto Press, 1997.

Bell, Daniel, *The End of Ideology: On the Exhaustion of Political Ideas in the Fifties*, Glencoe, Illinois, Free Press, 1960.

Bennett, R. B., *The Premier Speaks to the People: The Prime Minister's January Radio Broadcasts Issued in Book Form—The First Address*, Ottawa, Dominion Conservative Headquarters, 1935.

Berrigan, Daniel and Thich Nhat Hanh, *The Raft Is Not the Shore: Conversations toward a Buddhist–Christian Awareness*, Boston, Massachusetts, Beacon Press, 1975.

Berton, Pierre, *The Comfortable Pew: A Critical Look at the Church in the New Age*, Toronto, McClelland and Stewart, 1965.

Bissell, Claude T., ed., *Our Living Tradition: Seven Canadians*, Toronto, University of Toronto Press, 1957.

Blake, William, *Songs of Experience*, s. l., author and printer, W. Blake, 1794.

Blond, Phillip, *Red Tory: How the Left and Right Have Broken Britain and How We Can Fix It*, London, Faber and Faber, 2010.

Blum, William, *Killing Hope: U. S. Military and C. I. A. Interventions since World War II*, updated and revised edition, Monroe, Maine, Common Courage Press, 1995.

Borden, Robert Laird, *Robert Laird Borden: His Memoirs*, ed. Henry Borden, 2 vols., Toronto, Macmillan Co. of Canada, 1938.

Bos, Hildo and James H. Forest, eds., *For the Peace from Above: An Orthodox Resource Book on War, Peace and Nationalism*, Rollinsford, New Hampshire, Orthodox Research Institute, 2011.

Boswell, James, *The Life of Samuel Johnson, LL.D.*, 2 vols., London, Henry Baldwin for Charles Dilly, 1791.

Bridge, G. Richmond, ed., *Holy Living: Christian Morality Today—1986 Theological Conference*, Charlottetown, Prince Edward Island, St. Peter Publications, 1986.

Bryant, Darrol M., ed., *The Future of Anglican Theology*, New York, Edwin Mellen Press, 1984.

Burke, Edmund, *Burke, Select Works*, ed. E. J. Payne, 3 vols., Oxford, Clarendon Press, 1892–1898.

Callen, Barry L., *Clark H. Pinnock: Journey towards Renewal*, Nappanee, Indiana, Evangel Press, 2000.

Camp, Dalton, *Whose Country Is This Anyway?*, Vancouver, Douglas and McIntyre, 1995.

Canada, *Report on Social Security for Canada*, prepared by L. C. Marsh for the Advisory Committee on Reconstruction, Ottawa, King's Printer, 1943.

————, *Royal Commission Studies: A Selection of Essays Prepared for the Royal Commission on National Development in the Arts, Letters and Sciences*, Ottawa, E. Cloutier, Printer to the King, 1951.

Canadian Broadcasting Corporation, *Architects of Modern Thought, Third and Fourth Series: Twelve Talks for CBS Radio*, Toronto, Canadian Broadcasting Corporation, 1959.

Cantor, Norman F., *Inventing the Middle Ages: The Lives, Works, and Ideas of the Great Medievalists of the Twentieth Century*, New York, Quill–Morrow and Co., 1991.

Carrington, Philip, *The Anglican Church in Canada: A History*, Toronto, Collins, 1963.

Cassady, Carolyn, *Off the Road: My Years with Cassady, Kerouac and Ginsberg*, New York, W. Morrow, 1990.

Cayley, David and George Grant, *George Grant in Conversation*, Concord, Ontario, House of Anansi, 1995.

Chaucer, Geoffrey, *The Canterbury Tales*, trans. Nevill Coghill, Harmondsworth, Middlesex, Penguin Books, 1951.

Chomsky, Noam, *American Power and the New Mandarins*, New York, Pantheon Books, 1968.

————, *At War with Asia*, New York, Pantheon Books, 1969.

————, 'Necessary Illusions: Thought Control in Democratic Societies', *CBC Massey Lectures*, radio broadcast on CBC Radio, 28 November 1988–2 December 1988. Published as Noam Chomsky, *Necessary Illusions: Thought Control in Democratic Societies*, Montreal, CBC Enterprises, 1989.

————, *Hegemony or Survival: America's Quest for Global Dominance*, New York, Metropolitan Books, 2003.

Christian, William, *George Grant: A Biography*, Toronto, University of Toronto Press, 1993.

Christie, James, 'Jack in the World: The Social Vision of C. S. Lewis', *Pilgrimage: The Toronto C. S. Lewis Society Bulletin*, Vol. 9, No. 1, November 2001, pp. 1–16.

Clarkson, Adrienne, interview with George Grant, *First Person*, video broadcast on CBC Television, 2 June 1966. Published as George Grant, 'Individuality in Mass Society', in *Collected Works of George Grant: Volume 3, 1960–1969*, ed. Arthur Davis and Henry Roper, Toronto, University of Toronto Press, 2005, pp. 407–412.

Coleridge, Samuel Taylor, *Biographia Literaria; or, Biographical Sketches of My Literary Life and Opinions*, London, William Clowes and Sons, 1817.

Cooke, William, ed., *The Parish and Cathedral Church of St. James', Toronto 1797–1997: A Collaborative History*, Toronto, St. James' Cathedral and University of Toronto Press, 1998.

Copleston, Frederick C., *Religion and the One: Philosophies East and West*, New York, Crossroad Publishing Co., 1981.

Creighton, Donald Grant, *Harold Adam Innis: Portrait of a Scholar*, Toronto, University of Toronto Press, 1957.

————, *The Story of Canada*, Toronto, Macmillan of Canada, 1959.

————, *John A. Macdonald*, 2 vols., Toronto, Macmillan of Canada, 1965.

————, *The Forked Road: Canada, 1939–1957*, Toronto, McClelland and Stewart, 1976.

————, *Dominion of the North: A History of Canada*, new edition, Toronto, Macmillan of Canada, 1977.

————, *The Passionate Observer: Selected Writings*, Toronto, McClelland and Stewart, 1980.

Crouse, Robert D., *St. Augustine's Doctrine of Justitia*, unpublished MTh thesis, Trinity College, Toronto, 1957.

————, *Images of Pilgrimage: Paradise and Wilderness in Christian Spirituality*, Charlottetown, Prince Edward Island, St. Peter Publications, 1986.

Curry, Ralph L., *Stephen Leacock: Humorist and Humanist*, Garden City, New York, Doubleday, 1959.

Curtis, Adam, dir., *The Power of Nightmares: The Rise of the Politics of Fear*, video documentary broadcast on BBC2, 20 October 2014–3 November 2014.

Cuthbertson, Brian, *The First Bishop: A Biography of Charles Inglis*, Halifax, Nova Scotia, Waegwoltic Press, 1987.

Dart, Ron, 'Origen and Anthony: The Origenist Anthony contra Athanasius', unpublished essay, University of British Columbia, Vancouver, 1983.

————, 'R. C. Zaehner and the Primordial Tradition: A Critique', unpublished essay, University of British Columbia, Vancouver, 1983.

————, *The Red Tory Vision*, Dewdney, British Columbia, Synaxis Press, 1998.

————, *The Red Tory Tradition: Ancient Roots, New Routes*, Dewdney, British Columbia, Synaxis Press, 1999.

————, *Robin Mathews: Crown Prince of Canadian Political Poetry*, Dewdney, British Columbia, Synaxis Press, 2002.

————, *The Canadian High Tory Tradition: Raids on the Unspeakable*, Dewdney, British Columbia, Synaxis Press, 2004.

————, *The Spirituality of John Cassian*, Dewdney, British Columbia, Synaxis Press, 2005.

————, *Stephen Leacock: Canada's Red Tory Prophet*, Dewdney, British Columbia, Synaxis Press, 2006.

————, *George Grant: Spiders and Bees*, Abbotsford, British Columbia, Fresh Wind Press, 2008.

————, *Keepers of the Flame: Canadian Red Toryism*, Ste-Edwidge-de-Clifton, Quebec, Fermentation Press, 2012.

————, *Lament for a Nation: Then and Now*, New York, American Anglican Press, 2015.

Dart, Ron and Brad Jersak, *George P. Grant: Canada's Lone Wolf*, Abbotsford, British Columbia, Fresh Wind Press, 2011.

Dart, Ron and J. I. Packer, *In a Pluralist World*, Vancouver, Regent College Publishing, 1998.

Davis, Arthur, *George Grant and the Subversion of Modernity: Art, Philosophy, Politics, Religion, and Education*, Toronto, University of Toronto Press, 1996.

Dawson, Christopher, *The Spirit of the Oxford Movement*, New York, Sheed and Ward, 1933.

de la Roche, Mazo, *Whiteoak Chronicles*, London, Macmillan, 1940.

Denison, George T., *The Struggle for Imperial Unity*, London, Macmillan and Co., 1909.

Disraeli, Benjamin, *Sybil; or, The Two Nations*, 3 vols., London, H. Colburn, 1845.

———, *Benjamin Disraeli Letters*, ed. J. A. W. Gunn et al., 10 vols., Toronto, University of Toronto Press, 1982–2014.

Donne, John, *Devotions vpon Emergent Occasions and Severall Steps in my Sicknesse*, London, printed by A. M. and are to be sold by Richard Royston, 1638.

Dostoevsky, Fyodor, *The Brothers Karamazov: A Novel in Four Parts and an Epilogue*, trans. Constance Garnett, London, W. Heinemann, 1912.

———, *Crime and Punishment: A Novel in Six Parts and an Epilogue*, trans. Constance Garnett, London, W. Heinemann, 1914.

———, *The Idiot*, trans. Henry Carlisle and Olga Carlisle, New York, New American Library, 1980.

Dowden, Edward, ed., *Lyrical Ballads Reprinted from the First Edition (1798)*, London, David Nutt, 1891.

Drury, Shadia B., *Leo Strauss and the American Right*, New York, St. Martin's Press, 1997.

Egerton, George, ed., *Anglican Essentials: Reclaiming Faith within the Anglican Church of Canada*, Toronto, Anglican Book Centre, 1995.

Eliot, T. S., 'Mr. Leacock Serious', review of *Essays and Literary Studies* by Stephen Leacock, in *New Statesman*, Vol. 7, No. 173, 29 July 1916, pp. 404–405.

———, *Four Quartets*, New York, Harcourt, Brace and Co., 1943.

Elshtain, Jean Bethke, *Augustine and the Limits of Politics*, Notre Dame, Indiana, University of Notre Dame Press, 1995.

———, *Just War against Terror: The Burden of American Power in a Violent World*, New York, Basic Books, 2003.

Emberley, Peter C., ed., *By Loving Our Own: George Grant and the Legacy of Lament for a Nation*, Ottawa, Carleton University Press, 1990.

England, ed., *The Holy Bible, Conteyning the Old Testament, and the New: Newly Translated out of the Originall Tongues*, London, Robert Barker, 1611.

———, *The Book of Common Prayer, and Administration of the Sacraments and Other Rites and Ceremonies of the Church, According to the Use of the Church of England*, Cambridge, John Field, 1662.

Erasmus, Desiderius, *Moriae encomium; or, The Praise of Folly*, trans. John Wilson, London, William Leak, 1668.

———, *The Colloquies of Erasmus*, 2 vols., trans. N. Bailey, London, 1878.

Ewart, John S., 'A Perplexed Imperialist', *Queen's Quarterly Review*, Vol. 15, No. 2, October-November-December 1907, pp. 90–100.

Fairweather, Eugene Rathbone, *A Scholastic Miscellany: Anselm to Ockham*, Philadelphia, Pennsylvania, Westminster Press, 1956.

———, *The Oxford Movement*, New York, Oxford University Press, 1964.

Fairweather, Eugene Rathbone and Ian Gentles, eds., *The Right to Birth: Some Christian Views on Abortion*, Toronto, Anglican Book Centre, 1976.

Farrer, Austin, *Finite and Infinite: A Philosophical Essay*, Westminster, Dacre Press, 1943.

Farthing, John, *Freedom Wears a Crown*, ed. Judith Robinson, Toronto, Kingswood House, 1957.

Fiamengo, Marya, *North of the Cold Star: New and Selected Poems*, Ottawa, Mosaic Press–Valley Editions, 1978.

Flint, David, *John Strachan, Pastor and Politician*, Toronto, Oxford University Press, 1971.

Forbes, H. D., ed., *Canadian Political Thought*, Toronto, Oxford University Press, 1985.

Forsey, Eugene A., *A Life on the Fringe: The Memoirs of Eugene Forsey*, Toronto, Oxford University Press, 1990.

———, 'What Have These Reformers Wrought?', *The Machray Review*, No. 6, December 1997, pp. 34–39.

Forsey, Helen, *Eugene Forsey: Canada's Maverick Sage*, Toronto, Dundurn Press, 2012.

Frank, Erich, 'The Fundamental Opposition between Plato and Aristotle', *The American Journal of Philology*, Vol. 61, No. 1, January 1940, pp. 34–53.

Friskney, Janet Beverly, *New Canadian Library: The Ross–McClelland Years, 1952–1978*, Toronto, University of Toronto Press, 2007.

Fukuyama, Francis, *The End of History and the Last Man*, New York, Free Press, 1992.

Gadamer, Hans-Georg, *Dialogue and Dialectic: Eight Hermeneutical Studies on Plato*, trans. P. Christopher Smith, New Haven, Connecticut, Yale University Press, 1980.

———, *Truth and Method*, 2nd revised edition, trans. Joel Weinsheimer and Donald G. Marshall, London, Sheed and Ward, 1989.

Gairdner, William, ed., *After Liberalism: Essays in Search of Freedom, Virtue, and Order*, Toronto, Stoddart Publishing, 1998.

Gerin-Lajoie, Antoine, *Jean Rivard*, trans. Vida Bruce, Toronto, McClelland and Stewart, 1977.

Gilman, Richard Bertram, *Fountain Come Forth: The Anglican Church and the Valley Town of Dundas, 1784–1963*, s. l., s. n., 1963.

Ginsberg, Allen, *Howl and Other Poems*, City Lights Books, San Francisco, California, 1956.

———, *Your Reason & Blake's System*, Madras, New York, Hanuman Books, 1988.

Goa, David J., *A Regard for Creation: Collected Essays*, Dewdney, British Columbia, Synaxis, 2008.

Graham, David, ed., *We Remember C. S. Lewis*, Nashville, Tennessee, Broadman and Holman Publishers, 2001.

Graham, Roger, *Arthur Meighen: A Biography*, 3 vols., Toronto, Clarke, Irwin and Co., 1960–1965.

Granatstein, Jack L., *Who Killed Canadian History?*, Toronto, HarperCollins, 1998.

Grant, George, review of *The Higher Learning in America* by Robert M. Hutchins, 'The Bookshelf', column in *Queen's University Journal*, 18 January 1938, p. 3.

————, *The Empire: Yes or No?*, Toronto, Ryerson Press, 1945.

————, 'Adult Education in an Expanding Economy', *The Anglican Outlook*, Vol. 10, No. 7, May 1955, pp. 8–11.

————, *Philosophy in the Mass Age*, New York, Hill and Wang, 1960.

————, 'Tyranny and Wisdom: A Comment on the Controversy between Leo Strauss and Alexandre Kojeve', *Social Research*, Vol. 31, No. 1, Spring 1964, pp. 45–72.

————, 'Revolution, Responsibility, and Conservatism', address delivered at the Toronto International Teach-In, Varsity Arena, Toronto, held 8–10 October 1965. Published as George Grant, 'Realism in Political Protest', *Christian Outlook*, Vol. 21, No. 2, November 1965, pp. 3–6.

————, 'The Vietnam War: The Value of Protest', address delivered at a demonstration for peace in Vietnam, Toronto, 14 May 1966. Published as George Grant 'The Value of Protest' in *The George Grant Reader*, ed. William Christian and Sheila Grant, Toronto, University of Toronto Press, 1998, pp. 90–94.

————, *Technology and Empire: Perspectives on North America*, Toronto, House of Anansi, 1969.

————, *English-Speaking Justice*, Sackville, New Brunswick, Mount Allison University Press, 1974.

————, 'Dostoevsky's Christianity', lecture delivered at McMaster University, Hamilton, Ontario, 1976. Published as the fifth lecture in George Grant, 'Five Lectures on Christianity', in Ian H. Angus, Ron Dart, and Randy Peg Peters, eds., *Athens and Jerusalem: George Grant's Theology, Philosophy and Politics*, Toronto, University of Toronto Press, 2006, pp. 233–237.

————, 'Nietzsche and the Ancients: Philosophy and Scholarship', *Dionysius*, Vol. 3, December 1979, pp. 5–16.

————, review of *Benjamin Disraeli Letters* by Benjamin Disraeli, first and second volumes, edited by J. A. W. Gunn et al., in *The Globe and Mail*, 8 May 1982, p. E15.

————, *Technology and Justice*, Concord, Ontario, House of Anansi, 1986.

————, 'In Defence of Simone Weil', *The Idler*, No. 15, January-February 1988, pp. 36–40.

————, *George Grant: Selected Letters*, ed. William Christian, Toronto, University of Toronto Press, 1996.

————, *The George Grant Reader*, ed. William Christian and Sheila Grant, Toronto, University of Toronto Press, 1998.

————, *Collected Works of George Grant: Volume 1, 1933–1950*, ed. Arthur Davis and Peter Emberley, Toronto, University of Toronto Press, 2000.

————, *Collected Works of George Grant: Volume 2, 1951–1959*, ed. Arthur Davis, Toronto, University of Toronto Press, 2002.

————, *Collected Works of George Grant: Volume 3, 1960–1969*, ed. Arthur Davis and Henry Roper, Toronto, University of Toronto Press, 2005.

————, *Collected Works of George Grant: Volume 4, 1970–1988*, ed. Arthur Davis and Henry Roper, Toronto, University of Toronto Press, 2009.

————, *Lament for a Nation: The Defeat of Canadian Nationalism*, 40th anniversary edition, Montreal, McGill-Queen's University Press, 2005.

Grant, W. L., ed., *The Makers of Canada*, 12 vols., London, Oxford University Press, 1928.

Gray, Charlotte, *Sisters in the Wilderness: The Lives of Susanna Moodie and Catharine Parr Traill*, Toronto, Viking, 1999.

Gregory of Nyssa, Saint, *The Life of Moses*, New York, Paulist Press, 1978.

Griffiths, Bede, *Return to the Center*, Springfield, Illinois, Templegate Publishers, 1976.

————, *The Marriage of East and West*, Springfield, Illinois, Templegate Publishers, 1982.

Haliburton, Thomas Chandler, *The Clockmaker: Series One, Two and Three*, ed. George L. Parker, Ottawa, Carleton University Press, 1995

Hall, Stuart, ed., *Universities and Left Review*, periodical, London, Universities and Left Review Club, 1957–1959.

Harris, Susan and Nicholas Hatt, eds., *Recognizing the Sacred in the Modern Secular: How the Sacred Is to Be Discovered in Today's World*, Charlottetown, Prince Edward Island, St. Peter Publications, 2012.

Harrison, Ernest Wilfrid, *A Church without God*, Toronto, McClelland and Stewart, 1967.

Haslett, K. M., ed., *New Life: Addressing Change in the Church—St. James' Dundas Sesquicentennial 1838–1988*, Toronto, Anglican Book Centre, 1989.

Heidegger, Martin, *Being and Time*, trans. John Macquarrie and Edward Robinson, London, SCM Press, 1962.

Herbert, George, *The Temple: Sacred Poems and Private Ejaculations*, Cambridge, T. Buck and R. Daniel, printers to the University of Cambridge, 1633.

Herman, Edward S., *The Real Terror Network: Terrorism in Fact and Propaganda*, Boston, Massachusetts, South End Press, 1982.

Hooker, Richard, *The Works of Mr. Richard Hooker, Containing Eight Books of the Laws of Ecclesiastical Polity*, 2 vols., Oxford, J. Vincent for T. Tegg, 1839.

Hopkins, J. Castell, *The Canadian Annual Review of Public Affairs: 1907*, Toronto, Annual Review Publishing Co., 1908.

Horowitz, Gad, 'Tories, Socialists and the Demise of Canada', *Canadian Dimension*, Vol. 2, No. 4, May-June 1965, pp. 12–15.

————, 'Conservatism, Liberalism, and Socialism in Canada: An Interpretation', *The Canadian Journal of Economics and Political Science*, Vol. 32, No. 2, May 1966, pp. 143–171.

————, interview with George Grant, 'Horowitz and Grant Talk', *Canadian Dimension*, Vol. 6, No. 6, December 1969-January 1970, pp. 18–20.

Hume, David, *A Treatise of Human Nature*, 3 vols., London, John Noon, 1739, Thomas Longman, 1740.

Huntington, Samuel P., 'The Clash of Civilizations?', *Foreign Affairs*, Vol. 72, No. 3, Summer 1993, pp. 22–49.

————, *Clash of Civilizations and the Remaking of World Order*, New York, Simon and Schuster, 1996.

Hutchins, Robert M., *The Higher Learning in America*, New Haven, Connecticut, Yale University Press, 1936.

―――, ed., *Great Books of the Western World*, 54 vols., Chicago, Encyclopaedia Britannica, 1952.

Hutchins, Robert M. and Mortimer J. Adler, eds., *The Great Ideas Today: 1961*, Chicago, Illinois, Encyclopaedia Britannica, 1961.

Ignatieff, George and Sonja Sinclair, *The Making of a Peacemonger: The Memoirs of George Ignatieff*, Toronto, University of Toronto Press, 1985.

Ignatieff, Michael, *True Patriot Love: Four Generations in Search of Canada*, Toronto, Viking Canada, 2009.

Ingham, Michael, *Rites for a New Age: Understanding the Book of Alternative Services*, Toronto, Anglican Book Centre, 1986.

―――, *Mansions of the Spirit: The Gospel in a Multi-faith World*, Toronto, Anglican Book Centre, 1997.

Inglis, Charles, *The True Interest of America Impartially Stated: In Certain Strictures on a Pamphlet Entitled Common Sense*, 2nd edition, Philadelphia, Pennsylvania, James Humphreys, Jr., 1776.

Irving, John A., ed., *Philosophy in Canada: A Symposium*, Toronto, University of Toronto Press, 1952.

Isherwood, Lisa and Marko Zlomislic, *The Poverty of Radical Orthodoxy*, Eugene, Oregon, Pickwick Publications, 2012.

Jaeger, Werner, *Humanism and Theology*, Milwaukee, Wisconsin, Marquette University Press, 1943.

―――, *Early Christianity and Greek Paideia*, Cambridge, Massachusetts, Belknap Press of Harvard University Press, 1961.

James, William, *The Varieties of Religious Experience: A Study in Human Nature*, London, Longmans, Green and Co. 1902.

Jennings, Nicholas, *Before the Gold Rush: Flashbacks to the Dawn of the Canadian Sound*, Toronto, Viking, 1997.

Jewel, John, *The Works of John Jewel*, ed. John Ayre, 4 vols., Cambridge, Cambridge University Press, 1845–1850.

Jewett, Robert and John Shelton Lawrence, *Captain America and the Crusade against Evil: The Dilemma of Zealous Nationalism*, Grand Rapids, Michigan, W. B. Eerdmans, 2003.

John of Salisbury, *The Metalogicon of John of Salisbury: A Twelfth-Century Defense of the Verbal and Logical Arts of the Trivium*, trans. Daniel D. McGarry, Berkeley, California, University of California Press, 1955.

Keith, W. J., *Charles G. D. Roberts*, Toronto, Copp Clark Publishing Co., 1969.

Kerouac, Jack, *On the Road*, New York, Viking Press, 1957.

―――, *The Dharma Bums*, New York, Viking Press, 1958.

―――, *Lonesome Traveler*, New York, McGraw-Hill, 1960.

―――, *Desolation Angels: A Novel*, New York, Coward-McCann, 1965.

―――, *Vanity of Duluoz: An Adventurous Education, 1935–46*, New York, Coward-McCann, 1968.

Keynes, John Maynard, *The General Theory of Employment, Interest and Money*, New York, Harcourt, Brace and Co., 1936.

Kilbourn, William, ed., *The Restless Church: A Response to the Comfortable Pew*, Toronto, McClelland and Stewart, 1966.

————, ed., *Canada: A Guide to the Peaceable Kingdom*, Toronto, Macmillan of Canada, 1970.

King, William Lyon Mackenzie, *Industry and Humanity*, Boston, Massachusetts, Houghton Mifflin Co., 1918.

Kirby, William, *The U. E.: A Tale of Upper Canada*, Niagara, Ontario, s. n., 1859.

————, *Le Chien d'Or, The Golden Dog: A Legend of Quebec*, New York, Lovell, Adam, Wesson and Co., 1877.

Klein, Naomi, *No Logo: Taking Aim at the Brand Bullies*, New York, Picador, 1999.

Knowles, Norman James, ed., *Seeds Scattered and Sown: Studies in the History of Canadian Anglicanism*, Toronto, Anglican Book Centre, 2008.

Kroeker, P. Travis and Bruce K. Ward, *Remembering the End: Dostoevsky as Prophet to Modernity*, Boulder, Colorado, Westview Press, 2001.

Ladner, Leon Johnson, *The Ladners of Ladner: By Covered Wagon to the Welfare State*, Vancouver, Mitchell Press, 1972.

Langland, William, *The Vision of Piers the Plowman by William Langland Done into Modern English*, trans. W. W. Skeat, London, A. Moring, 1905.

LaPierre, Laurier et al., eds., *Essays on the Left: Essays in Honour of T. C. Douglas*, Toronto, McClelland and Stewart, 1971.

Laqueur, Walter, *A History of Terrorism*, New Brunswick, New Jersey, Transaction Publishers, 2001.

Laxer, James and Robert Laxer, *The Liberal Idea of Canada: Pierre Trudeau and the Question of Canada's Survival*, Toronto, James Lorimer and Co., 1977.

Leacock, Stephen, *Elements of Political Science*, Boston, Massachusetts, Houghton Mifflin Co., 1906.

————, *Greater Canada: An Appeal*, Montreal, Montreal News Co., c. 1907.

————, *Literary Lapses: A Book of Sketches,* Montreal, Gazette Printing Co., 1910.

————, *Essays and Literary Studies*, New York, John Lane, 1916.

————, *The Unsolved Riddle of Social Justice,* New York, John Lane, 1920.

————, *My Discovery of England,* Toronto, S. B. Gundy, 1922.

————, *Приключения в Плутория-клубе*, Moscow, Огонек, 1929.

————, *My Discovery of the West: A Discussion of East and West in Canada*, Boston, Massachusetts, Hale, Cushman and Flint, 1937.

————, *Last Leaves*, Toronto, McClelland and Stewart, 1945.

————, *While There Is Time: The Case against Social Catastrophe*, Toronto, McClelland and Stewart, 1945.

————, *Arcadian Adventures with the Idle Rich*, Toronto, McClelland and Stewart, 1989.

————, *Social Criticism: The Unsolved Riddle of Social Justice and Other Essays*, ed. Alan Bowker, Toronto, University of Toronto Press, 1996.

————, *My Recollection of Chicago and The Doctrine of Laissez Faire*, ed. Carl Spadoni, Toronto, University of Toronto Press, 1998.

————, *Sunshine Sketches of a Little Town*, ed. Carl Spadoni, Peterborough, Ontario, Broadview Press, 2002.

————, *On the Front Line of Life: Stephen Leacock: Memories and Reflections, 1935–1944*, ed. Alan Bowker, Toronto, Dundurn Press, 2004.

Leclercq, Jean, *The Love of Learning and the Desire for God: A Study of Monastic Culture*, New York, New American Library, 1961.

Leech, Kenneth, *Soul Friend: The Practice of Christian Spirituality*, San Francisco, California, Harper and Row, 1980.

————, *Subversive Orthodoxy: Traditional Faith and Radical Commitment*, Toronto, Anglican Book Centre, 1992.

Leech, Kenneth and Rowan Williams, *Essays Catholic and Radical: A Jubilee Group Symposium for the 150th Anniversary of the Beginning of the Oxford Movement, 1833–1983*, London, Bowerdean Press, 1983.

Lessing, Gotthold Ephraim, *Nathan the Wise, a Dramatic Poem, Written Originally in German*, trans. W. Taylor, London, R. Philips, 1805.

Lewis, Bernard, *Islam and the West*, New York, Oxford University Press, 1993.

————, *The Crisis of Islam: Holy War and Unholy Terror*, New York, Random House, 2003.

Lewis, C. S., *The Pilgrim's Regress: An Allegorical Apology for Christianity, Reason and Romanticism*, London, J. M. Dent and Sons, 1933.

————, *That Hideous Strength: A Modern Fairy-Tale for Grown-Ups*, London, John Lane, 1945.

————, *English Literature in the Sixteenth Century, Excluding Drama*, Oxford, Clarendon Press, 1954.

————, *Surprised by Joy: The Shape of My Early Life*, London, Geoffrey Bles, 1955.

————, *The World's Last Night and Other Essays*, New York, Harcourt Brace, 1960.

————, *The Discarded Image: An Introduction to Medieval and Renaissance Literature*, Cambridge, Cambridge University Press, 1964.

————, *God in the Dock: Essays in Theology and Ethics*, ed. Walter Hooper, Grand Rapids, Michigan, W. B. Eerdmans, 1970.

————, *The Abolition of Man; or, Reflections on Education with Special Reference to the Teaching of English in the Upper Forms of Schools*, New York, Touchstone Books, 1996.

————, *Mere Christianity*, New York, HarperCollins, 2001.

Lewis, Donald M., ed., *The Future Shape of Anglican Ministry*, Vancouver, Regent College Publishing, 2004.

Locke, John, *An Essay Concerning Human Understanding*, London, printed for Tho. Basset, and sold by Edw. Mory, 1690.

————, *Two Treatises of Government: In the Former, the False Principles, and Foundation of Sir Robert Filmer, and His Followers, Are Detected and Overthrown. The Latter Is an Essay Concerning the True Original, Extent, and End of Civil Government*, London, Awnsham Churchill, 1690.

Longfellow, Henry Wadsworth, *Evangeline: A Tale of Acadie*, Boston, W. D. Ticknor, 1847.

Lorimer, James, 'Robin's Egging Us on Again', *Books in Canada*, Vol. 6, No. 1, January 1977, p. 23.

Louth, Andrew, *The Origins of the Christian Mystical Tradition: From Plato to Denys*, Oxford, Clarendon Press, 1981.

Machray, Robert, *Life of Robert Machray*, Toronto, Macmillan Co. of Canada, 1909.

MacIntyre, Alasdair C., *After Virtue: A Study in Moral Theory*, Notre Dame, Indiana, University of Notre Dame Press, 1984.

———, *Whose Justice? Which Rationality?*, Notre Dame, Indiana, University of Notre Dame Press, 1988.

Macphail, Andrew, ed., *The University Magazine*, periodical, Montreal, s. n., 1907–1920.

Macpherson, Crawford Brough, *The Political Theory of Possessive Individualism: Hobbes to Locke*, Oxford, Clarendon Press, 1962.

———, *Burke*, Oxford, Oxford University Press, 1980.

Mair, Charles, *Tecumseh: A Drama*, Toronto, Hunter, Rose and Co., 1886.

Manning, Ernest C., *Political Realignment: A Challenge to Thoughtful Canadians*, Toronto, McClelland and Stewart, 1967.

Massolin, Philip A., *Canadian Intellectuals, the Tory Tradition, and the Challenge of Modernity: 1939–1970*, Toronto, University of Toronto Press, 2001.

Mathews, Robin, *This Cold Fist*, Ottawa, s. n., 1969.

———, *Canadian Identity: Major Forces Shaping the Life of a People*, Ottawa, Steel Rail Publishing, 1988.

———, *The Canadian Intellectual Tradition: A Modern People and Its Community*, Burnaby, British Columbia, Simon Fraser University, 1990.

———, *Treason of the Intellectuals: English Canada in the Post-Modern Period*, Prescott, Ontario, Voyageur Publishing, 1995.

———, *Being Canadian in Dirty Imperialist Times*, Vancouver, Northland Publications, 2000.

Mathews, Robin and James Arthur Steele, *The Struggle for Canadian Universities: A Dossier*, Toronto, New Press, 1969.

McCullum, Hugh, *Radical Compassion: The Life and Times of Archbishop Ted Scott, Tenth Primate of the Anglican Church of Canada (1971–1986)*, Toronto, Anglican Book Centre, 2004.

McGarvey, James A. 'Pete', *The Old Brewery Bay: A Leacockian Tale*, Toronto, Dundurn Press, 1994.

Merton, Thomas, *New Seeds of Contemplation*, New York, New Directions Books, 1961.

———, *Zen and the Birds of Appetite*, New York, New Directions Books, 1968.

———, *Peace in the Post-Christian Era*, Maryknoll, New York, Orbis Books, 2004.

Milbank, John, *Theology and Social Theory: Beyond Secular Reason*, Oxford, Blackwell Publishing, 1990.

Milbank, John and Simon Oliver, eds., *The Radical Orthodoxy Reader*, London, Routledge, 2009.

Milbank, John, Catherine Pickstock and Graham Ward, eds., *Radical Orthodoxy: A New Theology*, London, Routledge, 1999.

Miller, Arthur, *Death of a Salesman*, New York, Viking Press, 1949.

Mills, C. Wright, *The Power Elite*, New York, Oxford University Press, 1956.

Mills, David, ed., *The Pilgrim's Guide: C. S. Lewis and the Art of Witness*, Grand Rapids, Michigan, W. B. Eerdmans, 1998.

Milton, John, *Areopagitica*, ed. John E. Hales, Oxford, Clarendon Press, 1894.

Montgomery, Lucy Maud, *The Anne of Green Gables Collection: Six Novels in One Volume*, Oxford, Benediction Classics, 2012.

More, Thomas, *Utopia*, trans. Gilbert Burnet, London, Richard Chiswell, 1684.

Morgan, Bill and Nancy J. Peters, eds., *Howl on Trial: The Battle for Free Expression*, San Francisco, California, City Lights Books, 2006.

Morris, Audrey Y., *Gentle Pioneers: Five Nineteenth-Century Canadians*, Ontario, Paperjacks, 1966.

Morton, W. L., *The Canadian Identity*, Madison, Wisconsin, University of Wisconsin Press, 1961.

————, *The Kingdom of Canada: A General History from Earliest Times*, Indianapolis, Indiana, Bobbs-Merrill, 1963.

Murdoch, Iris, *The Sovereignty of Good*, London, Routledge, 1970.

Musto, Ronald G., *The Catholic Peace Tradition*, Maryknoll, New York, Orbis Books, 1986.

Nash, Knowlton, *Kennedy and Diefenbaker: Fear and Loathing across the Undefended Border*, Toronto, McClelland and Stewart, 1990.

Nelson, William H., *The American Tory*, Oxford, Clarendon Press, 1961.

Newman, John Henry, *The Idea of a University: Defined and Illustrated*, 3rd edition, London, Basil Montagu Pickering, 1873.

Nietzsche, Friedrich Wilhelm, *Thus Spoke Zarathustra: A Book for All and None*, trans. Walter Kaufmann, New York, Viking Press, 1966.

Oliver, Michael, ed., *Social Purpose for Canada*, Toronto, University of Toronto Press, 1961.

Orchard, David, *The Fight for Canada: Four Centuries of Resistance to American Expansionism*, Westmount, Quebec, Robert Davies Multimedia Publishing, 1998.

Paine, Thomas, *Common Sense*, Philadelphia, Pennsylvania, R. Bell, 1776.

Palmer, G. E. H., Kallistos Ware and Philip Sherrard, eds., *The Philokalia: The Complete Text*, 4 vols., London, Faber and Faber, 1983–1995.

Parrinder, Edward Geoffrey, *Mysticism in the World's Religions*, New York, Oxford University Press, 1976.

Pickstock, Catherine, *After Writing: On the Liturgical Consummation of Philosophy*, Oxford, Blackwell Publishing, 1997.

Pramuk, Christopher, *Sophia: The Hidden Christ of Thomas Merton*, Collegeville, Minnesota, Liturgical Press, 2009.

Puhalo, Lazar, ed., *Searching for Canada: The Red Tory Journey*, Dewdney, British Columbia, Synaxis Press, 2000.

Raleigh, Walter, ed., *The Complete Works of George Savile, First Marquess of Halifax*, Oxford, Clarendon Press, 1912.

Reckitt, Maurice, ed., *Christendom: A Journal of Christian Sociology*, periodical, Oxford, Blackwell, 1931–1950.

Rexroth, Kenneth, *An Autobiographical Novel*, Garden City, New York, Doubleday and Co., 1966.

Richardson, John, *Wacousta; or, The Prophecy: A Tale of the Canadas*, London, T. Cadell, 1832.

Robinson, Paul, 'The Chomsky Problem', *The New York Times*, 25 February 1979, pp. 3, 37.

Said, Edward W., *Orientalism*, New York, Vintage Books, 1978.

Sanzio, Raphael, *School of Athens*, fresco, Stanza della Segnatura, Vatican Palace, Rome, c. 1509–1511.

Sardar, Ziauddin and Merryl Wyn Davies, *Why Do People Hate America?*, New York, Disinformation Company, 2002.

———, *American Dream, Global Nightmare*, Thriplow, Cambridgeshire, Icon Books, 2004.

Saul, John Ralston, *Reflections of a Siamese Twin: Canada at the End of the Twentieth Century*, Toronto, Penguin Books, 1997.

Schmidt, Lawrence, ed., *George Grant in Process: Essays and Conversations*, Toronto, House of Anansi, 1979.

Seebohm, Frederic, *The Oxford Reformers John Colet, Erasmus, and Thomas More: Being a History of Their Fellow-Work*, 3rd edition, Longmans, Green and Co., 1887.

Sherrard, Philip, *The Greek East and the Latin West: A study in the Christian Tradition*, London, Oxford University Press, 1959.

Sibbald, Susan, *The Memoirs of Susan Sibbald (1783–1812)*, ed. Francis Paget Hett, London, John Lane, 1926.

Sibley, Robert C., *Northern Spirits: John Watson, George Grant, and Charles Taylor: Appropriations of Hegelian Political Thought*, Montreal, McGill-Queen's University Press, 2008.

Simons, John, ed., *The Challenge of Tradition: Discerning the Future of Anglicanism*, Toronto, Anglican Book Centre, 1997.

Skipton, H. P. K., *A Life of George Hills, First Bishop of British Columbia*, Victoria, British Columbia, Printorium Bookworks, 2009.

Smith, A. J. M., ed., *The McGill Fortnightly Review*, periodical, Montreal, s. n., 1925–1927.

Smith, Adam, *An Inquiry into the Nature and Cause of the Wealth of Nations*, 2 vols., London, W. Strahan and T. Cadell, 1776.

Smith, Denis, *Rogue Tory: The Life and Legend of John G. Diefenbaker*, Toronto, MacFarlane Walter and Ross, 1995.

Smith, Goldwin, *Canada and the Canadian Question*, London, Macmillan and Co., 1891.

Smith, Huston and Phil Cousineau, *The Way Things Are: Conversations with Huston Smith on the Spiritual Life*, Berkeley, California, University of California Press, 2003.

Smith, James K. A., *Introducing Radical Orthodoxy: Mapping a Post-Secular Theology*, Grand Rapids, Michigan, Baker Academic, 2004.

Snow, C. P., *The Two Cultures and the Scientific Revolution*, Cambridge, Cambridge University Press, 1959.

Southey, Robert, *The Poetical Works of Robert Southey: Complete in One Volume*, London, Longman, Brown, Green and Longmans, 1845.

Staines, David, ed., *Stephen Leacock: An Appraisal*, Ottawa, University of Ottawa Press, 1986.

Stevens, Geoffrey, *Stanfield*, Toronto, McClelland and Stewart, 1973.

Suiter, John, *Poets on the Peaks: Gary Snyder, Philip Whalen & Jack Kerouac in the Cascades*, Washington, District of Columbia, Counterpoint, 2002.

Sweet, William, ed., *Idealism, Metaphysics and Community*, Aldershot, Hampshire, 2001.

Swift, Jonathan, *A Tale of a Tub; Written for the Universal Improvement of Mankind*, London, J. Nutt, 1704.

Tadie, Andrew A. and Michael H. Macdonald, eds., *Permanent Things: Towards the Recovery of a More Human Scale at the End of the Twentieth Century*, Grand Rapids, Michigan, W. B. Eerdmans, 1995.

Tawney, R. H., *Religion and the Rise of Capitalism: A Historical Study*, Harmondsworth, Middlesex, Penguin Books, 1922.

Taylor, Charles M., *The Pattern of Politics*, Toronto, McClelland and Stewart, 1970.

―――, *Hegel*, Cambridge, Cambridge University Press, 1975.

―――, *Hegel and Modern Society*, Cambridge, Cambridge University Press, 1979.

―――, *Sources of the Self: The Making of the Modern Identity*, Cambridge, Massachusetts, Harvard University Press, 1989.

―――, *The Malaise of Modernity*, Concord, Ontario, House of Anansi, 1991.

―――, *A Catholic Modernity?*, Dayton, Ohio, University of Dayton Press, 1996.

―――, *Varieties of Religion Today: William James Revisited*, Cambridge, Massachusetts, Harvard University Press, 2002.

Taylor, Charles P. B., *Radical Tories: The Conservative Tradition in Canada*, Toronto, House of Anansi, 1982.

Teasdale, Wayne, *The Mystic Heart: Discovering a Universal Spirituality in the World's Religions*, Novato, California, New World Library, 1999.

Thobani, Sunera, 'It's Bloodthirsty Vengeance', speech delivered at Women's Resistance: From Victimization to Criminalization, Canadian Association of Elizabeth Fry Societies and Canadian Association of Sexual Assault Centres, Ottawa, 1 October 2001. Published as Sunera Thobani, '"It's Bloodthirsty Vengeance": Transcript of UBC Professor Sunera Thobani's Speech at the Women's Resistance Conference', *The Vancouver Sun*, 3 October 2001, p. A6.

Tolstoy, Leo, *War and Peace*, trans. Constance Garnett, 3 vols., London, W. Heinemann, 1904.

Torre, Michael D., ed., *Freedom in the Modern World: Jacques Maritain, Yves R. Simon, Mortimer J. Adler*, Mishawaka, Indiana, University of Notre Dame Press, 1989.

Treschow, Michael, Willemien Otten and Walter Hannam, eds., *Divine Creation in Ancient, Medieval and Early Modern Thought: Essays Presented to the Rev'd Dr Robert D. Crouse*, London, Brill, 2007.

Underhill, Francis and Charles Scott Gillett, eds., *Report of the Anglo-Catholic Congress*, London, Society of SS. Peter and Paul, 1923.

Walker, Susan, ed., *Speaking of Silence: Christians and Buddhists on the Contemplative Way*, New York, Paulist Press, 1987.

Walton, Izaak, *The Compleat Angler; or, The Contemplative Man's Recreation*, London, T. Maxey for Richard Marriot, 1653.

Ward, Bruce K., *Dostoevsky's Critique of the West: The Quest for Earthly Paradise*, Waterloo, Ontario, Wilfrid Laurier University Press, 1986.

Warren, David, ed., *The Idler*, periodical, Toronto, Idler Ltd., 1985–1993.

Weaver, Richard, *Ideas Have Consequences*, Chicago, Illinois, University of Chicago Press, 1948.

Weil, Simone, *Waiting on God*, trans. Emma Craufurd, London, HarperCollins, 1951.

———, *The Need for Roots: Prelude to a Declaration of Duties towards Mankind*, trans. A. F. Wills, London, Routledge and Kegan Paul, 1952.

Whillier, Wayne, ed., *Two Theological Languages by George Grant and Other Essays in Honour of His Work*, Queenston, Ontario, Edwin Mellen Press, 1990.

Williams, Rowan, *The Wound of Knowledge: Christian Spirituality from the New Testament to St. John of the Cross*, London, Darton, Longman and Todd, 1979.

———, 'Theology and the Contemplative Calling: The Image of Humanity in the Philokalia', lecture delivered at Father Alexander Schmemann Memorial Lecture, St. Vladimir's Orthodox Seminary, Crestwood, New York, 30 January 2010.

Willison, John and W. L. Grant, *Sir George Parkin: A Biography*, London, Macmillan and Co., 1929.

Wise, S. F., *God's Peculiar Peoples: Essays on Political Culture in Nineteenth-Century Canada*, ed. A. B. McKillop and Paul Martin Romney, Ottawa, Carleton University Press, 1993.

Wrong, George M. and H. H. Langton, eds., *Chronicles of Canada*, 32 vols., Toronto, Glasgow, Brook and Co., 1914–1916.

Yeats, William Butler, *Later Poems*, London, Macmillan and Co., 1922.

Zaehner, R. C., *Concordant Discord: The Interdependence of Faiths: Being the Gifford Lectures on Natural Religion Delivered at St. Andrews in 1967–1969*, Oxford, Clarendon Press, 1970.

Zernov, Nicholas and Militza Zernov, *The Fellowship of St Alban and St Sergius: A Historical Memoir*, Oxford, Fellowship of St. Alban and St. Sergius, 1979.

INDEX

171, 274; pluralism as the dogma of, 194, 205, 289 n. 8; principles of, 116, 176–177; progressive idea in, 109; and the Reformation, 111, 273; rejection of natural order in, 115; and religion, 204, 243; resistance to, in Orthodoxy, 254–255; roots and rise of, 109, 111, 116, 175–185, 219, 273; and the rural, 66; and Russia, 255; study of, 197; theology within, 243; thought in, distinguished from classical, 114; Tory–Anglican resistance to, 92–93, 99–100, 103, 115, 127, 137, 145, 153, 165, 211–212, 223–224; and tradition, 131, 223; underlying unity in ideologies of, 184; US as embodiment of, 116, 121; *see also* liberalism, Postmodern age
Mohammad Reza, Shah of Iran, 9, 11
monarchy, 124, 181, 217; *see also* aristocracy
Montgomery, Lucy Maud, 57
Montreal, 70, 252, 267–268
Montreal Declaration, 267
Montt, Efrain Rios, 11
Moodie, Susanna, 52, 74
moral order, *see* natural law
morality, *see* ethics
More, Thomas, 4, 17, 25, 119–120, 123, 127, 159. 217, 270
Morning Post, periodical, 281 n. 11
Morton, W. L., 76, 220
Mossadegh, Mohammad, 11
Muggeridge, Malcolm, 275
Mulroney, Brian, 55, 75, 81, 84, 145
multiculturalism, 180, 203
multigenerational connectedness, *see* continuity
Murdoch, Iris, 145, 151
Muslim Brotherhood, 14
'Muslim rage', 12
Musto, Ronald, 17, 19
My Discovery of the West, 143
mystery, 150–152, 255
Mystic Heart, The, 193
mysticism, *see* contemplation
Mysticism in the World's Religions, 194

Naropa Institute, 45
Nash, Knowlton, 87
Nashota House, 275
Nathan the Wise, 193

nation, nationhood, and liberty, 200, 202; meaning and sense of, 32, 52, 204; priorization of, over individual, 261; rights of, 82; security of, 125; sovereignty of, 51–53; standards of, 125; unity of, and community life, 73
National Policy, of J. A. Macdonald, 52, 63, 87
nationalism, as alternative to colonial way within empire, 59, 62–65, 141; as alternative to US colonialism, 27, 141; of Anglicanism, 72–73, 261; and the common good, 34; and the English tradition, 219; in France, 92; and Orthodoxy, 218; political identity of, 219; principles of, 34, 43; and spirituality, 218; tory form of, 5, 59, 93, 232; variations in expression of, 24, 85, 93, 144–145, 200; view of the state in, 25–26, 31; vision of, in Canada, 87; and war, 16; *see also* Canadian nationalism, toryism
natural law, natural order, 6, 109, 114–115, 124–127, 156, 178, 190–191, 212, 262; *see also* harmony, order
naturalism, 67, 71
nature, 71, 98, 127, 156, 186, 216, 262
Necessary Illusions, 22
necessity, *see* fate
Nelson, William H., 5
neo-conservatism, 215
neo-Constantinianism, 158, 194, 253
neo-Thomism, 111–112
neo-traditionalism, *see* perennialism
Netherlands, 3
network politics, 25
Neuhaus, John Richard, 6
New Atlantis, 99
New Democratic Party, 24, 57, 71, 85, 121, 123, 144, 188, 200
New Left, 38, 71–72, 77, 85, 93, 116, 144, 159, 188, 209, 211–212
New Left Review, periodical, 200
New Life, 171
New Right, 159
New Statesman, The, periodical, 224–225
New Testament, 118
New Westminster, Diocese of, 267–268
New York, 67, 111
New York Times, The, periodical, 29
New Zealand, 63

Newlove, John, 21
Newman, John Henry, 97, 132, 153, 233
Nicaragua, 11
Nicholls, David, 97
Nicholson, Graeme, 241, 251
Nicolas II, of Russia, 252
Nietzsche, Friedrich, 41, 44, 153, 212
Nisbet, Robert, 6
No Logo, 26
noblesse oblige, 215
Noel, Conrad, 101, 217–218
nominalism, 179–180, 184
North American Aerospace Defense
    Command, 90
North American Free Trade Agreement, 64
North Atlantic Treaty Organization, 90
North Cascades, 37
North–South thinking, about North
    America, 77
Northern Spirits, 244
Nova Scotia, 59, 162, 165, 242
Novak, David, 194
Novak, Michael, 6
Novum Organum, 99
nuclear question, *see* Bomarc Missile
    Crisis, Greenham Common, Litton
    Industries

Occam, William of, 179–180, 183–184
Of the Laws of Ecclesiastical Polity, 4,
    168, 247
Off the Road, 39
Old Brewery Bay, Orillia, 56, 72
Old Testament, 38, 119, 168
Oliver, Simon, 103
On the Front Line of Life, 236
On the Incarnation, 274
On the Road, 42
One Big Union, *see* Industrial Workers of
    the World
Ontario, 56, 73, 130, 133, 167, 230, 238,
    265
open theism, 156
openness, 101, 126, 184, 187, 189
opinion, perspectives, 115, 184, 187–189,
    203–204; *see also* hermeneutical
    agnosticism
Orchard, David, 53, 84
order, and Anglicanism, 101; displaced by
    liberty, 39; held in tension with liberty,
    141; or liberty, as guiding principle, 114;

in nationalism, 23–24, 34; as natural,
    moral, 114–115, 190; in toryism, 40, 46–
    47, 116, 207, 232; turn against, in
    liberalism, 111, 187; *see also* natural law
ordination of women, 169
organicity, organic connections, and the
    church, 225; and faith, 121, 126–127,
    147; and the nature of society and state,
    31, 55, 79, 111, 116, 141, 147, 219, 225;
    and toryism, 4, 72, 73, 92, 124;
    understanding of, 40, 120–121, 147; *see
    also* interdisciplinary way
*Origins of the Christian Mystical
    Tradition, The*, 275
Origins of Totalitarianism, The, 10
Orient, *see* East, Islam
Orientalism, 13
Origen, 274
Orillia, Ontario, 56–58, 65–66, 72–73,
    143, 236
orthodoxy, meaning of, 100, 103, 105
Orthodoxy, Greek–Russian Christianity,
    19, 103, 150–152, 212, 218, 251–257,
    273–277, 293 n. 4
Ottawa, 24
Our Living Tradition, 86
Owen, Derwyn, 147, 230, 234, 236
Oxford University, 97, 107–108, 113, 115,
    149, 151, 162–163, 242, 254, 256, 270,
    275
Oxford Movement, 102, 123
Oxford Movement, The, 165

pacifism, 15–17, 116, 149; *see also* peace
paideia, 131–139, 146; *see also* education
Paine, Thomas, 3, 5–6, 116, 184
Pakistan, 11, 13
paleo-conservatives, language of, 116
Palestine Liberation Organization, 11
Palestinians, 9
Palmer, Mitchell, 69
parish, 103, 105, 117, 122, 124–125, 165,
    171, 212, 229, 246, 264–265
*Parish and Cathedral Church of St.
    James', Toronto 1797–1997, The*, 234
Parkin, George, 59–60, 63, 129
Parliament of the World's Religions, 193
Parrinder, Geoffrey, 194
particulars, in philosophy, 179
party politics, 21–24, 26, 30–31, 79, 117–
    118, 123, 153, 200, 277; *see also* politics

CPSIA information can be obtained
at www.ICGtesting.com
Printed in the USA
BVHW08s1257270618
520186BV00002B/73/P

9 780996 324847